Beyond Criminology

3/23
$2—

Beyond Criminology

Taking Harm Seriously

Edited by Paddy Hillyard, Christina Pantazis,
Steve Tombs and Dave Gordon

Pluto Press
LONDON • ANN ARBOR, MI

Fernwood Publishing
BLACK POINT, NOVA SCOTIA

First published 2004 by
Pluto Press 345 Archway Road, London N6 5AA
and 839 Greene Street, Ann Arbor, MI 48106
www.plutobooks.com

and

Fernwood Publishing
Site 2A, Box 5, 32 Oceanvista Lane
Black Point, Nova Scotia B0J 1B0
and 324 Clare Avenue
Winnipeg, Manitoba R3L 1S3
www.fernwoodbooks.ca

British Library Cataloguing in Publication Data
A catalogue record for this book is available from the British Library

ISBN (Pluto) 0 7453 1904 1 hardback
ISBN (Pluto) 0 7453 1903 3 paperback
ISBN (Fernwood) 1 55266 148 2 paperback

Library of Congress Cataloging in Publication Data applied for

Library and Archives Canada Cataloguing in Publication
Beyond criminology : taking harm seriously / edited by Paddy Hillyard ... [et al.].
Includes index.
ISBN 1–55266–148–2

HV6028.B49 2004   361.1   C2004–903820–6

10   9   8   7   6   5   4   3   2   1

Designed and produced for Pluto Press by
Chase Publishing Services, Fortescue, Sidmouth, EX10 9QG, England
Typeset from disk by Stanford DTP Services, Northampton, England
Printed and bound in the European Union by
Antony Rowe Ltd, Chippenham and Eastbourne, England

Contents

List of Figures and Tables

FIGURES

TABLES

List of Abbreviations

ACPO	Association of Chief Police Officers
ALO	Airline Liaison Officer
ANC	African National Congress
CACD	Court of Appeal (Criminal Division)
CCA	Centre for Corporate Accountability
CCRC	Criminal Cases Review Commission
CPS	Crown Prosecution Service
DHS	Department of Homeland Security
DND	Drugs for Neglected Diseases
DTO	detention and training order
ECHR	European Court of Human Rights
EEA	European Economic Area
EPA	Environmental Protection Agency
ESRC	Economic and Social Research Council
EU	European Union
FAO	Food and Agriculture Organisation
FBI	Federal Bureau of Investigation
FOD	Field Operations Directorate
GATS	General Agreement on Trade and Services
GATT	General Agreement on Tariffs and Trade
GDP	gross domestic product
GMO	genetically modified organisms
HSE	Health and Safety Executive
ICCPR	International Covenant on Civil and Political Rights
ICD	International Classification of Diseases
ILO	International Labour Organisation
IMF	International Monetary Fund
INS	Immigration and Naturalisation Service
ITO	International Trade Organisation
LDC	least developed country
LFS	Labour Force Survey
MOU	memorandum of understanding
NAFTA	North American Free Trade Agreement
NAO	National Audit Office
NASS	National Asylum Support Service

NSPCC	National Society for the Prevention of Cruelty to Children
OECD	Organisation for Economic Cooperation and Development
OP	organo-phosphorous
PCA	Police Complaints Authority
PLO	Palestine Liberation Organisation
POA	Prison Officers' Association
PPP	Purchasing Power Parity
PRO	Public Record Office
PTSD	post-traumatic stress disorder
R&D	research and development
SIAC	Special Immigration Appeals Commission
SMR	Standardised Mortality Ratio
TRIPS	Trade and Related Property Rights
UK	United Kingdom
UN	United Nations
UNCTAD	United Nations Conference on Trade and Development
UNHCR	United Nations High Commissioner for Refugees
UNICEF	United Nations Children's Fund
US	United States
WHO	World Health Organisation
WTO	World Trade Organisation

1
Introduction

A number of years ago, at the annual conference of the European Group for the Study of Deviance and Social Control, a long-standing debate within and around criminology (re)emerged as a dominant theme of discussions outside the formal sessions – namely, what is the theoretical rationale and political utility of retaining a commitment to the analysis of crime, (criminal) law and the criminal justice system? During those discussions, an alternative focus, around the notion of social harm, was explored as well as the theoretical feasibility and policy potential of an alternative set of discourses.[1] The exploration of these issues was developed subsequently at a conference in 1999 organised and hosted by colleagues at the School for Policy Studies, University of Bristol. Since then we have presented a number of conference papers on various aspects of social harm. This book is a product of all these deliberations.

The principal aim of a social harm approach is to move beyond the narrow confines of criminology with its focus on harms defined by whether or not they constitute a crime, to a focus on all the different types of harms, which people experience from the cradle to the grave. The range and type of harm people experience during their life course are, of course, extremely varied. Many will suffer food-poisoning, others will die in car crashes or be run over by a car, some will fall off ladders doing DIY in the home, a large number will die or be injured either going to work or while at work, others will die or will be disabled for life from medical mistakes or other factors such as super bugs in hospitals, many will suffer considerable financial loss as a direct result of mis-selling of pensions, endowment policies and other financial products. Some of these events will be captured by the criminal law. Most of the events, however, will not be seen as criminal and categorised in a variety of different ways from 'outcomes of the market economy' to 'accidents' or 'mistakes'. Yet for the person who dies, whether it is from a deliberate act, 'accident' or indifference they are still dead with all the social and economic consequences for their family and friends. Similarly, if a person is injured or they 'lose' their life savings, the immediate harm is the same whether it is socially constructed as a crime or a mistake. Thus, it is a central premise of this book that it makes no sense to separate out harms, which can be defined as criminal, from all other types of harm. All forms of harms we argue must be considered and analysed together. Otherwise a very distorted view of the world will be produced.

Our argument is not that the harms resulting from events, acts and omissions, which are defined in the criminal law, are unimportant or that criminology as a discipline does not have a contribution to make to the understanding of harm. On the contrary, a number of the harms arising from events which are defined as criminal are socially, economically and psychologically very damaging and have widespread consequences. Our argument is that a number of consequences arise as a direct result of the bracketing of crime from other harms and focusing extensively on criminal harm. It provides a highly partial, biased and distorted view of the nature and extent of harms people experience during their lifetime and makes any attempt to explain the origins of criminal harms suspect. Moreover, it helps to perpetuate the belief that the solution to many different forms of social harm is by criminalizing them and ratcheting up and broadening the aims of the criminal justice system. More fundamentally, it leads to a neglect of much more damaging and dangerous forms of harm.

The book seeks to explore a number of different types of harm and to make a theoretical contribution to discussions around the conceptualisation of the notion of harm, as well as attempting to explain why so much harm takes place. To this end the book brings together a number of chapters written by the four editors, as well as a number of specifically commissioned chapters to explore various aspects of the study of social harm. We make no claims to provide a definitive text on the subject. There are a number of obvious gaps in the substantive harms considered and the theoretical ideas are in their infancy. This is inevitable in embarking on a new enterprise. Nevertheless, the book provides the broad contours of a social harm perspective and lays down a challenge to move beyond criminology to a more holistic analysis of the vagaries that are likely to befall all of us.

The book opens with an analysis by Paddy Hillyard and Steve Tombs of the key features of the debate as it currently stands between, on the one hand, those who would retain a commitment to 'crime' and criminology and, on the other hand, those who would abandon criminology for a social harm perspective. To this end, the chapter begins by highlighting several criticisms of criminology, criticisms raised in particular by a diverse group of critical criminologists over the past 30 to 40 years.

While these are hardly new, the rehearsal of these is an important starting point for a discussion of the potential of the development of an alternative discipline. The chapter then proposes a number of reasons why a disciplinary approach organised around a notion of social harm may prove to be more productive than has criminology hitherto: that is, may have the potential for greater theoretical coherence and imagination, and for more political progress.

There is no simple assumption here, or throughout the pages that follow, that a social harm approach has a necessary superiority over criminology, and that the study of each has potential advantages over the other. While there certainly are potential problems to be faced in any shift away from criminology towards a social harm approach, arguments can be made for this shift to occur. It is our view that the contributions presented in this volume represent a significant testimony both to the limits of criminology and, more importantly, to the possible advantages of a disciplinary approach based around a concept of social harm. It also needs to be emphasised, however, that, even if we are to accept that there are an array of merits and disadvantages to each discipline, then there *are* bases for evaluating or arbitrating between these competing claims. For us, as critical social scientists, key questions that must be asked of a discipline are to what end, and for whom, does it seek to produce knowledge? The more adequate discipline, then, is the one which produces knowledge more likely to enhance social justice. Ultimately, the issue of any shift from criminology to a social harm approach must be resolved from the viewpoint of a politics informed by social justice.

A central thesis of the book is that much harm is 'the social wreckage of neo-liberal globalisation'.[2] In Chapter 3 Steve Tombs and Paddy Hillyard therefore present a theoretical framework to explain the production of harm based on a critique of economic policies in general, and the neo-liberal paradigm in particular. The first part of the chapter explores some of the principal characteristics of this model: the growing concentration of economic power, the moves to further deregulation, the hegemony of the project and, perhaps most important of all, the exponential increases in the levels of inequality in the world. The second part of the chapter attempts to develop an initial typology of the different forms of harm which are directly or indirectly produced by the neo-liberal model of economic progress. While the chapter provides an overarching explanation, we would not argue that everything could be explained by a political economy approach. Custom, tradition, gender, race and other factors are all important as illustrated in other chapters.

One of the considerable ironies of the apparent triumph of western liberalism is that it exists alongside the chaos of war, crime and poverty. These phenomena occur not only in developing countries but also in the developed world. In the most advanced democratic society in the world, as Jamil Salmi points out in Chapter 4, 20 per cent of the children live in poverty, 3.5 million people are homeless, one-third of all families go hungry on a regular basis, 42 million live without health insurance, 23,000 people are murdered and 50,000 rapes are reported every year. To top it all, it has the highest concentration of jailed people in the world. How can such staggering levels of violence coexist, he asks, alongside capitalism and democracy? To understand violence he develops a systematic analytical framework to explore its various dimensions and then identifies the patterns and relationships linking the various manifestations of violence to the prevailing economic, social and political power structures in an effort to establish accountability.

Another considerable irony of the apparent triumph of western liberalism and its rhetoric of rights and responsibilities is the utter indifference it shows to the production of harm. In Chapter 5 Simon Pemberton seeks to identify the processes which operate in capitalist society to promote moral indifference among its population to the suffering of others. He begins by pointing out the lack of interest of mainstream criminology in the topic before assessing the contribution of critical criminology. He provides a perceptive comparison between the importance given to the concept of intention and how it is central to the definition of crime and the notion of moral indifference. While the latter is potentially far more harmful than much intentional criminal events, it carries little or no opprobrium. In the second part of his chapter he attempts to develop a theory of moral indifference building upon Bauman's work.

In Chapter 6 Tony Ward argues that instead of all the harms caused by the state being incorporated into a social harm approach, they should be covered by a notion of state crime – defined as a form of organisational deviance involving human rights violations – and this topic should form part of criminology. This would further make the expanding cadres of students signed up for criminology courses aware that even on the most narrowly legalistic definition, serious crime is predominantly the activity of governments and government officials. Another important reason is political. Criminology, he suggests, should be part of the process of labelling and sanctioning this extensive form of harm. He touches on the political economy of state harm and argues that there are clear economic connections between state violence and economic conditions depending on whether the state is 'strong' or 'weak'. The final section of his chapter outlines two possible ways of studying state harms that lie outside the concept of crime.

Miscarriages of justice are commonplace in any criminal justice system. In the United States they have received considerable attention in the context of the death penalty and in the United Kingdom (UK) there have been a number of very high-profile cases where innocent people have been found guilty of crimes which they did not commit and as a consequence have spent many years in jail before finally being released. In Chapter 7 Michael Naughton adopts a social harm approach to reorientate definitions of miscarriages of justice away from high-profile wrongful convictions to embrace the mundane routine successful appeals against criminal conviction. He catalogues the types of victims and the variety of forms of harm they experience as a result of a conviction which is overturned on appeal. He thus opens up an uncharted and little discussed but very important form of harm within the criminal justice system. Thus the chapter is not so much a critical engagement with the underlying theoretical or methodological tenets of a social harm approach, but a sympathetic *application* to illuminate the promise of a social harm approach in the specific area of wrongful criminal convictions. Its primary aim is to show the ability of a social harm approach to raise questions that have not hitherto been posed and, simultaneously, contribute to the establishment of new agendas for social problems.

In Chapter 8 Joe Sim considers what he terms as the 'victimised state' – the ideological construction of the nature and extent of violence and dangers facing prison and police officers. He deconstructs the official data concerning deaths and injuries sustained by these state servants, and challenges the social construction of these groups as 'victimised'. He compares the approaches to the deaths of prison and police officers with deaths in state custody and police-induced deaths on the roads and considers the theoretical implications generated by the political and cultural fixation with the 'victimised state'. In particular, he explores the links with the reinforcement of authoritarian law and order policies. There is a need, he suggests, to reflect on the *moral* underpinnings of state interventions and the role that regressive visions of morality play in defining and redefining the nature of these interventions. When a police or prison officer is murdered, the plaintive iconography that is mobilised must be challenged in order to try and avoid a further intensification in the state's clampdown and the production of yet more harm.

Decomposing bodies washed ashore on beaches, frozen bodies found in the undercarriage wheels of aircraft and stacked bodies in lorry containers are just some of the horrific outcomes for people who have attempted to leave their homes and start a new life elsewhere. Thousands upon thousands of men, women and children have died, and are dying annually. In a powerful and disturbing chapter (Chapter 9) Frances Webber details the widespread harm stemming directly from exclusionary immigration and asylum policies, which she dissects with detailed precision. Migration itself, she argues, has been redefined as a crime against the new economic order. Public policies in this context, far from being benign, cause widespread death throughout the world. To legitimise the wholesale criminalisation and exclusion of victims of globalisation, politicians harness and exploit popular racism and xenophobia. In so doing they provide aid and comfort to the far right and encourage the spread of racist violence.

While people die seeking a better life, many people die working. In May 2002, the International Labour Organisation (ILO) estimated that 2 million workers die each year through work-related accidents and diseases. This is more than 5,000 every day and it is considered to be a large underestimate of the true figure. In Chapter 10 Steve Tombs details some of the main killers in the workplace, such as cancers and respiratory disease. He also analyses the extensive social, psychological and financial harm work-related death causes before presenting the results of a detailed statistical audit undertaken into the work of the Health and Safety Executive (HSE) – the government body with primary responsibility for enforcing health and safety law in Britain. He specifically examines the work undertaken by the HSE's 'operational inspectors' – those inspectors who inspect workplaces, investigate reported injuries, and decide whether or not to impose enforcement notices or to prosecute. The chapter adds to the body of evidence that clearly indicates that the criminal law *does not* offer effective occupational health and safety protection.

Death is also the theme of Chapter 11. Danny Dorling examines 13,000 murders committed in Britain between January 1981 and December 2000. In a highly original contribution he rejects the dominant criminological conceptualisation of murder with its detailed focus on individual murderers, the victims and the modus operandi. Instead, he treats murder in a Durkheimian problematic as a social fact and, therefore, much more than the sum of individual acts and relates the data to social structures and social change. In particular, he shows that the majority of murders are concentrated in the poor parts of Britain.

He addresses two central questions: why are some people much more likely to be murdered than others and why are the rates of murder in Britain changing as they are? This is perhaps the most challenging part of the chapter and raises a number of issues, which takes us beyond the traditional criminological gaze. He analyses the murder rates by age cohort and discovers that for one particular group of men – those men born in 1965 and after – their murder rate is generally increasing as they age. Most of these men left school in the summer of 1981, which was the first summer for over 40 years that a young man living in a poor area would find work or training very scarce. The situation then got steadily worse as the Conservative government pursued a neo-liberal economic agenda, which decimated the manufacturing sector in Britain. Dorling concludes that those who perpetuated the social violence and those who voted them in are the prime suspects for most of the murders in Britain.

In Chapter 12 Christina Pantazis takes a life course approach to the study of harm endured by women and girls in the developing world. These harms often result in death, disability or other serious injuries. Yet they have been largely ignored by criminology – a theme raised at the outset. The unique contribution of the chapter lies in bringing together a very wide range of research covering different regions of the developing world and detailing the most significant harms – both in terms of extent and impact – experienced by females at different stages of their lives. The analysis makes for grim reading. It illustrates that the cause of a significant amount of harm in the world stems from gender oppression, economic interests, social customs and other factors. As well as showing the widespread and devastating harm which women and girls experience worldwide during their lives, it illustrates the many advantages that a life course approach can bring to the study of social harm.

In Chapter 13, aptly entitled 'Heterosexuality as Harm: Fitting In', Lois Bibbings considers ways of applying a social harm analysis to heterosexuality – a hegemonic concept if ever there was one. She provides a fascinating analysis showing how heterosexuality in western societies is considered to be the only appropriate form of sexual expression and 'real sex' requires sexual intercourse. 'Fitting in' is thus a *sine qua non* of sexual activity and all other forms or practices are judged against this appropriately erect and wholly embracing construction – they are either not real sex or beyond the pale (or 'pole'?). Gender is also a crucial aspect of this analysis. For example, as she puts it: 'The male always comes first, is dominant and the norm against which the Other is measured … the female comes second (if she comes at all)'.

In the second half of the chapter she explores the harm caused by the hegemonic ideology of heterosexuality in two concepts: in the family and in medicine. She begins with the family and details how the cosy heterosexual family unit centring upon a man and a woman, married or unmarried, who cohabit in a sexual relationship and reproduce is taken as the norm, causing untold harm to those who wish to live in other forms of relationship – such as gays and lesbians, and intersex or transsexuals people. Her second example focuses on medicine and continues with the theme of fitting in. She describes a number of examples of the way surgery is used to remove or reshape healthy body parts to enforce versions of heterosexual conformity among men and women. The examples include clidoridectomy, circumcision and the surgical treatment of intersex people. The chapter concludes by briefly recognising the numerous other spheres – work, health, education, politics, to list a few – to which a social harm approach could be applied to deconstruct the dominant construction of heterosexuality.

In Chapter 14 Roy Parker focuses on children and explores the harm that children suffer and the harm that they are considered to do. He traces the different types of harm to specific children, with an emphasis on physical and sexual abuse rather than with neglect. Interestingly from a harm perspective, he argues emotional abuse is now being taken more seriously. He raises the important question of where the principal responsibility may lie: with parents, schools, care homes, penal establishments, the state or the market, which is increasingly targeting children. He explores the varied and often-inconsistent responses to the harms caused by children before making the point that no clear-cut distinction can in fact be made between the harm done to children and the harms that children do. There is considerable evidence to suggest that the children who harm have often been harmed themselves. The harm can take a variety of forms from inconsistent or erratic parenting to extensive physical attacks. In such a context, he asks, is it possible to apply the notion of criminal intent? The relationship between the two is complicated and variable. He concludes by suggesting that if harms were better documented and understood and their relative severities gauged, more appropriate policies might be adopted.

The leaders of the world have repeatedly committed themselves to eradicating poverty over the past 40 years. Unfortunately, they have singularly failed to act despite the necessary technological and economic resources being available to fulfil these commitments. In Chapter 15 Dave Gordon discusses poverty, the world's largest source of social harm. Poverty causes more death, disease, suffering and misery than any other social phenomena. Over 10 million young children die in the world each year and, in over half of these deaths, malnutrition is a contributory cause. Yet the cost of preventing these deaths is relatively small, $13 billion per year for ten years would provide basic health and nutrition for every person on the planet. By comparison $30 billion was spent on pizza in the United States (US) in 2002 (Pizza Marketing Quarterly, 2003). The reasons why world leaders and policy-makers are indifferent to the death and suffering of the 'poor' is that they are an indirect consequence of the capitalist global economic system. Since no one intended all these children to die young their deaths are seen as unfortunate but not unjust. Similarly, policy-makers are unwilling to risk the likely small political harm of redistributing 0.2 per cent of the world's income to the 'poorest' (the amount needed to provide basic social services for all) even though they may desire an end to world poverty. Social harm, unlike criminology, provides a theoretical framework for examining the effects of unintended harms and therefore has something meaningful to contribute to debates on poverty – the greatest social cause of premature death on the planet.

A central premise of the book is that criminal harm forms a very small and largely insignificant proportion of the vast bulk of harms which take place daily. It is our hope that the book illustrates the types of issues and themes which we consider should be at the centre of a social harm perspective. Taken together the chapters provide a selection of the range of harms people are likely to experience during their lives, most of which will never be captured by the criminal law. In particular, the volume of preventable death is thousands of times greater than the number of deaths which are labelled as homicides. Thus the book as a whole provides a challenge to the distorting and distorted approach of criminology as an intellectual discipline. It cannot be seen as objective when it ignores so much of the more destructive and damaging harms while showing a concern with vast amounts of trivial harm both nationally and internationally. It will always be a suspect discipline as long as it bases its endeavours on a narrow set of events defined by those organisations which create so much harm – nation states. It is time to move beyond criminology and to begin to take harm seriously.

2
Beyond Criminology?

Paddy Hillyard and Steve Tombs

There are good reasons why this is an important moment to rehearse the criticisms and debate the issues around criminology and social harm. To begin with, van Swaaningen, in his recent analysis of critical criminology (1997, 1999), has argued that the 'heyday' of critical criminology has passed and that 'criminology has shifted away from epistemological and socio-political questions and returned to its old empiricist orientation as an applied science ... fuelled by the political issues of the day, and geared by the agenda of its financiers' (van Swaaningen, 1999: 7). Similarly, Muncie has noted that the critique of 'crime' and criminology advanced by 'radical criminologists' in the 1970s is a 'debate that remains unfinished', having been 'foreclosed by the growing hegemony of realist approaches' in the 1980s onwards (Muncie, 1999: 6). While we may not agree with all of the details of van Swaaningen's (nor, indeed, Muncie's) analysis of the state of critical criminology, his call for the rejuvenation of critical criminology requires an assessment of the prospects of criminology *per se*, and it is in the spirit of this exigency that a reassessment of the limits of a criminology is necessary, and all the more fruitful if this is an exercise which assesses the merits or otherwise of criminology alongside an alternative set of discourses.

Let us turn, then, to a brief statement of some of the key criticisms of criminology that have been advanced, largely in the past 30 to 40 years, by a range of critical social scientists. We shall do so by focusing critically upon the concept of crime, which remains central to the discipline of criminology, processes of criminalisation and the criminal justice system. Where we refer to 'crime', then, we are referring to the dominant construction of crime to which criminology has been, and remains, wedded.

A BRIEF 'CRITICAL' CRITIQUE OF CRIMINOLOGY

Crime has no ontological reality

Perhaps the most fundamental criticism of the category of crime is that it has no ontological reality. Everyone grows up 'knowing' what crime is. From a very early age children develop social constructions of robbers and other criminal characters who inhabit our social world. But in reality there is nothing intrinsic to any particular event or incident which permits it to be defined as a crime. Crimes and criminals are fictive events and characters in the sense that they have to be constructed before they can exist. This is a point that has been made time and time again by numerous writers: Box, Christie, Hulsman, Mathiesen, De Hann and Steinert, to name a few. Crime is thus a 'myth' of everyday life.

The lack of any intrinsic quality of an act which defines an event as crime can be emphasised by reference to a variety of 'crimes'. Thus, for example, street violence, theft or unauthorised taking of a motor vehicle, rape, credit card fraud, the use or sale of certain illegal drugs, and the (consensual) nailing of a foreskin to a tree, are all defined as crime and thus should all be (and often are) reacted against with punishment. However, these 'problematic situations' as Hulsman (1986) calls them, can and do occur in totally different kinds of situations and for different reasons. Hulsman argues that since there is a heterogeneity of problems that are dealt with under the heading of 'crime', a standard response in the form of the criminal justice punishment cannot *a priori* be assumed to be effective. Further, he has pointed out that people who are involved in 'criminal' events do not appear in themselves to be a special category of people. In short, unless we have a story about what is crime and who is a criminal, it is impossible to recognise either. This is not to deny, of course, that there are some very nasty events which everyone calls crimes.

Criminology perpetuates the myth of crime

Criminology has not been self-reflective and has, on the whole, accepted the notion of crime. So much is it considered to be an unproblematic concept that few textbooks bother to query it. *The Oxford Handbook of Criminology* is illustrative. The first two editions (Maguire et al., 1994, 1997) contained no discussion of the notion of 'crime'. It was not until the third edition that this lacuna was corrected with a chapter by Lacey (2002). This provides a comprehensive analysis of the relationship between legal and social constructions of crime and she adopts the notion of 'criminalisation' to show the ways in which these two different constructions of crime constantly interact. However, she does not go as far as Hulsman and suggest that there is no ontological reality to crime and there is no sustained analysis of the way the criminal law fails to capture the more damaging and pervasive forms of harm.

At the same time, despite the post-modern critique of theory, criminology is still producing meta-theory to explain 'crime' or producing another cook's tour from Lombroso through to strain theory. There is still a belief within criminology that it is possible to explain why people commit 'crime' notwithstanding that 'crime' is a social construct. The focus is still on *content* rather than on the social, political and economic *context* of the production of the regimes of truth. As Carol Smart pointed out, 'the thing that criminology cannot do is to deconstruct crime' (1990: 77).

'Crime' consists of many petty events

The term 'crime' always invokes a certain level of seriousness, both popularly and – to a large extent – academically. However, the vast majority of events which are defined as crimes are very minor and would not, as Hulsman (1986) has pointed out, score particularly highly on a scale of personal hardship. A perusal of the *Criminal Statistics for England and Wales*, until 2002 an annual Home Office publication, illustrates this point. The police record the detail of hundreds of criminal events most of which create little physical or even financial harm and often involve no victim. In addition, many of the petty events defined as crimes are often covered by insurance and individuals are able to obtain compensation for the harm done or, indeed, for harms which either have not occurred or have been greatly exaggerated. There appears to be some expectation that since the potential harm has been insured against, it is legitimate and not seen as criminal by people making false claims in order to recover some the outlay for the costs of insurance.

It is important to emphasise that this inclusion of vast numbers of petty events which would score relatively lowly on scales of seriousness is not simply a function of the definition of crime in the criminal law. We need to be clear that among those events that get defined as crime through the law, there are processes of selectivity in terms of which crimes are selected for control by criminal justice agencies, and how these events, once selected, are then defined by the courts, so that some rather than others are defined more seriously through the consistent attaching of harsher punishments. Thus Reiman presents a 'pyrrhic defeat theory' of criminal justice policy and systems, in which he argues that: 'the definitions of crime in the criminal law do not reflect the only or the most dangerous of antisocial behaviours'; 'the decisions on whom to arrest or charge do not reflect the only or the most dangerous behaviours legally defined as criminal'; 'criminal convictions do not reflect the only or the most dangerous individuals amongst those arrested and charged'; and that 'sentencing decisions do not reflect the goal of protecting society from the only or the most dangerous of those convicted by meting out punishments proportionate to the harmfulness of the crime committed' (Reiman, 1998: 61).

'Crime' excludes many serious harms

Many events and incidents which cause serious harm are either not part of the criminal law or, if they could be dealt with by it, are either ignored or handled without resort to it. Box, of course, developed this point in his classic book, *Power, Crime and Mystification* (1983), raising issues around corporate crime, domestic violence and sexual assault, and police crimes, all largely marginal to dominant legal, policy, enforcement, and indeed academic, agendas, yet all at the same time creating widespread harm, not least among already disadvantaged and powerless peoples.

There is little doubt, then, that the undue attention given to events, which are defined as crimes, distracts attention from more serious harm. But it is not simply that a focus on crime *deflects* attention from other, more socially pressing, harms – in many respects, it positively *excludes* them. The aim to preserve the label 'crime' for a discrete range of phenomena was, after all, the essence of Tappan's (1947) celebrated response to Sutherland's (1940, 1945, 1949) attempt to delineate a criminological focus upon 'white-collar crime', and this definitional issue continues to exercise those who would focus upon corporate and state crimes in particular (Friedrichs, 1992, 1998a, 1998b). Thus efforts, which have attempted to treat corporate or state crimes, have, in both areas, consumed a substantial amount of time and intellectual effort in the exercises of setting out, and then justifying, how and why certain activities of states and corporations can and should be treated through criminology. This is, as argued elsewhere with respect to the usage of the term 'safety crimes', more than an irritation – it has profound effects on the enterprise itself (Tombs, 2000). Thus in the context of 'safety crimes', a focus upon recorded occupational injury entails reference to over 1 million workplace injuries per year in Britain; restriction to the term 'crimes' means making reference to 1,000 or so successfully prosecuted health and safety offences. These are enormous differences, and have implications in terms of what can be done with such data conceptually, theoretically *and* politically (Tombs, 2000). Thus, while retaining a commitment to crime and law, attempts to introduce currently marginal concerns into the discipline of criminology (and, indeed, criminal justice) – for example, offences by the state or corporations – have raised enormous theoretical and practical tensions. Indeed, Christie (1986) has argued that these are not simply tensions, but necessary facets of criminal justice systems.

Constructing 'crimes'

In the absence of any intrinsic quality of an event or incident to differentiate them, the criminal law uses a number of complex tests and rules to determine whether or not a crime has been committed. One of the most important tests is the concept of *mens rea* – the guilty mind. It applies principally to the individual but not exclusively. For example, the highly questionable concept of conspiracy is used to prosecute groups of people (Hazell, 1974). In some contexts the simple failure to act is sufficiently blameworthy to be a crime. Each of these tests is an artifice in a number of respects. It is, for example, impossible to look into a person's mind and measure purpose, to understand what was going through their minds at the time or indeed what a reasonable person would think and/or do. Therefore, *mens rea* has to be judged by proxy through examining the person's words and deeds and speculating as to the likely responses of a fictitious ideal/ordinary person. In addition, it is questionable whether a magistrate or jury in making a decision on guilt would actually arrive at their decision by the mere process of applying the appropriate technical legal test(s).

Law's complex reasonings in relation to defining crime, while not exclusively focused on the individual, have an individualising effect which extends beyond the notion of intent *per se*. Thus, even where intent is not the issue in determining liability – such as in the case of corporate manslaughter – then the individualising ethos of criminal law has militated against such successful prosecutions, while in contexts where this charge has been raised, such as following the Zeebrugge or Southall 'disasters', then charges of manslaughter have been raised against relatively low-level individuals on the scene of the incident – namely, the assistant bosun or the train driver (see Tombs, 1995; Slapper and Tombs, 1999: 30–4, 101–7; and Chapter 10, passim).

It is also worth noting that the notion of intent presupposes, and then concretises, a moral hierarchy which, once examined, is counter common-sensical, certainly from the viewpoint of social harm. This point is made originally – to the best of our knowledge – by Reiman in a simple but striking fashion. Reiman contrasts the motives (and moral culpability) of most acts recognised as intentional murder with what he calls the indirect harms on the part of absentee killers, by which he means, for example, deaths which result where employers refuse to invest in safe plant or working methods, where manufacturers falsify safety data for new products, where illegal discharges are made of toxic substances into our environment, and so on. Reiman notes that intentional murderers commit acts which are focused upon one (or, rarely, more than one) specific individual, a point which we know holds for contemporary Britain, despite moral panics about 'stranger danger'; thus in such cases the perpetrator – whom in many respect fits our archetypal portrait of a criminal – 'does not show general disdain for the lives of her fellows' (Reiman, 1998: 67). Reiman contrasts such forms of intentional killing with the deaths that result from 'indirect' harms. For Reiman, the relative moral culpability of the intentional killer and the mine executive who cuts safety corners is quite distinct and, he argues, contrary to that around which law operates; the mine executive

> wanted harm to no-one in particular, but he *knew his acts were likely to harm someone* – and once someone is harmed, the victim is someone in particular. There is no moral basis for treating *one-on-one harm* as criminal and *indirect harm* as merely regulatory. (Reiman, 1998: 67–70)

Thus, Reiman concludes, the former is less likely to represent some generalised threat to others than is the latter. For Reiman, and his point is a convincing one, indifference is at least if not more culpable than intention, and ought to be treated as such by any criminal justice system (see Pemberton, Chapter 5 in this volume). Yet the greater moral culpability that is attached both legally and popularly to acts of intention can also allow those implicated in corporate crimes to rationalise away the consequences of their actions (see Slapper and Tombs, 1999: 105–7, 118–22; and Chapter 5, passim).

Criminalisation and punishment inflict pain

Defining an event as a 'crime' either sets in motion, or is the product of, a process of criminalisation. The state appropriates the conflict and imposes punishment (Christie, 1977). The state – via the criminal justice system – proceeds to seek to inflict suffering, once a crime and a criminal have been defined. It inflicts punishment on offenders, of which the prison sentence is the ultimate option and symbol (Blad et al., 1987). Christie (1986) is very deliberate in calling this process 'pain delivery'. The criminal justice system delivers pain in all forms of punishment. He rejects the claims that prison, for example, seeks to rehabilitate, deter or provide just deserts.

Indeed, the inflicting of pain by the state through the criminal justice system is a process that involves a number of discrete, but mutually reinforcing, stages: defining, classifying, broadcasting, disposing and punishing the individual concerned. Furthermore, these very processes create wider social harms which may bear little relationship to the original offence and pain caused. For example, they may lead to loss of a job, a home, family life and ostracism by society. Moreover, such processes foreclose social policy or other responses to events (see below).

'Crime control' is ineffective

The crime control approach has manifestly failed. On almost any publicly stated rationale upon which legitimacy has been sought for them, criminal justice systems are ineffective. Moreover, even on the basis of a narrow definition of 'crime', the number of events defined as 'crime' has been increasing steadily for many years with only a small recent downturn (Home Office, 2003a). Many of those who are defined as criminal return to crime after the infliction of pain. For example, a recent report in the UK claimed that 'of those prisoners released in 1997, 58 per cent were convicted of another crime within two years. 36 per cent were back inside on another prison sentence' (Social Exclusion Unit, 2000: 1). If a car broke down on nearly 60 out of every 100 journeys, we would get rid of it.

The criminal justice system does not work according to its own aims. The criminal justice system is supposed to do something about certain problems (crime) in society. It operates by processing those individuals (criminals) held responsible for certain actions. And the problem is seen to be solved if the offender has received a criminal justice system punishment. In his classic text *Prison on Trial* (1990), Mathiesen collates evidence from a wide range of sources (penal, sociological and criminological) regarding the defensibility of prison. He argues that no theoretical rationale for the prison – be this based upon individual prevention, rehabilitation, incapacitation, individual deterrence, general prevention or some pure neo-classicist calculation of proportional just punishment – is able to defend the prison. Yet despite the fact that it has never been able to work according to any stated rationales, it continues to exist, indeed proliferate. Pilger has recently observed that in the US, 'more people are now employed in what are known as the "prison industries" than in any of the country's top 500 corporations, with the exception of General Motors' (Pilger,

1998: 70). Thus Mathiesen (1990) calls the prison a fiasco, arguing that we still have prisons because there exists a pervasive and persistent ideology of prison in our societies and he sets out several ideological functions in advanced welfare state capitalistic societies for the prison. In short, to broaden Mathiesen's point, crime control activities have *actual* rationales beyond those of crime control.

'Crime' gives legitimacy to the expansion of crime control

Because crime is so often considered in isolation from other social harms it gives legitimacy to the further expansion of the crime control industry. As Christie (1993: 11) has pointed out, this industry solves two major problems that confront modern societies: differential access to paid work and the uneven distribution of wealth. It does this by providing profit and work while producing control of those who would otherwise cause trouble. Successive governments since the 1990s have made crime control a top priority. In the UK the amount committed to law and order has increased faster than any other area of public expenditure and, as a result, more and more people's livelihoods are dependent on crime and its control. Modern social orders are thus being increasingly characterised by an unacknowledged but open war between young males, mainly from poor and deprived backgrounds, and an army of professionals in the crime control industry (Box, 1983; Christie, 1993; Reiman, 1998). At the same time, many manufacturing industries have diversified to provide the equipment in the war against crime.

As Hulsman (1986) has pointed out, the criminal justice system is characterised by a fundamental uncontrollability. For Henry and Milovanovic, conventional crime control efforts fuel the engine of crime: 'Control interventions take criminal activity to new levels on investment and self-enclosed innovation. [...] Public horror and outrage call for more investment in control measures that further feed the cycle' (1996: x–xi).

Indeed, modernist criminological research, with the production of 'scientific results', plays its part in this circle by concretising and affirming reality (ibid.). More generally, numerous new courses in crime, criminology and criminal justice have been established in UK universities to train the personnel, while there have been large expansions in the collection and analysis of criminal intelligence and in the dissemination of crime news.

'Crime' serves to maintain power relations

The concept of crime maintains existent power relations in a myriad of, more or less subtle, ways. First, although the criminal law has the potential to capture some of the collective harmful events perpetuated in the suites and in corridors of the state, it largely ignores these activities and focuses on individual acts and behaviours on the streets. This is in part a product of the individualistic nature of judicial reasoning and its search for the responsible individual. In part it is also a product of the centrality of the notion of a very particular version of crime and its discourses in our culture. Second, by its focus on the individual, the structural determinants which lead to harmful events – such as poverty, social deprivation and the growing inequalities between rich and poor – can be ignored. Third, the crime control industry is now a powerful force in its own right; it has a vested interest in defining events as crime. Fourth, politicians use crime to mobilise support both for their own ends and to maintain electoral support for their parties. Finally, recalling Reiman's 'pyrrhic defeat theory', he argues that the net effect of the way in which the social reality of crime has been created in and reproduced through the criminal justice system and criminal justice policy is the perpetuation of 'the implicit identification of crime with the dangerous acts of the poor' (Reiman, 1998: 61). Thus crime in many different sets of relationships serves to maintain existing power relations.

Indeed, since its inception, criminology has enjoyed an intimate relationship with the powerful, a relationship determined largely by its failure to subject to critique the category of crime – and disciplinary agendas set by this – which has been handed down by the state, and around which the criminal justice system has been organised (Foucault, 1980a; Cohen, 1981; Garland, 1992, 1997).

THE POTENTIAL OF A SOCIAL HARM APPROACH

This section outlines some reasons why a disciplinary approach organised around a concept of harm may be more theoretically coherent and imaginative, and more progressive politically. Taken together, these concerns, encompassing the deleterious activities of local and national states, and of corporations, upon people's lives, whether in respect of lack of wholesome food, inadequate housing or heating, low income, exposure to various forms of danger, violations of basic human rights, *and victimisation to various forms of crime*, produces a sense of a need for a disciplinary home which could embrace a range of harms that affect many people throughout their life cycle. We have therefore sought a disciplinary approach that may encompass harms which are deleterious to people's welfare from the cradle to the grave. Of course, when we speak of people's welfare, we refer not (simply) to an atomised individual, or to men and women and their families, the social units which often experience harm. For it is clear that various forms of harms are not distributed randomly, but fall upon people of different social classes, genders, degrees of able-bodiedness, racial and ethnic groups, different ages, sexual preferences, and so on. Further, one focus of a social harm approach might be upon harms concentrated upon particular geographical areas, so that, notwithstanding the enormous ideological baggage that follows such a term, it might be possible to deploy the term 'community' positively within social scientific discourses. The notion of a 'harmed community' could embrace groups of people in some form of collectivity who are physically or financially harmed by whatever means.

Defining harm

This still, of course, leaves an awful lot of work to be done in terms of defining precisely what is meant by social harm. And in this respect, this represents precisely the same problem that has long confronted criminology, though one largely avoided or ignored, certainly by 'mainstream' criminology. Intuitively, as we have stated, we would want the term to embrace a wide range of events and conditions that affect people during their life course. At the same time, one possible problem with a social harm approach is with its broadness, its encompassing nature. Here, we begin to mark out, tentatively not least since many of the chapters in the book elaborate substantially upon what we have to say, the range or types of harms of humans with which a social harm approach would be concerned.

A social harm approach would first encompass *physical* harms. These would include premature death or serious injury through clinical iatrogenesis, violence such as car 'accidents', some activities at work (whether paid or unpaid), exposures to various environmental pollutants, assaults, illness and disease, lack of adequate food or shelter, or death, torture and brutality by state officials.

It would also include *financial/economic* harm which would incorporate both poverty and various forms of property and cash loss. This latter sub-category is highly problematic, because our society operates on the principle of financial loss as the motor force of our social organisation – but we are thinking particularly here about a variety of forms of fraud, which includes pension and mortgage 'mis-selling', mis-appropriation of funds by government, private corporations and private individuals, increased prices for goods and services through cartelisation and price-fixing, and redistribution of wealth and income from the poorer to the richer through regressive taxation and welfare policies. Widening the notion of financial or economic harm would entail taking cognisance of the personal and social effects of poverty, unemployment, and so on.

Another possible and much more problematic area concerns *emotional and psychological* harm. These types of harms are much more difficult to measure and relate to specific causes. However, there is evidence, as some of the chapters in this book show, that these types of harms are significant in many different contexts.

Finally, a developed understanding of social harm could include reference to *cultural safety* (Alvesalo, 1999: 4), encompassing notions of autonomy, development and growth, and access to cultural, intellectual and informational resources generally available in any given society.

There are obvious objections to be raised at such attempts to even begin to define harms. At best, it could be objected that harm is no more definable than crime, and that it too lacks any ontological reality; at worst, it might be objected that definitions of harm descend into a pure relativism, the production of particular political orientations to the world. We shall return to these objections below. Here, however, two points need emphasis.

First, defining what constitutes harm is a productive and positive process – much more positive than simply pointing to a list of inquiry delimited by an existent body of (criminal) law. Indeed, a social harm approach is partially to be defined in its very operationalisation, in its efforts to measure social harms. The point is that if we are attempting to measure both the nature and the relative impact of harms which people bear, it is at least reasonable to take some account of people's own expressions, and perceptions, of what those harms are! Thus a field of inquiry is (partially) defined by people's understandings, attitudes, perceptions and experiences rather than preordained by a state. Part of the 'problem' of defining social harm, then, is not a problem at all, but a positive aspect – its definition is partially constituted by its operationalisation.

Second, these objections seem to be premature and overly pessimistic. There are many examples where, despite some social phenomenon being difficult to define, we attempt to access and measure this via a series of indicators. What matters is what these indicators are, and how they are selected. For example, in the 1990s, the British government began to attempt to measure the 'quality of life', at first sight a highly intangible phenomenon. Yet, despite the fact that this is hardly a readily definable phenomenon, a number of proxy measures have been used. Again, these may be subject to dispute, but these disputes are about the substantive details rather than the validity or viability of the exercise.

While we need to accept, then, that there are real difficulties in, first, identifying a range of harms that might fall within the rubric of social harm, and, second, developing a valid series of means of measuring these, we view these more as technical issues *in*, rather than as insuperable obstacles *to*, the development of such a disciplinary enterprise. Indeed, were we to fall at the first hurdle of definition in any attempt at an extended consideration of the utility of a social harm approach, then we would be accepting that criminology was a more useful set of discourses simply because its referent objects – law, crime – allowed it to proceed less 'controversially'. This would be problematic to say the least – witness the vast amount of energy devoted to attempting to include white-collar, corporate or state crimes within this discipline. Rather than fall at this hurdle, then, let us explore what arguments can be proposed in favour of the development of a social harm approach. In the following section, we propose six such arguments which would produce a range of theoretical, conceptual, empirical and policy-oriented benefits.

The vicissitudes of life

Perhaps the greatest benefit of an analysis of harm is that it would be the basis for developing a much more accurate picture of what is most likely to affect people during their life cycle. Harm could be charted and compared over time. While crime is charted temporally and, increasingly, spatially, it is seldom compared with other harmful events. Hence crime statistics produce a very distorted picture of the total harm present in society, generating fear of one specific type of harm and perpetuating the myth of crime. A comparative and broader picture would allow a more adequate understanding of the *relative* significance of the harms faced by different groups of individuals. Finally, a stress upon social harm would also facilitate a focus upon harms caused by chronic conditions or states of affairs – such as exposure to airborne pollutants or to various health hazards at work, poor diet, inadequate housing, unemployment, state violence, and so on – as opposed to the discrete events which tend to provide the remit of criminology and the criminal law. All of these foci would be of benefit for individuals, but they could also provide a basis for more rational social policy – policies, priorities and expenditures could be determined more on the basis of data, less on the basis of prejudice and mantra (the seemingly irresistible need to reduce 'crime figures'). Thus a focus on harm could have benefits for local and national states – though we have to recognise that such a focus would present a potential threat to these states, since state activities (or inactivities) are likely to be highlighted as *sources* of harm.

The allocation of responsibility

The study of harm permits a much wider investigation into who or what might be responsible for the harm done, unrestricted by the narrow individualistic notion of responsibility or proxy measures of intent sought by the criminal justice process. It allows consideration of corporate and collective responsibility. Thus, while the responsibility for serious rail crashes is often impossible to determine legally in any satisfactory fashion, companies involved in looking after the track and the train operators surely bear some moral responsibility for the multiple-fatality incidents? Indeed, the UK's Law Commission (1996) has recently recommended that criminal responsibility should be extended to corporate bodies. While this would enlarge the scope of the criminal law, overall the restricted scope of criminal responsibility would remain. A study of harm allows a sharper focus on political and ministerial responsibility. In the UK, ministerial responsibility appears to have been increasingly watered down in recent years if the failure of ministers to resign in the face of major disasters and other harm events is any indication. The study of harm also raises the interesting new possibility of the allocation for responsibility in the failure to deal adequately with social problems. Dorling in Chapter 11, for example, has indicated that some areas have experienced no homicides between 1981 and 2000 while other areas have experienced ten or more; these latter areas are highly correlated with poverty. Clearly, structural rather than individual factors are responsible. This conclusion thus raises the interesting question of whether the allocation of responsibility lies solely with the individual murderer or also with those who have either failed to eradicate or reproduced poverty in these areas.

Policy responses

A social harm approach might allow greater consideration to be given to appropriate policy responses for reducing levels of harm. The aim of welfare should be to reduce the extent of harm that people experience from the cradle to the grave. As we have indicated the focus of criminology and the use of the criminal law tend inevitably to generate responses to illegality which entail some form of retribution or punishment on the part of the state; what is more, these processes are in the hands of judges, magistrates, barristers, and so on, who are largely unrepresentative of general populations, and in whose hands systems of 'justice' have time and time again proven to operate problematically (as can be seen, for example, in Chapter 7). A social harm approach, however, triggers quite a different set of responses to harm. Requiring policy responses entails a politicisation of an issue – rather than handing it over to unelected, largely unaccountable and certainly non-representative elites. Thus responses to social harms require debates about policy, resources, priorities, and so on. Notwithstanding the limitations of formal political processes in so-called western liberal democracies, these are surely more appropriate fora for debates than relatively closed and elite-dominated criminal justice systems.

Of course, this shift from criminal justice to a broadly defined social policy raises questions of efficacy and justice. There are some who might wish to extend the scope of the criminal law to deal with activities and omissions that are hitherto either non- or 'inadequately' criminalised. For example, at least since Sutherland coined the term 'white-collar' crime in 1939, there have been successive generations of criminologists who have argued for the more effective criminalisation of white-collar and corporate offenders, not least in the name of some form of social justice – that is, an argument that if lower-class offenders are to be treated harshly, then an equality of pain should extend to other types of offenders. Such arguments have gone largely unheeded, so that the treatment of such offenders at all stages of the legal process remains highly favourable when compared with lower-class offenders (Slapper and Tombs, 1999; and Chapter 10, passim).

This suggests something to us about the nature of the system – the criminal justice system – to which these arguments are directed. Moreover, it needs to be added that even if 'successful', such arguments may tend to legitimate the existence of an extended system of social control, within which the weakest and most vulnerable members of our societies have always suffered disproportionately. Further, but relatedly, such calls for more effective criminalisation need to be aware of the 'flexibility' of this system and the obduracy of its highly unequal functioning. Thus, those of us who have proposed reforms in the way in which corporate offenders, for example, are treated, must be clear that whenever we speak of policy implications, or propose reforms in relation to treating corporate offences as crimes, that these reforms may then be developed in ways that we had not intended. That is, 'progressive' reforms which seek to alter the basic workings of a highly unequal criminal justice system can and are often turned on their head, and may ultimately serve to exacerbate existing structures of inequality and vulnerability; the intentions behind proposals clearly do not determine their actual uses (Alvesalo and Tombs, 2002).

Mass harms

A social harm approach might more accurately chart instances of mass harm. A basic weakness with crime and criminology, as we have seen, is that they are fundamentally related to the actions, omissions, intentions of, and relationships between, individuals and hence have problems embracing corporate and state 'crime'. All too often, the debates around these issues become entangled in ultimately somewhat sterile arguments regarding whether or not such harms do or should constitute crimes. Basically we have here attempts to squeeze into a discipline organised around individualistic notions of action and intention harms – both chronic and acute – caused by routine practices, Standard Operating Procedures, lines of organisational responsibility and accountability, general modus operandi, cultures of fear, indifference and thoughtlessness, and so on, on the part of bureaucratic entities which are not reducible to the actions, motives and intentions of the individual human agents who constitute them. There is, quite simply, a lack of fit.

Equally great efforts are *then* expended – if 'crimes' have been identified – in attempting to determine effective policy responses within the existing criminal justice system. This enormous effort might better be used in determining more appropriate public policy responses. Thus, for example, developing mechanisms to render the activities of internal security services involved in 'anti-terrorist' activities more transparent and publicly accountable are likely to be more effective than using the criminal law to determine which particular individuals bear what degree of responsibility for particular transgressions, such as the effects of a 'shoot to kill policy'; proposing changes to governance structures, or the nature of corporate ownership *per se*, is likely to prove more effective than seeking to identify individual company directors who might represent the corporate mind and who thus had the information to have prevented a particular 'accident' or 'disaster' occurring. The point is not that remedies through the criminal or civil law are worthless, but that remaining wedded to crime, law and criminal justice produces a myopia among many criminologists to wider, and at least potentially more effective, social and public policy responses.

Challenges to power

Foucault, apart from being very rude about criminology, did draw attention to the importance of the relationship between power and knowledge, and the need to resist the operation of power as it is articulated in all forms of relationships. In particular, he alerted us to the production of what he calls 'regimes of truth', and this should lead us to ask of claims to knowledge, who is producing these discourses and for what reasons? (Foucault, 1979). Many feminists have also engaged in a long-term critique of discourses around crime and criminology, with some arguing for an abandonment of criminology (cf. Smart, 1990; Carlen, 1992). A similar position has been taken by some of the Marxists who worked within and around the National Deviancy Symposium in Britain.

By contrast, and with no little irony, it is worth reiterating, as we have already noted, that there is perhaps *less* fundamental questioning now of the nature of criminology as a set of discursive practices, or as a discipline, than was the case 30 or 40 years ago. This is attributable, not least, to the decline of theorising within criminology, the pressures to gain external funding for academic research, the increased focus upon short-term utility as a basis for such research, and so on (Cohen, 1981; Rock, 1994; Hillyard and Sim 1997; Partington, 1997; Holdaway and Rock, 1998; Hillyard et al., 2004). If Foucault is a frequent reference point for contemporary criminology, the epistemological significance of much of Foucault's work seems to have passed criminology by.

One source of a challenge to the dominant discourse around crime and criminology could be a new discourse or discipline around social harm. This is not to claim that this discipline could escape the power-knowledge nexus. Indeed, the establishment of a discipline around social harm would not enter virginal discursive terrain, since states have historically defined harm in individualistic terms, terms which are institutionalised through medico-legal discourses and professions. But while a social harm approach can seek to develop social explanations, the origins of criminology render a shift from individualism highly problematic. Thus we are arguing that in its explicitly political starting point (see below), in its basis in intellectual reflexivity, in its commitment to the resurrection of subjugated knowledges, a social harm approach might entail a more progressive form of power-knowledge than that which criminology has come to represent in its 100-year plus history.

It should be noted here also that such an approach is likely to pose quite different challenges for structures of power embedded within and around local and national states. All too often, the products of criminological reasoning have been used to bolster states, providing rationales for the extensions of state activities in the name of more effective criminal justice. Since the products of research around social harm are likely to implicate states, then the relationship with states will be quite different – there is likely to be less symbiosis in terms of activity and interests. Indeed, the seemingly increasingly close and complex links between local states and local, national and transnational capital mean that these challenges are both political and economic. In respect of challenges to existent power structures in these senses, then, an emphasis upon social harm may have far greater transformative potential than criminology.

A critique of risk

Discourses of risk are currently popular following the work of Giddens (1991) and Beck (1992), in particular. Our society is increasingly conceptualised as a 'risk society' where insurance has become the key mechanism by which we deal with the lottery of life. A new form of knowledge based around actuarial decisions, probabilities and databases is being developed. Feeley and Simon (1992), as is well known, have applied the notion of risk to developments in penal policy and argue that there has been a shift away from a focus on rehabilitation and reform to a focus on risk. The penal system is now concerned about reducing the risk in the control of dangerous populations and an actuarial criminology has replaced a rehabilitative criminology.

We would argue that a discourse around harm would pose a challenge to the overly individualistic (Pearce and Tombs, 1998) and apolitical (Rigakos, 1999) forms of analyses embraced by the notion of risk as it is dominantly being interpreted and developed. Risk has long historical roots located in the marketplace and associated with the problems and difficulties concomitant with the accumulation and investment of capital. It was then developed within the chemical and nuclear industries, not least as a way of defining legal corporate and state activity through reference to technicist calculations such as cost-benefit analysis, quantitative risk assessment, notions of acceptable risk based on the cost of a life, and so on (Pearce and Tombs, 1996). As Garland (1997) suggests, insurance has promoted a form of 'responsibilities autonomy' and 'de-dramatised' the social conflicts that arise out of economic life. Harm focuses on collectivities not in order to calculate individual risk but to seek a collective response to its reduction. It opens up discussions about the conflicts in economic life around the differentials in wealth and life chances. A social harm approach would, in this sense, be more positive.

CRIMINOLOGY, SOCIAL HARM AND JUSTICE

It must be emphasised again that we are not arguing that a social harm approach has a necessary superiority over criminology. The key issue is that where there are competing claims then these must be judged according to which approach will produce greater social justice. This is ultimately a political question. Moreover, we would argue that these political questions must be addressed at both the strategic and the tactical levels. In a longer-term, strategic sense, criminology is to be abandoned since its focus upon crime, law and criminal justice has always been inadequate in that such a focus entails some reproduction of what Braithwaite has called 'a class-based administration of criminal justice' (Braithwaite, 1995: 118). But this is not to deny the politically progressive tactic of approaching crime, law and criminal justice as sites or objects of struggle, which facilitate the development of focused political action.

A shift to a social harm approach is not, then, to entail any necessary abandonment of such struggles. However, a commitment to a focus upon social harm does carry with it two clear corollaries. First, that intellectual and political activity does not privilege law as a site of activity or struggle; and, second, that intellectual and political activity can address harm without making reference to law. These are short- and medium-term tactical political issues. Moreover, they are tactics that cannot adequately be adopted from the starting point of criminology, which is necessarily pulled towards dealing with crime, law and criminal justice.

A shift to 'social harm', then, entails no *restriction* of our work and political activity to law, while at the same time no simple abandonment of this focus. While critiques of criminology – rehearsed above – are well made, they may tend towards a reification of criminology *as is*, when one of the tasks of critical criminologists has been, and surely remains, to reshape the nature and boundaries of the discipline. The problem for us is when this tactical aim is confused with a strategic end. Criminology can be refashioned, but only within limits. We certainly recognise the force of Carlen's argument, that it is perfectly possible for any form of critical social science to recognise the ideological power of the empirical referent without one's radical enterprise being subverted by it:

> there is no reason why they [radical theorists] should not *both* take seriously (that is recognise) *and* deny the empirical referent's material and ideological effects [...] the very task of theory is to engage in a struggle for power over the 'meaning of things'. (Carlen, 1992: 54, 62; emphasis in original)

Thus one can accept the poverty of dominant criminological discourses, and approach these as an object of struggle. However, strategically, and in the longer term, because there are certain necessary elements, or rules of formation, of this discipline, then this struggle can only have a limited range of outcomes (albeit more or less favourable).

In general, then, it is our view that all forms of theorising and intellectual practice tend to reify, support and indeed enhance that very phenomenon which is at the centre of their activity. Disciplines produce and reproduce their objects of study. Thus, no matter how deconstructive, radical or critical a criminology is, in the very fact of engaging in criminology, this at once legitimates some object of 'crime'.

In this context, it is worth emphasising that we have referred in this chapter constantly to the *potential* of criminology and the *potential* of a social harm approach. But criminology has been established as a discipline for well over 100 years and, while it would be simply wrong to claim that criminology has not contributed to any progressive social change, it is at least instructive that we must still couch progressive effects largely in terms of potential. Indeed, there is significant room for debate as to whether or not these particular instances of progressive social change could not have been achieved more effectively through means quite different from criminology and reference to, or use of, the criminal law. Even if we take the benign view, and grant criminology its progressive effects, then it remains clear that the costs of this progress, as criminology has established itself as a discipline, have been high. As is now well documented, one of the consistent effects of the category of crime and criminal justice systems – both largely accepted by most criminologists and forms of criminology – is the reproduction and exacerbation of social and economic inequalities. As Reiman (1998) so succinctly put it in the title of a now classic text, a key effect of the carnival mirror of harms around which criminal justice systems are organised is that *The Rich Get Richer, the Poor Get Prison*. Indeed, the contours of this carnival mirror are not incidental, but integral, to the nature of contemporary criminal justice systems. And it is this integral nature which explains the obduracy of dominant social constructions of crime – reproduced, of course, by criminologists – in the face of the enormous amount of critical scrutiny to which these have been, and remain, subject.

While criminology may have, and criminologists certainly have been, responsible for important and progressive theoretical and practical work, the efforts of over 100 years' focus on the object of crime have been accompanied by: a depressing and almost cyclical tour around a series of cul-de-sacs in search of the 'causes' of crime; vastly expanded criminal justice systems which, at the same time, have proven unsuccessful on the basis of almost any publicly provided rationale for them; and ever increasing processes of criminalisation, as a succession of critical criminologists have demonstrated. If criminology is now well established as a discipline, the costs of legitimacy and professionalisation have been, and continue to be, high when measured against any index of social justice. On the other hand, we would argue that in some respects an alternative discipline, such as that based around social harm, could barely be less successful. But it also entails pitfalls, and some might argue that these are more problematic than those entailed in 'doing' criminology, since the dangers associated with the latter activity are at least known (formally), while those attendant upon 'doing' social harm are relatively unknown.

In the short to medium term, then, we should note that whether or not a new disciplinary focus is to emerge, we must accept that raising issues of social harm does not entail making a simple, once-and-for-all choice between representing these as *either* crimes *or* harms; each may form part of an effective political strategy. What we would add is that it is crucial that whether/when we speak of crime or harm, we must be clear about which we are speaking on particular occasions, that is, description and analysis must not slide between the two, not least due to the risk of opening up such work to charges from critics that it lacks rigour or displays bias, for example. In this respect, the development of a discipline organised around social harm may prove progressive, since it provides a further disciplinary basis from which, and series of outlets within which, treatments of social harm may – where deemed appropriate – proceed.

3

Towards a Political Economy of Harm: States, Corporations and the Production of Inequality

Steve Tombs and Paddy Hillyard

One of the least discussed, but most offensive, effects of New Labour government in Britain since 1997 has been the virtual institutionalisation of what Hutton referred to in 1995 as the '30/30/40 society' (Hutton, 1995: 195 and passim). With their variously stated commitments to retaining, and even extending, central aspects of the neo-liberal architecture erected on the rubble of social democracy by four successive Conservative governments, Blair's administrations have presided over a continuing, regressive redistribution of wealth, income and life chances for most groups of people.

Since setting its stall out immediately through, on its first full day of office, relinquishing control over a key element of fiscal policy – interest rates – to a group of non-elected bankers, and then, in its first foray into social policy, imposing cuts in single parent benefit, the New Labour government has consistently sought to represent itself as the government which cannot buck the market – though it has been busily reconstituting that market, embracing the private sector and opening up almost all areas of what remains of the welfare state to the vicissitudes of the market and the whip of the financial analyst's evaluation.

At the same time, one area in which New Labour governments have seen themselves as retaining considerable room for manoeuvre has been with respect to 'crime' and 'criminality'. These terms are used advisedly, not simply in the sense that each term is a social construction, but because their ambit has been expanded significantly since 1997. Thus these terms have been extended to encompass a wide range of 'antisocial behaviours', typically engaged in by young people – first, 'teenagers', and more recently, children as young as eight years old. Other favoured targets of criminal justice interventions have been 'asylum seekers', 'unfit' parents, 'aggressive beggars', 'sex offenders', and, most recently, 'terrorists' or their sympathisers. Crucial in this extension of the reach of criminalisation has been the importing of the phrase 'community safety' – which we might interpret as freedom from or the absence of harms – into the criminal justice lexicon, notably via the Crime and Disorder Act 1998. Moreover, in the local audits which this Act required, the term 'community safety' has been used to target traditional kinds of deviance, notwithstanding the fact that it is in principle a relatively inclusive term, while the Home Office, in its guidance to local authorities on the drawing up of a crime audit and community safety strategy, issued no explicit guidance excluding the range of social harms produced by corporations and local states themselves (Whyte, 2002). Yet, *as if natural*, the disorders and insecurities upon which local community safety strategies have focused have almost overwhelmingly been confined to the *activities of* (rather than the harmful *experiences suffered by*) the marginalised 30 per cent of the population (see also Hallsworth, 1999).

Thus a further effect of this redefinition of the 'problems' of crime and criminality has been to reproduce, indeed exacerbate, the political myopia towards the offences and harms produced by the *least* socially excluded or marginal members of our societies – namely, the relatively powerful, the high status offenders and dominant organisations whose crimes are usually captured within the (albeit unsatisfying) rubric of 'corporate and white-collar crime' (Tombs, 2002). Foucault's celebrated analysis of the emergence of the 'the criminological labyrinth' (Foucault, 1977: 252) – within which 'the perception of another form of life was being articulated upon that of another class and another human species ... [a] zoology of social sub-species and an ethnology of the civilizations of malefactors' (ibid., 253; cited in Sumner, 1994: 36) – retains its relevance. The gaze of the political spokespeople of the victims of crime, as well as of contemporary academic criminology, remains overwhelmingly cast downwards.

Thus if one thinks of the major issues that have affected people's quality of life in the UK in the past quarter of a century, one immediately realises that these have remained untouched by either the rhetoric or practices around crime, law and order. Notable here are state violence and the variety of associated crimes committed in Northern Ireland, the BSE and various food scandals, the case of Harold Shipman and his ability to continue to murder for years largely thanks to the complacency of a self-regulating professional body, the depressing series of rail disasters that have caused hundreds of deaths and misery for tens of thousands, the enormous toll of deaths brought forward by pollution, and the sets of cases of so-called pensions and endowment 'mis-selling' which, taken together, probably represent the most widespread and devastating instances of corporate crime ever committed on these islands (Clarke, 1998; Ryle, 2002). What is striking is that each of these events raises issues about law, its enforcement, and the social (in)ability to pursue powerful actors through the criminal justice system – in other words, they all fall firmly within the supposed terrain of academic criminology (Hillyard et al., 2004).

Shifting focus to the US, the archetypal capitalist society, we find that the problems of neo-liberal economic policy become daily more apparent. For example, levels of personal and business debt have rocketed to new heights, the trade deficit at the end of 2002 stood at $450 billion, growth struggles around the 1 or 2 per cent level, and foreign ownership of American assets has risen to nearly $7 trillion. It is not difficult to predict that there will be a crash and other multinationals will join Enron, Worldcom and others in ignominy. When the first bank collapses the reality of the fragility and nonsense of the neo-liberal paradigm may sink home. Meanwhile the gap between the rich and the poor increases, while those at the bottom of the pile eek out an existence from garbage cans on the margins of society. Park benches are redesigned to move on the homeless and those who use their initiative to cut out a living on the streets by illegal means find them themselves in prison. In April 2003 there were over 2 million people in US jails and prisons. As in Britain, these inequalities prevent social mobility and cement the class structure, a structure which in the US is highly racialised[1] and feminised (see Garfinkel and McLanahan, 1988). In both countries, one of the most important social phenomena has been the growth in women's employment – yet once these economies stall it is precisely these jobs that will be the first to go, with disastrous social consequences for the increasing number of households requiring two incomes to sustain their (usually hardly luxurious) standard of living. In these contexts, the neo-liberal economic paradigm is fundamentally harmful – it wrecks lives and creates harm on a wide scale – and these features are not some aberration, but integral and necessary aspects of this form of economic and political organisation.

The trends in Britain, the US and elsewhere in the northern and the industrialising countries in the southern hemispheres clearly demonstrate that the major *events* affecting the lives of most people are produced within the (increasingly complex) state–corporate network: they are harms systematically produced by the state, in its local and central forms, and by private business, from the local trader through to the multinational corporation. Yet if this statement is true with respect to events, it is even more significant with regard to the *conditions*, the states of affairs that determine people's quality and longevity of life. Thus, states and companies combine to produce not only unequal distributions of income and wealth, but also differentially distributed access to healthcare, social and welfare services, education, employment, housing stock, for example. In addressing the production of social harm, we are inevitably led to the need to understand the interrelated functioning of the most powerful social actors – states and private businesses. A framework for understanding the increasing imbrication of these formally discrete public and private bodies forms a key focus of this chapter.

More specifically, the aims of this chapter are two-fold. The first section explores some of the more theoretical issues concerning the neo-liberal economic model and, in particular, the relationship between states, markets and the law. It then explores some of the principal characteristics of the model: the increasing concentration of economic power and the moves to further deregulation, globalisation as a 'hegemonic project', the growing inequalities and, most importantly, the dogma that perpetuates the view that the neo-liberal model is the only way for progress to be achieved. The second section of the chapter then introduces the notion of harm and analyses some of the different forms of harm, which are directly or indirectly connected to capitalism in general, but its neo-liberal version in particular.

THE 'NEW' INTERNATIONAL ECONOMY

The past 30 years or so have witnessed a key series of economic, political, social and cultural shifts, central to which has been the emergence of neo-liberalism, a particular version of capitalist ideology and organisation in which free markets and minimal states are central (Pearce and Tombs, 1998: 3–33). Thus, reflecting upon the 1990s, Anderson has defined the 'principal aspect' of this decade as 'the virtually uncontested consolidation, and universal diffusion, of neo-liberalism' (Anderson, 2000: 10), with this 'neo-liberal consensus' finding 'a new point of stabilization in the "Third Way" of the Clinton-Blair regimes' (ibid.: 11). For some commentators, the end of the twentieth century signalled the once-and-for all triumph of the political shell of liberal democracy and a free market economic order (Fukuyama, 1992), and the death of all forms of socialism and social democracy (Gray, 1998; Callaghan and Tunney, 2000). If such apocryphal claims are taken at all seriously, one should expect to find severe implications for the willingness or ability of nation states to regulate capitalist corporations effectively.

Most of the ideas informing this new neo-liberal economic paradigm are associated with the work of the Chicago School. It has been enormously influential in the reorganisation of the British and American economies (and, of course, internationally), in terms of the organisation of interactions between national economies, and as tools of powerful international organisations in their dealings with developing economies.

Neo-liberalism, states, markets and the law

The discourses around the neo-liberal model seldom mention the role of the state and for many it is assumed that the state has been eclipsed by the rise of the corporation. It is important, therefore, to enter into some theoretical consideration of the nature of states, markets and corporate activity. We seek to utilise some of the insights of a Marxist analysis here, a mode of analysis which itself seems to have been organised off academic agendas in the past two decades (Pearce, 2003).

The first point to make is that, both historically and contemporaneously, it is clear that capitalist forms of production may be organised in a series of quite different ways within a variety of political and social 'shells', producing quite different effects (see Pearce and Tombs, 1998). That is, capitalism as a system is neither unified nor homogeneous – which is not to deny certain essential features that define it. Within the construction of different forms of capitalism, the state plays a key role (Jessop, 1982, 1990). For instance, state activities are preconditions for the risk-taking activities of entrepreneurs. States help to constitute capital, commodity, commercial and residential property markets, produce different kinds of 'human capital' and constitute labour markets, and regulate the employment contract. Further, the state plays a role in constituting economic enterprises through specifying rules of liability and possibly specifying rules of incorporation. These are put in place by regulatory instances that include, but are not exhausted by, regulatory agencies.

These schematic observations partly explain why regulation is a necessary function of a state even in the quintessential market economy. While 'the ideological notion of latent or implicit markets which only need freeing figures strongly in neo-liberal rhetoric' (Sayer, 1995: 104), this contrasts with the overwhelming empirical and theoretical evidence attesting to markets as social constructions. The creation, maintenance and development of 'markets' require coordinated, extensive and ongoing involvement of the state and other institutions (Sayer, 1995). A key instrument of this work by states is effected through law in its various forms.[2]

While criminal law polices the boundaries of capitalism and plays a key role in disorganising its potential opponents (Pearce, 1976), civil law is essential to its functioning (Pashukhanis, 1978). Legal regulation of economic transactions depends upon the acknowledgement that actors are in some specific senses legal subjects. In the case of the modern business corporation, it also plays a key role in its very constitution as a legal subject and in its organisation. The limited liability business corporation is a trading company construed as having its own legal personality, independent of its members. It has directors legally empowered to determine its business goals and the use of its assets and managers to organise specific profit-making activities. Its shareholders usually play some role in selecting its directors and are entitled to a share of its profits but, other than the monies that they have invested in the company, are immune from the consequences of its actions or debts (Perrott, 1981: 83–4). It is this last feature, in particular, that means that this organisation is built upon a structure of irresponsibility (Pearce, 1995; Tombs and Whyte, 2003). The generalisation of this legal form, with its attendant privileges, and other elements of the advanced capitalist legal model, is one of the key and underemphasised aspects of the process of globalisation. Furthermore, it is in the transnational context that we find the development of civil law in a direction that not only recreates many elements of (pre-democratic) British common law but also goes significantly beyond these. The most useful way to understand this is by a brief digression into aspects of the emergence of some key international institutions.

During the Second World War it became clear to those opposing the Axis Powers that it was necessary to set up a series of organisations to regulate political, social and economic relations between and within states. Thus the United Nations (UN) gradually emerged over a four-year period beginning in 1941 and, during the Bretton Woods Conference of 1944, the International Monetary Fund (IMF) and the World Bank were created. The IMF and the World Bank were initially mandated to end world poverty and placed under the control of the UN's Economic and Social Council and in 1947 a new body was proposed, the International Trade Organisation (ITO), under UN control and subject to its social mandate. American pressure prevented the creation of the ITO and also, in 1947, led to the creation of a new organisation, the General Agreement on Tariffs and Trades (GATT), with a more restricted mandate not directly answerable to the UN. In 1947, the IMF and the World Bank were reconfigured so that their mandate and decisions were more controllable by the wealthiest nations, particularly the US (Barlow and Clarke, 2001: 54–9).

Since 1951, European trade barriers have been increasingly attenuated, so that the European Union (EU) integrates politically and economically a substantial number of European nation states. Since 1994, the US, Canada and Mexico have become significantly more economically integrated through the North American Free Trade Agreement (NAFTA). In 1995, GATT was effectively replaced by the World Trade Organisation (WTO) which, although nominally democratic, is also effectively under the control of the wealthiest nations (Wallach and Sforza, 1999; Barlow and Clarke, 2001).[3] The policies of these countries in turn are largely dictated by the interests of the major corporations active within them – although this by no means guarantees a total coincidence of interests between the wealthiest nations, nor between these individually or collectively and specific corporations.

For our purposes what is most significant about these changes is that, in the name of 'free trade', there has been and continues to be moves to develop international law in a way that significantly limits the ability of national governments to determine the nature of their social, political, legal and economic systems. For example, Chapter 11 of the NAFTA agreement has been used to challenge directly a number of decisions made by governments concerning environmental and safety and health regulations. It allows corporations to sue the government of a NAFTA member-country for any lost profit, resulting from that government's actions.[4] Further, judgments in such cases are made by secret tribunals and are premised on an assumption, made explicit in the WTO's Agreement on Technical Barriers on Trade, that environmental standards must be both 'necessary' and least 'trade restrictive' (Barlow and Clarke, 2001: 80). Clearly these 'criteria' are based on the neo-liberal dogma that increased trade *per se* is intrinsically good.

Furthermore, the rationale for damages lies in another doctrine developed by right-wing American lawyers. This is the doctrine of 'takings', which provides an expansive new definition of property rights. Epstein (1989) argued that regulations 'are takings under the Fifth Amendment ("… nor shall private property be taken for public purpose without just compensation"), so government must pay those businesses or individuals whose property values are in someway diminished by public actions' (cited in Greider, 2001: 4). The logic of this position is relatively clear: if there is a conflict between property rights and other social values – claims for the common good, and the rights of those who own little or nothing – the minority who own the bulk of the wealth will see their rights secured. This will even be true when the government intrudes into the 'private sphere' in order to protect society's general health and welfare. A blatant attempt to demand such a legal regime might prove politically problematic in most democratic countries – hence its use as a legal rationale in such arms length decision-making bodies as the tribunals of NAFTA and the WTO is both a sly way to achieve similar goals as well as providing a basis for claiming that it is external pressure, not an internal political demand, that leads to their national implementation. Right-wing politicians and the US Council for International Business were already discussing these ideas in the mid-1980s well before the NAFTA negotiations and before the creation of the WTO (Greider, 2001: 5). Clinton's Democratic administration proved a willing participant in such discussions (MacArthur, 2001). Once again, then, we have a clear example of an unholy alliance between politicians, academics and business leaders.

Finally, it should be noted that the power of the advocates and beneficiaries of 'free trade' would be augmented significantly – and, some argue, disastrously (Gatswatch, 2001) – through the extension of the General Agreement on Trade and Services which is currently being negotiated at the WTO (GATS, originally agreed at the WTO in 1994). Legal mandates to 'liberalise' services will open up crucial markets for private corporations, given that the value of international trade in services amounted even in 1999 to $1,350 billion, or 20 per cent of the world's cross-border trade, these figures being an understatement; moreover, for the past 20 years, trade in services has been expanding more rapidly than trade in goods (WTO, 2001). The effect of any such agreement being extended would be to undermine significantly government's ability to regulate, extend to almost any service provided by national governments, and massively increase the power and reach of northern-based multinationals in developing economies (Gatswatch, 2001). In short, GATS would remove the final remaining legal barriers to the creation of a truly global marketplace.

In this context, it is now possible to consider some of the key characteristics of neo-liberal economies *per se*. One dominant feature of neo-liberal economic regimes has been the concentration of economic power – and they seem firmly set on inexorable paths towards even greater concentration. Within both the US and the UK economies, there were a series of key merger movements over the last century (Jones, 1982). None could be accounted for adequately in terms of the greater efficiency of those companies who benefited the most (ibid.; Pearce and Tombs, 1998). A perhaps more plausible interpretation of these trends is to be found in the desire to secure ever greater market share and greater absolute corporate incomes while cutting costs, as a means of staving off (or perhaps redistributing the effects of) long-term declines in rates of profitability. Following Marx, the level of competition/oligopoly serves as a means of redistributing surplus value among firms – it cannot affect the level of surplus value, and thus the rate of profit, at the level of the economy as a whole.

The 1990s saw further mergers and the emergence of oligopoly on a global scale (Pearce and Tombs, 2002: 192–5). One net effect of these general restructurings has been to augment the dominance of existing, and the creation of some new, extraordinarily large economic actors. An examination of the most recent available data on the gross domestic product (GDP) of all 30 Organisation for Economic Cooperation and Development (OECD) member states with the annual revenues of the world's largest corporations is instructive: on the basis of such data, *of the 50 largest economies, 24 are states, 26 are corporations*; Exxon-Mobil, now the world's largest corporation, has a revenue greater than the GDP of 14 OECD states.[5]

'Globalisation' as a hegemonic project

A second important feature of the neo-liberal paradigm is that globalisation has now assumed the mantle of a hegemonic project. A widespread belief is circulating, to the effect that this new phase of capitalist development (even, for some, a stage of post-capitalism) renders the efforts of states, regulatory agencies and oppositional social forces increasingly redundant. This 'new orthodoxy', or 'common sense' (Harman, 1996), now widespread in political, cultural, popular and academic contexts (Hirst and Thompson, 1996: 1, 4), proclaims, in its strongest variants, the emergence of a new, globalised economic order. It emphasises the primacy of markets, capitalist production and the minimised role of nation states. Irrespective of whether, and in what forms, globalisation actually 'exists', it is clear that the discourses of globalisation now exert enormous power over governments of advanced capitalist economies, not least the current British and US governments. Thus the *discourses* of globalisation have assumed the status of a hegemonic truth, a new orthodoxy (Harman, 1996; Hirst and Thompson, 1996; Weiss, 1997). It is the 'perceived dictats' (Goldblatt, 1997: 140) of this orthodoxy which governments invoke as they seek to attract or retain private capital through various forms of de- and re-regulation, impose massive cutbacks in the social wage, and more generally reproduce the 'political construction of helplessness' (Weiss, 1997: 15); and it is this orthodoxy to which transnational capital points as it seeks to increase its leverage over national states, and both intra- and inter-national sources of resistance.[6] Thus, for our considerations, the key implication of the hegemony of discourses of globalisation is that governments can exert less political control over economies

– economic management is relegated to the task of overseeing the operation of 'free' markets – and over the key actors in these economies, namely corporations and, most significantly, multi- or transnational corporations. Having accepted – more or less willingly – the dictats laid down through the discourses of globalisation, governments *discipline themselves* to the extent that they either eschew, or at best exercise supreme caution in imposing, additional 'burdens' – that is, regulation, or more specifically the costs arising from so-called 'social' regulation and the effects of corporate competitiveness – upon business.

What we want to suggest here is that the very emergence of arguments and claims around globalisation represents part of a project of hegemonic reconstruction. One immediate observation is that if the idea of globalisation has become a very powerful one, then this has emerged, not in any 'free-floating' sense, but as it is propagated in forms that are linked to certain agents, institutions and practices. If we view globalisation as 'hyper-liberalism' (Cox, 1993b: 272), it is possible to link this idea to the claim by some that there has occurred a conscious process of hegemony (re)construction, key agents of which have been large multinational companies, right-wing governments and politicians, particularly from the US and Britain, and right-wing academics (Gill 1990; Cox 1993b; Snider, 2000).

Globalisation tendencies are symbiotically linked to deflationary macro-economic policies. Of course, such policies, in the name of 'adjustment', have been rigorously pursued within many national states under pressure from a range of international economic and financial institutions including the IMF, the World Bank, the G-8,[7] the OECD and, more recently if at least post-Seattle increasingly infamously, by the WTO. Moreover, the role of such institutions embraces normative as well as material elements (Pauly 1994; Price 1994; T. Young 1995). Thus, more generally, Gill and Law argue that 'during the 1970s and the 1980s, the emphasis, certainly with regard to economic policy, has shifted towards *a definition of questions and concepts* which is more congruent with the interests of large-scale, transnational capital' (Gill and Law, 1993: 104, emphasis added; Strange, 1994).

The construction of this new hegemony, then, relies not just on material power (the ability of capital and national states to distribute benefits and disadvantages), but also on a moral and intellectual leadership, so that the ideas associated with globalisation become predominant to the extent that they seep into popular consciousness, ruling out alternatives, and integrating into the ranks of the (relatively) advantaged some 'subordinate' groups while (often safely) consigning to economic and social marginalisation and exclusion whole segments of populations (Pearce and Tombs, 1996). This hegemony seeks to organise off political agendas notions of state regulation of, or intervention in, corporate activity and discussions of the social wreckage produced by economic policies. It further organises from political agendas the ability of states to address social problems via social policy, where such policy involves expenditures. Of course, academic discourse plays a not insignificant role here, and more generally in constructions of the 'feasible' or 'acceptable' (Snider, 1990; 2000; Moran, 1998; and see Pearce and Tombs, 1998: 223–46; Hillyard et al., 2004).

Neo-liberalism's 'political realities'

Thus the utilisation and development of the idea of globalisation has involved the creation of a new set of economic and political 'realities' – realities which constrain the possible, the desirable and the feasible within and beyond national states. This has profound implications for those who would seek to improve protective regulation, and for the greater provision of goods and services through a public sector. In this sense of the creation of new discursive terrains, terrains which set these limits, it makes sense to speak of an increase in the structural power of capital.

These new political realities are now observable in a number of areas. First, any country which wishes to be a member of the new club must make its economy business friendly. This has been most observable in Britain where a succession of New Labour ministers have stated the aim of the Labour government as being to make Britain the most business friendly environment in the world (see Osler, 2002, passim). Second, states must look favourably on the competitive context of their key corporate players and make sure that they are on an 'even playing field'. This involves being extremely generous in terms of corporate welfare and corporate taxation. Excessive corporate welfare has been recently justified on the basis of the need to develop 'national champions' to compete in the so-called global marketplace. Yet this practice of state welfare to corporations has long been central to the development of corporate capital, and operates on an international, not simply domestic, scale (see, for example, Ruigrock and van Tulder, 1995). The commitment to corporate welfare was heightened under Reagan and Thatcher (Chomsky, 1999: 66–8), and maintained by more recent administrations in both the US and UK. Beyond national governments, the IMF has been identified as a key source of corporate welfare (Mokhiber and Weissman, 1999a: 74–6; see also Mokhiber and Weissman, 1999b).

At the same time, based on the 'reality' of their ability to locate in a range of localities, transnationals are able to continue to exert pressures on governments to reduce the tax 'burden' (Toynbee, 2002). It is no coincidence that the years since 1980 have seen across almost all OECD states reductions in levels of corporate taxation (Mishra, 1999: 41–4). Citing figures from a report by the US General Accounting Office, Mokhiber and Weissman note that in each of the years 1989 to 1995, almost a third of the largest corporations operating in the US 'paid no US income tax. More than six out of ten large companies [assets of $250 million or more, or sales of at least $50 million] paid less than a million dollars in federal income tax in 1995' (Mokhiber and Weissman, 1999c: 1). Donohoe claims 'US corporations receive more annually in government subsidies than they pay in taxes' (2003: 81). A recent series of exposés by Nick Davies on corporate taxation in the UK has documented how the Inland Revenue adopts a generally laissez-faire approach to collection of corporate taxes, writing off non-payment or failing even to investigate corporate tax returns, and thus not collecting even the diminished sums owed once government-led concessions and corporate devised avoidance schemes have worked their effect on the corporate tax bill (Davies, 2002a, b, c).

Most fundamentally, then, we inhabit an era in which business interests – which are by definition sectional interests arising out of activity conducted for private motives – are increasingly represented as 'general' or 'national' interests. We are increasingly persuaded that what happens to individual businesses and business in general matters to us. When a poor quarterly performance on the part of a company, or a drop in the London Stock Exchange, is reported to us it is represented as necessarily and indeed generally bad news. Further, business activity is increasingly represented as *a good end in itself*, as opposed to what it actually is – namely a *means* to some other end, whether this is profits, wages, or various socially necessary and (perhaps) socially useful goods and services.

Intimately related to the increasing moral capital of capital is the emergence of discourses of deregulation. Thus many have argued that the period since 1979 has also been one characterised by *deregulation*, accompanied ideologically by commitments to enterprise – and enterprise can also be expressed as the valorisation of risk – which have become so engrained in certain circles that they are almost unquestioned truths.

Alongside this valorisation of private economic activity has occurred a sustained attack on state, public and, in particular, regulatory activity. Bureaucracy has become a pejorative term, the public sector increasingly understood in terms of waste and inefficiency, while the phraseology of 'burdens on business' and 'red tape' to refer to law regulating economic activity has become very common currency, with the unquestioned implication being that such burdens and tape should be reduced as far as possible.

Whereas large public subsidies to, low taxation for, and re-regulation of the corporate sector are seen as simply new political realities, similarly unavoidable is the new fact that welfare for those who have to bear the brunt of the vagaries of the market is seen as a burden, increasingly disciplinary regulation the only option. In the US the scope of and access to welfare has been steadily reduced in recent years. Underpinning these moves has been a highly racist agenda in so far that much welfare involves a transfer from white to black people. These changes have found intellectual support in right-wing academia, and the argument that welfare produces dependency and an underclass. The drive to contract the welfare system is particularly stark in relation to the provision of occupational pensions and healthcare schemes by employers. These are increasingly being seen as a burden. Morgan Stanley, one of America's leading investment banks, circulated a memorandum to North American clients in November 2002 telling them that they should pull out of unionised firms. It described pension plans as 'toxic' for shareholders and stated that union firms are more likely to provide retirement and heathcare benefits which could eat into corporate profits (*Guardian*, 23 November 2002).

Britain may not have yet gone as far as America in contracting its welfare state, but many American ideas have found favour with both Conservative and Labour governments, such as the reduction of unemployment insurance as a right, welfare-to-work initiatives, tax credits rather than direct public subsidies and a preparedness to do nothing as the corporate sector stops making pension provision for its employees – nothing, that is, except urge that workers save more, while raising the idea of a 'flexible' retiring age as a euphemism for an extension of people's working lives (Jones, 2002: 4). At the same time, it has encouraged the use of Private Finance Initiatives to fund current and capital expenditure showing a reckless disregard for the welfare of the next generation who will be forced to pay for the current generation's welfare improvements before being able to access health, education and employment provision for themselves and their children. In the wider world, pressure to reduce public spending leading to a reduction in social welfare has been the cornerstone of many 'structural adjustment' packages implemented by the IMF and the World Bank, with devastating consequences.

Most of the most generous social policies which guarantee support in health, housing, education and income maintenance are supported by progressive taxation and they achieve substantial redistribution of wealth from the better off to the weaker sections of society. Now there is a widespread belief that progressive taxation policies are anathema to growth and that nation states that go along this route will be uncompetitive in the global market. In such a context there is nothing to address the growing levels of inequalities, nor ameliorate their consequences, which are currently being experienced by most advanced industrial societies and many countries have begun to dismantle the programmes built-up through years of struggle.

THE 'NEW' INTERNATIONAL ECONOMY AND HARM PRODUCTION

The capitalist economic system, while creating large benefits for sections of the world's population, has always produced a wide range of social harms. As Marx so cogently showed, harm production is a necessary and essential part of the system. The state, as we have suggested above, is often complicit in the processes of capitalism's harms while at the same time producing its own forms of harms in a variety of different ways. Contradictorily, states, while producing significant harm to their own and other's citizens, do develop policies to prevent harm or, where such harms occur, to help those individuals affected. The production and control of harm, therefore, involves a complex interrelationship both between states and the corporations that operate within the capitalist system, and between different elements of the state itself.

We would further argue that the neo-liberal form of capitalism is both quantitatively and qualitatively more harmful than other forms – and at the same time, governments are much more reluctant to prevent the harms caused or to alleviate their impact through the provision of a wide range of policies and support networks. It is difficult, however, to develop a comprehensive picture of the nature and extent of harm produced by either the dynamics of the capitalist system, and, in particular, its neo-liberal version, or the range of harms caused directly or indirectly by the state. Thus, while there has been a substantial amount of work rooted in a generic – but usually taken-for-granted – notion of 'crime', neither corporate nor state illegalities have figured significantly in such work. Further, if unsurprisingly, nor has there been any attempt ever made to develop a generic concept of 'capitalist harm'. Closest to such an enterprise have been perhaps analogous and certainly useful attempts to set out typologies of human need, violence and, of course, human rights.[8] There is also an important body of work which focuses upon the relationship between neo-liberalism and the systematic production of specific harms – the stunning collection edited by Jim Yong Kim and colleagues (Kim et al., 2000) or the articles that fill *The International Journal of Health Services* [9] are exemplary instances of such work around health. The contributions that are included in this text provide concrete analyses of various specific areas of harm.

Notwithstanding what follows, we wish to provide here a few illustrations of the nature and extent of different harms under a series of broad headings. Thus while it is premature to attempt to develop any typology of harm, it is possible to categorise loosely the main types of harms which are produced by the capitalist system, in general, and neo-liberalism, in particular, into four main groups: the harms which occur as a direct result of the *dynamics of the market*, and in particular the intimately related and growing *inequalities* which this organisation of economic and social life systematically produces; harms produced during the *production and distribution* of goods and services, and harms produced as a result of the *consumption* of goods or services. We shall discuss each of these loose categories in turn, simply as a way of illustrating the range of harms with which any political economy of harm must grapple.

Markets and inequalities

Perhaps the most extensive and far-reaching harms stem from the very operation of market-based economies. The new economic order – based upon the extension of market-based logic and discipline to all areas of economic (and social) life and all corners of the globe – is fundamentally characterised by growing inequalities both within and between states. As Gordon illustrates in this volume (Chapter 15), the sheer scale (and trends in) inequalities between and within states are startling.

However, these increases in inequality are hardly uniform. Thus, trends towards greater poverty and income inequality in the 1980s were the most marked in those welfare regimes pursuing a 'liberal deregulatory' (Esping-Andersen, 1999) strategy: for example, during the 1980s, the lowest decile earners lost, relative to the median, 8 percentage points in Australia, 11 in Canada, 13 in New Zealand, 23 in the UK and 29 in the US (ibid.: 154; see also Fritzell, 1993). Gottschalk et al. (1997) and then Froud et al. (1999) are among others who document the peculiarity of the US and UK in terms of inequality.

These inequalities have, of course, a range of manifest origins. Some are a direct result of the *self-imposed* fiscal constraints placed upon government spending within neo-liberal states. Some are quite straightforward consequences of decisions of government, such as budgets which redistribute wealth from the poor to rich (see Pantazis and Gordon, 2000). Other inequalities, and associated harms, are a direct result of the constant demand for profit, which can only be achieved in the short term by cutting the costs of production – for example, paying the minimum wage, or less. Yet further inequalities and associated harms are produced either as a result of the volatile international capital markets where currency speculation creates economic havoc within countries or from the demands of institutions like the IMF, the World Bank or WTO.

What is clear is that a key characteristic of the harms produced systematically by markets and their inequalities is that they are a necessary effect of states permitting unaccountable world institutions and corporations to act in a relatively unconstrained fashion. Market-produced inequalities are, of course, explained in neo-Chicagoan terms by the maxim that the competitive nature of neo-liberalism produces losers as well as winners. And, indeed, there are devastating harms which arise from the growing inequalities which the neo-liberal economic model produces. There are the direct harms experienced by significant sections of the population who are forced to live at or below subsistence level and there are the indirect harms created such as poor health, illiteracy and antisocial and criminal behaviour. Supporters of this form of economic activity argue that inequalities are essential for progress, innovation and the overall success of the system – and that the trickle down of wealth subsequently reduces poverty. Yet, there is considerable evidence to suggest that the greater the inequalities the more unstable the system. A large proportion of conventional criminal behaviour has its origins in deprivation, and lack of income and material possessions, in a context in which material possessions and conspicuous consumption are the dominant values in capitalist social organisation. Moreover, in many communities, both in the developed and developing world, the production and distribution of illegal drugs provide the only means to a standard of living above the poverty level. As crime rates increase, more and more resources are made available to deal with crime and other dysfunctional behaviour that arise from subsistence existence, thereby reducing the amount of resources available for education, health and other social services.

Production, distribution and consumption

The harms caused in the production, distribution and consumption of goods and services are now reasonably documented, and include a range of physical, financial and psychological harms. In this section, we focus upon three different forms of harms to illustrate some of the many types of harm that emerge from the production, distribution and consumption of goods and services within neo-liberal economies: namely, environmental destruction, the production or consumption of food and, rather differently, the harms which emerge as a consequence of the very differential production and distribution founded upon the ability to pay rather than human need, the central basis of a market-based system – and here we illustrate the point via reference to the pharmaceutical industry.[10]

If we turn first to focus upon environmental harm, we find a chilling set of consequences of the production and distribution activities of corporations and their relationships with states. To illustrate these, we focus here on data pertaining to the US, since this is the world's largest economy, it is the home of the world's largest multinationals, and it is the world's richest economy, despite which there are massive and increasing levels of inequality, so that if significant segments of the population are being consigned to the margins of the world's largest economy, then one can expect to find an even more skewed distribution of quality of life across the rest of the globe. A recent survey of evidence relating to environmental degradation in the US and its consequences for social justice within and beyond that state is particularly helpful (Donohoe, 2003).

In the US in particular, and the industrialized north in general, the inequality of resource use and its consequences are stark: on average, one North American uses as much commercial energy as two West Germans, three Japanese, 16 Chinese or 1,072 Nepalese (Gordon and Suzuki, 1990: 211). Put differently, the US contains 5 per cent of the world's population, yet accounts for 25 per cent of world energy consumption and 72 per cent of its hazardous waste production (Donohoe, 2003: 580). Globally, the richest 25 per cent of countries account for 63 per cent of global emissions, the poorest 20 per cent contributing just 2 per cent (ibid.; see also Smith, 1997: 25, 15).

Returning to the US specifically, its Defense Department is the world's largest consumer of oil, while generating 'half a billion tons of toxic waste per annum, more than the top five chemical companies combined' (Donohoe, 2003: 582). Within the US, industry and car use are the primary and secondary contributors to air pollution, and, within this, trucks and buses account for almost three-quarters of the estimated cancer risk from auto-related pollution, while levels of airborne pollutants endanger almost 133 million Americans (Donohoe, 2003: 575). Moreover,

The US Environmental Protection Agency (EPA) has estimated that 250,000 cases of aggravated asthma and 15,000 deaths from cardiopulmonary diseases could be eliminated each year if the agency's standards for ozone and particulates are implemented ... Unfortunately, the implementation has been blocked by heavy lobbying from oil, gas and other industries. (Donohoe, 2003: 575)

Standards of water quality in the US are declining, the Clean Water Act of 1972 is under review (for retrenchment not expansion!), and cases of ill health caused by unfit tap water are numerous – for example, an outbreak of *Cryptosporidium* affected over 400,000 people in Milwaukee in 1993 (Donohoe, 2003: 576; see also Snider, 2003). Even bottled water is not a safe resort for the consumer – it has recently been estimated that between 25 and 40 per cent of bottled water on sale in the US is simply repackaged tap water (Donohoe, 2003: 576).

On toxic pollutants more generally, US industry adds 25 billion pounds of toxic pollutants to the environment each year (Donohoe, 2003: 577). The effects are too numerous to mention, but as examples: 2 million children in the US are at risk of neurological damage due to lead exposures, exposures which particularly threaten Afro-American children living in inner-city areas; 45 million US citizens, a disproportionate number of whom come from lower socio-economic status neighbourhoods, live within 4 miles of the 1,000-plus designated 'Superfund' sites;[11] and the EPA estimates that farm workers suffer up to 300,000 pesticide-related acute illnesses and injuries per annum (Donohoe, 2003: 577).

The second example of harm caused in the production, distribution and consumption of goods focuses on deaths and illnesses arising from consumption itself. Though the most harmful substance consumed today is tobacco, the analysis here focuses on the production and consumption of the food we eat. There are now well-documented links between food consumption and health (Baggot, 2000). The dynamics of the market and the ever-present demand to increase profits creates an environment in which concerns about safety are not being prioritised. The example of genetically modified organisms (GMOs) is a case in point. The health and environmental effects remain unknown. Yet, the big US multinationals are determined to push ahead with their production. GMOs are now used to plant 25 per cent of America's corn crop and 30 per cent of its soya beans; moreover, 'at least 60 per cent of convenience foods now sold in the US contain genetically altered ingredients. No labelling is required' (Donohoe, 2003: 580). Convenience foods, unsurprisingly, are disproportionately marketed and consumed by lower socio-economic groups. The European Union's reluctance to whole-heartedly endorse GMOs has now led to a trading dispute between the US and the EU.

The consequences of not prioritising safety and health concerns are only too apparent in beef production and the subsequent development of vCJD, which has so far killed nearly 50 people in the UK. While the origins of the disease are far from certain they clearly lie deep within the system of food production and the interrelationship between the state and corporations. It is accepted that the immediate cause of death is a result of the transfer of a prion from cattle to humans. But there are a number of theories about the cause of cattle developing mad cow disease – yet whichever of these is most accurate, they tend to have in common that they locate the cause of the problem with the lack of control over the development of food production practices, particularly the use of waste materials or chemicals. Just how many cases of vCJD there will be in the coming years is a matter of conjecture. A new study suggests that there could be as many as 6,600 cases (Ahlstrom, 2002).

Another major area of concern involves the indiscriminate use of antibiotics, some of which are for growth promotion only, in animal foods. It is now widely believed that this has created a situation in which certain bugs are now untreatable by modern medicine and that resistant super bugs are now spreading from poultry to humans. Already, one of the strains of the Salmonella bug is resistant to a number of different antibiotics and this is particularly worrying, as this form of food poisoning has shown a large increase in recent years in Britain. It was only in 1999 that the supermarket Tesco and the high-street retailer Marks & Spencer decided to no longer stock chickens that had been fed antibiotic growth promoters and EU regulations now ban a number of antibiotics because of concerns. Yet, both antibiotic growth promoters and antibiotics continue to be used on a large scale. In 2001 some 43 tonnes of antibiotic promoters and ten times the amount of antibiotics – 463 tonnes of the stuff – were sold in Britain (Purvis, 2003). These figures provide another example of the way health concerns go largely unheeded in the drive for profit and cheaper food.

The responsibility for the regulation and reduction of harm lies with states. But states in certain political circumstances are prepared to conspire with corporations to deceive the population about some disasters as illustrated in the so-called 'cooking oil' scandal in Spain in the 1980s where a number of people were sent to prison for contaminating cooking oil which it was alleged was the cause of hundreds of deaths and deformities. Even the World Health Organisation (WHO) supported the Spanish government's line. However, research by Dr Antonio Muro y

Fernandez-Cavado, who was Director of the La Paz Children Hospital in Madrid, suggested early on in the developing crisis that rather than cooking oil, people were being poisoned when eating salads and that organo-phosphorous (OP) chemicals were responsible. He was sacked from his job, which gave him time to investigate further the 1,000 or more deaths and more than 25,00 serious injuries. He eventually produced conclusive evidence that the cause was indeed the heavy contamination of OP on tomatoes grown in Almeria in the southeast corner of Spain. As Bob Woffinden has shown, various political and industrial interests coincided to cover up the real cause of the poisoning. The multinational chemical companies would have had much to lose if OPs were declared to be the cause. The Spanish government could not afford a scandal of this dimension. It would have ruined the fledgling economic miracle of Almeria, which forced fruit and vegetables into rapid growth under long tunnels of plastic sheeting, and perhaps would have damaged the tourist industry. The cover-up shows how public interest can be of little concern to government and multinationals alike. Many deaths and injuries could have been avoided if the truth had been admitted and some of the devastating consequences for public health avoided (Woffinden, 2001).

Each of these examples illustrates the dangers from the mass production of food in the current economic environment. Governments are reluctant to intervene because of the enormous pressures from the vested interests all along the food chain. The need for employment opportunities, the commercialisation of scientific developments and, above all, profits make it increasingly difficult for governments to oppose many of the developments taking place in food production or to impose adequate regulatory regimes. The various scandals noted above will no doubt join a long line of food production disasters over the coming years as the neo-liberal economic paradigm remains unchallenged.

Finally in this section, we wish to give the briefest indication of the harms which emerge as a consequence of the very differential production and distribution founded upon the ability to pay rather than human need, the central basis of a market-based system – and here we illustrate the point via reference to the pharmaceutical industry, and what it does *not* produce. As Cohen (2002) has noted, recent decades have seen the emergence of innovative drug treatments that have helped mitigate or cure everything from life-threatening disease (such as cardiovascular disease and cancer) to the unpleasant marks of ageing (including baldness and impotence). But what she terms 'this health revolution' – one that has resulted in considerable gains in life expectancy and health improvements in some parts of the world – has in fact left most of the world's population behind.

Thus drug research and development (R&D) for diseases that disproportionately affect poor people in developing countries is at a virtual standstill. Of the 1,393 new drugs approved between 1975 and 1999, only 16 (or just over 1 per cent) were specifically developed for tropical diseases and tuberculosis, diseases that account for 11 per cent of the global disease burden (Cohen, 2002). The 'neglected diseases' are those mainly affecting people in developing countries, for which treatment options are inadequate or do not exist, and for which R&D is insufficient or non-existent. Thus, according to the World Health Organisation:

14 million people die each year from communicable diseases such as malaria, TB, sleeping sickness and kala azar. An estimated 97 percent of deaths from communicable diseases occur in developing countries, with the poorest people in those nations disproportionately affected. Infectious and parasitic diseases account for 25 percent of the disease burden in low- and middle-income countries, compared to only three percent in high-income countries. (Cohen, 2002)

The ravages of communicable diseases are worsening as some 'old' diseases reappear. While global expenditures on health R&D are increasing dramatically – with all industry eyes on the US market and the diseases of the rich, only 10 per cent of global health research is devoted to conditions that account for 90 per cent of the global disease burden. 'Heavy reliance on an increasingly consolidated and highly competitive multinational drug industry to generate new medicines has left the development of life-saving drugs subject to the forces of the market economy' (Torreele, co-chair of the Drugs for Neglected Diseases (DND) Working Group, cited in Cohen, 2002).

Pharmaceutical companies simply lack any financial incentive to invest in the development of new treatments for diseases that affect people who cannot afford to pay. People in developing countries, who make up about 80 per cent of the world population, only represent about 20 per cent of worldwide medicine sales. All of sub-Saharan Africa totals less than 2 per cent of the global pharmaceutical market. Industry leaders acknowledge their narrow focus, and (as the case of HIV treatments has recently, and graphically, illustrated) will maintain this doggedly. And this makes good neo-liberal economic sense – pharmaceutical companies top the US industry performance list for return on investment, with a 39 per cent return for shareholders, according to *Fortune* magazine (Cohen, 2002).

CONCLUSION

If the period since the mid-1970s has undoubtedly been one of significant economic and political changes across the globe, it is clear from our particular attention to the role of, and consequences in, the UK and the US that *politics matters* a great deal in the creation, encouragement or permissioning of these trends and the mediation of these effects of 'economic' change (MacEwan, 1999: 66–98).

As we argued earlier, states are neither victims of, nor passive agents within, generalized economic processes (Weiss, 1998: 204–8, and passim). This was reinforced where we noted, for example, the peculiarity of trends in inequality and poverty in the US and UK, and the wider contextual point that OECD countries have experienced quite different trends in both inequality and poverty during this period (Gustafsson and Palmer, 1997; Jantti and Ritakallio, 1997; Navarro, 1999). Indeed, in one OECD state, Finland, a relatively recent but paradigmatic example of a corporatist welfare state (Pekkarinen, 1997), the 1980s were a decade of *equalising* incomes (Andersson, 1996: 68) and *decreases* in poverty (Gustafsson and Uusitalo, 1990; Jantti and Ritakallio, 1997).[12] Thus, in recent studies of the changes in the welfare states – and both the sources and effects of these changes – in all OECD countries, Navarro has documented a heterogeneous range of experiences (Navarro, 1999; Navarro and Shi, 2001). Navarro is led to conclude that:

> *the changes in the welfare state respond primarily to political rather than economic forces.* The current emphasis on globalisation as the cause of these changes has an apologetic function, defending the inevitability of such changes. Yet globalisation is not a cause but a symptom of the state of class relations in the developed capitalist countries ... the social democratic countries have actually been among the most integrated internationally, without 'globalisation' being a handicap for the extensive development of their welfare states. Actually the extensive welfare state development was a *condition* for their competitiveness and integration into world markets. (Navarro, 1999: 48; see also, Therborn, 1986; MacGregor, 1999; Navarro, 2000)

Consistent with Navarro's use of the term 'political forces', when we say that *politics matters*, this refers not merely, or even mainly, to the nature of governments, but more importantly to the balance of class forces, the nature and history of institutions, the character of particular national state formations and so on (Moran, 1998). Moreover where politics matters particularly is in terms of the differential nature and levels of social harm that it may or does produce: thus, as Navarro and Shi have recently noted, following Virchow, politics *is* public health in the most profound sense (Navarro and Shi, 2001: 10).

As we have noted, the political forces in the ascendancy in both the US and the UK for the past quarter of a century have been neo-liberal. This was of course the case under Reagan then Bush, and Thatcher then Major, but we should be clear that Clinton (then George W. Bush) and Blair have each headed governments explicitly committed to maintaining the fundamentals of the neo-liberal consensus (Pollin, 2000), even where some of these governments have adopted the 'Third Way' mantle. Indeed, the most insidious consequence of the adoption of neo-liberalism in its 'Third Way' guise is that the view that 'there is no alternative' 'acquires full force once an alternative regime demonstrates that there are truly no alternative policies' (Anderson, 2000: 11).

Let us be clear about the implications of the above analysis. There is little or no theoretical or empirical evidence that globalisation *per se* autonomously places constraints upon states and thus governments. Quite the opposite in fact. A much more plausible explanation is that those governments and nation states that have most enthusiastically pursued neo-liberal policies – rationalised, whether consciously or not, via the discourses of globalisation – have been pivotal actors in producing inequality and social harm. This imposition of neo-liberal economics on both sides of the Atlantic (and beyond) has had real material consequences, as we indicated above, and as is demonstrated throughout this text, in terms of recent trends in inequality and poverty and associated factors such as health, education, housing and the provision of basic goods such as clean water and air.

At the same time, the state has reconfigured its regulatory activity of private business activity significantly since the early 1980s. In some cases, this has meant the material and ideological undermining of regulatory bodies, leading to their virtual emasculation, or at least significantly reduced capacity. Somewhat differently, where the state has withdrawn from the provision of key services, handing over the provision of such services to the private sector, it has constructed opaque, largely non-accountable, and ultimately ineffectual regulatory quangos. Now, the absence or diminished capacity of external state regulation has important consequences in terms of the production of harm. For in general, the lessons of the relationship between corporate activity and the absence of or diminution in regulation are clear, if unnervingly simple: corporations have a tendency to lie, cheat, poison and kill; they produce death and emiseration in ways often aided, even encouraged, by state and governmental cynicism, callousness and duplicitousness; and they do so in a fashion which is often both calculated and routine. In an era of business–labour 'partnership', these are terribly unfashionable statements, but they seem to us to be incontrovertible (Tombs, 2002).

There are at least four implications of this analysis of the neo-liberal economic paradigm and its associated harm production for criminology, implications which underpin the significance and timeliness of the considerations engaged in throughout this text.

First, the harms which are defined as criminal and hence the subject of criminological investment form a very small proportion of the total harms produced either directly or indirectly as a consequence of the blind pursuit of the paradigm. The harms we have described are not simply more numerous, but they are qualitatively different. While the individual murderer will kill one or a few people at any one time, the acts or omissions by corporations or states will lead to the death of hundreds or thousands of people and loss and injuries to many more. The estimated 10,000 deaths in France as a result of the heat wave in August 2003 and the failure of the government and, in particular, the medical services to take remedial action after a possible disaster was anticipated illustrates only too well the differences between the two forms of harm. Similarly, in terms of property offences, the scale of corporate and state destruction far outweigh the harm carried out by criminals. The harm done by the young kid who cuts down a tree and is prosecuted for criminal damage pales into insignificance in contrast to the logging companies who destroy huge rain forests essential for the survival of the world's eco-systems.

Second, this analysis has argued that any adequate understanding of the vast scale of harm that affects people from the cradle to the grave must be understood in terms of political imperatives and the economics of the neo-liberal paradigm. They cannot be explained by a focus on individual acts or omissions. The vast majority of harms are structurally determined. Of course, individuals are responsible at some point, but they act collectively following the dictates of the neo-liberal paradigm.

Third, criminology, in failing to discuss, let alone analyse, the harms discussed in this chapter and indeed throughout this book contributes to the political myopia towards the social wreckage which we all witness around us.

Finally, the analysis provides an explanation for the increasing criminalisation of sections of the population. Neo-liberal governments – increasingly bereft of the means or inclination to devise social policy responses to social problems – have turned increasingly towards the extension of the criminal justice system and the criminalisation of economically marginalised groups and individuals and their families. As Braithwaite has recently – and succinctly – put it: 'While the welfare state is wound back, the punitive state is not' (Braithwaite, 2000: 227). Thus the sphere of criminal justice is increasingly characterised by an increasing trend towards purchasing via the market the means of safety and security on the part of the new middle classes while at the same time the criminal justice system delivers more repressive technologies of control and penal policies aimed at the marginalised or excluded poor (Garland, 1996; Stenson, 2001; Sullivan, 2001). The latter become increasingly subject to 'punitive segregation' (Garland, 2001). Far from a stake-holder society, as New Labour would have it, it is increasingly becoming a shackle-holder society (Downes, 1997), and it is a society in which corporate and state harms appear to be less, rather than more, likely to be encompassed within an albeit significantly expanded criminal justice system.

4

Violence in Democratic Societies: Towards an Analytic Framework[1]

Jamil Salmi

In democratic countries, the violent nature of the economy is not perceived; in authoritarian countries, it is the economic nature of violence which is not perceived.

Bertolt Brecht

On 21 October 1989, the Berlin wall fell, announcing the collapse of the Soviet empire and the demise of twentieth-century socialism. In a much-celebrated article published the same year, a senior official of the US Department of State, Francis Fukuyama, announced the 'end of history', celebrating 'the unabashed victory of economic and political liberalism and the universalisation of western democracy as the final form of human government' (Fukuyama, 1989: 37). Indeed, the Cold War is over and capitalism has prevailed; such terms as market economy, freedom and democracy can now be interchangeably used.

And yet, how do we reconcile the triumph of western liberalism with the chaos, war, crime, terror and poverty that dominate the media, compounded by the devastating impacts of 11 September 2001? This grim reality is not exclusive to the unruly former republics of the Soviet Union, the now defunct fundamentalist Taliban regime of Afghanistan, and the fanatical regimes of Saddam Hussein and the generals of Myanmar; this is also very much the reality of the rich, democratic societies of our planet. For example, 20 per cent of the children in the US – the wealthiest nation in the world – live in poverty, 3.5 million people are homeless, one-third of low-income families go hungry on a regular basis, 42 million citizens live without health insurance, 23,000 people are murdered, 50,000 rapes are reported every year and the country boasts the highest concentration of jailed people in the world. Do these staggering statistics reflect accidental events and crises, or do they attest to the fact that violence coexists, in a significant fashion, with capitalism and democracy?

The following three dimensions will be explored in an effort to address these questions:

1. establishing the different categories of violence;
2. applying the violence analytical framework; and
3. the biased reports of violence.

The analysis undertaken here is guided by the assumption that violence is not a random phenomenon, in most cases, but an event associated with specific causes and responsibilities. Fundamentally this chapter reflects a strong belief in the existence of universal human rights and, in this context, the notion of harm represents the effects of violence on the victim regardless of their society, culture, gender or character. Whether Chinese or Swiss, Muslim or Jew, man or woman, experiences such as torture, hunger, fear, lack of political freedom and self-determination are harmful. The degree of tolerance towards various manifestations of harm may differ from one person to the other, and from one culture to the other, but there are common experiences of oppression, suffering and alienation, which affect all human beings alike.

ESTABLISHING THE DIFFERENT CATEGORIES OF VIOLENCE

> The world has enough for every man's need but not for every man's greed.
>
> Mahatma Gandhi

Violence is often narrowly equated with images of war (as in Afghanistan and Iraq), murders (as in Washington DC), or riots (as in Indonesia); by definition, however, violence is any act that threatens a person's physical or psychological integrity and can be classified analytically in different forms. Four main categories of violence are: (1) direct violence; (2) indirect violence; (3) repressive violence; and (4) alienating violence.

Direct violence

When people write or talk about violence, it is usually direct violence they refer to. Direct violence covers all physical acts that result in deliberate injury to the integrity of human life. Examples include homicides (genocide, war crimes, massacres of civilians, murders) and forms of coercive or brutal actions that cause physical or psychological suffering (forced removal of populations, imprisonment, kidnapping, hostage taking, forced labour, torture, rape, maltreatment). The atrocities inflicted on the Muslim populations of Bosnia and Kosovo by the Serbian army and police throughout the 1990s are a sad illustration of this category of violence. The Turks' brutal treatment of the Armenians throughout history is another such case. The Turks severed the tongue of Armenians speaking their native language in the seventeenth century, and attempted, three centuries later, to eliminate the entire Armenian population in 1915.

Indirect violence

Indirect violence is a category intended to describe harmful, sometimes deadly situations, which result from human intervention but involve no direct relationship between the victims and the institutions, population groups or individuals responsible for their plight. Two subcategories of this type of violence are *violence by omission* and *mediated violence*.

Violence by omission draws on the legal notion of non-assistance to persons in danger. A legal penalty is imposed, in some countries, on citizens who refuse or neglect to assist victims threatened by actions or phenomena that are technically avoidable or controllable by society. Applying this notion of 'criminal failure to intervene' at the social or collective level is an effective approach in dealing with this form of violence. Two such cases that exemplify this category of violence are the Holocaust and, more recently, the massacre of Tutsis in Rwanda. Some historians argue that the US State Department had sufficient information of Adolf Hitler's 'final solution' as early as 1942 (Morse, 1967), but only after President Roosevelt read the secret memorandum entitled 'Acquiescence of this Government in the Murder of the Jews' in January 1944 did he dispatch the US army to rescue the victims of the Nazi extermination plans. Richard Breitman, in his recent publication, documents a similar failure of Britain, under Anthony Eden's government, to intervene and prevent mass executions of Jews (Breitman, 1999). Eden's refusal to act on compelling British intelligence informed by monitoring German radio communications was attributed to his alleged strong anti-Semitic sentiments. More recently, the US government, under Bill Clinton's presidency, has been accused of overlooking the mass slaughter of 800,000 Rwandan Tutsis in 1994, with the full knowledge of the annihilation from US intelligence agencies (Power, 2001).

This violence by omission approach applies not only to the lack of protection against physical violence, but also to the lack of protection against social violence (hunger, disease, poverty), accidents, natural catastrophes, occupational and health hazards. In countries where resources are abundant but unequally distributed, those who do not have equal access to resources are victims of poverty – 'the greatest terror', according to Mark Twain – and people exposed to lack of protection from social violence such as mass hunger and income equality are also victims of violence by omission. French forces that occupied Indochina in 1945 contributed indirectly to the death by starvation of 2 million Vietnamese by denying them access to existing rice stocks after the crop failed (Zinn, 1980: 461). Another form of this type of violence is income inequality, which is on the rise both within and across nations. With 1.2 billion people living on less than one dollar a day, it is clear that the benefits of globalisation have remained out of reach for nearly half of the developing world's population (World Bank, 1997: 12). The income of the richest 20 per cent of the populations in Brazil, Guatemala and Jamaica is, for example, more than 25 times that of the poorest 20 per cent (United Nations Development Program, 2000: 34).

Another example of this subcategory of indirect violence is those who are victims of accidents and this is exemplified in the absence of strict gun control laws in the US. In December 1998, for example, a woman in New Jersey was shot dead by her ex-husband even after a judge served a restraining order against the ex-husband and the police confiscated his gun. But the angry ex-husband purchased another gun in a neighbouring county only 10 miles away. A significant degree of responsibility, it could be argued, for this incident and the several thousand gun accidents, suicides and murders reported each year, could be directed to the gun manufacturers, the US government and perhaps largely to Congress members – many of whom accept campaign contributions from the National Rifle Association.

The impact of natural disasters is another form of indirect violence – when it is recognised that human intervention could have lessened the impact of seemingly uncontrollable acts of God. For example, experts established that the 1985 Armero catastrophe in Colombia would not have claimed so many lives if the Nevada del Ruiz volcano had been carefully observed and the population evacuated before the fateful mudslide (Vanhecke, 1985).

While violence by omission is a passive form of indirect violence, *mediated violence* is, in contrast, the result of a deliberate human intervention in the natural or social environment whose harmful effects are indirect and often delayed. All forms of ecocide that destroy or damage our natural environments are examples of mediated violence. During the Vietnam and Afghanistan wars, US and Soviet armies used the defoliant Agent Orange – primarily intended to destroy crops in enemy territory – which caused genetic malformations among babies in infected areas and cancer among war veterans. The sale of pesticides and medical products banned in the country of origin (US, Europe) to developing countries is another illustration of this type of violence.

Another form of mediated violence is, paradoxically, embargos against repressive regimes that are often motivated by generous principles of solidarity with populations suffering under a dictatorial regime. A former United Nations Children's Fund (UNICEF) representative in Haiti documents in a recent publication the devastating impact, on the children and women of that country, of the UN-imposed embargo against the illegal government of General Cédras (Gibbons, 1999). Many civilians died in the countryside of common diseases due to the embargo on petrol that disrupted traffic.

Repressive violence

Repressive violence refers to the most common forms of human rights violations – including civil, political and social – that are traditionally documented and monitored by international NGOs such as Amnesty International or Human Rights Watch. Civil rights are violated when people are denied freedoms of thought, religion, movement or equality before the law (including the right to a fair trial). Political rights are violated in countries with no genuine democracy, fair elections, freedom of speech and free association. Social rights are violated in countries that deny the freedom to form trade unions or participate in strikes.

Alienating violence

Based on the assumption that a person's wellbeing does not come exclusively from fulfilling material needs, the notion of alienating violence refers to denying a person the right to psychological, emotional, cultural or intellectual integrity. Such rights manifest in the empowerment at work or in the community, the opportunity to engage in creative activities, a young child's need for affection – child psychologists are now examining the crucial role of 'emotional intelligence'– the feeling of social and cultural belonging, and so on. Examples of alienating violence emerge primarily in countries with deliberate policies of ethnocide that threaten the cultural identity of an entire linguistic or religious community. The recent Australian movie *Rabbit-proof fence* (2003) showed in a vivid manner the plight of 'half-caste' children forcibly taken away from their Aboriginal family to be integrated into 'civilisation', defined of course as the civilisation of white people. Between 1931 and 1970, thousands of children were abducted from their family, transported like cattle in trains reminiscent of the later Nazi death trains, raised and educated in special camps, to be eventually adopted by white families (if the skin of the child was fair enough) or placed in forced servitude (if the skin of the child was considered to be too dark). Indigenous populations in several African and Latin American countries are, as a result of discriminatory cultural policies, being gradually assimilated and losing their identities. Other forms of alienating violence rampant in many regions are racism and any form of prejudicial practices against particular groups in society, such as homosexuals or the elderly.

Freedom from fear is a key dimension of alienating violence. Millions of people are victims of direct violence – such as war, civil strife, repression and the aftermath – and are afflicted daily with anxiety, apprehension and dread. Palestine, Israel, Colombia, Northern Ireland, Liberia, Chechnya and Burundi are present-day examples of troubled regions. Throughout the world, people living in urban areas with high crime rates are also affected by feelings of anxiety. A recent survey conducted in Latin America indicates that, even in a large metropolis like Buenos Aires with relatively low levels of crime, a high proportion of people live in fear. The rapid growth of security products and services in both industrialised and developing countries attests to the fact that this dimension of alienating violence is rampant. In President Roosevelt's 1941 Annual Message to Congress, he declared that 'freedom from fear' was one of four essential freedoms he intended to preserve for the American people, together with freedom of expression, freedom of worship and freedom from want.

APPLYING THE VIOLENCE ANALYTICAL FRAMEWORK

The law in its majestic equality forbids the rich and the poor alike to sleep under bridges, to beg in the streets and to steal bread.

Anatole France

To fully understand the role of violence in a society, a systematic and objective analysis of the varying dimensions of violence must be undertaken. By applying the proposed violence analytical framework – a mechanism for examining complex forms of violence – patterns of interconnections and causal relationships can be drawn from a methodical analysis of the *geographical*, *historical*, *ideological* and *institutional* facets of violence.

Violence can be analysed in different geographic settings using the same methodological screen. The murderous suicide attacks perpetrated by Palestinian youths against Israeli civilians, for example, must be viewed alongside the inhumane treatment of the Palestinians, including murder of civilians during military actions, extra-judicial assassinations, the use of civilians as human shields, the torture of presumed activists, the bulldozer destruction of homes (sometimes with women and children trapped inside), the demolition of archaeological, historical and religious landmarks, illegal occupation of land, daily discrimination and humiliations, and so on. Examining the complex economic and social relationships across national borders reveals harmful linkages – a European child's marvel with her or his first electronic game as compared with an Asian child worker's exhaustion at assembling electronic components for the game.

Outlining historical patterns of violence is another analytical approach in applying this typology. Nobel Prize winner Bishop Desmond Tutu of South Africa illustrates the relationship between colonialism and the growth of the western economies in a statement: 'when the missionaries first came to Africa they had the Bible and we had the land. They said, "let us pray." We closed our eyes. When we opened them, we had the Bible and they had the land.'

Comparing different realities across ideological boundaries can be undertaken using this framework. The typology of human rights violations can be used for capitalist and communist societies, kingdoms and republics, secular and fundamentalist regimes alike. For example, when examining the defunct Soviet Union through this framework, the human cost of socialism as it operated in that context becomes clear. Tales of terror, massacres, mass executions, deportation of entire population groups, purges and concentration camps dominate the history of the Soviet regime, reflecting unprecedented levels of institutionalised state terrorism.[2]

Defining the roles and responsibilities of different institutions – including individuals, groups, firms, governments and multinational companies – is another approach to applying this typology. Two such cases that illustrate the institutional dimensions of violence can be found in a disputed Latin American region and in Bosnia. Thousands of Bolivians and Paraguayans died during a war triggered by a border dispute between 1932 and 1935; but in reality it was a war by proxy between two giant oil companies – Standard Oil of New Jersey and Shell Oil – competing for control of the Chaco oil fields. In Srebrenica, Bosnia, Serb troops massacred about 7,000 civilians (men and boys) in July

1995 under the watchful eyes of the UN armed forces (FORPRONU). Conclusions of several official inquiries, notably by the French and Dutch parliaments and the UN itself, have faulted the international community for failure to intervene in what was considered one of the worst massacres in Europe since the Second World War. The US government overlooked the mass slaughter of Bosnian civilians; the French military, which commanded the UN troops, refused to order air strikes to protect the victims; and the Dutch soldiers under the UN flag remained passive. The resignation of the Dutch Prime Minister in April 2002 is a first example in modern times of a country owning up to its sins of omission in an honourable way (Rossigneux, 2001; Power, 2002). But neither the UN nor the US and French governments have acknowledged responsibility for their passive complicity.

The proposed violence framework is also helpful in identifying harmful situations in democratic societies where, theoretically, human rights are fully protected by the rule of law. The European Court of Justice recently condemned the French government for use of torture by police against common criminals. Amnesty International has launched a campaign against capital punishment in the US – one of the few countries in the world, together with Iran, Pakistan and Somalia, where the death penalty can still apply to young people under the age of 18.

In applying this framework, it is important to note that a particular occurrence of violence might fall under several categories at the same time. Slavery, for example, can be classified under each of the four categories of violence. The manhunt in West Africa, the forced voyage to North America and the denial of freedom illustrate the direct violence dimension; the slaves' living conditions exemplify the indirect form of violence; the denial of all rights falls under repressive violence; their uprooting from Africa, assimilation into a completely foreign culture and society and denial of basic dignity as human beings constitute the alienating violence. The 'delicate' practice used in nineteenth-century Cuban plantations to preserve the continuity of the slave population illustrates dramatically the relationship between individual cruelty and the significance of slavery as an economic system: to discipline pregnant slaves, a hole dug in the ground protected the baby of the pregnant slave who could be whipped without any damage to her precious cargo (Galeano, 1981: 119).

Table 4.1 summarises the main dimensions of the proposed violence analytical framework and indicates possible levels of responsibility.

Table 4.1 Typology of different categories and forms of violence

Category	Perpetrator			
	Individual	Group	Firm	Government
Direct violence (deliberate injury to the integrity of human life)				
murder	X	X		X
massacre		X		X
genocide				X
torture	X	X		X
rape and child sex	X	X		X
maltreatment	X	X		X
female circumcision	X	X		
forced resettlement	X	X		X
kidnapping/hostage taking		X	X	X
forced labour (including child labour)	X	X	X	X
slavery				
Indirect violence (indirect violation of the right to survival)				
Violence by omission (lack of protection against ...)				
poverty			X	X
hunger			X	X
disease			X	X
accidents				X
natural catastrophes				X
Mediated violence (harmful modifications to the environment)		X	X	X
Repressive violence (deprivation of fundamental rights)				
Civil rights				
freedom of thought		X		X
freedom of speech		X		X
freedom of religion		X		X
right to a fair trial				X
equality before the law				X
freedom of movement				X
Political rights				
freedom to vote				X
freedom of association				X
freedom to hold meetings				X
Social rights				
freedom to go on strike			X	X
freedom to form a union			X	X
protection of private property				X
Alienating violence (deprivation of higher rights)				
alienating living/working conditions	X	X	X	X
racism	X	X		X
social ostracism	X	X		X
cultural repression		X		X
living in fear	X			X

THE BIASED REPORTS OF VIOLENCE

Your disease is called non conformism. Your course of treatment is
four walls.
> Soviet doctor welcoming a dissident in a psychiatric ward
> (Boukovsky, 1972: 28)

Reports of the various manifestations of violence and harm in the
media are often biased. Four common types of biases can be identified:
(1) superficiality; (2) lack of proportion; (3) excessive individualisation;
and (4) ideological one-sidedness.

A common form of bias in reporting violence is *superficiality* – the
tendency to cover the most sensational images and stories of violence
and human rights violations without providing relevant contexts,
explanations, causes, linkages and patterns. The presentation of violent
acts, presented as isolated events, convey inaccurately that people
are always confronted with tragic accidents, unfortunate mistakes,
involuntary blunders or unforeseen side effects. The assassination
of a Turkish diplomat by an Armenian terrorist, for example, was
reported without mention of the Turkish government's 90-year refusal
to acknowledge the 1915 Armenian genocide. Another such case is
the news of the My Lai massacre, which was broadcast in 1968 at the
height of the Vietnam war. The American public was outraged, but the
emphasis of their reaction was not on the US army's brutal, systematic
assassination of Vietnamese civilians presumed to be opponents during
Operation Phoenix but on the one person supposedly responsible for the
My Lai massacre, Lieutenant Calley. The same happened with the 2004
abuse scandal at the Abu-Ghraib detention centre in Iraq. The official
US response has been to blame a few soldiers rather than looking at
the chain of command and the interrogation policy guidelines behind
the abuse cases.

The *lack of proportion* in media is another form of bias that presents
the most spectacular events of the day without considering the magnitude
of the phenomenon. In January 1999, Serb forces brutally murdered
45 people in the Kosovo village of Racak, just two months before the
NATO military intervention. This event dominated international media
and triggered the failed peace conference in Rambouillet. Meanwhile,
hundreds of people were being murdered in Sierra Leone, Angola and
Congo without any press coverage.

Excessive individualisation in the media is a third form of biased
reporting that isolates individual actions and behaviours from a
social context. Riots in Liverpool, Brixton and Birmingham in 1981

and 1985 were officially branded as the work of 'a few hooligans lacking spirituality' (Cassen, 1981). News reports failed to correlate the outbreak of violence with the deterioration of employment and housing conditions, the recrudescence of racism and police harassment of black immigrants in the concerned districts. In an earlier reference to the December 1998 murder of a woman by her ex-husband, the local press focused on the individual crime without any recognition of the social responsibility of authorities that failed to prevent a dangerous person from buying a gun.

A final bias in the media is *ideological one-sidedness* when coverage of crimes or violations is defined by ideological views of those in power. Palestinian freedom fighters are referred to as 'terrorist criminals' by the same Israeli leaders (Begin and Shamir to name only two) who had proudly described themselves as freedom fighters in the 1940s when they violently attacked British occupation troops. British authorities referred to the leading members of the Jewish terrorist organisation Stern – responsible, among other violent acts, for the bomb planted in the King David hotel which killed several soldiers – as 'terrorists'. In February 1994, a Jewish settler killed 29 Palestinian worshipers and was then killed by survivors of the attack. With the approval of the Israel Supreme Court, his tombstone was inscribed with the words 'holy' and 'martyr'.

An examination of common reactions of governments accused of human rights violations illustrates biases in reporting violence. Results of research undertaken using data from Amnesty International reveals that all governments – whether from the political left or the right, socialist or capitalist, republics or kingdoms – tend to respond in the same way (Salmi, 1991). Typically, they hide behind one of five types of responses. The first approach is to accuse critics that they are meddling in the internal affairs of a sovereign country. A second reaction is the denial of charges brought forward by Amnesty International as fabricated lies. Another reaction is an insistence that those defended by Amnesty International are criminals and not political prisoners: thus, the dissident Sakharov was no more a political prisoner in the eyes of the Soviet Union than Bobby Sands was in the eyes of Margaret Thatcher, or Dennis Banks, the famous Indian American activist of the 1970s, in the eyes of the US government. A fourth reaction is to accuse Amnesty International of being ideologically biased. Communist countries accuse the human rights organisation of representing the interests of imperialism and capitalism, while capitalist countries accuse Amnesty International of being an agent of communism. Finally, the same governments who reject Amnesty International's intrusion in their internal affairs recommend that the human rights organisation examines closely the internal affairs of their enemies. During the Iraq–Iran war, for example, Iraq recommended that Amnesty International monitor human rights violations in Iran, and vice versa.

CONCLUSION

Capitalism is the extraordinary belief that the nastiest of men for the nastiest of motives will somehow work for the benefit of all.

John Maynard Keynes

To understand fully the role of violence and the related extent of harm inflicted upon various population groups or individuals in a democratic society, or in any society for that matter, the following are recommended. First, a systematic analysis of the varying dimensions of violence existing in that society must be undertaken and the violence analytical framework proposed here can help facilitate this type of analysis. Second, on the basis of this analysis, it is necessary to identify the patterns and relationships linking these manifestations of violence to the prevailing economic, social and political power structures, in an effort to establish accountability. An objective and methodical examination of the complex forms of violence can help prevent the biased conceptions and provide an accurate and holistic view of its role in a given society. Lenin himself wrote that 'you should not judge classes, parties or people by what they say, but by what they do in reality'.

5

A Theory of Moral Indifference: Understanding the Production of Harm by Capitalist Society

Simon Pemberton

The concept of moral indifference seeks to capture the moral silence/ inactivity of capitalist societies to the human suffering caused by their organisation. The events of 11 September in 2001 are perhaps one of the starkest examples of moral indifference. On this day, the western world collectively grieved the tragic loss of 3,045 people in the attacks upon the World Trade Center, New York and the Pentagon, Washington. However, there is little doubt few of these tears were shed for the victims of the 'global economy' who also died on that day: the 24,000 people who died of hunger, the 6,020 children who died from diarrhoea or the 2,700 children who died of measles (*New Internationalist*, November 2001: 19). These victims of the 'global' economy are a material reality of the current organisation of the 'global' relations of production. However, global capital and nation states of the western world have succeeded in persuading their populations of quite the opposite. While many in the western world perceive the attacks on New York and Washington to be acts of murder, few would consider the habitual suffering of those in the developing world as anything other than a natural disaster.

These examples demonstrate that capital and the political elites of capitalist society are habitually locked into a process of legitimating this suffering to civil society. Thus, in order to maintain the hegemony that gains the consent of subordinate groups for the present organisation of capitalist society, the harm caused by the relations of production must be justified. Consequently, capitalist ideology must be equipped to validate the socially mediated harm which claims the lives of the 'have-nots' of both the developing and developed worlds. An important aspect of this ideological process is the creation of moral indifference, in both perpetrators of these acts and their bystanders. The aim of this chapter is to identify the processes that promote moral indifference among capitalist society to the suffering of others.

To achieve this aim the chapter is divided into two parts. The first part will reflect upon the contributions of critical criminology to the notion of moral indifference, in order to identify aspects of this work which the social harm perspective can build upon. In light of these observations, the second part will be devoted to the development of the concept of moral indifference from a social harm perspective. In order to achieve this the chapter will draw upon Zygmunt Bauman's work on morality.

CRITICAL CRIMINOLOGY AND INDIFFERENCE

With the exception of critical criminology, the discipline of criminology has largely ignored the question of moral indifference to harm. The interest in this notion for critical criminologists stems from their concern with the criminalisation of the marginalised. This has led to a questioning of the discourses which support the processes of 'selective criminalisation' in capitalist societies and the criminal law's obsessive focus upon the intentional acts of individuals.

The criminologist Steven Box (1983) is highly critical of the legal rationality which, for him, prioritises intentional acts for criminal sanction. Box argues that to avoid the question of indifference is to remain silent upon a significant amount of human suffering: evil should not be unrecognised merely because it is as banal as indifference; indifference rather than intent may well be the greater cause of avoidable human suffering ... (Box, 1983: 21).

Box, drawing on the seminal work of Reiman (1979), makes the observation that the popular distinction made between acts of intention and acts of indifference is based upon a 'common sense hierarchy of morality' (Box, 1983: 21). In this hierarchy it is usually considered 'morally worse to intend harm than to be indifferent to whether harm results from one's behaviour' (ibid.: 21). Box seeks to challenge this widely accepted view, by arguing that if an individual intends to harm, this does not automatically demonstrate a disdain toward humanity because it is directed at a specific person. On the other hand, he contends that if an individual is indifferent to the consequences of their actions and someone is harmed, then this displays disdain for humanity in general.

There are certainly compelling aspects to Box's argument which deserve greater attention. Box claims that 'indifference rather than intent may well be the greater cause of avoidable human suffering' (ibid.: 21). There is considerable support for this contention. Consider, for example, different types of physical harm in the UK. In any one year in England and Wales there are between 750 and 850 homicides. In comparison, deaths largely stemming from indifference far exceed these figures. An estimated 20,000 people every year die from health conditions related to pollution (Committee on the Medical Effects of Air Pollutants, 1998); around 300 people die every year from fatal injuries received while at work (Health and Safety Executive, 2001); and over 3,000 die in road traffic accidents (Department of Transport, Local Government and the Regions, 2002).

Box also points out that 'the intent to harm someone may be less immoral (or at least no more immoral) than to be indifferent as to whom is harmed' (1983: 21). This argument serves to challenge the dominance of legal discourse and the moral/ethical codes it perpetuates. In western jurisprudence there is an implicit hierarchy of morality. This can be seen most clearly in the English law of manslaughter. This is governed by what is called the 'identification' doctrine, which specifies that the culpability of a company may be determined by the actions of one of its 'controlling officers'. A company is indictable for manslaughter only if a controlling officer's actions have fulfilled the prerequisites for the crime (see *R* v. *P&O European Ferries* (Dover Ltd) (1990) 93 Cr App R 72). In order to bring a successful prosecution, the reckless mind and actions of the individual must be connected to the event concerned. To prosecute 'traditional' crime it is a relatively simple task to connect the thinking part of the crime to its commission. However, this becomes problematic when attempting to demonstrate that an individual in a large corporation with a highly complex division of labour has fulfilled all of the prerequisites of a criminal offence. As a result, the legal doctrine has made it extremely difficult to bring successful prosecutions for manslaughter against corporations. The first successful prosecution was brought in 1994 following the tragic events at Lyme Regis when three children died canoeing. Significantly, the company, OLL Ltd, was a one-man operation, and identifying the company with the actions and omissions of the managing director was relatively easy (Lacey and Wells, 1998).

A well-publicised failed prosecution occurred following the Zeebrugge ferry disaster. A total of 192 people died due to the sinking of the Townsend-Thoresen ferry, the *Herald of Free Enterprise*, which left port with its bow doors open. The prosecution collapsed due to insufficient evidence. The judge concluded that there was no senior member of the company who could be identified as reckless to the risk of the ferry sailing with its doors open. The failure arose from the individualistic nature of the criminal law and its accompanying notions of culpability and intention. In contrast, the notion of indifference is less concerned with positivist notions of culpability and focuses on those organisations and bodies responsible for developing and maintaining cultures where public safety is ignored principally because of the need to make a profit.

To understand indifference in a case like Zeebrugge, the economic context surrounding these events must be considered. During the mid-1980s the competition in the cross-channel ferry market was acute. One of the destabilising factors in this market was the British government's decision to privatise Sealink UK Ltd, which unleashed market forces into a sector previously dominated by state owned operators (C. Boyd, 1992). It resulted in intense competition which forced several companies into bankruptcy or into radical programmes of restructuring, a situation that was further exacerbated by the immanent opening of the Channel tunnel. Crainer points out that the fears of the ferry operators over the anticipated competition from the tunnel soon turned into 'bullishness as they recognised that the tunnel was unlikely to eliminate completely the need for cross-channel ferries' (1993: 22). This mood was evidenced in the comments of one Townsend-Thoresen representative, who suggested that it was possible to 'build a fleet of ships to equal the capacity of the tunnel and at half the price' (cited in Crainer, 1993: 21). There is little doubt that a competitive ethos permeated the company and one outcome was an emphasis upon achieving the optimum number of crossings.

The pressure for a 'quick turn around' at port, 'to sail at the earliest moment', was identified in the Sheen inquiry as one of the underlying reasons for the ferry's departure with the bow doors still open (Crainer, 1993). An internal Townsend-Thoresen memorandum stated that, *'sailing late out of Zeebrugge isn't on'* (C. Boyd, 1992), and all masters and officers were required to explain to the Townsend hierarchy why delays of as little as ten minutes had occurred (Crainer, 1993). To summarise, the Zeebrugge case is an example of the inability of the criminal law to punish the consequences of moral indifference. This is primarily a product of the liberal structure of the criminal law and the implicit individualistic legal and political consciousness attributed to the nature of a criminal actor and act. The inability of the criminal law should be coupled to a lack of political will to adapt the law to these situations. This reluctance is evidenced in the failure of successive British governments, both Conservative and Labour, to implement the recommendations of the 1996 Law Commission on corporate manslaughter.

Stan Cohen's (1993) work on state crime provides a number of insights into how such tragic events can occur and, in particular, the symbolic machinery which promotes cultures of indifference and creates bystanders to harm. His work seeks to understand the denial of state crimes by populations who should be ideologically opposed to them. His analysis focuses upon a specific section of the population: 'the enlightened, educated middle class, responsive to messages of peace and co-existence' (Cohen, 1993: 103). For Cohen, this focus is important because those observers who support the actions of the state have no reason to object to these harms.

It is indisputable that Cohen's work is a valuable contribution to any discussion of indifference. Consequently, there are compelling reasons to envisage a theory of denial as part of a theoretical continuum with indifference because the notion of denial allows analysis of the symbolic machinery required by capitalist society to ensure indifference to harm.[1] However, his approach is also symptomatic of the tensions which exist in the reasoning of critical criminology. In general, critical criminology has become tied to the 'common sense hierarchy of morality' (Box, 1983: 21) as a consequence of the discipline's proximity to legal discourse and the criminal justice system, notwithstanding important exceptions (for example, Reiman, 1979; and Box, 1983).

Cohen (1993) defines state crime as 'gross violations' of human rights, which he argues can be equated to traditional criminal offences such as murder and rape. In adopting this legalistic approach, Cohen places great importance on the use of the normative frameworks of human rights conventions and international law. He rejects the Schwendingers' (1975) expansive use of human rights to define starvation and poverty as state crimes as a 'moral crusade'.[2] Furthermore, he criticises the Schwendingers' approach for collapsing together socially injurious action, such as genocide, with economic exploitation, which he considers to be 'hardly morally equivalent categories' (Cohen, 1993: 98).

Cohen's work demonstrates the ambiguity for critical criminologists in the use of legal discourses. Clearly there is significant political utility in using pre-existing definitions of criminal harm and his approach forms a powerful counter discursive tool to the proponents of the 'law and order' project to demonstrate the disproportionate levels of human suffering inflicted through state crime when compared to traditional crime. British and American forces' recent invasion of Iraq was considered by many legal experts to be illegal (*Guardian*, 17 March 2003). As a consequence, the deaths of some 5,000 to 7,000 civilians may be defined as murder (*Guardian*, 13 June 2003). This is undeniably a persuasive argument to highlight the extent of the harm caused by nation states and the inconsistencies inherent in the 'law and order' project.

The disadvantage of such an approach is related to two interconnected points: it narrows society's imagination to harms envisaged by the criminal justice system and it reaffirms the moral hierarchy of intentional acts over acts of indifference. From this perspective, Cohen's (1993) assertion that genocide and economic exploitation do not fall into equivalent moral categories is contestable and a strong case can be made for seeing genocide and economic exploitation within a comparable moral category. Cohen's distinction between genocide and economic exploitation fails to acknowledge the current reality: that economic exploitation has resulted from the relations of production actively sought by global capital and accommodated by the policies of nation states. This point is illustrated by the arguments of Chossudovsky (1997) who likens the economic exploitation of the developing world, performed through the deliberate manipulation of market forces, to a process of 'economic genocide'. For Chossudovsky the policies of the IMF, World Bank and WTO have been instrumental in the manipulation of market forces for the benefit of transnational corporations. Thus, these supra national governmental bodies have remained indifferent to the consequences of their economic policies to the benefit of global capital.

Another form of 'economic genocide' is the use of economic policy as a tool of imperialist power – for instance, the UN sanctions (primarily led by Britain and America) against the former Iraqi regime after the invasion of Kuwait. However, the grave consequence of the denial of vital medical supplies and food were the deaths of an estimated 500,000 children in the years between 1991 and 1998 (Pilger, 2002: 62). After resigning from the UN, Dennis Halliday, the former Assistant Secretary-General, remarked: 'I had been instructed, to implement a policy that satisfies the definition of genocide: a deliberate policy that has effectively killed well over a million individuals, children and adults' (cited in Pilger, 2002: 56). However, the British and American governments remained indifferent to the costs of the sanctions, in order to weaken the uncooperative President Saddam Hussein. This indifference is evidenced in the then US Ambassador to the UN Madeleine Albright's infamous remark: 'I think this is a very hard choice, but the price – we think the price is worth it' (cited in Pilger, 2002: 64).

In order for an act of indifference to fall into the equivalent moral category as intention, an actor or a group of actors must be shown to be capable of intervening. Hence, into this moral category should be placed harm acts in which indifference has been demonstrated to be the implicit causal factor. Undeniably, the nation states of the developed world possess the ability to intervene in these economic processes and ultimately the harm these cause.[3] They could demand a different set of economic policies. Yet they have for the last 30 years supported the loans and structural adjustment packages of the IMF and World Bank to which the developing world has been increasingly subjected for the benefit of the developed world. Many countries have been actively encouraged to reduce their welfare systems, to deregulate labour markets, to privatise state owned industry, all for the benefit of global capital and at a huge cost to their populations (Townsend, 2002).[4]

The consequences of this process are evidenced in the findings of the United Nations Conference on Trade and Development (UNCTAD) 2002 report, which found that over the last 30 years, the number of those living in extreme poverty in least developed countries (LDCs) has more than doubled – from 138 million in the late 1960s to 307 million in the late 1990s (UNCTAD, 2002a).[5] The report was clear: the proposed trend of the least developed countries' descent into further poverty should be located in the 'current form of globalisation' (UNCTAD, 2002b). In any event, it seems almost irrelevant whether harm occurs from either economic exploitation or genocide when the results of both are preventable. The levels of suffering are equally unpalatable, be they the 6 million victims of the Holocaust or the estimated 30,000 victims of the global economy who perish daily from hunger and preventable diseases.

DEVELOPING A THEORY OF INDIFFERENCE

The previous section demonstrated the need to develop a notion of moral indifference, which can capture the processes that cause the vast majority of avoidable human suffering in contemporary society. In order to achieve this aim the following section is divided into two parts. The first will describe the basic concepts which underpin Bauman's theory of morality, before engaging with the critiques which this has provoked. The discussion of these critiques will provide a space to suggest the appropriate adaptation of these concepts for use in a social harm analysis. The second attempts to 'contextualise' Bauman's writings with relevant examples of moral indifference in capitalist society.

Bauman's sociological theory of morality

Integral to Bauman's (1989) development of a sociological theory of morality is his rejection of Durkheim's notion of morality. Durkheim's notion of morality was guided by his concern with the need for social integration. In this light, moral systems are viewed as crucial to the preservation of a society, through the application of constraints to the pre-societal drives of human nature which are essentially cruel and selfish. Bauman argues that the acceptance of Durkheim's notion of

morality has profound consequences for social theory which in general
has viewed pre-social or a-social motives as incapable of being moral.
The factory system has served as a dominant metaphor to convey the
idea that societies produce moral behaviour. For Bauman, however, such
an analysis fails to acknowledge the interrelationship between power and
the social authority to pass moral judgement. This is illustrated by the
dilemma legal practice and jurisprudence faced after the Holocaust, the
possibility that morality results from 'insubordination towards socially
upheld principles' (Bauman, 1989: 177). Hence, Bauman argues that the
challenge for social theory is to reject the notion that the production of
morality results from the conscience collective and to accept an analysis
of the actor as the source of moral behaviour.

Bauman considers that the process of socialisation is concerned with
the manipulation of moral capacity *not* its production. He believes moral
behaviour to be possible through the 'context of coexistence' (1989: 179)
and draws upon the work of French philosopher Emmanuel Levinas,
for whom 'being with others' is the essential defining characteristic
of being human and forms our first and foremost responsibility. This
responsibility is unconditional and is not dependent on prior knowledge
of the other. Central to the argument is the notion that responsibility
is the primary structure of subjectivity. Thus, the subject is constituted
through the responsibility it takes for the other; a responsibility
which is based neither upon legal obligation nor the calculation of
reciprocal benefit.

If we accept that responsibility is the defining characteristic of
subjectivity, then morality becomes the 'primary structure of the
intersubjective relation in its most pristine form' (Bauman, 1989: 183).
Bauman concludes that the very essence of morality is the duty to the
other and this overrides all other interventions: 'morality is not a product
of society. Morality is something which society manipulates' (ibid.).

In his later work, *Life in Fragments* (1995), Bauman seeks to develop
the notion of moral action existing independent of norms. He draws
upon Vetlesen's analysis of Eichmann in which he argues that Eichmann's
'indifference to the meaning of suffering to the infliction of pain' should
be understood in the context of his 'objectifying attitude towards his
fellows, as opposed to a participatory-empathic one' (Bauman, 1995:
57). Eichmann's crimes were supported by the codification of the
German state – an example of the objectification process – and for
Bauman this provides justification to adopt the participatory empathic
stance. This stance rejects the notion of ethical codification, because
it is devoid of *'empathy and emotional participation in the suffering of
others'* (Bauman, 1995: 57, emphasis added).[6]

Bauman's rejection of Durkheim's stance and the adoption of a pre-social foundation for morality has been the source of several critiques. He has been accused of espousing a non-sociological theory of morality (Shiling and Mellor, 1998; Junge, 2001). Junge's critique challenges Bauman's theory of morality upon two fronts. First, Junge argues that Bauman's approach to morality does not include a notion of mutuality, which he considers as a prerequisite of social action. Consequently, Junge argues that Bauman's gift of morality is 'poisoned with the fragility of non mutual action' (2001: 110). For Junge, Bauman's theory lacks a normative code which ensures a connection between the two parties, or the culmination of the moral relationship. The absence of this connection is the reason why he argues that Bauman's notion of moral action could never constitute a social situation.

In response to Junge, it can be argued that Bauman's notions of pre-social morality and 'being for the other' are of great importance to those engaged in critical work. Primarily, Bauman's stance allows a notion of power to exist in the study of morality. If the notion of reciprocity is introduced into the equation, then the relationship becomes loaded. Once mutuality exists, 'being for the other' changes in nature. Automatically certain preconditions are attached and once they cease to exist responsibility may be withdrawn. In a global society where power is distributed unequally according to class, gender and ethnicity, those who find themselves in positions of power are also those who naturally should be demanded more frequently to assume responsibility for the other. An illustration of this can be found in the debates which surround the aid given by developed countries to the developing world. A common argument that arises against the donation of aid is the 'waste' of aid through the 'corruption' which exists in many developing countries. In this context, 'being for the other' is negated, because of the actor's perception that a mutuality of responsibility should exist – the responsibility of these countries to spend this money appropriately. If 'being for the other' is unconditional, then a moral obligation is borne by the developed world, whatever ideological and historical disputes exist over the responsibility for the suffering of these people.[7]

The second aspect of Junge's critique follows from the first. He challenges the notion that 'being for the other' without being with the other is an essentially existential responsibility. He claims that Bauman has provided an asymmetric basis for moral action, which rejects the fundamental notions of sociology, intersubjectivity, reciprocity and symmetric relations. Hence, Junge seeks to reformulate Bauman's theory through the introduction of reciprocity to partner responsibility: reciprocity being the normative ideal upon which the structure of interaction is founded. As a consequence of this alleged lacuna, he claims that Bauman's theory is incapable of sociological investigation. In other words, he envisages 'being for the other' establishes a moral party of two and the notion of 'reciprocity' completes this situation, as no longer are we free to return the moral gift, but obliged to do so.

Modernity, characterised by large state bureaucracies and industry, has made the social situation to which Junge alludes impossible. This is because an actor, within a bureaucratic structure, is capable of making decisions where the effects are felt by others unknown to them. Hence, Bauman places a theoretical emphasis upon the notion of 'being for the other', for this very reason, that these structures have detached us from the reality of our actions. It is empirically impossible to conceive of the notion of reciprocity in this situation. For example, a victim of corporate harm would rarely meet face-to-face with the boardroom perpetrator. Thus Junge's analysis lends itself to interpersonal confrontations, which characterise 'blue collar' crime.

Furthermore, it is erroneous not to envisage norms being able to arise from Bauman's notion of 'being for the other', although it is accepted that this would not appear to be Bauman's intention. Part of the problem stems from Bauman's ambiguity over the use of ethical codes.[8] However, the obvious strength of Bauman's work is the insights it offers on the underpinning values of modernity and late modernity as potential sources of immoral action within these societies. Yet it does not appear to offer comment upon norms or codes that provide the conditions in which 'being for the other' may thrive. It is of great importance for those engaged in critical scholarship to be able to distinguish between circumstances which are advantageous to moral thinking and moral action and those that are not. Political strategies may then be organised to promote alternative spaces in the neo-liberal hegemony in which 'being for the other' thrives.

The notion of 'identification' from the work of Christie (1993) can be helpfully added to Bauman's theory. This will meet some of the concerns of critical scholarship while remaining faithful to the notion of 'being for the other'.

In the seminal text *Crime Control as Industry*, Christie describes some of the possible reasons for Norway's resistance to the trend in rising prison populations across Europe. He argues that the activities of Norwegian group KROM have played a major role in influencing penal policy. It is composed of a variety of 'stake-holders': practitioners, politicians, liberals, journalists and prisoners, and every year it holds a meeting in the mountains. While Christie concedes that those who have extreme 'law and order' agendas do not participate in these meetings, people attend from a diverse range of background. In spite of this diversity, the group produces a 'joint moral community', which is characterised by empathy and provides a situation in which 'pictures of monsters do not thrive' (1993: 39–40). This community is underpinned by *informal standards for what it is considered acceptable to do in the name of punishment, and also the view that these standards are valid for all human beings* (ibid.: 40, emphasis added). The reasons why these standards exist, for Christie, are almost impossible to identify for certain. However, he surmises that the standards exist because of the actor's 'imaginary power', 'the capacity to see oneself in the other person's situation' (ibid.). He concludes that this process of 'identification' operates upon general standards for all, which prevent extreme measures resulting, because the group's reference point is: 'it could have been me, found guilty, brought to prison' (ibid.).

In this Norwegian example, the people's behaviour matches the characteristics of Bauman's 'being for the other': the responsibility to the prisoner is not contingent, it exists for all human beings. Furthermore, the empathy which exists for the prisoner's plight results from the 'participatory empathic stance' people assume, and 'being for the other' has become institutionalised into the group's activities. The individual moral reasoning displayed by these individuals has given rise to an intersubjective framework of moral norms. While the moral behaviour arose independent of this normative framework, the process of identification has ensured that 'being for the other' remains central to their moral reasoning. In short, the notion of identification provides a tool with which to identify intersubjective frameworks that promote 'being for the other' and challenge moral indifference.

'Contextualising' Bauman

Having discussed and developed Bauman's theories of morality, the following section seeks to demonstrate how his analyses of morality provide insights for a social harm perspective using the concept of moral indifference. In *Modernity and the Holocaust*, Bauman (1989) demonstrated the facets of modernity which made the Holocaust possible. He specifies a number of processes that result in the moral manipulation of actors and are instructive of the moral indifference to harm production that occurs in the corporation and the state.

The first process which Bauman identifies is the relationship between 'social proximity and moral responsibility'. Bauman argues that moral manipulation begins with the neutralisation of the moral responsibility for the other through the physical or spiritual separation of society. This process was integral to what he terms the 'social suppression of moral responsibility', the second of these processes. In the case of the Holocaust, once the Jew was removed from everyday life and personal intercourse, and no longer belonged to the realm of moral duty, the bureaucracy and the technology of the Holocaust could become a reality. Accordingly, the Jews were legally defined as subordinate to the majority of the population. They were dismissed from the labour market and eventually 'ghettoised'.

These processes were deliberately designed to separate the victim group from the rest of the population and to secure the general population's indifference to the outcome which followed. As a consequence of this physical separation and the neutralisation of moral 'outrage', annihilation was not a startling deviation, but rather the logical outcome of this process. Thus, once this policy decision had identified the problem group, the further the sequence of stages moved away from the original definition, then increasingly decision-making was based upon rational/technical judgements as opposed to moral considerations. These stages were designed with one overriding objective: to create physical and mental distance between the groups in order to achieve the social suppression of moral responsibility. Modern industrial societies are characterised by the same separation between decision-makers and individuals and hence there is an inherent danger of moral indifference to actions that fall outside people's sphere of experience.

The third process Bauman identifies is the 'social production of distance'. He contends that due to the relationship between human proximity and morality, 'morality seems to conform to the law of optical perspective' (Bauman, 1989: 192). Thus, as distance increases, responsibility for the other would appear to be reduced. Moral indifference is inherent in the structures of industrial society because the effects of human action far exceed an actor's moral visual capacity. In these societies, the 'intermediary' has become an important factor in this process, ensuring that individuals do not experience the consequences of their actions. The intense division of labour and the extensive chain of commands, which characterise industrial societies, have served to mediate between the initial policy decision and its consequences, releasing these participants from their responsibility to the other. The process of task splitting in modern societies ensures responsibility to the 'mini moral community' of the bureaucracy or the production line, as opposed to the other.

There are many examples of corporate harm which illustrate Bauman's theory of the Holocaust. One of the most infamous cases involved the Pinto car made by Ford. It was introduced in 1970 to the American small car market previously dominated by European and Japanese manufacturers. During production a design fault was identified, namely that the fuel tank was prone to rupture in the event of low speed impacts. On the basis of a cost benefit analysis, Ford decided it would cost the company less to pay compensation for injury and the loss of life than it would to recall the vehicle and put right the fault. The observations of Dennis Gioia, a Recall Coordinator with Ford during the production of the Pinto, illustrate the manner in which a capitalist division of labour creates mini moral communities. Recalling the company loyalty which permeated its employees during the 1970s fuel crisis and influenced their everyday decisions, Gioia states:

> It did not fit the pattern of recallable standards; the evidence was not overwhelming that the car was defective in some way, so the case was actually fairly straightforward. It was a good business decision, even if people might be dying. (1996: 145)

Gioia went on to relate how during his tenure as Recall Coordinator his concerns for those at risk from Ford cars soon evaporated because allowing such concerns to 'surface was potentially paralysing and prevented rational decisions about which cases to recommend for recall' (ibid.). His experiences demonstrate the capability of modern society to negate moral impulses and produce moral indifference to the consequences of wealth accumulation.

Gioia's account is illustrative of the continuum upon which indifference and Cohen's theory of denial exist. In Gioia's account, he describes his own participation in the negation of his moral impulses, through the strategy of neutralisation – a characteristic of denial. In Cohen's notion of implicatory denial, the person attempts to neutralise the reality of their actions by seeking to negotiate a different construction of an event. In Gioia's case, this was achieved by what Cohen terms 'authorisation' (1993: 110): when 'acts are tacitly approved of by those in authority' internal moral urges are replaced by, in this example, the moral code of the company and the concerns for profit.

Bauman's focus in *Modernity and the Holocaust* is upon the immoral potential of societies characterised by large bureaucratic and industrial structures. However, Bauman's recent work has sought to develop a sociological theory of morality in the context of late/post-modernity. This analysis focuses upon the consequences for morality in a period of significant restructuring in the bureaucratic and industrial structures. These changes have occurred as a result of the reorganisation of global capital, which was set in motion during the 1970s, and has been facilitated by the subsequent dominance of neo-liberal values in the policies of many nation states. Bauman's analysis concentrates upon the 'by-products' of the demise of social democracy, and in particular the increasing levels of exclusion from the labour market and the subsequent subjection of this population to strategies of control.

A central element of his argument is that there have been fundamental changes in the work ethic (Bauman, 1998). While it once supplied a disciplined labour force, a burgeoning work force is no longer a sign of economic health. Instead, corporations, dictated by the short-term concerns of shareholders for increased dividends on their investments, continually strive for minimal labour overheads. Hence, Bauman contends that the role of the work ethic has become: 'an effective means to wash clean all the hands and consciences inside the accepted boundaries of society of the guilt of abandoning a large number of their fellow citizens to permanent redundancy' (Bauman, 1998: 72).

The work ethic is used by capitalist societies to create images in its own reflection of those who threaten its order: these visions 'tend to be self portraits of the society with minus signs' (Bauman, 1998: 73). Importantly, those marginalised from the labour market suffer the double bind of exclusion, through their non-participation in the sphere of consumerism, as well as exclusion from the labour market. Ignored by these two processes of integration, this section of the population has become the 'by-product' of capitalist society. The sight of society's 'by-product' serves as a warning to the current participants in the market, and constantly affirms the work ethic to them. Consequently, the plight of the losers has become increasingly dire, as collective responsibility for these people evaporates: the welfare system is exchanged for the criminal justice system, as a means of dealing with them.

In 'Social Issues of Law and Order', Bauman (2000) seeks to understand the processes in which societies have attempted to impose order upon those who do not abide by the norm of the work ethic. He argues that this shift in the work ethic has had a fundamental influence upon penal policy in western countries. Prisons once served as a means of moral correction, where the deviant was educated in the ways of the work ethic. The purpose of prisons – 'factories of discipline' – has been diminished by the emergence of the 'Super Max' prison. These prisons, which Bauman describes as 'factories of exclusion', have exchanged techniques of discipline for techniques of immobilisation.[9]

Bauman suggests that the reason for this loss of a sense of collective responsibility for the losers in the current organisation of the relations of production has been their expulsion from the 'universe of moral obligations' (Bauman, 1998: 77). He argues this has been achieved through the link between poverty and criminality:[10]

As actual or potential criminals, the poor cease to be an ethical problem – they are exempt from our moral responsibility. There is no more a moral question of defending the poor against the cruelty of their fate; instead there is the ethical question of defending the right and proper lives of decent people against assaults likely to be plotted in mean streets, ghettos and no go areas. (Bauman, 1998: 77)

Accordingly the work ethic has ceased to be a statement of moral sentiments, and has become a tool of what Bauman terms 'adiaphorisation' (1998: 78). This is a process which removes 'ethical opprobrium' for morally unconscionable acts. It is achieved when an action is declared neutral, through the application of an alternative moral criterion, which is unaccountable to other moral codes. In the context of late modernity, moral thinking in capitalist societies has come to be colonised by the concerns of economic rationality (Titmuss, 1970; Fevre, 2000). It has become the dominant moral code and has replaced 'being for the other' with the 'sober, rational calculation of costs and effects' (Bauman, 1998: 81). Consequently, the work ethic has become an aspect of 'adiaphorisation', as it supplies a benchmark to evaluate whether those enduring suffering are worthy of our compassion.

The following anecdote serves to illustrate this notion of 'adiaphorisation'. It is taken from the American satirist Michael Moore:

In my first film, *Roger & Me*, a white woman on Social Security clubs a bunny rabbit to death so that she can sell him as 'meat' instead of as a pet. I wish I had a nickel for every time in the last ten years someone has come up to me and told me how 'horrified' and 'shocked' they were when they saw that 'poor little cute bunny' bonked on the head. The scene made them physically sick. Some had to turn away or leave the theatre. Many wondered why I would include such a scene. The Motion Picture Association of America (MPAA) gave *Roger & Me* an R rating in response to that rabbit killing ... But less than two minutes after the bunny lady does her deed, I included footage of a scene in which the police in Flint opened fire and shot a black man who was wearing a superman cape and holding a plastic toy gun. Not once – not ever – has anyone said to me, 'I can't believe you showed a black man being shot in your movie! How Horrible! How disgusting! I couldn't sleep for weeks'. After all, he was just a black man, not a cute, cuddly bunny. (2002: 59)

This passage provides a vivid example of the moral indifference which exists in capitalist society to the suffering of excluded populations. Following Bauman's notion of 'adiaphorisation', the indifference of the cinema audience to this suffering can be explained primarily by the socio-economic position of young black Americans. An estimated 20 per cent of young black men are neither at school nor working compared to 9 per cent of white men (COEA, 1998). Furthermore, estimates suggest that black males' median earnings for full time work were $150 less than white male employees (ibid.). Black males are more likely than their white counterparts to be at the periphery of consumerism and the labour market. In addition, the process of 'adiaphorisation' is underpinned by racist ideologies which link poverty and black criminality together. Gilroy (2002), for example, argues that racist discourses often attempt to locate explanations of black criminality in a cultural rejection of the work ethic. Through the application of the work ethic, the 'toy gun' wielding victim is removed from the 'universe of moral obligation'. His fate is an irrelevance to a society where moral obligations are reserved for the 'deserving', who operate within the economic sphere. Ultimately, 'adiaphorisation' secured the indifference of the audience to this human suffering and their moral opprobrium for the suffering of 'that' rabbit.

CONCLUSION

This chapter has outlined the possible development of a theory of moral indifference, based on the work of Bauman and the prospective benefits it holds for the social harm paradigm. Hopefully, this chapter has persuaded the reader of the need for critical scholarship to awaken the consciousness of populations to the human suffering caused by the social relations of capitalist society. However, due to the restrictions of space a number of important issues were only briefly dealt with or excluded from this discussion. I would like to outline these issues here to demonstrate the paths upon which future discussions of this concept may develop.

The first issue is the role that moral indifference plays in the constitution of capitalist hegemony. As suggested in the introduction the role of moral indifference performs a wider function in sustaining the organisation of capitalist society. This hegemony is an integral feature of the acceptance of a historical bloc's harm production and without it the stability of the bloc would be seriously questioned. In line with Gramsci's (1999: 234) observation, it could be argued that the notion of moral indifference is of paramount importance to capitalist societies' hegemonic capability to 'organise permanently the impossibility of internal disintegration'.

The second issue is concerned with Bauman's later writings on morality and his theorisation of the processes of marginalisation. Bauman's description of marginalisation is pitched at a highly abstract level. In order to understand the operation of moral indifference in capitalist society, the reality of the political economy of marginalisation is fundamental to this analysis. Thus, empirical grounding of Bauman's theories within a political economy analysis would further develop the notion of moral indifference.

The final issue reflects upon the possible drawbacks of moral indifference. As an underdeveloped concept, moral indifference is open to interpretation. At present the notion of moral indifference, like social harm, is ambiguous in nature and at risk from unwanted interventions from the right. This is a particular concern given the dominance of 'New Right' and 'Third Way' discourses over popular moral debates. However, the presence of these discourses merely demonstrates the importance for the left to develop theories of morality, which challenge the 'legitimacy' of the harm produced by capitalist society.

ACKNOWLEDGEMENTS

Thanks go to the editors for their insightful comments and painstaking scrutiny of this chapter. Also I would like to thank Sarah Pemberton for her critical engagement with earlier drafts.

6
State Harms

Tony Ward

This chapter seeks to explicate the concepts of state *crime* and state *harm*. State crime is a form of organisational deviance involving human rights violations by state agencies (Green and Ward, 2000). But states also cause harm in ways that are not deviant but, on the contrary, are central to their normal functioning. Indeed, unless 'harm' is restrictively defined, virtually any state practice could be considered harmful to someone. The first section of this chapter accordingly seeks to construct a reasonably narrow definition of 'harm' as applied to state practices. The second section discusses state crime and very briefly sketches a criminological approach to the state. The third section sketches an account of the political economy of state crime/harm. Finally the chapter outlines two possible ways of studying state harms that lie outside the concept of crime. Some kinds of state harm may be studied as part of criminology, not because they are themselves crimes but because they form part of the context in which certain kinds of criminal behaviour occur. Alternatively, social harm, including state harm, may be seen as a completely autonomous field of study, overlapping with criminology but asking different questions about a much broader subject matter.

DEFINING 'HARM'

In a broad sense, 'harm' may be 'conceived as the thwarting, setting back, or defeating of an interest' (Feinberg, 1984: 33). In this sense, any political decision can be considered harmful to someone. Political institutions exist to resolve conflicts of interest. In politics there are winners and losers, and those who lose out necessarily suffer harm in the broad sense. For example, if taxes are increased, my interest in maximising my income is set back. Moreover, as Jeremy Bentham observed, 'to make a law is to do evil' – by restricting liberty and threatening violators with sanctions – 'that good may come' (1970: 54). If 'state harm' is not to embrace all of politics and law, we need to focus on a narrower category of serious harms.

One category of especially serious harms involves the thwarting of 'basic welfare interests' (Feinberg, 1984: 57), or basic human needs (Doyal and Gough, 1991). These are interests in those elements of freedom and wellbeing that are necessary for human beings to function effectively as purposive agents (Gewirth, 1978). They include such things as life, physical and mental health, freedom from severe pain, freedom from confinement or coercion, and sufficient education and financial resources to enable one to play a part in the life of one's society. Except for certain people whose goals or capacities are of an unusually limited kind, anyone who is unable to secure these basic interests will be seriously harmed.

Serious harms of this kind are of particular relevance to the study of states. States universally claim to protect (some) people against these kinds of harms and they universally claim the right to inflict harms of this type in some circumstances, such as punishment and warfare. The ideology and international law of human rights, to which virtually all states notionally subscribe, embodies these two claims. Human rights law proclaims, on the one hand, the duty of states to respect and secure the basic welfare interests of all human beings, and on the other hand, the right of states to invade those basic interests in order to enforce the law, fight defensive wars, maintain public health, and so on.

Some writers equate the term 'harm' with *wrongful* invasions of interests (Feinberg, 1984) or with violations of human rights (Gewirth, 1982). Human rights violations can be equated with wrongful infringements of basic welfare interests or human needs. The Schwendingers (1975) propose to equate human rights violations in this sense with *crimes*. So do Kauzlarich et al. (2001), whose concept of state crime includes many of the normal, taken-for-granted policies and practices of capitalist states:

For example, the poor, racial and ethnic minorities, and women are explicitly or tacitly victimized by the state partly because of its support for larger structural and cultural definitions of worth, power, authority and prestige. Ultimately, stratification produces inequality in social relationships between the state, groups of citizens, and the interests of capital. To the extent that the state supports immoral and illegal inequalities and their harmful manifestations, a state can be in whole or in part considered responsible for victimization. (Kauzlarich et al. 2001: 176)

Social stratification can certainly be seriously *harmful*, especially when it erodes what Rawls (1971: 440) calls the 'primary good of self respect' – the sense of being an agent whose purposes are worthwhile and capable of achievement. Green and Ward (2000) object to definitions of *crime* along these lines on the grounds that by including inequalities that are widely accepted as legitimate (or at least within the fair range of debate in a democratic society) they break the conceptual link between crime and deviance. But what Kauzlarich et al. are trying to do is to develop a *victimology* of state crime, which is a different enterprise from that of studying state crime as a form of organisational deviance. It is not unreasonable to say that people whose lives are blighted by unemployment or ill health, for example, as a result of government policies have been *victimised* by the state. What this perhaps suggests is that the concept of harm is a better foundation for victimology than that of crime.

The concept of 'harm' should arguably be defined more broadly still, to include serious harms (invasions of basic welfare interests) that do not infringe human rights standards. If one accepts that there are circumstances in which states can justifiably coerce, imprison or even kill people, without violating their human rights, then it seems more honest to say 'these people have been seriously harmed, but with good reason', than to deny that they have been harmed at all. For the purposes of this chapter, therefore, a 'state harm' is an invasion by a state agency of any person's[1] basic welfare interests, whether such invasion is justified or not. I shall now consider the arguments for and against working with the narrower concept of state *crime*.

STATE CRIME AND STATE HARM

How 'state crime' (or for that matter 'harm') should be defined depends on the purpose for which one is using the terms. If one is discussing international criminal law, a crime is a breach of that law. If one is using 'crime' as a term of moral and political opprobrium, a state crime is any behaviour by a state that one regards as grossly immoral. If one is discussing criminology, then the term 'crime' should be confined to behaviour that is in some sense deviant (Green and Ward, 2000). The reason is simple: deviant behaviour is what criminology is about. (I take 'criminology' to be a convenient shorthand for 'the study of the deviance and social control', not exclusively confined to criminal law.) But this raises two questions: what is deviant behaviour, and why work within a discipline dedicated to studying it?

Deviance is not an inherent quality of an act, but results from the application of a rule by a social audience (Becker, 1963). The best definition of this slippery concept that I can suggest is the following. An act is deviant where there is a social audience that (1) accepts a certain rule as a standard of behaviour, (2) interprets the act, or similar acts of which it is aware, as violating the rule, and (3) is disposed to apply significant sanctions – that is, significant from the point of view of the actor – to such violations. The matrix of an actor, a rule, an audience and a potentially significant sanction is what defines the essential subject matter of criminology. The work on state crime that Penny Green and I are engaged on (Ward and Green, 2000; Green and Ward 2000, 2004) is based on the idea that in many but not all violations of human rights in contemporary global society,[2] all these elements are present. The relevant actors are state agencies. The relevant rules are rules of international law, domestic law and social morality, as interpreted by audiences that include domestic and transnational civil society, international organisations, other states and other agencies within the offending state itself. The relevant sanctions include legal punishments, censure or rebellion by the state's own population, damage to the state's domestic and international reputation, and diplomatic, economic and military sanctions from other states.

How do these elements combine to make up a distinctively criminological interpretation of behaviour? At risk of rather drastic oversimplification, I would suggest that nearly all criminological theories fall into two groups. First there are those that interpret deviance as instrumental and (to a more or less limited degree) rational behaviour. The potential reaction of the audience is a cost of the behaviour that the actor either takes into account or fails to appreciate. Rational choice theory, control theory and Mertonian anomie theory are all variations on this theme, as are virtually all attempts to explain corporate crime. Kauzlarich and Kramer (1998) show that this perspective can be quite easily adapted to explain many kinds of state crime.

The second major approach interprets crime as a form of *performance*. Explanation focuses on the meaning of an action to an audience and to the actor. In this perspective the proscription of an act by a rule is not necessarily a disincentive to its performance. The rule is part of what confers social meaning on an act. The transgressive character of certain actions may enhance their value as ways for people to define, to themselves and others, the kind of actors they are. Variations on this line of argument can be found in subculture theory (Cohen, 1956), labelling theory, in work on 'accomplishing masculinity', and in Katz's (1988) account of the 'seductions and repulsions' of crime.

Katz's work is particularly significant because although it is mainly concerned with individual deviance he makes a point of beginning and ending his argument with examples of state crime. He concludes that western governments, like armed robbers, often murder because they feel compelled to maintain a tough image rather than because it achieves any tactical objective.

The criminological explanation of state crime needs to draw on both of these two approaches to behaviour that is both a form of organisational deviance and, in many instances, a form of extreme interpersonal violence. As organisations, state agencies tend to be strongly goal-oriented and instrumentally rational (Kauzlarich and Kramer, 1998) but it is unlikely that some of the extreme forms of personal violence engaged in during, for example, war or genocide can be explained satisfactorily without paying attention to the dimension of performance. The two approaches I have sketched are not mutually exclusive. The impact of a performance on its audience (based on its disregard for rules) can be one means of achieving instrumental goals. This is how state (or anti-state) terrorism works, insofar as it does work. Sometimes, however, the actions of state terrorists appear so tenuously connected to instrumental goals that some observers suspect that the performance is an end in itself (for example, Aretxaga, 2000; Mahmood, 2000).

Interested readers will be able to decide for themselves how successful our (Green and Ward, 2004) attempts at explanation are. But, a sceptical reader might ask, why bother? Why are we so keen to bring state crime within the framework of a discipline whose contributions either to knowledge or to human welfare have so far been less than spectacular?

One reason is pedagogic. Criminology is an expanding subject in UK universities and is also an important element in many law degrees, where it serves to bring a relatively sociologically informed and (one hopes) critical perspective to bear on the study of legal rules and their enforcement. As a matter of simple intellectual honesty, it is important to point out to our students that *even on the most narrowly legalistic definition, serious crime is predominantly an activity of governments and government officials.* War crimes, genocide, torture and corruption – activities proscribed by national and international criminal law and predominantly committed, or at least connived at, by governments – are the leading forms of illegal force, and possibly also of fraud, in the modern world.

State crime is impossible to quantify with any precision, but two findings give an idea of its scale. Rummel (1996) calculated that on the best available estimates over 169 million people were murdered by governments from 1900 to 1987 (this figure excludes those deaths in wars not attributable to war crimes, which Rummel estimates at 35 million). Zvekic (1998) shows that according to victimisation surveys, being asked for a bribe is the second most prevalent form of victimisation (after consumer fraud) in all but the industrialised world. But victimisation surveys can tap only experiences of 'petty corruption', not the much more serious 'grand corruption' involving senior officials and major firms (Moody-Stuart, 1997). Admittedly there are also large dark figures for corporate fraud and individual tax evasion (which are likely to be more rampant than corruption in the richest economies). Nevertheless the enormous sums believed to have been stolen by the world's leading kleptocrats – $45 billion by the Suharto family in Indonesia, $12 billion by Marcos in the Philippines, $8–9 billion by Mobuto in former Zaire, $4 billion by Abacha in Nigeria[3] – make corruption a plausible contender to be the world's leading form of property crime, if not in absolute financial terms, then at least in terms of the damage done to the economies affected.

The second reason for studying state crime is political, and is implicit in the concept of state crime itself. State crime is organisational deviance that is defined as such by, *inter alia*, domestic and transnational civil society. Civil society includes the academic criminological, legal and sociological communities (see Ward and Green, 2000). Criminology is therefore itself a minor part of the process of labelling and sanctioning state crime. Encouraging greater criminological attention to state crime can be expected to produce political effects, however marginal, either for good or ill. The good effects will consist of encouraging the imposition of formal or informal sanctions that encourage states to comply with human rights norms (Risse et al., 1999). The ill effects will consist of encouraging sanctions that are either counterproductive or, worse, themselves inflict death and suffering on innocent people.

Unfortunately this reasoning also suggests at least three worrying drawbacks to the concept of state crime. First, it could be argued (perhaps most tellingly from an abolitionist perspective) that the concept of 'crime' is inherently dangerous because it encourages the assumption that the appropriate response is punishment.[4] When states take it upon themselves to punish other, 'rogue', states the consequences can be extremely destructive, as we have seen in Afghanistan and Iraq. In response to this, it can be pointed out that any reasonably impartial account of state crime is bound to highlight the extensive 'criminal record' of some of the would-be guardians of global law and order, notably the US (see, for example, McClintock, 1985; Chomsky, 1989;

Blum, 2000) – and thereby undermine the prevailing rhetoric about 'rogue states'.

The second drawback lies in the self-referential nature of the definition of deviance: state crime is what social audiences so label, but criminologists are themselves part of the social audience. What, then, are we to do about those state harms that are *not* effectively labelled as deviant, but that we believe ought to be? Again the American and British actions in Afghanistan are a prime example. Given the overwhelming domestic approval (at least in the US) and international acquiescence that greeted this intervention, it seems difficult to argue that it is an example of organisational deviance in the sense defined above (the war on Iraq is another matter). The case can be made, however, if one equates deviance with illegitimacy (cf. Ward and Green, 2000). That is, one can argue that even though the American action was accepted by most important audiences as being justified by international legal standards, it was actually not so justified if those standards are properly applied (Green, 2002; Mandel, 2002). But there is an undeniable tension here between theoretical consistency and political commitment.

Closely related to this is the third drawback, which lies in the ambiguous nature of human rights discourse. In analysing this problem, we (Ward and Green, 2000) have made use of Gramsci's concept of hegemony, as extended to international relations by Robert Cox (1993a). Hegemony is a form of domination based on the acceptance by both the rulers and the ruled of an ideology that makes the rulers' actions appear to serve universal interests when in reality they serve sectional interests. On the international scene, a hegemonic bloc made up of the US, its allies and international institutions promotes an ideology of human rights, 'good governance' and so-called free trade, which gives an appearance of universalism to a strategy that promotes the interests of rich states and of international capital. The consequences of this can be seen in the spectacular increase in international inequality,[5] which denies millions of people in the poorest countries the most basic rights to life, health and subsistence. Paradoxically, we argue, it is precisely the *genuine* universality of human rights – their grounding in basic welfare interests that really are common to nearly all human beings – that makes them such an effective tool of global hegemony. In practice, the universalism of human rights is deceptive because of the selective manner in which powerful states and institutions uphold them, neglecting economic and social rights and those violations of civil and political rights that are deemed to be committed in a good cause.

A critic of our approach might argue that to recognise as 'crimes' only those human rights violations that actually attract some significant form of censure and sanction is merely to reinforce the existing selectivity in the denunciation of human rights violations. One response to this would be to point out that, precisely by making the distinction between harms (or rights violations) and crimes, our approach actually highlights the selective nature of international censure. Another response is that the study of state crime, as we define it, by no means excludes gross economic harms such as famines. On the contrary, much poverty, famine and disease is a direct result of state crimes of corruption, war and repression (de Waal, 1997; Green and Ward, 2004).

THE POLITICAL ECONOMY OF STATE HARM

It is with some trepidation that I embark on a brief discussion of this enormous subject. There are, however, some fairly simple connections between economic conditions and state violence which can be outlined without entering into any very sophisticated theoretical analysis.

One of the more promising approaches to studying the criminal or harmful behaviour of state elites builds on the work of Tilly (1985, 1992) and Levi (1988) in political science, and starts from the assumption that states are predatory organisations seeking to maximise their revenue. Notable applications of this approach to state crime are Reno's (1999) work on West Africa and Smart's (1999) on China.

Tilly compares states to 'protection rackets': coercive entrepreneurs who extract revenues in exchange for protection against threats that are partly real, partly illusory and partly created by themselves. He argues that in the military competition between states in early modern Europe, 'state makers developed a durable interest in promoting the accumulation of capital' (1985: 172). Such states offered protection at relatively efficient rates, enabling capitalists to retain a large proportion of their capital while providing finance for the state's military expansion. Agencies such as courts and parliament subjected state coercion to a measure of control and predictability, which is essential to the existence of stable property rights. Faced with popular resistance, states extended the protection of law, representative institutions and other benefits to wider sections of the population.

Such concessions helped to foster what Levi calls 'quasi-voluntary compliance' (1988: 52) – that is, compliance that is underpinned by coercion but which is forthcoming even when the immediate risk of coercive sanctions is low. Quasi-voluntary compliance, as Levi points out, greatly reduces monitoring and enforcement costs. It enables states to extract more revenue, but requires them to spend some of it in a way that will be perceived as promoting the common interests of the taxpayers.

Thus there are fairly straightforward economic reasons for states to accept restraints on their power to harm. However, certain states (commonly but perhaps misleadingly called 'weak states') never develop this degree of self-restraint, while others find the price of maintaining such legitimacy too high.

Weak states

Weak states, or 'quasi-states' (Jackson, 1990: 21), are entities that enjoy recognition as states in international law (with the substantial economic and political benefits such recognition confers) but lack the resources and administrative capabilities to offer their populations much in the way of protection, legal rights or public services. Such states – largely concentrated in sub-Saharan Africa – are predatory organisations which do not appear to serve the interests of any class in the indigenous population, unless the state elite or 'bureaucratic bourgeoisie' (Theobald, 1990: 95) is considered a class in its own right (Schatzberg, 1988). Weak states in this sense appear particularly prone to civil war (of a kind fought with little regard to military convention), state terror and genocide (Holsti, 1996; Kaldor, 1999).

A number of reasons can be cited for this apparent autonomy of weak states from class interests. First, the indigenous bourgeoisie is unlikely to be a powerful political force, and cannot become such a force without an effective state to protect its interests (Reno, 1999). Second, state elites are likely to identify their interests as lying in the promotion of capitalist development only if they have, in economic jargon, a low 'discount rate': that is, if they value long-term gains nearly as highly as short-term ones (Levi, 1988). The acute political instability of weak states forces rulers to focus on the short-term maintenance of their military power and patronage networks. Third, in contrast to early modern European states, weak states need little internal support in order to maintain their military power. Ruling elites typically inherited military resources from the former colonial power and were able to maintain them during the Cold War through superpower sponsorship (Tilly, 1985, 1992). Even without such sponsorship, armaments of a relatively low-tech kind are cheap and readily available (unfortunately, from the rulers' point of view, they are equally available to insurgents). And fourth, states can ally themselves with *foreign* commercial interests, trading access to lucrative raw materials for commercial and military support (Reno, 1999). Even military/political organisations that lack internationally recognised statehood can be acceptable partners for western firms if they have a sufficiently effective monopoly of violence to provide secure access to resources, as Charles Taylor showed in the days when he controlled much of Liberia but was not yet its recognised president (Ellis, 1999; Reno, 1999).

In a looser sense, weak states include those which, though not as chaotic as Liberia, are still *relatively* weak in terms of their ability to meet demands from their population, guarantee security and raise living standards. Gurr (1986) argues that such 'weak' states are relatively likely to resort to violence. Welsh (2002), in a careful survey of East Asian states, argues that those that are 'weak' in this sense, because they lack resources and bureaucratic professionalism, have the highest levels of state violence (particularly killing) and also of vigilantism. She also argues that a combination of globalisation, economic crisis and pressure from western institutions is tending to weaken Asian states and promote further violence.

'Strong' states in crisis

As Hall et al. (1978), building on Gramsci, argue in a classic analysis, economic crisis also tends to push 'strong' states – those with high levels of legitimacy or hegemony – in the direction of greater repression or authoritarianism. The reason, again, is quite straightforward. 'Hegemony' describes a condition in which laws and policies aimed at promoting the prosperity of a capitalist economy are widely accepted as serving universal interests, not just those of a dominant class. To create this impression of universal benefit requires that certain real material benefits and economic and political concessions are accorded to subordinate classes. In times of economic crisis these concessions appear too expensive, or too detrimental to the interests of capital, and the state elite sees a need to cut them back. Such retrenchment naturally tends to provoke resistance, but by defining those who resist as a threat to public order and the common good the state aims to legitimise the repressive measures necessary to defeat the resistance.

This bald account of course leaves unanswered many complex questions about the precise nature of the linkages between the state elite (or elites), the dominant class or bloc, and various elements of 'civil society' which play a key role in orchestrating consent – questions which Hall et al. discuss in meticulous detail. But in broad outline it fits such episodes as the policing of the British miners' strike (Green, 1990; Jefferson 1990) and, in a much more extreme form, the murderous Argentine military regime of 1976–82 (Pion-Berlin, 1989; Feitlowitz, 1998; Marchak, 1999) – which, for all its brutality, enjoyed a wide measure of middle-class support.

State socialism (or state capitalism)

Since the focus of this book is on capitalist societies it is not necessary to enter into discussion of the political economy of so-called communist states – those in which the state elite directly controls the means of production. But no account of state harm can ignore the catastrophic social harms inflicted by such states in the twentieth century: above all, the famines, combined with state terror, suffered by the rural populations of the USSR and China. While recent scholarship suggests that Stalin's 'great terror' killed 'only' about 2 million people (Getty and Naumov, 2000), the Ukrainian famine is estimated to have killed 7–8 million in 1933 alone, and the Chinese famine of 1958–61 over 30 million (Becker, 1996: 46, 270).

Both these famines were entirely 'man-made' – that is, state-made – disasters. Both resulted from essentially similar causes, according to Becker (1996). The Soviet and Chinese states, bent on rapid industrialisation of their economies, both expropriated grain or rice in quantities which did not leave peasants enough to eat. Both imposed methods of collective farming that resulted in drastic lowering of output (in the Chinese case particularly, this was compounded by the use of pseudo-scientific farming methods that would supposedly produce miraculously increased yields). Both blamed the failures of collective agriculture on 'class enemies' and responded with terror. In both cases the information about production supplied to the central state by local officials was wildly inaccurate. A more recent example of catastrophic famine in a command economy is the situation in North Korea. The causes appear to be rather different from the Russian and Chinese examples, but state policies are again a primary factor (Noland et al., 2001).

BEYOND STATE CRIME? AGENDAS FOR RESEARCH

State harm, even in the restricted sense proposed above, has many more manifestations than violence and death. Does the entire range of state policies that cause, or fail to prevent, serious harm comprise a coherent field of study? In the remainder of this chapter I want to sketch two possible agendas for research on state harm. I focus here primarily on stable capitalist states such as the UK and US.

Contextualising criminology

The first, and less ambitious, agenda sees the study of social harm essentially as a kind of supplement to criminology. The focus here would be on those harms which, though not amounting to crimes in themselves, form an important part of the context of criminal or deviant activity. The most obvious example is the harm done by the criminal justice system itself, but this falls within criminology's existing remit. A less obvious example is provided by Stuart Henry's argument for conceptualising the deviant activities of participants in the informal economy as a 'crime of omission of the state' (1991: 256). One need not be convinced by Henry's case for an extremely broad concept of 'crime' to agree with him that the political decisions that perpetuate the informal economy are both intrinsically harmful and an important context for understanding street crime. Dorling in Chapter 11 of this volume makes a similar argument concerning murder.

A third example is the harm resulting from the persecution of more or less harmless forms of deviance. Anything that prevents lesbians, gay men, transgender people or sadomasochistic practitioners (Beckmann, 1999) from living out their sexual identities freely and openly is, prima facie, a violation of the 'primary good of self respect' (Cornell, 1995), and accordingly a form of social harm. It perhaps makes more sense to focus on the harm done by social control than on the deviance of the individuals concerned. A similar argument could be applied to some forms of drug use.

Finally, an important area for research 'beyond criminology' – though one in which I claim no expertise – is surely the harm done by compulsory schooling (Beckmann and Cooper, 2003). As Carlen and her colleagues argue, it is important to distinguish between schooling and education:

> When ... we talk of education we refer to all those processes which develop a person's emotional, mental and physical capabilities. By schooling, we [mean] ... the training of pupils by teachers according to a curriculum ... [E]ducation can occur as a result of, without or despite schooling, and ... schooling can variously involve education and/or its opposite – the stunting or limitation of emotional, mental and physical capabilities ... [T]he degree of education received via schooling is mediated by class structure, gender differentiation and racism – and ... by the prevailing political economy and dominant educational ideologies. (Carlen et al., 1992: 4)

The question this raises is how far what is conventionally called 'juvenile delinquency' could be construed as an attempt to escape or counteract the harm done by schooling – particularly harm to the 'primary good of self-respect', the sense of being a person who counts, who can achieve something (the classic work of Cohen, 1956, and Willis, 1977, contains pointers in this direction). Searle (2001) and Cooper (2002) provide some vivid examples of how children's self-respect is denied by teaching and school discipline, often leading to resistance and exclusion from school, which causes further harm.

A new field?

All the above proposals involve only modest ventures 'beyond criminology'. A different, more challenging agenda for the study of social harm sees it as a completely different subject from criminology. Whereas criminology focuses on definitions of, reactions to and motives for deviant behaviour, the new discipline (I confess to a lingering affection for the proposal to call it 'zemiology') would ask the same sort of questions about harm. Although harm and deviance are closely related (people who label any given behaviour as deviant tend also to perceive it as harmful) they are distinct areas of study, and I do not see why they cannot exist side by side. Social sciences (sociology, social geography, social anthropology, and so on) often have large overlaps between their fields of study, but approach them from different perspectives.

State harms can be divided into three classes:

Acknowledged harms – activities that the state acknowledges as both harmful and illegitimate, often the subjects of trials, public inquiries, truth commissions, and so on;
Contested harms – where a state agency is accused of causing harm but denies either the existence of the harm or its own responsibility: for example, Gulf War Syndrome; and
Putatively legitimate harms – where the state acknowledges doing something harmful (for example, putting people in prison) but claims justification for it.

Harms that are straightforwardly *acknowledged* – where the state's acknowledgment fully concurs with the victims' claims – appear to be relatively rare (see Hayner, 2001). There are also some harms that are almost universally accepted as legitimate, even by those on the receiving end. But it seems likely that a great majority of all instances of (alleged) state harm will be the subject of conflicting claims about their existence, degree and legitimacy, and/or about the apportionment of blame for them. By focusing on these pervasive claims, and counter-claims the study of state harm could achieve some coherence as a (sub-)discipline, despite the enormous diversity of the harms in question.

Contested harms can be analysed from either of two perspectives. One is on the lines of Cohen's (2001) sociology (or social psychology) of denial. Here one first establishes that the behaviour in question really is both harmful and illegitimate and then studies the various ways in which states deny that it is really happening (literal denial), or that it is what it appears to be (interpretive denial), or that it matters (implicatory denial). There might also be some cases where one has to apply this perspective in reverse: that is, to study the reasons why state denials of things *that really didn't happen* fail to carry conviction.

The second perspective involves adopting a neutral stance towards the reality or legitimacy of the harm and studying the various rhetorical, legal and political strategies by which state agencies and their critics seek to gain acceptance for their point of view. Particularly instructive examples of this approach to contested harms come from studies by sociologists of law and/or science of 'mass toxic torts' involving alleged harms either by state agencies (for example, the 'Agent Orange' litigation: Schuck, 1986; Jasanoff, 1995: 196–8) or corporations (for example, the litigation over birth defects allegedly caused by the drug Bendectin™ (Edmond and Mercer, 1997; Sanders, 1998). Many but not all such studies aim to 'deconstruct' whatever version of events was eventually endorsed as true (Smith and Wynne, 1989; Jasanoff, 1995).

In embarking on such 'deconstructive' accounts of the 'truth' about state harm (or social harm in general), it is important to bear in mind Hacking's distinction between 'indifferent' (or natural) and 'interactive kinds' (1999: 103–9). That is, there are some classes of things that cause harm irrespective of how their effects are described by human beings: for example, nuclear radiation. I do not claim to know whether, and if so how, radiation can cause leukaemia in the unborn children of exposed fathers, but I have argued that the rejection by a British court of the claim that it does so can be understood in terms of the relative coherence and plausibility of the narratives constructed by scientists and lawyers on both sides (Ward, 1998). This line of argument in no way denies that there is a truth of the matter, one way or the other. Radiation is a 'natural kind' of phenomenon that has certain causal powers independent of human knowledge of those powers. Our knowledge of those properties is socially constructed; the causal powers themselves are not (Bhaskar, 1998).

Post-traumatic stress disorder (PTSD), on the other hand, is something that seems very likely to be of an 'interactive kind'. That is, it seems likely that the real and often terrible distress suffered by war veterans or disaster victims, for example, is to some extent influenced by the sufferer's awareness that it is, or is not, classified as PTSD (Hacking, 1995; A. Young, 1995). Here it makes some sense to say that the harm itself, and not just our knowledge of it, is socially constructed (not that this makes it any less disabling). What makes this area something of a minefield is that sociological or historical narratives about the social construction of harm can look very much like the narratives put forward by state or corporate actors to deny the harm or deny responsibility for it (Ward, 1999). A prime example is Showalter's (1997: 134–43) highly controversial account of Gulf War Syndrome (which is critical of journalistic accounts sympathetic to the veterans but strikingly uncritical of scientific claims by government agencies). What we have in Gulf War Syndrome is a contested harm where the contest partly turns on how far the harm is natural and how far it is socially constructed. Ironically, the usual bias of social scientists (and humanities scholars like Showalter) against organic explanations and in favour of social ones turns out here to favour the state.

The *legitimation* of state harm raises intricate conceptual questions (Beetham, 1991; Ward and Green, 2000), and rather than attempt to unravel them in the abstract I shall use the following intriguing incident as a case study. In 1994, a constable in the Avon and Somerset Constabulary pleaded guilty to common assault against a 14-year-old boy whom he had 'clipped round the ear' because he was one of a 'gang' whose disorderly behaviour was disturbing to elderly residents. He was fined £100 and ordered to pay £50 compensation.

> What followed was an extraordinary degree of public approbation of the constable's behaviour, criticism of the court ruling, and even offers to pay his fine. The *Star*, *Sun* and *Mirror* newspapers were reportedly inundated with some 64,000 telephone calls declaring their support for the constable and concern that he was being punished for using 'good, old-fashioned police methods'. In a phone-in poll, 98 per cent of nearly 72,000 respondents said that PC Guscott was right to do what he had done. According to police sources, over 16,000 people signed a petition backing the constable as he was subsequently reprimanded by his Chief Constable in an internal disciplinary hearing. (Lee, 1998: 1)

Here we have an action that is clearly harmful and also illegitimate on one of the three dimensions identified by Beetham (1991): it breaks institutionalised rules. It is acknowledged as such by the court and the Chief Constable and by Guscott himself – though in such a way as to define it as an act of *individual* deviance and not as a state crime. Yet on the other dimensions identified by Beetham, it appears to be the law itself, rather than Guscott's action, that lacks legitimacy at least as far as a certain section of the public is concerned. They do not see the law as being 'justified by shared beliefs', and their letters and petitions can be construed as a demonstration of consent, not to policing under the rule of law, but to minor extra-legal violence. Rather than the assault, it becomes Guscott's own treatment (perhaps not so much the fine as his public degradation) that becomes a 'contested harm'.

From a standpoint of commitment to human rights, one would surely want to say that the court was right – Guscott's action was illegitimate (even though one could imagine 'legitimate' responses to the situation that might be more harmful). So why is this illegitimate conduct accepted as legitimate by a significant social audience? There are essentially two possibilities. One is that they regard banging on a pensioner's door and kicking the cat flap as the sort of conduct that justifies what would prima facie be a violation of human rights. But then one wonders whether the response would have been the same if Guscott had assaulted an adult in comparable circumstances. The other possibility is that the relevant section of the public does not regard unruly adolescents – or children in general – as fully human persons with rights (see Parker in Chapter 14 of this volume).

This small incident illustrates a number of important points about legitimacy. First, it is important to distinguish between what 'the public' *perceives* as legitimate, what *really is* legitimate according to the rules and values that the state itself claims to uphold, and what is right according the analyst's own normative standards. Second, the work of legitimation, as Gramsci (1971) stressed, is largely done not by the state itself but by elements of civil society such as newspapers – which do not *invariably* dance to the precise tune played by the 'primary definers' (Hall et al., 1978: 57) such as the police and the courts. Third, legitimacy has several elements, and the same conduct may score high on one dimension of legitimacy and low on another. Fourth, there are two ways of legitimising harm: one is to argue that it is justified in the particular circumstances of the case; the other is to suggest, more or less openly, that the harm is acceptable because of *who the victim is.* The latter, which is all too common where people have been harmed or killed by the police (Scraton and Chadwick, 1987), is particularly dangerous. In its most extreme form, the exclusion of a category of victims from perpetrators' 'universe of obligation' makes genocide possible (Fein, 1990; see also Pemberton in Chapter 5 of this volume).

CONCLUSION

It appears possible to construct a reasonably coherent field of study centring on the ways in which states cause, deny and legitimise (or acknowledge and repair) social harms. The seminal works of Hall et al. (1978), Christie (1982, 2000), Bauman (1989)[6] and Cohen (2001) give some indication of how such an agenda might be pursued. I must confess that I do not feel much inclined to explore this route further myself – trying to understand state *crime* is enough work for one lifetime! But if any reader feels tempted to venture further along the way, this chapter will have served its purpose.

7

Re-orientating
Miscarriages of Justice

Michael Naughton

This chapter looks through a social harm lens at the issue of miscarriages of justice in England and Wales. It argues that a social harm approach is useful in reorientating definitions of miscarriages of justice because it moves beyond existing understandings of the number of victims of wrongful conviction to the various forms of harm caused in the most apparently routine of successful appeals against criminal conviction. This shifts notions of miscarriages of justice onto new and more productive territory by bringing into focus a scale of victims, and a variety of forms of harm that are engendered by wrongful convictions, which previously has not been sufficiently acknowledged or subjected to appropriate critical appraisal. In essence, then, this chapter is not so much a critical engagement with the underlying theoretical or methodological tenets of a social harm approach. Rather, it is more of a sympathetic *application* to illuminate the promise of a social harm approach in the specific area of wrongful criminal convictions. The primary aim is to show the ability of a social harm approach to raise questions that have not hitherto been posed and, simultaneously, that may contribute to the establishment of new agendas for social problems.

The chapter is presented in three parts. First, the limitations of the existing terrain on miscarriages of justice are briefly explicated. Then, the utility of a social harm approach in redefining miscarriages of justice is outlined. Finally, a social harm approach is applied to the issue of successful appeals against criminal conviction to provide the beginnings of a more adequate depiction of the *trails of harm* of miscarriages of justice, not only to the direct victims, but also more widely.

THE LIMITATIONS OF THE EXISTING TERRAIN

The existing work on miscarriages of justice in England and Wales, whether from campaigning organisations (see for example, Action

Against False Allegations of Abuse, 2002a; INNOCENT, 2002; Merseyside Against Injustice, 2002; The Portia Campaign, 2002), the media (for example, Woffinden, 1998; Goodman, 1999; Gillan, 2001; Foot, 2002), academic sources (for example, Green, 1995: 8; Nobles and Schiff, 1995: 299; Sanders and Young, 2000: 9), the criminal justice system and/or the governmental sphere (for example, Royal Commission on Criminal Justice, 1993: chapter 11), has not generally addressed the question of the scale of the miscarriage of justice phenomenon in any systematic way. Rather, all eyes have, hitherto, been generally directed towards cases of successful appeal against criminal conviction that were brought about through the post-appeal procedures of the Criminal Cases Review Commission (CCRC) after they have previously exhausted existing appellate opportunities. This is evident in the extent to which debates on the issue tend to revolve (still) around the same few notorious cases – Guildford Four, Birmingham Six, Bridgewater Four, M25 Three, Cardiff Newsagent Three, Stephen Downing and, most recently, the case of Robert Brown – which gives the impression that miscarriages of justice are exceptional occurrences of wrongful imprisonment. A profound limitation with this *exceptionalism* is that successful appeals that are achieved through the post-appeal procedures of the CCRC represent only a tiny fraction of the total annual number of successful appeals within England and Wales. Indeed, since the CCRC started handling casework in March 1997, there have been only about seven successful appeals per annum that have derived from a referral back to the Court of Appeal (Criminal Division) (CACD) from the CCRC (Naughton, 2003a).

Existing discourses, then, exclude the thousands of cases that are successful in appeal each year at the Crown Court for criminal convictions given in Magistrates' Courts. They also exclude the hundreds of cases that are successful in appeal each and every year at the CACD for criminal convictions given in the Crown Court. As this translates numerically, in the decade 1991–2000, the CACD abated over 2,670 criminal convictions – a yearly average of 267 (see Lord Chancellor's Department, 2000: 13). In addition, there are around 3,500 quashed criminal convictions a year at the Crown Court for convictions obtained at the Magistrates' Courts (Lord Chancellor's Department, 1998, 1999, 2000). In the context of these figures, existing approaches to miscarriages of justice can be conceived as providing a poor depiction of the scale and everyday occurrence of wrongful criminal convictions in England and Wales. Contrary to popular perceptions and dominant definitions, wrongful criminal convictions can be conceived as a very ordinary, routine feature of the criminal justice system.

At the same time, the existing discourse on the harmful consequences of miscarriages of justice is also insufficient. For, in addition to being almost predominantly aimed at the direct individual victims in exceptional cases of wrongful imprisonment, it tends to conceive the harm caused to such victims in the narrow confines of the denial of civil and politico-legal rights. This is at the expense of an analysis that would encompass both social and economic rights. The existing discourse is also largely silent about many other forms of harm that are engendered by wrongful convictions. Little or no consideration is given to the broader forms of harm to victims of miscarriages of justice and to their husbands, wives, partners, children and other relatives and friends. In addition, the inherent economic consequences of excessive public expenditure on wrongful convictions, which takes away from other areas of need (health, education, housing, and so on), need to be included for an adequate depiction of the consequences of wrongful convictions, but are also currently omitted (Naughton, 2001).

The existing terrain, then, mitigates against analyses that might more adequately and appropriately depict the *scale* of wrongful criminal convictions in England and Wales as indicated by the many thousands of successful appeals that occur annually. It also obscures an extensive range of additional dimensions of *harm* that accompanies wrongful criminal conviction, not only to the direct victims, but other people too. Existing approaches can, therefore, be conceived as serving a number of functions. They subjugate, marginalise and/or disqualify potentially effective forms of 'counter-discourse' on the real nature and full extent of the harmful consequences of wrongful criminal convictions (see Foucault, 1980b: 80–7).

A SOCIAL HARM APPROACH

It is within such a context that a social harm approach can be utilised to reorientate definitions of miscarriages of justice and provide a more adequate depiction of the harm that they cause. As argued in Chapter 2 in this volume, criminology gives undue attention to many events and incidents that are defined as 'crime', and, hence, detracts attention away from other events and incidents which often involve a comparable or even greater amount of serious harm to victims. For example, while there is an annual average of over 1 million recorded workplace injuries in Britain, only 1,000 or so are successfully prosecuted as 'crimes' and, hence, become subject to some form of critical analysis. As a consequence, injuries at work are minimised and marginalised and this has profound implications in terms of what can be done with such data conceptually, theoretically *and* politically. It is, therefore, necessary to focus the analysis on workplace harm and not solely on those cases defined as crimes.

In a similar way, there is a parallel utility in attempting to reorientate definitions of miscarriages of justice to include all successful appeals to provide a more adequate depiction of the number of wrongful convictions and the harm that they engender. To conceive of either workplace injuries or miscarriages of justice as exceptional occurrences that amount to a handful of cases each year is inadequate. A social harm approach to miscarriages of justice, therefore, requires a reorientation of how they are conceptualised and defined, and how the harm from miscarriages of justice is quantified: 'what one measures, and how one measures it, makes an awful lot of difference to what one finds and the range of responses that then appear to be feasible' (Hillyard and Tombs, 2001: 11). From such a perspective, an analysis of successful appeals against criminal conviction can produce a more comprehensive 'voice' and/or set of analyses of the harm that accompanies the possible scale of miscarriages of justice.

To aid in the provision of a more accurate picture of the vicissitudes of such phenomena as wrongful convictions, Hillyard and Tombs (2001: 11) have sketched a definitional framework for a social harm approach along the following lines: *social harm* 'would encompass notions of autonomy, development and growth'; *physical harm* 'would include torture and brutality by state officials'; and *financial harm* would incorporate 'misappropriation of funds by government'. In the specific context of the harmful consequences of wrongful convictions I would extend this definitional framework to include a notion of *psychological harm* that would cover any psychological or emotional distress arising from events and behaviours outside of an individual's control.

These different types of harm have a resonance, not only to the victims in exceptional cases of wrongful conviction, but also to victims of routine wrongful convictions. Moreover, a developed social harm approach would emphasise the *indirect* forms of harm that are currently neglected. The remainder of this chapter uses Hillyard and Tombs's definitions and the added definition of psychological harm to explore successful appeals against criminal conviction to extend existing accounts and provide a more adequate depiction than currently exists of the harmful consequences of wrongful criminal convictions.

THE HARMFUL CONSEQUENCES
OF MISCARRIAGES OF JUSTICE

There has been an almost total neglect of, and, hence, a general absence of information about, the harm caused to victims in routine wrongful convictions, that is, victims who are routinely successful in appeal in either the CACD or the Crown Court. So, while statistical data on the *number* of victims that are routinely wrongly convicted each year are available, the available information of the *harm* to victims of miscarriages of justice has been largely restricted to biographical accounts of victims in exceptional cases. This impacts upon the following analysis by restricting it to an exploration of the available material on exceptional cases. This is not to imply that the exceptional cases that are cited are necessarily exceptional from a social harm perspective. On the contrary, there is enough available evidence to suggest that the harm caused to victims in routine cases of successful appeal against criminal conviction is often comparable with the victims in high-profile cases. For instance, the general social and psychological harm to victims of wrongful convictions for paedophilia, which may or may not incur a custodial sentence, and the knock-on effects to their families/friends/communities, has been well documented (see, for example, Action Against False Allegations of Abuse, 2000, 2002b; False Allegations Support Organisation, 2002). Moreover, the small amount of evidence that exists about successful appeals against wrongful convictions in Magistrates' Courts illustrates the far-reaching harmful consequences of wrongful convictions for routine criminal offences such as drink-driving offences – victims lose jobs, go to prison, some even attempt to commit suicide (Ford, 1998a). With this in mind, what follows is an attempt to initiate a systematic project on the harmful consequences to victims of routine wrongful convictions. This contribution is not exhaustive. The strategy is to provide insights of some of the more prominent forms of social, psychological, physical and/or financial harm that victims of exceptional wrongful conviction might experience to both enhance existing critical voices and encourage further research into routine cases.

Social harm

As indicated, in terms of the additional forms of harm to the direct victims of wrongful conviction, a social harm approach would emphasise forms of social harm that relate to being deprived of a partner's support and/or to a parent's absence during a child's upbringing, which can have associated impacts upon both the absent parent and the child's health and life-chances. This was exemplified in a recent statement by Paddy Hill (Birmingham Six) in which, he declared, 'Me, I died in prison, inside' (cited in Hattenstone, 2002). This suggests that he will probably never get over the social harmful effect of his 16 years of wrongful imprisonment, during which his wife divorced him and his children grew up in children's homes without him (see also, Geffen, 1999). The social harm to Michael O'Brien (Cardiff Newsagent Three) was equally severe. During his ten years of wrongful imprisonment, he was also absent from his son's life. Perhaps, even more agonising, however, his second child, a daughter, suffered a cot death when she was two months old. His wife subsequently left him, and his father, who was reported to have been 'broken' by his son's wrongful imprisonment, drank himself to death (Hill, 2001).

Another form of social harm experienced by many direct victims of wrongful conviction is the stain on their reputations despite a successful appeal. Annette Hewins was successful in a routine appeal in the CACD in February 1999 for an arson attack that killed three people. As she asserted: 'I was exonerated by the courts but not in the community in which I live. That won't happen until the investigation is officially reopened and the killer is caught … until … [the] murderer is found … I will carry the stigma. Injustice doesn't cease just because you walk free from the court of appeal' (cited in Roberts, 1999). To be sure, a feature of many wrongful convictions is the 'whispering campaigns' about the guilt of the victims that continue long after the victims, which achieved a successful appeal (see Dyer, 1997; White, 1997; *The Times* 10 July, 1998; *The Times*, 1 December 1998). These brief examples give an insight into the likely forms of social harm to victims of wrongful convictions. Gareth Peirce (cited in Gillan, 2001) has described one form of social harm that almost all victims of wrongful imprisonment are likely to share: 'They [victims of wrongful imprisonment] come out with no money and no counselling. They have no references, it is difficult to open a bank account, and you can't get a mortgage. They have no GP. You don't belong.'

In addition to the harms experienced by the individual victims of miscarriages of justice, there are profound social effects upon the families and friends of the victims. In some cases the harm caused in terms of the anger, anguish, pain, suffering and sheer frustration of the family and friends of the wrongly convicted can be just as severe as that of the people they support, and can have profound and long-lasting effects upon their own lives. For example, Ann Whelan, the mother of Michael Hickey, one of the Bridgewater Four, was singled out following the successful appeal in the Bridgewater case for the 19 years that she had campaigned tirelessly and relentlessly for their release (Leonard, 1997). Prior to the wrongful conviction of her son, for his alleged part in the murder of Carl Bridgewater, Ann Whelan had no interest in the criminal justice system. Her son's conviction, however, changed everything and will probably define the remainder of her life, as well as the life of her son. A letter to *The Times* in July 1998 suggests that her campaign is far from completed. She complained that in the twelve months since the quashing of the Bridgewater convictions nothing had been done to bring to account those responsible for the unjust convictions of the men. In particular, she pointed out that there had been no inquiry into how such a 'horrendous' miscarriage of justice could have been perpetrated and no effort had been made to find the real killer. She regarded this state of affairs as a terrible indictment of the law, the judicial system and the Home Office. She further asserted that the men and the public deserve to see immediate action by the Home Office, Crown Prosecution Service (CPS) and the police. She concluded that no doubt the authorities hoped that, following the successful appeals, the problem would go away. This, she said, will not happen. 'In acquitting these innocent men they have completed only half the task and must be reminded of this in no uncertain terms' (Whelan, 1998). In October 2002, Whelan (2002) reported that she was experiencing socio-psychological harm because of her son's continuing mental health problems. Such narratives of the social consequences of wrongful convictions to the lives of families and/or friends of victims are also a common theme of other campaigns against miscarriages of justice (see Birnberg, 1998; Hale, 2002).

The overturn of wrongful convictions raises questions about the real perpetrators of the crimes. The approach that I have adopted would point out that there are significant forms of social harm to the families and friends of the victims of crime. For example, the release of the three surviving members of the Bridgewater Four (Pat Molloy, the 'fourth' member, died in prison in 1981) gave rise to the awkward question: 'Who, then, did murder Carl Bridgewater?' (Graves, 1997). This question had long since been regarded as closed in the public's mind. There had been a general belief and conviction, particularly among Carl's Bridgewater's former community, that justice had been done. Even after a *Rough Justice* television programme, which was helpful in the final referral of the case back to the CACD, Carl Bridgewater's father had asserted: 'I am firmly convinced that those men killed our son and are serving just sentences' (*Daily Mirror*, 27 July 1996). With the quashing of the Bridgewater Four's convictions, however, this position was called into question and it raised the possibility that someone else might have been responsible for Carl's murder. As yet, the case of who killed Carl Bridgewater remains officially unsolved. However, as Tongue said: 'memories of the killing will fester like an open wound unless the case of who killed Carl is solved' (cited in Weaver, 1997). This emphasises that both the general fear of crime and the re-emergence of forms of social and/or psychological harm to the families and friends of the victims of criminal offences is a real consequence of the public knowledge of wrongful convictions (Steele, 1995; Graves, 1997; Leonard, 1997; Shaw, 1998; Buncombe, 1999; Roberts, 1999; *Liverpool Echo*, 31 March 2000; Hale, 2002).

There is a further important consequence of a social harm approach for the victims of miscarriages of justice. The failure to convict those persons guilty of serious offences should be as much a concern from a criminal justice perspective as from a harm approach. When an innocent person is wrongly convicted, a perpetrator of a serious crime is *not* convicted and they remain at liberty, then there is the potential for them to commit more serious crime, and, hence, cause more harm.

Psychological harm

Perhaps the most serious and profound of the associated consequences to the direct victims of wrongful convictions is the psychological harm that they experience. This was highlighted, for example, in 1996 when Adrian Grounds, a psychiatrist at the Institute of Criminology at Cambridge, examined Gerry Conlon of the Guildford Four and four of the Birmingham Six. He found that they were all suffering from irreversible, persistent and disabling PTSD. He compared their mental state with that of brain damaged accident victims or people who had suffered war crimes. He concluded that it often made them impossible to live with (Pallister, 1999a).

Four years after Grounds's examinations there was evidence that the traumas continue for at least some of the members of the Guildford Four. In a newspaper article that appeared in June 2000, eleven years after his release, Gerry Conlon (one of the Guildford Four) claimed that he was 'still going through a terrible time, getting dreadful flashbacks' (Pallister, 2000). Adding support to Grounds's earlier findings he asserted that his 'psychiatrist [had told him] that he has never experienced a worse case of post-traumatic stress syndrome, worse even than the soldiers in the Falklands war' (Pallister, 2000).

Paul Hill (another member of the Guildford Four), stated in a BBC television programme, broadcast in June 2000, that he did not think there was 'anybody alive who [could] come out of that experience and not be scarred' (Pallister, 2000). He continued that the most poignant thing about his case for him was that the judge had 'expressed regret that the death penalty was not an option' (Pallister, 2000).

A social harm approach would also highlight that there are wider ranging socio-psychological harms arising from miscarriages of justice. The very legitimacy of the criminal justice system ultimately rests on its ability to deliver on its stated aims to be 'just', 'fair' and 'efficient' (Criminal Justice System Online, 2003). Miscarriages of justice highlight the failure of the system to meet those objectives and may have a profound and troubling effect upon each and every member of society. It signals a failure of judicial legitimacy that must urgently be addressed (JUSTICE, 1989; Regan, 1997: 6).

Physical harm

Victims of miscarriages of justice can also be subjected to a variety of forms of physical harm by the state as a consequence of their wrongful convictions and/or wrongful imprisonment. The case of Keith Twitchell, for example, provides a pertinent illustration. For his alleged part in an armed raid on a local factory in which a security guard was killed and £11,500 stolen, eight or nine police officers handcuffed Twitchell's wrists to the back legs of the chair upon which he was sitting. Next a plastic bag was placed over his head and pressed against his nose and mouth. This suffocation procedure was repeated until finally his resolve was broken and he agreed to sign the statement put in front of him. For his 'confession', Twitchell served 13 years of wrongful imprisonment. Quashing his conviction in the CACD, Lord Justice Rose emphasised that the case was: 'yet another appeal ... [in which] ... a significant number of police officers ... some of whom rose to very senior rank, behaved outrageously, and in particular extracted confessions by grossly improper means, amounting in some cases to *torture*' (Pallister, 1999a, emphasis added).

In George Lewis's successful appeal case it was revealed that he was head-butted, punched in the head and threatened with a syringe as police officers questioned him after his arrest in 1987 for two armed robberies and a burglary that he did not commit. The officer who assaulted him was the late John Perkins, a detective constable with the West Midlands Serious Crime Squad, which has since been disbanded. It subsequently emerged that the squad secured at least 49 prosecutions on the basis of false confessions or other forms of fabricated evidence (Ford, 1998b; Pallister, 1999a).

An analysis of the Bridgewater case reveals a similar story. Most disturbingly, no forensic evidence of any kind against the four was ever submitted to any court. No fingerprints of the men were found.

No murder weapon was ever found. And there were no witnesses. On the contrary, the only forensic evidence and witnesses known to the police clearly indicated that it was someone else who might be guilty. The police suppressed this and the entire prosecution case was based almost solely on the 'confession' of Patrick Molloy that occurred after days of violent interrogation, during which his teeth were broken and he was consistently hit around the face and head. For the first ten days he was denied access to a solicitor. During this time his food was heavily salted and he was denied liquids. In desperation he drank from the toilet. His sleep was interrupted regularly during the night. In the end, when he was traumatised and weakened by the experience, he was offered immediate bail if he signed a confession linking the other three to the murder. This he signed as DC John Perkins held him by the hair and read his 'confession' in his ear while DC Graham Leeke wrote it down (Regan, 1997). When Patrick Molloy was allowed access to a solicitor he immediately retracted any statement that he had made, but to no avail. When the remaining three of the Bridgewater Four were freed on bail by the CACD in 1997 Lord Justice Roch made the assertion that: 'It now seems that Mr Molloy was interviewed by officers who were prepared to deceive him into making confessions' (Graves, 1997).

Financial harm

Finally, in addition to the social, psychological and/or physical harmful consequences of miscarriages of justice, the financial costs of wrongful convictions need to be encompassed by a social harm approach. These include compensation to victims of miscarriages of justice, which currently amounts to an annual average of £6 million. They also include the estimated £85 million a year that it costs publicly funded legal services to provide legal representative support to victims of miscarriages of justice at their original trials in which they are wrongly convicted, and then funding them again to overturn their wrongful convictions. They include a further estimated £65 million a year in terms of containing the wrongfully convicted in prison (Naughton, 2003b). In these three areas alone, wrongful convictions are currently costing in excess of £180 million per year. When other relevant financial costs are also considered such as the running of the CCRC, the Police Complaints Authority (PCA), the costs to the welfare system in terms of supporting families when victims are wrongly imprisoned, and so on, the total costs of wrongful convictions run into many hundreds of millions of pounds each year.

This analysis could be accused of stretching the argument too far. As no human system can be perfect, it is inevitable that some miscarriages of justice will occur. Accordingly, it is also inevitable that the provision of safeguards to attempt to prevent and remedy miscarriages of justice when they occur is a necessary requirement in a liberal democratic society and it will incur a financial cost. The problem with this argument is that the system doesn't *sometimes* get it wrong. As shown above, contrary to public perceptions and the stated aims of the criminal justice system, there are in excess of 3,750 successful appeals against criminal conviction every year in England and Wales. This expenditure on miscarriages of justice is not only wasteful, but it is money which could be spent on essential social services. The excessive amount of money spent on wrongful criminal imprisonment could be spent on deprived school children. The excessive amount spent on compensation to victims of wrongful criminal charges/convictions could be spent on the countless scores of people that are denied necessary hospital treatments. The excessive amount spent on legal fees could be used to improve the criminal justice system so that miscarriages of justice do not occur in the future.

CONCLUSION

This chapter has attempted to demonstrate the promise of a social harm approach in the analysis of miscarriages of justice. In so doing, the beginnings of a more adequate and appropriate depiction of the harmful consequences of wrongful convictions was provided. It covered not only those cases of successful appeal that result from a referral back to the CACD from the CCRC but, also, more routine wrongful convictions that occur in Magistrates' Courts and the Crown Court. A social harm approach would, thus, move beyond existing definitions by incorporating a scale of wrongful convictions and a more holistic understanding of the harmful consequences engendered, which have not previously been acknowledged or subjected to critical appraisal. Thus, while more research is undoubtedly required on the precise forms of harm in the thousands of routine wrongful convictions that occur each year, it seems equally clear that a social harm approach contributes to the establishment of a new agenda for the future study of miscarriages of justice.

What has been absent from the foregoing analysis, however, is any mention of the potential methodological problems or weaknesses or undeveloped aspects of a social harm approach in appraising the promise of a social harm project to wrongful convictions. It seems fitting to conclude on a more critical note by looking at some of the more obvious dilemmas that would also need to be taken into account in a social harm approach to wrongful convictions. Not least, there is a range of issues relating to the inherent subjectivity and relativism of social harm analyses in the sense that 'harm' is an irreducibly value-laden norm. Clearly, and most basically, some individuals will tend to get more easily upset (psychological harm), or more easily hurt (physical harm), than others in the event of experiencing very similar wrongdoings against them. This could play out to the effect that the treatment of individuals by state agencies such as the police and prison service, for example, that upset or hurt those individuals who are predisposed to psychological anxiety or more vulnerable to physical harm would be defined as harmful and, hence, 'criminal'. By the same token, however, similar, or even the same treatment during police interviews and/or imprisonment would *not* be defined as harmful and, hence, not 'criminal', if they occurred to individuals not so predisposed. To give an almost caricatured sense of the problem, would the wrongful imprisonment of someone prone to claustrophobia represent a worse 'crime', because it incurred more harm to the victim, than the wrongful imprisonment of someone who did *not* have that condition?

The serious point behind such a scenario concerns the relationship between harm and *injustice*, a complex connection, which the logic of a social harm approach seems to oversimplify. This is an issue because the injustice of a wrongful conviction might have little to do with the exact amount of harm experienced. An individual would be no less unfairly treated because he/she did not complain about their psychological deterioration in prison while hoping for the repeal of their sentence. This emphasises an inevitable subjectivity/relativism in calculations of harm. For example, to take a case of economic harm, a £50 parking fine to a millionaire would cause little bother to that individual's daily life. However, the same penalty dealt out to a person on state benefits would probably account for a week's groceries, thus constituting a disproportionate amount of harm to the latter individual in relation to the same treatment. While there would undoubtedly be some additional 'justice' in a kind of sliding scale of penalties according to harm, the effectiveness of the resulting system and the intrusive contestability of case-by-case relativities would be unlikely to create consistency of expectation, a prerequisite of *any* system of law/justice.

ACKNOWLEDGEMENTS

Thanks to Steve Tombs, Paddy Hillyard and Gregor McLennan for insightful and most helpful comments on earlier drafts.

8
The Victimised State and the Mystification of Social Harm

Joe Sim

> Selective shortsightedness is the main feature of standard analyses
> of violence in democratic capitalist societies. This syndrome shows
> itself in the form of attitudes and statements that are out of phase
> with the reality of the phenomenon observed. (Salmi, 1993: 4)

In 1973, Stan Cohen published a short essay entitled 'The Failures of
Criminology' in which he identified a number of significant 'matters'
that criminology as a discipline had failed to address and which had
resulted in criminologists adopting a position of 'political timidity'.
These 'matters' were 'intimately concerned with questions of values,
political conflict and power'. They included: the failure of criminologists
to recognise the 'overreach' of the criminal law and the nature of its
enforcement; their failure to address white-collar and 'respectable'
criminality; and their failure to confront the centralised control exerted
by the Home Office over the research agenda (Cohen, 1988: 51–2).

Cohen also addressed one other key area of omission. This related
to the question of violence. As he noted:

> In analysing the causes of violence, criminologists have not understood
> the problems raised by violence associated with various forms of
> ideological conflict (race, class, national, religious) ... criminologists
> either have tried to extrapolate straight from their traditional models
> (so militants suffer from 'unresolved authority problems') or have
> abandoned the debate completely by saying that such questions are
> for political science to deal with. (Ibid.: 52)

What has happened in the 30 years since Cohen critiqued the myopia
of criminologists in this area? In some respects, there has been definite
progress made in moving towards a more analytical and sociologically

informed understanding of violence, its antecedents and manifestations. This development has been built on a number of important theoretical and methodological insights arising in particular from the work of critical criminologists who have eschewed the restricted, empiricist categories of analysis and the 'zombie concepts' which have dominated the discipline (Beck, cited in Bauman, 2002: 82).[1] In contrast, these criminologists have drawn their academic inspiration from a range of different disciplines and their theoretical orientation in recognising the complex relationship between the utilisation of violence and interpersonal and structural processes of power.[2]

However, despite these progressive and encouraging developments, mainstream criminologists have continued to operate within a theoretically reductionist and politically regressive paradigm for analysing violence. Take the question of definition. While feminist work, with its emphasis on the normality of male violence, has mounted a series of profoundly important theoretical and political challenges to the positivist discourse of individual abnormality, this epistemological shift has not impacted on criminology in general where the conceptualisation of violence remains overwhelmingly based on a legal definition of the phenomenon (see Pantazis in Chapter 12 of this volume). This has produced an analysis which is 'superficial, out of proportion, trivialised, individualised and one-sided' (Salmi, 1993: 4). Furthermore, this legal definition focuses on intent as opposed to omission, on events rather than processes. Therefore, in relation to key areas such as deaths generated by environmental pollution and deaths at work, the narrow and circumspect definition articulated through official discourse has failed to capture the nature, extent, impact and consequences of the injuries and deaths generated by a labour process geared towards profit maximisation and safety minimisation (personal communication, Steve Tombs).

The concentration on legally defined violence within the mainstream of the discipline has led to the neglect and negation of a range of other activities and processes, often officially sanctioned and inevitably denied, which also have immense physical and psychological repercussions on those individuals and groups who are degraded and brutalised by them (Cohen, 2001). This point is particularly relevant to the question of institutionalised state violence. As Richard Edney has argued, there is a 'dearth of scholarship' with respect to explaining state violence in general and prison violence in particular. This is:

> partly the result of a tendency of researchers, usually criminologists, to ignore or underplay the significance of a prison officer's contribution

to the lives of prisoners while incarcerated ... The scholarship that we do have and, in particular, criminology has [sic] bemoaned the lack of access to prisons to conduct proper research. The problem is thus presented as being of a technical nature rather than criminology's inability to conceive of the state as criminal, and its lack of a theoretical understanding of state violence. (Edney, 1997: 289–90)

For Edney, this situation has developed despite the existence of a body of academic and prisoner-generated literature which points to the endemic role of violence – physical and mental – within the prison's institutional framework. However, this literature – marginalised and neglected – is based on the subjugated knowledge of prisoners. The implications of this neglect are profound:

Criminology and its fixation with methodology, objectivity, restrained language and appropriate form does not know what to do with these writings. So it ignores them ... and the result is a criminology which is partial, irrelevant and seemingly produced solely for the pleasure of researchers rather than a serious attempt to comprehend violence in all its forms. (Ibid.: 290)[3]

Furthermore, when state violence in prisons (and other institutions) is discussed it is usually conceptualised in rigorously positivist terms, the result of an individual, unmanageable state servant deviating from cultural and institutional norms that are otherwise benevolent and supportive. For the liberal Prison Reform Trust, for example, most staff carry out their duties with 'skill and integrity' (Lyon, 2003: 3). Taking this position, of course, means that the often-insidious role of many staff in maintaining the vulpine order of the prison is ignored.[4] Thus in their major study, *Prison Violence*, Edgar and his colleagues singularly fail to address either violence committed by staff or the fear and uncertainty experienced by prisoners with respect to the state's capacity for unleashing violence against them, especially in the bleak shadow of the prison's segregation unit (Edgar et al., 2003).

This critique leads to another issue that has been marginalised in mainstream criminology (and indeed in critical criminology as well). This relates to the level of violence sustained *by* state servants during the course of their duties.[5] At first glance, this issue may seem less important than the physical and psychological destruction of 'deviant' bodies and minds by state servants. However, as both Gramsci and Althusser have pointed out, the production and reproduction of an inequitable social order requires a state form that is capable both of serious repression while actively engaging in constructing a popular, common sense, interpellated consciousness around the myriad range of issues, activities and events that are part of the everyday world in which human beings live and work. Thus, building a consensus around the essential benevolence of state institutions and their servants – particularly police and prison officers – while simultaneously socially constructing these same servants as living in perpetual danger from the degenerate and the desperate, has been central to this process. The hegemony concerning the 'truth' surrounding the dangers faced by prison and police officers, while contested and contingent, nonetheless operates as a powerful, ideological mechanism for securing the legitimacy of the criminal justice system and the wider definitions of social order that this system upholds and defends.

This chapter, therefore, presents a critical analysis of the dangers facing state servants by focusing on what has been termed 'the victimised state' (Sim, 2000/2001: 26). First, it deconstructs official data concerning the deaths and injuries sustained by prison and police officers,[6] and challenges the social construction of these groups as perennially victimised by the predacious criminal inside and outside the walls of penal institutions. Second, it contrasts these data with the role that the state plays as the victimiser with respect to two substantive areas: deaths in state custody and police-induced deaths on the roads. Finally, the chapter considers the theoretical implications generated by the political and cultural fixation with the perennial victimisation of state servants, explores the links between this victimisation and the reinforcement of authoritarian law and order policies, and considers some strategies that might be adopted by critical criminologists to challenge the intensification in the state's authoritarian power which consistently underpins the 'Iron Times' (Hall, 1988: vii) in which we live.

HARM, RISK AND PRISON OFFICERS

Arguably, the social construction of prison officers as perennial victims of violence has become normalised to the point where it is now taken for granted by the majority of academics, politicians, media experts, policy-makers and the public. Inevitably, this allows their representative body, the Prison Officers' Association (POA), effectively to remain beyond definitional challenge concerning violence against its members. As the prison crisis has deepened, and the politics of law and order has intensified, so successive Home Secretaries have uncritically accepted the POA's position as the primary definers of penal reality in relation to assaults and violence. This 'standing influence', as the association's first General Secretary perceptively phrased it (Cronin, 1967: 75), has transcended the bitter and, from the perspective of prisoners, detrimental conflicts between the POA, prison managers, civil servants and politicians that have dominated the penal landscape since the early 1970s (Fitzgerald and Sim, 1982).

Thus, the POA can be understood in classical moral entrepreneurial terms. In acting as *the* primary definer around this profoundly important social issue, its leaders, with unconditional rank-and-file support, have been able to 'establish the initial definition of the topic that commands the field' (Hall et al., 1978: 58). And while Schlesinger and Tumber have rightly argued that it is important not to adopt a reductionist position when discussing the POA (and indeed the Police Federation), and to recognise that there are 'distinctive positions over current policy' with respect to different state fractions (Schlesinger and Tumber, 1994: 40), it is equally important to note that the undisputed claim to authority and the symbolic position that prison and police officers command, have allowed the association to construct a clear and precise definition of the 'truth' around the normalised nature of prison violence and the risks and dangers faced by its members. The ideological power of this 'truth', which reproduces and reinforces the broader populism concerning the difficult job that state servants do, is such that alternative definitions of social reality remain subjugated and muted. Indeed, those who do attempt to articulate alternative definitions that challenge the nature and extent of violence experienced by state servants are insidiously positioned as 'heartless (they don't care about the officer who is victimised) and naïve (they don't live in the "real" world)' (Sim, 2000/2001: 26).

What, therefore, does a critical analysis indicate about the violence faced by prison officers? Two points are worth making. First, it is clear that individual officers, at particular moments, do experience violence and, occasionally, death at the hands of prisoners. Crucially, however, this violence is neither as widespread nor as common as the POA claims. Take the issue of prison officer deaths. Table 8.1 notes that 29 officers died between 1988 and 2000. The majority of them – 19 (66 per cent) – died from heart attacks while on or off duty. This figure rises to 80 per cent if the category of 'on duty' is considered alone. In contrast, one officer – or 3 per cent of the total – was murdered on duty.

The nature and number of these deaths therefore raise serious questions about the kind of dangers prison officers face in their everyday lives and what is harmful to them as they carry out their duties. Why, for example, are the dangers generated by a sedentary lifestyle which may then be generating heart attacks not given the same political and populist attention as the rare death-inducing attack on an officer by an individual prisoner? Furthermore, death is not a one-way process that only touches prison officers when they are on or off duty. It also affects prisoners and those in other institutions who are theoretically supposed to be in the care of the state. In 1999 alone there were 117 self-inflicted deaths in British prisons. Altogether, between 1990 and 1999, 1,350 people died in police cells, psychiatric hospitals and prisons in England and Wales (Sim, 2000/2001: 26).[7]

Table 8.1   Prison officer deaths, 1988–2000

Cause of death	On duty	Percentage	Off duty	Percentage	Total	Percentage
Heart attack	16	80	3	33	19	66
Suicide	–	–	3	33	3	10
Accident	1	5	1	11	2	7
Illness	–	–	2	22	2	7
Road traffic accident	2	10	–	–	2	7
Murder	1	5	–	–	1	3
Total	**20**	**100**	**9**	**99**	**29**	**100**

Source: adapted from a personal communication from HM Prison Service, 22 December 2000.

What about the question of assaults on prison officers? Again, this issue is usually discussed in emotive, and ultimately unhelpful, terms. For example, speaking to the in-house *Prison Service News* in 1999, the former Prisons Minister Paul Boateng argued that 'it is very important that we ensure that prison officers receive the same consideration as any other victim of crime *when they are subject to some of the appalling assaults that are visited on them*' (cited in *Prison Service News*, October 1999: 15, emphasis added). In making this statement, Boateng uncritically reinforced the image of the prison as a highly dangerous and harmful place for staff. There are, however, a number of points that can be made which provide a different perspective on this issue.

First, it is important to note that the official definition of assault in prison ranges from 'the most serious of assaults to *incidents involving little physical contact*' (Home Office, 1997: 5, emphasis added). This means that *serious* assaults on staff in prison are not as common as would first seem. In fact, only around 8 per cent of assaults on staff are serious (personal communication, HM Prison Service, 13 June, 2000).

Second, as Table 8.2 indicates, in 1999 there were 6,318 assaults involving prison staff *and* prisoners in England and Wales. However, assaults on staff amounted to 4 per 100 of the population while assaults on prisoners were 5 per 100 of the population. These data, in themselves, therefore raise some very important issues concerning *who* is actually at risk in prison. It is clear that prison staff members are assaulted. Nonetheless, the social construction of the prison as a dangerous and harmful place for staff *alone* is theoretically and politically problematic, particularly when the dangers faced by prisoners are also considered.

Table 8.2   Assaults on prison staff and prisoners, England and Wales, 1999

Assaults	Number	Number per 100 population
On prison staff	2,556	4
On prisoners	3,344	5
On others	418	1
All assaults	**6,318**	**10**

Source: adapted from *Hansard*, 6 March 2000: cols 543–4.[8]

Third, the National Audit Office (NAO) has indicated that the harm faced by prison staff may come from areas that are totally unrelated to the dangers posed by prisoners. For example, in 1997–98, over one-third of the days lost at work were due to musculoskeletal problems or injuries sustained. In addition:

> Absences caused by assaults on duty have been falling gradually over the last four years … One-fifth of all time lost for both prison officers and other staff was due to psychological conditions, such as stress, anxiety and depression, which were the most important causes of absences of between six months and one year, at almost 40 per cent. Research in three prisons suggested that further work is needed to establish the extent to which work-related stress is caused by problems with the style of management in prisons. (National Audit Office, 1999: 2)

The NAO concluded that 'sickness arising from accidents and assaults in prisons represents a small proportion of absence, with roughly five per cent of sickness arising from accidents and at least two per cent from assaults' (ibid.: 52).

The NAO's investigation formed the basis for the subsequent inquiry conducted by the House of Commons Committee of Public Accounts which reported in 1999. The committee was also concerned about high levels of sickness among prison staff. In 1997–98 this resulted in:

a total of 485,000 prison officer working days [being] lost to sickness absence ... Some 1,180 of [the Prison Service's] 23,000 officers were unavailable for duty due to ill-health on any one day, the staffing equivalent of seven medium-sized prisons. (Committee of Public Accounts, 1999: x)

The inquiry pointed to research conducted in three different prisons, which indicated that 40 per cent of staff 'cited harassment and bullying by managers as a cause of work-related stress' (ibid.: xiv). Furthermore, in his evidence to the committee, the Director General of the Prison Service conceded that 'some staff will claim to have back injuries when they may not be as serious as they are', although he felt that new policies being pursued by the Prison Department would change this situation (ibid.: 14). By 2000–1 the situation had indeed changed. The number of working days lost through sickness had *increased* to almost 597,000. This averaged out at '13.6 working days per member of staff per year, or 2,600 officers per year across the Service. This equated to a cost to the Service of £65,651,771' (Her Majesty's Prison Service, 2001: 76).

Thus, the prison *may* be a physically and psychologically dangerous place but the question is: dangerous for whom? For prison officers, the source, nature and extent of the danger that confronts them is much more complex than the discourse of the 'dangerous prisoner', the prism through which prison violence is explained and understood. The harm they experience stems from a structure and culture which not only pays little regard to occupational health and safety, but also often allows them to claim they are the victims of physical injuries and psychological stress which are both overdramatised and underscrutinised. Finally, there is one other important point to note. Stress does not impact on prison officers equally as they are not a homogeneous group. Arguably, for those staff who wish to engage in caring, therapeutic work and who are then pejoratively labelled as 'care bears', it is the daily and insidious drip-feed of punitive aggression emanating from the prison's formidable culture of masculinity, rather than the likelihood of a prisoner-induced assault, that has the greatest impact on their self-esteem and the levels of stress and psychological harm they experience (Sim, 2002: 316).

RISK, HARM AND POLICE OFFICERS

If the harm done to prison officers can be linked symbolically to the social health or otherwise of society, then the death of a police officer arguably has a significance that carries even more symbolic weight. When a police officer is killed on duty as at Shepherds Bush in 1966, in Blackpool in 1971, in the inner-city disturbances in 1985 or in Manchester in 2003, these killings ultimately come to represent 'a potent symbol of lawlessness' (Chibnall, 1977: 54) in a society degraded and scarred by hostility to authority and order. However, as with the data concerning the dangers facing prison officers, the data relating to the police can also be critically deconstructed. Again, this deconstruction reveals a more complex picture compared with the simplistic thesis of individual dangerousness articulated within official discourse and by academics such as Robert Reiner who, in his influential book *The Politics of the Police*, maintained that 'the police officer faces, behind every corner he turns or door-bell he rings, some danger, if not of firearms at least of fists' (Reiner, 1985: 87).

In a debate in the House of Lords in 1982, the Earl of Onslow compared the murder rate of police officers in England and Wales with the murder rate in other countries:

> In 1978 in the USA there were 19,560 murders. That is an astronomical number – more than the number of grouse shot at Bolton Abbey and that is quite a lot. In England there were 620. On the murder of policemen, which people rightly get exercised about: in the USA in 1979 there were 106 such murders and in 1980 104. During the period 1969–78 there were 1,123 law enforcement officers feloniously killed in the United States. How many were there killed in England? There were 13, my Lords. We are not dealing with an open season for policemen, we are dealing with the very occasional, exceptional crime … I have some figures which have come from *Police Review* of the numbers of policemen per 100,000 killed in a series of 16 nations … what is the English score my Lords? It is 1.3. It is the lowest of all the figures issued in this report. (*Hansard*, 24 March 1982: col. 1038)

These early figures can be set against data from this period concerning members of the public who died at the hands of the police. Between 1970 and 1980 at least twelve people died in England and Wales after being shot by different forces or because the individuals concerned were involved in demonstrations. Additionally, 'between 1972 and 1982 there were 411 deaths in police custody (or otherwise with the police) including 275 (67 per cent) due to unnatural causes or suicide' (Gilroy and Sim, 1987: 96).[9] More recent data reveal a similar picture. Between 1994 and 1998, 28 police officers died on duty. As Table 8.3 indicates, 21 of these deaths, or 75 per cent of the total, were due to the involvement of officers in road traffic accidents. In contrast, four officers were murdered. This represented 14 per cent of the total. The remaining three (11 per cent) died after collapsing in the office, from a heart attack while baton training and in a helicopter crash (personal communication, Her Majesty's Inspector of Constabulary, 27 July 2000).

Table 8.3   The causes of police officer deaths, 1994–98

Year	Road traffic accidents	Murder	Other	Total
1994	4	1 (stabbed)	1 (heart attack on baton training	6
1995	3	1 (shot)	–	4
1996	7	1 (stabbed)	–	8
1997	3	1 (stabbed)	–	4
1998	4	–	2 (one collapsed in the office; one killed in helicopter crash)	6
All Years	**21 (75%)**	**4 (14%)**	**3 (11%)**	**28 (100%)**

Source: adapted from *Hansard*, House of Lords, 10 November 1999: cols 175–6.

In contrast,[10] between 1994 and 1997–98, 215 people died in police custody while the equivalent figure for the period 1994 to 1998–99 was 282 (*Hansard*, 12 July 2002: col. 1251).[11]

What about assaults on police officers?

Over 20 years ago the Metropolitan Police Commissioner Sir David McNee published his report on the policing of London for 1981, the year of serious public order disturbances in the capital. Despite the seriousness of the disturbances which put the police in the front line of confrontation, McNee revealed that the number of days lost through officers being injured *on* duty coincided almost directly with the number of days lost through officers being injured *off* duty. There were nearly 60,000 in each category:

> When further information was requested from Scotland Yard, a spokesman in the Yard's statistical branch stated that some officers were involved in road traffic accidents when travelling to work, some fell off ladders and others were injured playing sports. These figures are significant given that a central element in the police's argument about policing London is the danger involved in tackling criminals and in public order situations. (Greater London Council, 1982: 2)

More recent figures raise further questions concerning the violence officers face. Surveying data for the period 1991 to 1996–97, Her

Majesty's Inspectorate of Constabulary argued that while there was 'a widespread view' in the police service that assaults against officers 'were increasing significantly', they found that this view 'was not wholly supported by the findings of this Inspection' (Her Majesty's Inspectorate of Constabulary, 1997/98: 3). The Inspectorate went on:

> Official figures indicate that since 1991 assaults on police officers had been steadily decreasing despite wide fluctuations in some forces ... Assaults classified as serious increased in 1995/96 and 1996/97, with a 4.1 per cent increase also in minor assaults in 1996/97 ... if the Metropolitan Police figures (which have been affected by a reclassification) are excluded, the serious assaults in fact decreased by 36.4 per cent and the overall increase reduced from 4.4 per cent to 4.0 per cent. (Ibid.)

Tables 8.4 and 8.5 develop this argument further. As Table 8.4 indicates, between 1997 and 1998 there were 29,100 prosecutions for assaults on police officers, a figure that implies common everyday violence against them. However, closer examination of this global figure reveals a different picture. First, in just over 8,500 cases – 29 per cent of the total – the individuals prosecuted were not convicted. Second, in just over 18,000 cases – 62 per cent of the total – the individuals were given a non-custodial sentence. In other words, in 91 per cent of cases, the individuals were either found not guilty or given a non-custodial sentence. This latter figure suggests that despite the dominance of a retributive law and order discourse, the assaults were not severe enough for the courts to consider imprisoning the accused. In fact, less than 10 per cent of the cases resulted in immediate custody for the defendant.

Table 8.4 Numbers cautioned, convicted and sentenced for assaults on the police, 1997 and 1998

Disposal	1997	1998	Total
Cautioned	1,609	1,528	3,128
Prosecuted	14,837	14,263	29,100
Convicted	10,375	10,214	20,589
Non-custodial sentences	9,152	8,934	18,086
Immediate custody	1,223	1,280	2,503

Source: adapted from *Hansard*, House of Lords, 1 February 2000: cols 29–30.

Table 8.5 illustrates the percentage increase/decrease in injuries sustained by police officers in England between 1997–98 and 1998–

99. As the data indicate, although the injuries caused by assaults and violence – 527 (31 per cent) and 448 (25 per cent) – formed the biggest categories in each of the two years, they still constituted the minority of injuries sustained by officers during these years. It is also worth noting that the combination of officers 'slipping and tripping' and officers 'being injured while handling, lifting or carrying' were higher in percentage terms – 33 per cent and 36 per cent respectively – than the category for officers being injured through assaults and violence. In addition, the number of injuries caused by assaults and violence actually *fell* over this two-year period from 527 to 448, a drop of 18 per cent.[12]

Table 8.5 Injuries to police officers in England, 1997–98 and 1998–99

Category	1997–98	1998–99	Percentage Change
Exposed to or contact with harmful substance	21 (1%)	36 (2%)	+ 4.2
Injured by an animal	35 (2%)	51 (3%)	+ 31
Struck by moving vehicle	52 (3%)	73 (4%)	+ 29
Injured while handling, lifting or carrying	238 (14%)	326 (18%)	+ 27
Falls from height	87 (5%)	103 (6%)	+ 16
Struck by moving, flying or falling object	134 (8%)	154 (9%)	+ 13
Strike against something fixed or stationary	83 (5%)	94 (5%)	+ 12
Slip, trip or fall on same level	326 (19%)	324 (18%)	– 1
Other kind of accident	184 (11%)	160 (9%)	– 15
Injuries caused by assault or violence	527 (31%)	448 (25%)	– 18
Total	**1687 (100%)**	**1769 (100%)**	**+ 5**

Source: adapted from *Hansard*, House of Lords, 1 February 2000: cols 29–30.

As with prison officers, these data highlight a key element involved in the risks police officers face on a daily basis, which again has remained beyond criminological scrutiny. This relates to the risks generated by their working environment. These risks arise out of health and safety procedures – or the lack of them – in their everyday working lives and provide a sharp contrast with the social construction of officers as enduring everyday victimisation from those labelled and categorised as the desperate and the depraved.[13]

There is a further issue to be considered here. The injuries sustained by individual officers, either through assaults or through health and safety failures at work, can be contrasted with the deaths and injuries they and members of the public sustain as a result of their involvement in what has become a contentious public and political issue, road traffic accidents.

In May 2002, the Police Complaints Authority (PCA) published a major study of the deaths and injuries generated and sustained by the police in road traffic accidents (Police Complaints Authority, 2002). Citing early research in this area, the PCA noted that between 1990 and 1993 there were 1,117 victims of police vehicle accidents which resulted in 92 fatalities. Crucially, 'nearly 80% of the fatalities were suffered by members of the public' (ibid.: 6). Turning to their own research, the PCA pointed out that between 1998 and 2001, a further 91 people died in 85 incidents involving police vehicles, while deaths resulting from police pursuits had increased by 409 per cent between 1997 and 2002 (ibid.: i and 1). Finally, the report noted that while there were methodological issues around the interpretation of the data, the initiation of pursuits had *more* to do with the infringement of traffic laws than with any danger to the public or police: 'only around one third of the pursuit/follows ... [were] initiated for what would be regarded as non-traffic crimes' (ibid.: 33).

THEORISING THE VICTIMISED STATE

What are the theoretical implications for the analysis developed here? There are six issues in particular I want to explore.

First, in their cultural history of the British state, Philip Corrigan and Derek Sayer noted that '"the State" never stops talking' (Corrigan and Sayer, 1985: 3). In making this important point about 'state talk', Corrigan and Sayer recognised that the power of the state in capitalist societies extended beyond its material role in terms of confronting internal problem populations and external enemies, to the cultural and symbolic position occupied, and the interventions made, by the different institutions in civil society. They further noted that the state is involved in:

> *moral regulation*: a project of normalising, rendering natural, taken for granted, in a word 'obvious', what are in fact ontological and epistemological premises of a particular and historical form of social order. Moral regulation is coextensive with state formation, and state forms are always animated and legitimated by a particular moral ethos. (Ibid.: 4; emphasis in the original)

These insights are useful for thinking about the issues that have been raised in this chapter. The murder of a state servant, particularly a police officer, represents a profound, symbolic moment in the culture and politics of a society triggering, as it does, an outpouring of popular sentiment and political rage. Such deaths signify that the social body is on the brink of moral collapse and is therefore in need of an increased injection of law and order to revive it and inoculate it from the further spread of those diseased degenerates who threaten its healthy equilibrium. The fabric of the society has been so torn and desecrated by these deaths that it can only be repaired (and the death revenged) by weaving the thread of social control ever tighter through the sharp needle of authoritarianism. 'State talk', and the moral populism generated by this 'talk', thus plays a crucial discursive role in this repressive process through the mobilisation of a highly restricted definition of the danger confronting the consecrated guardians of the social order.

Second, the few state servants who die in violent circumstances become, for the many who follow their lives and deaths in the mass media, the embodiment of a set of mystical, eternal values to which the society should aspire. Thomas Mathiesen's brilliant insight into the panoptic *and* synoptic nature of contemporary power relationships is useful here (Mathiesen, 1997). As he notes, contemporary forms of social control are not only built on a deeply embedded system of surveillance where the few survey the lives of the many, but in addition, 'we have seen the development of a unique and enormously extensive system enabling *the many to see and contemplate the few...*' (ibid.: 219; emphasis in the original). Thus the lives and deaths of individual state servants – the few – become the undiluted focus for the grief and outrage of the many. At the same time, the distorting and dislocating social divisions which are integral to contemporary modernity and which underpin and give meaning to the violent activities of individuals, organisations, corporations and states, remain on the ideological and political periphery as the society expiates its guilt through also focusing on the lone individual who carried out what is inevitably portrayed as an act of wanton barbarity. Thus, this solitary individual is situated at the centre of the gaze of the many through the defining circuits of a mass media whose capacity for engaging in the 'dramatisation of "evil"' remains undiminished, indeed has intensified, since Frank Tannenbaum coined the term over 60 years ago (Tannenbaum, cited in Lilly et al., 1989: 122).[14]

Third, the 'ideological mystification' (Box, 1983) surrounding violence *against* state servants operates through a dialectical process sustained by *exaggeration* in relation to the numbers who are assaulted and murdered and *overdramatisation* in relation to the seriousness of the violence against them. At the same time, violence committed *by* state servants is also mystified ideologically through a process of *individualisation* and *circumspection*. As noted earlier, this means focusing on the few 'bad apples' allegedly responsible for institutional violence while narrowly defining the nature and extent of the violations against those who are in the care of the state. This dialectical process has allowed powerful interest groups such as the POA and the Police Federation virtually to monopolise the debate about the violence and danger faced by their members. In a Gramscian sense, this accreditation, consecrated and blessed by the vast majority of the mass media and political spokespersons, has been integral to the construction of a commonsense, populist discourse concerning what state servants do and *what is done to them* on a daily basis.

Fourth, in terms of prisons, one of the key ideological consequences in the social construction of prison officers as perennial victims of prisoner brutality is that dangerous situations inside are 'conceptualised as events that are faced by, and done to, state servants rather than as processes which are also engaged in by them' (Sim, 2000/2001: 26). This construction distracts attention away from the institutionalisation of physical violence within the state and from 'something about which people seldom talk: namely, *the mechanisms of fear*' (Poulantzas, 1978: 83), which are mobilised against prisoners (and the confined in general).

Poulantzas' neo-Marxist analysis has been echoed by the decidedly non-Marxist, ex-Chief Inspector of Prisons, Sir David Ramsbotham, who in a number of excoriating reports has highlighted the detrimental experiences of prisoners when confronted by a staff body that conceptualises them as less-than-human. In a report on Dartmoor, Ramsbotham found that:

> 25 per cent of those who felt unsafe on their first night ... did so because of 'the attitude of staff' ... while 11 per cent of respondents reported insulting words and behaviour by other prisoners, the number reporting this conduct from staff more than doubled to 24 per cent. We believe from these indications that there was a pattern of verbally abusive behaviour at Dartmoor. Additionally we were told many times that when in E Wing (Segregation Unit), prisoners could hear screaming, shouts of 'Don't kick me' and verbal insults shouted by staff, such as 'Vermin to exercise' ... [A] prisoner said: 'The staff are very rude and threatening to inmates in general – they talk to us like dogs, threats made all the time, people are afraid to complain. People like myself who try are labelled as troublemakers. This prison is very bad'. (Her Majesty's Chief Inspector of Prisons for England and Wales, 2002: 37)

Fifth, the data presented above raise a number of important issues around the concept of risk and how it has been theorised in contemporary criminology. Risk, and its impact on criminal justice policy, has dominated many of the recent debates in criminology, particularly with respect to the shift towards the actuarialism of the 'new penology' and the social construction of the responsible subject (Feeley and Simon, 1992). It has also had a profound impact on the ideologies and practices of many criminal justice and mental health professionals (Gray et al., 2002a). However, not only are there serious conceptual and methodological problems in uncritically applying risk to the field of mental health and crime, particularly with respect to the issue of predictability (Madden, 2002; Outen, 2003), but the data in this chapter suggest that criminologists (and indeed so-called 'practitioners') need to develop a more comprehensive definition of what the concept means if it is to have any analytical viability. This would involve shifting their professional gaze away from an overwhelming concern with, and concentration on, the behaviour of the powerless and the risks they pose, to considering how the powerful *have* utilised and *continue* to utilise their self-referential propensity for being *at risk* to justify and legitimate political and policy clampdowns. One effect of this analysis would be belatedly to turn the criminological gaze upwards towards the powerful and identify how the discourse of the risks faced by state servants, *historically and contemporaneously*, has been central to the legitimisation of their power and the implementation of authoritarian policies.

Finally, the on-going construction of state servants as perennial victims reflects a more general contemporary political development which is tied in with the role of the 'respectable' victim in the intensification of reactionary criminal justice and social policies. Austin Sarat, for example, has noted how 'the voice of the victim', articulated through victim impact statements, has legitimated 'the return of revenge' with respect to the use of capital punishment in the US (Sarat 1997: 182). Sally Robinson has pointed out that the 'perceived disempowerment of white men has produced a backlash against feminism, civil rights and entitlement programmes understood to be at odds with white men's interests'. The backlash – in this case legitimated by the social construction of white male victimisation – has threatened to 'erode the gains' made by liberationist movements in the last three decades (Robinson, 2000: 190–1). David Garland has also argued that 'the sanctified persona of the suffering victim has become a valued commodity in the circuits of political and media exchange' (Garland, 2001: 143).

In 2002, the victimisation of the respectable also underpinned the New Labour government's proposals for the indefinite detention of individuals *who had not committed a crime* but who were allegedly suffering from 'Dangerous and Severe Personality Disorder'. These proposals were legitimated by a number of high-profile murder cases, including those of Megan and Lin Russell and Sarah Payne, as well as the moral panics around paedophiles. According to Gray et al., 'the government is making no excuses that the primary objective is risk management and public protection and society's interests are being elevated above all others' (Gray et al., 2002b: 3).[15]

This backlash has been reinforced by the interventions of groups such as the Victims of Crime Trust and Protecting the Protectors (the protectors in this case being the police). These organisations are not only unconditionally supported by the main political parties[16] but also have become a ubiquitous presence in the mass media. As in the US, the ideological cement for this support is the 'spectre of the predator criminal', which is the 'ever-present image' (Surette, 1996: 185). It is an image that is refined, articulated and disseminated by these pressure groups via the mass media, and in a classic spiral of amplification is reflected back to them by an increasingly fearful public whose idealisation of the past, and trepidation about the future, legitimates the populist clampdown in the present. Finally, and most obviously, in the aftermath of the destruction of the Twin Towers in New York, the media-inspired images of Arab victimisers as 'sleazy "camel jockeys", terrorists and offensively wealthy "sheikhs"' (Said, 1993: 42), juxtaposed with the desecration and victimisation of rational and cultured western institutions, has inevitably led to the introduction of draconian, anti-terrorist legislation by states across the world and legitimated the suspension of already fragile civil liberties, the abrogation of the rule of law and the normalisation of special powers (Statewatch, 2001; Hillyard, 2002).

CONCLUSION

In many ways mainstream criminology remains conspicuously yoked to the liberal theoretical and methodological prescriptions that underpinned the discipline's genesis during the Enlightenment and legitimated its historical, though incomplete, colonisation by the powerful. Arguably, this colonisation has become intensified in the 30 years since Stan Cohen published 'The Failures of Criminology', to the point where the discipline's compliant snout is now immersed in a financially lucrative trough brimming with the swill of state, corporate and commercial research interests (Hillyard et al., 2004). This has made it virtually impossible, and indeed unthinkable, for those in the mainstream to develop either the consciousness or the critical concepts necessary to move beyond the legalistic definition of crime and victimisation that still prevails within the discipline and the suffocating theoretical and political orthodoxy of evaluation studies, and 'what works', which have become the template for much of what criminologists 'do' in the early twenty-first century.

At the same time, critical criminology has continued to move forward by building on the theoretical insights developed by earlier generations of scholars. This has been particularly evident with respect to extending the definition of crime and victimisation to incorporate and include the social harms experienced differentially by the powerless across different phases of their life cycle (Hillyard and Tombs, 1999). This development has provided a further challenge to the myopic circumspection of conventional criminology and its reliance on the barren, legalistic definition of crime discussed earlier.

However, the arguments in this chapter also suggest that critical criminologists need to think differently in order to develop a more nuanced approach to the question of state power and social control. In particular, they need to reflect on the *moral* underpinnings of state interventions and the role that regressive visions of morality play in defining and redefining the nature of these interventions. In other words, at moments of deep crisis when a police or prison officer is murdered, the plaintive iconography that is mobilised – sanctified, incorruptible guardians of social order – justifies a further intensification in the state's clampdown. This is a profoundly moral process as these deaths resonate with broader, hegemonic visions of terminal social breakdown which themselves are underpinned by a deep psychic anxiety about the nature and direction of the social order. In turn, they play a central discursive role in the reconfiguration of that order onto a more authoritarian terrain.

Finally, it is important to think about strategies of resistance that might challenge and neutralise the contemporary onslaught of state-defined images of victimisation. There are two strategies, in particular, that should be considered. First, it is important to note, as Bob Jessop has done, that the state is not a 'real subject' and that it 'does not exercise power'. Rather 'it is always specific sets of politicians and state officials located in specific parts of the state system' who 'activate specific powers and state capacities inscribed in particular institutions and agencies' (Jessop, 1990: 367). This is an important point as it opens up the possibility of contingencies within, and contradictions between, state institutions and state officials. This, in turn, raises the question of how hegemonic alliances can be constructed between critical academics and more progressive fractions operating within the state, a question that has been neglected in critical thinking (Sim, 2003).

This point is illustrated by the debates surrounding capital punishment which occurred in 1969 when parliament discussed the repeal of the Murder (Abolition of the Death Penalty) Act 1965. This Act had suspended hanging for five years. The Police Federation and the POA lobbied for its return, as ever citing the murderous dangers their members faced. James Callaghan, the Home Secretary, responded by challenging the meaning attributed to the figures presented by the Federation and the POA and concluded that he 'simply [did] not believe, on the basis of those figures, that it can be established that capital punishment is necessary for the protection of the forces of law and order' (cited in Block and Hostettler, 1997: 265).[17] The debate concluded with parliament finally abolishing capital punishment. This example, although over three decades old, raises profoundly important theoretical, political *and* strategic questions for contemporary, critical academics with respect to the *limitations* imposed on the state as a result of internal conflicts and contradictions between its different fractions and networks of power. At the same time, for critical criminologists, making alliances with more progressive networks within the state without compromising their commitment to developing a 'criminology from below' (Sim et al., 1987: 7) can generate a serious challenge to the nefarious influence of reactionary state fractions such as the Police Federation and the POA. It is a strategy that these academics should consider if they are to contribute to overhauling and abolishing the many iniquitous and inequitable policies pursued within the contemporary criminal justice system.

The second suggested strategy is more modest and circumspect. Critical criminologists should re-engage with the criminal justice data generated by the state. While the political class in England and Wales has consistently emphasised that the good governance of society should be based on the control of information, one of the great paradoxes of this position is that the state, historically and contemporaneously, has generated and continues to generate a plethora of data on a range of social issues, a fact ruthlessly exploited by Marx in the nineteenth century in his forensic dissection of the capitalist labour process. To some extent, this political and methodological tradition of critically dissecting official data has been lost to the point where critical criminologists need to reconnect with it as one way of constructing an alternative epistemology with respect to the nature and impact of contemporary state power. Recent (and forthcoming) critical research and writing has gone some way towards achieving this goal (Ballinger, 2000; Tombs, 2000; Hillyard et al., forthcoming, as well as Dorling in Chapter 11, Pantazis in Chapter 12 and Tombs in Chpater 10 of this volume), but more of this work is needed to demystify what the state and its servants do (and what they do not do) to maintain an often brutalising social order. In engaging in this exercise, critical criminologists can contribute to the redemption of a discipline beset by the intellectual compromises engendered by its history of timidity towards the activities of the powerful and the theoretical ossification generated by its contemporary obsession with the reductionist, morally bankrupt discourses of evaluation and 'what works'.

ACKNOWLEDGEMENTS

This chapter was first presented as a paper at the annual conference of the Socio-Legal Studies Association Conference at the University of Bristol in April 2001. Thanks to those who attended the session for their comments. Thanks also to Steve Tombs and Dave Whyte for their exhaustive comments on an earlier draft and for their help with the data; to Anette Ballinger and Paddy Hillyard for various discussions; to Adam Edwards and Pete Gill for the discussion about police victimisation; and to Gerry Cordon for the musical trips on the 'magic, swirling ship'. Finally, thanks to the Nuffield Foundation for providing the grant that allowed me to research prison healthcare in 1999. The ideas for this chapter were generated as a result of this research.

This chapter is for Adrian Mellor.

9

The War on Migration

Frances Webber

Do you remember the shock, the incredulity of the first time you read about the frozen body of an asylum seeker falling from the sky, after stowing away in the undercarriage of a jet aircraft? How quickly we become inured to the horror of such stories, as deaths in transit become more and more frequent and commonplace: deaths by drowning in the waters of the Gibraltar strait or the Atlantic; body parts being caught in the nets of Sicilian fishermen; deaths by asphyxiation in the searing, suffocating heat of a container lorry stuffed with legal goods and illegal people; deaths by falling from precarious footholds on or under international trains; deaths by murder at the hands of ship's crew on the orders of a captain unwilling to pay the fine levied for having stowaways on board.

Thousands upon thousands of men, women and children have died, and are dying annually as a result of exclusionary immigration and asylum policies. They are dying because migration itself has been redefined as a crime against the new economic order. And as politicians harness and exploit popular racism and xenophobia in order to legitimise this wholesale criminalisation and exclusion of the victims of globalisation, they provide aid and comfort to the far right and encourage the spread of racist violence.

DEATH BY POLICY

On Boxing Day 1996, the crew of an old rusting freighter the *Yiohan* forced over 300 passengers off the ship and on to a small craft designed for a third of that number. Over 280 drowned when the boat went down. Four years later, fishermen in Sicily were still hauling in corpses and body parts with their catches (*Observer*, 10 June 2001). The tragedy received very little press coverage: only the *Observer* ran the story, as an exposé of the ship's captain. Such incidents have become too common to be newsworthy, unless they happen on our doorstep or they contain something out of the ordinary. Almost 4,000 immigrants, mainly Moroccans, died between 1997 and 2001 crossing the Gibraltar strait from Morocco in small boats; hundreds or thousands more have died off the coast of Italy coming from Albania and in the voyage to the Canary Islands from North Africa (ERB, 2001; ERB, 2003a). There was blanket coverage in the British press of the discovery of the bodies of 58 Chinese asylum seekers in a lorryload of tomatoes at Dover in June 2000 – but it focused on the distress of those who had found the bodies and on the criminality of those who had brought them, rather than attempting to understand the issues thrown up by the deaths. There was precious little sympathy for the victims, or for their relatives, who were frequently unable to come forward to identify bodies of their loved ones because of their own irregular status and the Home Office refusal to offer immunity from deportation (CARF, 2000d; CARF, 2000e; *Guardian*, 20 June 2000, 5 July 2000).

This lack of curiosity as to the reasons is startling in view of the relative novelty of the phenomenon of mass illegal migration to western Europe and the extraordinary lengths people go to in their attempts to reach a safe haven here – or to ensure that a relative does. It is now common knowledge that Sri Lankan Tamils, Turkish Kurds, Iranians, Somalis, Kenyans, Cameroonians, Nigerians, Afghans, Algerians, Chinese, Bosnians, Croatians, Albanians, Kosovans have frequently sold everything they have, or mortgaged their entire future, to finance their northward or westward journey or that of an oldest or only son. A detailed analysis of the reasons for migration is beyond the scope of this chapter. But why is it necessary to sacrifice so much for the journey, when air travel is so cheap? Why, in the age of mass travel, when flying halfway round the world for a week's holiday is not uncommon, is the journey from east to west, from south to north so arduous and dangerous, costing a fortune and frequently a life?

The policies responsible for these deaths began to be devised in the 1970s, when economic recession exposed fundamental shifts in the nature of the economies and thus the labour needs of post-industrial societies. As the avenues of economic migration closed down, wars of decolonisation, proxy wars, ethnic conflicts, environmental devastation, and mass pauperisation through neo-colonial looting, western trade protectionism and international debt burdens all gave rise to unprecedented levels of forced migration. The west's response has been both increasingly ferocious and concerted.

BORDER CONTROLS

The first way of preventing the arrival of unwanted migrants is to strengthen border controls. In Europe, Germany was the first country to impose visa requirements on nationals of countries from which asylum seekers were arriving, in 1980, and other European countries including Britain soon followed suit. In 1985–86, Britain imposed visa requirements on Sri Lankans[1] in response to the numbers of Tamils fleeing ethnic pogroms, following this up with visas for other Commonwealth countries including India, Pakistan, Nigeria and Ghana.[2] Visa requirements were calculated to prevent the entry of asylum seekers.[3] Austria deployed 2,000 military personnel on its borders in the 1990s. They simply turned away all undocumented immigrants, including would-be asylum seekers. Italy's immigration police performed a similar function at Italian airports, resulting in extraordinarily low rates of reception of refugees throughout the 1990s. And in the United States, Clinton's Illegal Immigration Reform and Responsibility Act 1996 (IIRRA) allowed immigration officers summarily to remove aliens with no valid documents.[4]

To enforce the exclusionary policy, governments reached for carrier sanctions – fines for airlines and shipping companies which carried undocumented passengers, or passengers with false travel documents. Carrier sanctions, used by the US, Canada and Australia, introduced in Britain in 1987 and now compulsory for all EU member states,[5] represented a quantum leap in immigration control. Carriers are now fined £2,000 per passenger in the UK (from $1,000 to $3,300 per passenger in the US),[6] forcing airlines and shipping companies into immigration control functions. Carriers are liable for passengers with false documents, or documents not belonging to them, if the falsity is 'reasonably apparent', under the carriers' liability law, the Immigration (Carriers' Liability) Act 1987, now section 40 of the Immigration and Asylum Act 1999. In Canada, airlines can reduce their liability by entering a memorandum of understanding (MOU) with the Canadian immigration authorities, whereby it agrees to carry out document screening as specified by the Canadian immigration authorities; make use of technological equipment provided by the Canadian immigration authorities to detect forged documents; take photocopies of documents which the airline suspects may be forged; and allow the immigration authorities to carry out additional passenger screening (Amnesty International, 1997). There is no automatic exemption from financial penalties for passengers subsequently granted refugee or humanitarian status. Hopes that the EU directive would require such an exemption were dashed when the draft directive was modified before its adoption in June 2001.

Immigration officials are then needed to provide training to carriers' check-in staff, and to advise airlines on better and faster systems for integrating checking-in and passport and visa checks, and so a network of airline liaison officers grew up, posted in the airports of all the main countries of origin and transit of refugees. The British government took the logic further in July 2001 by posting immigration officers at Prague airport to examine passengers themselves, to prevent the boarding of those (mainly Roma) passengers suspected of intending to claim asylum in the UK.[7] The next generation of carrier sanctions requires carriers to obtain advance authority to carry passengers, which will require them to check individual passengers' eligibility for entry to the destination country before allowing them to board.[8]

The compatibility of carrier sanctions with international refugee law has been repeatedly questioned (Feller, 1989; Ruff, 1989), and the United Nations High Commissioner for Refugees (UNHCR) and Council of Europe have repeatedly condemned them as forcing refugees to resort to smugglers (see Council of Europe, 1991, 2000a, 2000b; UNHCR, 2000), but no UK court has declared them unlawful, despite challenges by British Airways and Hoverspeed (Macdonald and Webber, 2001: 12.9). There is no doubt, however, that the combination of visa controls and carrier sanctions makes legal travel to western countries impossible for refugees and other forced migrants, and forces them into lying to embassy officials so as to obtain visit or study visas, or buying false documents, or travelling clandestinely so as to by-pass immigration controls. Increased vigilance at embassies and checking of documents and eligibility at ports abroad, including the increasing use of bio-data such as palmprint and iris recognition,[9] have limited the options further, so that for many the only possibility for those forced by political necessity or impelled by economic need to travel west or north is clandestine travel.

As more and more people resort to clandestine travel, physical security measures proliferate – fences, searchlights, armies, helicopters, sniffer dogs, x-ray, thermal imaging and night vision devices; a huge security industry has been created to detect and prevent illegal entry, in a mirror image of the smuggling industry. When Spain joined Schengen in 1989, it was funded by the EU to spend hundreds of millions of pesetas fortifying the frontiers of its North African enclaves, Ceuta and Melilla, with barbed wire, closed circuit TV and monitoring equipment (Webber, 1991). The wire has got higher and higher ever since.

These developments were mirrored in the US, where President Clinton launched Operation Gatekeeper in 1994. It doubled the number of border patrol agents along a 14-mile stretch of the US–Mexico border heavily used by undocumented immigrants. The operation pushed migrants away from the relatively safe coastal corridor towards the mountains and deserts straddling the border east of San Diego, and an estimated 1,600 migrants died in the four years after the initiative, through cold in the mountains or heat and dehydration in the desert (CARF, 1999a). Despite campaigners' efforts to raise awareness of the deaths, and to save lives, another thousand and more migrants are known to have died from similar causes trying to cross the 2,000-mile border between 1998 and 2001 (*Guardian*, 21 July 2001). Volunteers have sited water tanks throughout the desert areas and fill them up regularly.

Physical prevention continues in Europe. In 1999, the German border with Poland and the Czech Republic boasted the highest density of border guards in the world (CARF, 1999a). On the Greek border with Turkey, would-be immigrants have been killed by land mines and by border guards (IRNA, 2001). Stringent border controls in Europe have been extended increasingly east and south, as the 'accession' countries (the states bordering the EU, ten of which joined on 1 May 2004) and the Mediterranean states dependent on EU trade, aid and cooperation sign association agreements obliging them to take on the role of buffer state cum border police for the EU. As one of the measures required for joining the EU, Poland, whose frontiers with Ukraine and Belarus are already policed from 156 watchtowers by a national border guard equipped with helicopters and vehicles with night sight and thermovision, is recruiting over 3,000 more border guards, bringing the immigration police strength up to 18,000. It will also buy seven new helicopters and two light aircraft, and will decrease the distance between watchtowers. Critics have complained that the measures amount to a new 'iron curtain' (*Independent*, 31 July 2002). Immigration officers from Ukraine, a candidate state some way behind Poland in the accession queue, have been taken on a tour of the US–Mexican border to learn about border control methods and technologies (CARF, 2002b). Turkey has become another of western Europe's gatekeepers – a particularly inappropriate role given its own continuing repression of its Kurdish minority.[10] In May 2002, the frozen bodies of 19 Iranian asylum seekers, including six women and nine children, were discovered in melting snowdrifts in the mountains of southeast Turkey (*Guardian*, 3 May 2002). Turkey does not recognise the right of non-Europeans to claim asylum, and holds them in camps for months, sometimes years, while the UNHCR attempts to find resettlement countries for them.

The states from which refugees are fleeing are also recruited into the west's war on immigration. Readmission clauses, which require countries of origin to take back their nationals who are expelled from EU countries, have become a mandatory feature of trade and aid agreements (Peers, 2003a). The Lomé Convention of February 2000 requires African, Caribbean and Pacific countries to agree to take back not only their own nationals but also anyone else EU member states want to get rid of, as the price of trade cooperation. At the Tampere summit of October 1999, the principle of using the EU's economic and political muscle to enforce return and readmission agreements with countries of origin and transit was endorsed (Statewatch, 1999). Over 70 countries, including some of the poorest in the world, now have obligations to readmit their own nationals under treaties with the EC,[11] and countries of origin of asylum seekers are increasingly being recruited to prevent the departure of their own citizens, by strengthening exit controls. The Sri Lankan government was required to introduce laws criminalising illegal exit by the UK government (Statewatch, 1999). China agreed to more efficient exit controls, and a crackdown on illegal immigration to the west, as the price for western countries' support in its bid to join the WTO (Beijing Review, 2002). Sold as 'anti-trafficking' measures (EU Council, 2002) they are yet another barrier to the flight of refugees from persecution or intolerable conditions.

INTERCEPTION

Visa controls, the creation of 'buffer zones' around western Europe, the export of controls to countries of origin and transit, the carrier sanctions and the network of Airline Liaison Officers (ALOs) and preboarding immigration officers to enforce them are some of the measures designed to intercept and turn away refugees and migrants before they arrive. More bellicose measures are now being employed. The US navy, emulating southeast Asian states' response to the Indo-China refugee crisis of the 1970s, began physically intercepting boats carrying Haitian refugees in the 1990s, refusing to allow them to land in the US and returning them to Haiti without determining whether they qualified as refugees. The US Supreme Court upheld the legality of this action in a landmark case which many observers believe was determined more by political considerations than by international law obligations,[12] and US patrols continue to intercept and turn back boats with undocumented passengers without screening them for refugee status (CMRA, 2002). The Haitian case encouraged other governments in the view that the obligations of the 1951 Convention do not apply extra-territorially. In August 2001, the Australian government decided on similar action after its coastguard ordered a Norwegian vessel in its waters, the *MV Tampa*, to go to the rescue of a sinking Indonesian fishing boat. The *Tampa* rescued over 400 Afghan refugees from the boat, and sought permission to land them, but Australian officials refused. The prime minister described the refugees (including many women and children) as terrorists, and the ship's captain was told to land them instead on the tiny Pacific island of Nauru for Australian immigration officials to process their claims there. The government then passed laws retrospectively validating its action (Willheim, 2002).

Europe has followed the US and Australian lead. The French navy has intercepted a merchant ship alleged to be carrying hundreds of illegal migrants (*Guardian*, 18 March 2002), while the Italian government has taken powers to intercept boats in international waters, and a senior minister has advocated the use of lethal force against 'boat people'.[13] In June 2003 an RAF Nimrod intercepted two boats carrying illegal immigrants from Morocco to Lanzarote in a joint operation run by the Spanish Guarda Civil and supported by the Portuguese navy and the British and French air forces. The exercise was part of Operation Ulysses, a joint military venture between Spain, the UK, Italy, Portugal and France, which began patrolling the Mediterranean in February 2003 and later extended its operations to the sea between the African coast and the Canary Islands. With observers from Greece, Norway, Holland, Germany, Poland and Austria, it is a pilot for an EU-wide interception force.[14]

All of these measures do nothing to deter the desperate; they simply push up yet further the price of migration, both financial and human, as they force smugglers to find new routes or other ways of bringing their human cargo to the west. Since the Spanish civil guard introduced a new surveillance system in the Gibraltar strait – the 9-mile stretch of water separating Europe from Africa – the numbers caught crossing the strait have dropped by 78 per cent. But in the first half of 2002, nearly half of the more than 6,000 migrants who were apprehended on Spanish beaches had endured a 60-mile Atlantic voyage to the Canary Islands from the Saharan coast of Africa (*Independent on Sunday*, 4 August 2002). Hundreds of bodies of sub-Saharan Africans are now washed up on Lanzarote and Fuerteventura's beaches every year, and thousands more are known to die by cold or drowning during the 15- to 20-hour Atlantic voyage.

Closer to home, over 500 asylum seekers tried to storm the entrance to the Channel Tunnel on Christmas Day 2001, crossing two fences, one electrified, to get in, only to be repelled by riot police with tear gas

(*Guardian*, 28 December 2001; *Hansard*, 28 February 2001). In February 2001, an Iraqi refugee died and another broke both legs after leaping 20 feet from a bridge onto a moving train heading for Britain through the Channel Tunnel. In May 2001, nine Romanians, including a three-year-old child, squeezed into a hatch under a Eurostar train and travelled to Britain in sub-zero temperatures at speeds of up to 186 miles per hour (*Guardian*, 3 March 2001). Services had to be suspended in September 2001 to allow the tracks to be cleared after up to 15 asylum seekers were found injured on railway lines in Kent.

In August 1999 two boys aged 14 and 15, Tounkara Fodé and Yaguine Koita, both Guinean, froze to death in the undercarriage of a plane from Conakry to Brussels. On their decomposing bodies, found ten days later by a passing mechanic, was found a handwritten plea to 'the citizens of Europe' begging for help for Africans in the struggle against war and poverty (IRR, 1999). More wheel-arch stowaways have died since. A stowaway who fell from a plane as it took off from Gatwick Airport on Christmas Day 2000 was believed to be a Cuban asylum seeker who had been in the wheel arch for the Havana–Cancun–London trip. He was the second person to have died and fallen from an aircraft in two days. The body of another man was found on Christmas Eve on an 80-acre Surrey field beneath the busy flightpaths for Gatwick and Heathrow. Stowaway Mohammed Ayaz plunged 20,000 feet to his death from a jet coming in to land at London's Heathrow Airport in June 2001 after hiding in the plane's undercarriage. In April 2002 another stowaway's body was found in the undercarriage of an aircraft which had flown from Entebbe, Uganda, to London.[15]

In November 2000, German prosecutors considered prosecuting a 27-year-old Romanian stowaway, found unconscious and suffering from hypothermia inside the undercarriage of a passenger jet, for endangering air traffic. The only other known survivor has been Pardeep Singh, who in October 1996 survived a ten-hour flight from Delhi in temperatures of minus 60 celsius, which killed his brother Vijay. Home Office officials refused Pardeep asylum and the immigration minister said that to allow him to stay on compassionate grounds would encourage others to breach immigration controls (NCRM, n.d.).

The latest attempt to stop spontaneous refugee arrivals in Europe is the proposal for offshore refugee processing in 'regional protection areas' and 'transit zones', presented to the EU by Britain in a discussion paper in March 2003. Regional protection areas would be centres close to refugee-producing countries where refugees would be held for an initial period of six months and then, if they could not go home, would be 'processed' for resettlement in a participating state. Transit zones would be on the periphery of western Europe. Those asylum seekers who 'jumped the queue' and arrived in western Europe would be fingerprinted, photographed and immediately transferred to a 'transit zone' in Croatia or Albania (Amnesty International, 2003; Home Secretary, 2003). Although not agreed, the proposals remain on the table.

CRIMINALISATION

The small boats in which the migrants travel to the Spanish islands are increasingly skippered by children, employed to avoid the increasingly steep sentences handed down to adult smugglers who are caught. The smuggling of people has become big business in the past 15 to 20 years, as legal alternatives have been blocked. Ten thousand dollars is not uncommon as the price of getting to western Europe, Canada, the US or Australia from Sri Lanka or Iraq. The passengers of an English man sentenced in July 2002 to ten years in prison by a Greek court for smuggling 72 illegal immigrants in the yacht he was skippering claimed they had paid up to $20,000 dollars for the 30-hour trip from Izmir, in Turkey (*Independent*, 25 July 2002).

The growth of people-smuggling is a direct result of the policies of exclusion. But instead of leading to a reappraisal of those policies, it has led to the cranking up of penalties. In the UK, the penalty for assisting illegal entry went up from seven to ten years' imprisonment in 1999, and increased to 14 years in 2002. A UN survey of 45 countries in October 1999 showed an average punishment of between five and 15 years' imprisonment, sentences comparable with drug smuggling and much higher than smuggling firearms (which received sentences of between one and ten years) (Backers, 2001; CARF, 2001b; Morrison, 2001a, 2001b). People-smuggling may be a humanitarian response to a need, in the tradition of 'underground railroads' conveying escaped slaves north in the US in the nineteenth century, or Jews and resistance fighters out of Nazi occupied territories during the Second World War, or it may be solely motivated by commercial considerations. But little distinction is drawn in the criminal justice systems of the destination countries between the humanitarian and commercial smugglers, with humanitarian smugglers going to jail, at least in the UK, just as commercial ones do (albeit for shorter periods).[16]

Of even more concern is the failure by destination countries to distinguish adequately between smuggling and trafficking, although they are the subject of two separate protocols to the UN Convention on Transnational Organised Crime, signed in December 2001. Trafficking, as distinct from smuggling, involves the exploitation by the trafficker of the person trafficked, either by sale or forms of slavery. Sometimes this arises because the person cannot afford the cost of being smuggled, and becomes bound to the trafficker until the debt is paid. Sometimes women and children are sold or kidnapped for sexual exploitation (see Pantazis in Chapter 12 of this volume). But too often, no distinction is drawn in the criminal law between trafficking and smuggling. And although the EU has agreed on measures to outlaw trafficking,[17] it has so far failed to help the victims of trafficking by granting residence rights, despite the recommendation in the UN Protocol of December 2001.

The concern expressed by western governments for 'victims' of smugglers and traffickers is often belied by the treatment of those 'victims' as criminals themselves. Article 31 of the Refugee Convention, recognising that many refugees would be unable to enter countries of refuge legally, prohibited the imposition of penalties on those who entered illegally and claimed asylum promptly. In the UK, a High Court case in 1999 exposed the routine criminal charging, conviction and imprisonment of would-be asylum seekers who had entered the country on false documents – a practice which violated Article 31. Picked up at the airport, they were usually not given the chance even to claim asylum, but were taken the following day to the Magistrates' Court on criminal charges of possession of false documents, where they received six to nine months' imprisonment before they knew what was happening.[18] And although the 1999 court case stopped the imprisonment of smuggled asylum seekers on criminal offences, it did not stop their detention as illegal immigrants – which is lawful under the Convention.

DETENTION

Australia's policy of deterrence of asylum seekers includes mandatory detention for all who arrive illegally – in other words, virtually all asylum seekers, including children – for the whole of the asylum process, which can take up to three years. Detainees, including Afghans, Iraqis, Iranians, Sri Lankans and Vietnamese, are held in camps such as that in Woomera, a former missile base in the desert of central Australia. Conditions there are grim, and the desperation of detained asylum seekers sparks frequent hunger strikes and occasional mass break-outs (*Independent*, 30 March 2002). In January 2002, a freeze on refugee processing provoked protest action in which some detainees sewed their lips together, while others drank detergents or shampoo and others still tried to hang themselves (*Independent*, 25 January 2002). In the US, there is mandatory detention for everyone subject to 'expedited removal', that is, all who have illegally arrived, and although those with a 'credible fear' of persecution may be released, many are detained – particularly Haitian asylum seekers, who may be put in the same facilities as criminals, strip-searched and shackled (CMRA, 2002).

Organisations concerned with refugees such as the UNHCR deprecate the detention of asylum seekers. The numbers of asylum seekers held in detention in the UK, however, doubled between 1997 and 2001, and despite condemnation from the UN Human Rights Commission, over half were still held in prisons in late 2001 including torture victims. Although detention in prisons is being phased out, the detention of asylum seekers is increasing, and extends to children. A Scottish parliamentary delegation to Dungavel Removal Centre in April 2002 found 'no justification for the detention of children'. It expressed a number of other concerns including the lack of accountability by the private provider, the length of time asylum seekers are detained and the lack of good grounds for detention (Scottish Parliament, 2002). Detention under the Immigration Acts is unlimited in time, and immigration detainees, unlike criminal suspects, enjoy no statutory right to bail. Detainees may spend days, weeks, months or years in detention: the longest is six years' detention without charge, trial or crime,[19] while a Kurdish mother and her four children were detained for over a year before being deported in August 2003. Three of the four children suffered psychiatric damage as a result of their lengthy detention, during which they received no education.[20] A system of automatic bail hearings provided for in a 1999 Act was never implemented, and the provisions were repealed in 2002. It was only in 2000 that detainees had a right to written reasons for their detention, and even now the reasons provided are formulaic and uninformative.

Immigration detention has been privatised in the UK for decades, and staff are paid similar wages to security guards (with a small increment for riot training). At an official inspection in 1998, detainees at Campsfield immigration detention centre said staff were rude, racist and threatened them with removal to prison or back to their own country if they complained (Her Majesty's Chief Inspector of Prisons, 1998). Detainees in prisons were even worse off, treated like criminals but with none of the privileges of the 'criminal' prisoners. Fifty detainees who went on hunger strike in HMP Walton, Liverpool, in 2001 claimed they were insulted, spat on, given inedible and time-expired food and sedated for control purposes.[21] There have been deaths from excessive force in detention, too. The nephew of Patrice Lumumba was killed by prison guards at Pentonville prison, where he was detained, in October 1991 (Amnesty International, 1993). But it is the fact of detention, its perversity and its inhumanity as a way of treating exhausted and vulnerable people, the lack of intelligible reasons for it and its indefinite and uncertain duration, which cause the most distress. 'I had been in prison in my own country before, but now I felt betrayed because I came to seek asylum and now I was being taken to prison' (Ashford, 1993:52). The most common response of asylum seekers to detention is precisely this sense of betrayal, of unfairness – and despair, which not infrequently manifests itself in attempts at self-harm or even suicide. Kimpua Nsimba was an asylum seeker from Zaire who was detained when he arrived in the UK in 1990 because immigration officers could not find an interpreter who spoke his language, Lingala. He hanged himself five days later in the toilets; no one had spoken to him during that time and he had not been told why he was detained or for how long. At his inquest, it emerged that detention staff had no training in suicide prevention. The inquest was also notable for the coroner's remark that the deceased had not really been detained, since he had been free to return to his own country. A 16-year-old who was held at Campsfield for over a year suffered mental breakdown, but his repeated complaints of auditory hallucinations were treated with paracetamol, and he remained in detention after a serious and almost successful suicide attempt.[22]

In December 2001 Yarl's Wood, a brand new detention centre, was opened near Bedford, to house 900 asylum seekers, making it the biggest in Europe. It featured 5-metre high walls of chain-link fencing topped by a triple line of barbed wire; security devices rivalling those in high-security prisons, including microwave detection units, pan and tilt dome cameras – but, in common with the other six immigration detention centres in England and Wales, no sprinklers. The Bedfordshire Fire Brigades Union said it had warned Group 4 Security, the private company running Yarl's Wood, of the need for sprinklers in the building, which was built in ten months at a cost of £100 million (see NCADC, 2002). In February 2002, it caught fire during a protest by detainees at the alleged manhandling of an elderly and sick detainee. Police did not allow fire-fighters access to the building until 'order had been re-established'. A guard told the criminal trial of detainees charged with riot and affray that officers were told to lock the detainees into the burning building – an order which was obeyed (*Guardian*, 23 July 2003). It emerged that Group 4 Security was initially treated as a suspect and investigated for corporate manslaughter, and police spent months sifting through the ashes of the centre before satisfying themselves that no detainees had died in the fire. Witnesses to the events were deported before the trial, preventing the defendants from obtaining their testimony (ibid.; *Guardian*, 22 March 2002; *Independent on Sunday*, 12 May 2002). Thirteen persons were originally charged but two absconded before the trial began. Of the eleven who went to trial seven were acquitted of all charges, three were found guilty of violent disorder and one person of affray (see NCADC, 2002; CARF, 2003).

Liberty is upheld in all western countries as one of the primary human rights – the Universal Declaration of Human Rights Article 3; International Covenant on Civil and Political Rights Article 9; and the European Convention on Human Rights Article 5 – and protected by *habeas corpus* laws. But immigrants' rights to freedom are given scant protection. In a 1987 UK case, one of the most senior judges described the release from detention of those arriving in the UK as 'an act of grace',[23] and eight months' detention of asylum seekers was held not excessive.[24] It was, however, universally believed that detention could only be justified by a risk of absconding. But in 2002 the House of Lords ruled that such a justification was unnecessary, when it upheld detention by nationality at Oakington, a former military barracks which holds 400 asylum seekers including women and children.[25] Asylum seekers from a list of countries from where asylum claims are most likely to be refused are held there for seven days while their claims are processed, simply because processing is easier that way.

The segregation of asylum seekers from mainstream society has been the theme in welfare provision, too. In the UK, since 1996, immigrants and asylum seekers have been unable to access basic 'safety net' welfare benefits and public housing available to the rest of the population. Prohibited from working, destitute asylum seekers have sought help from local councils. Dispersal began as an ad-hoc response by local councils in London and the southeast to their obligations to this new constituency of destitution; they paid councils and private providers in areas where accommodation was more plentiful, although run-down, to take 'their' asylum seekers for them. In 1999 the Labour administration returned responsibility for asylum seekers from local to national government, but institutionalised dispersal, setting up the National Asylum Support Service (NASS), a branch of the Home Office, to buy in support and accommodation services from public and private suppliers.

The dispersal system in Britain was modelled on European precedents, even though these showed that compulsory dispersal provided 'a perverse incentive for genuine refugees to live illegally instead of applying for asylum' and had led to an increase in racism and neo-Nazi activity (ARC, 1999). Dispersal means that destitute asylum seekers must submit to transportation to an unknown, unchosen and

frequently hostile destination. Conditions in dispersal accommodation
are frequently squalid, in

> the twilight zones of the unregulated private housing sector where,
> huddled in bedsits, shared houses, overcrowded hostels and bed and
> breakfasts, they face private landlords who see in them a lucrative
> business opportunity ... Asylum seekers are herded into dormitory
> conditions, [where] food is often inedible, sanitation deplorable,
> heating insufficient and fire and safety regulations ignored. (Fekete,
> 2001: 33–4)

On occasion, asylum seekers are removed to dispersal accommodation
by force, as in the case of a Kosovan family with three children, who
sought to remain close to the father's adult son in north London. Police
bundled the family into a van and forced them onto a train to Hull,
where the family discovered that they had been sent to a hostel for the
mentally ill (ARC, 1999). A Kurdish family subjected to serious racial
attacks when they were dispersed from London to a Glasgow housing
estate were ordered to return there on pain of losing all support when
they fled back to London after their schoolboy son was stabbed in
September 2001.[26]

The voucher system, like dispersal, started in the UK as an ad-
hoc measure and was institutionalised into law by the New Labour
government in 1999. Asylum support was to be largely in kind rather
than cash, and the humiliation involved in presenting vouchers for goods
in supermarkets was an integral part of the experiment. It was meant as a
deterrent. But destitute refugees could not return to their home countries
and had no alternative means of support since work was prohibited.
They had no option but to swallow the humiliation in the supermarket
queue as they asked in vain for change (the government 'sold' the voucher
scheme to supermarkets on the basis that they would not be required to
give change), as vouchers presented were insufficient, or cashiers decided
that yoghurt was a luxury food for which vouchers could not be used
(Refugee Council, 1997). A vociferous and lengthy campaign in which
Bill Morris, the black general secretary of the Transport and General
Workers' Union, played a leading part, eventually secured the abolition
of the food voucher scheme in late 2001 – but then the government came
up with other plans which were even worse.

LIVING IN A BUBBLE

The new welfare scheme, set out in the Nationality, Immigration and
Asylum Act 2002, was designed to achieve the total segregation of

asylum seekers from society. Only those with their own means, or who could rely on the support of family, friends or community for the time it takes to process the claim (anything from three months to three years) would be able to live in the community. Those needing support would be sent to one of 15 self-contained rural accommodation centres, with their own barracks-style housing, medical and educational facilities, miles away from the nearest town. Leaving the centres, even overnight, could result in forfeiting the asylum claim. In a suitably grisly twist, one of the 750-bed centres was to be built next to the site of a pit full of 13,000 rotting carcasses of cattle buried during the foot and mouth epidemic of 2001, from which five tankers of liquid a day were still being drained in May 2002, although that site was abandoned following protests (*Independent*, 15 May 2002). As well as local anger at the government's lack of consultation, the proposals provoked furious opposition among teachers and others concerned with children, who pointed out that integration into mainstream schools brings emotional stability for traumatised refugee children, while the children benefit the schools by their outstanding academic performance once they have learned English (NUT, 2002). But the purpose of the centres is not to assist with the recovery of asylum seekers from traumatic experiences, or to help them integrate into a new society. Even though by the summer of 2002 over half of all asylum seekers were allowed to remain in the UK (*Independent*, 31 August 2002), accommodation centres are designed for deterrence and removal. As Home Secretary David Blunkett told parliament,

The difficulty sometimes with families whose removal has been attempted is that their youngsters have become part of a school, making it virtually impossible in some circumstances to operate the managed system to which we should all sign up unless we believe in completely open borders, which would be an interesting free enterprise experiment – eventually the system would give and people wouldn't want to come here anymore as it would no longer be attractive, which would be crackers and a crazy piece of politics. (*Hansard*, 24 April, 2002, 353)

Thus the Home Secretary's rationale for making asylum seekers live in a limbo away from society is that they become too well integrated to be easily removed, and they must be removed in the interests of 'managed migration'.

STARVING THEM OUT

While the proposals for segregated education were hitting the headlines, other provisions, passed quickly and quietly through parliament, excluded large numbers of asylum seekers and others from support altogether. They came into force in January 2003, and their effect has been devastating. Section 55 of the 2002 Act excludes from all support childless 'late claimants', that is, asylum claimants who did not claim as soon as 'reasonably practicable' after arrival in the UK – unless denial of all support would breach their human rights.[27] Home Secretary David Blunkett told parliament that the section would only be used against those who abused the asylum system just to get support. But in practice, officials were instructed to refuse support to all childless asylum seekers who failed to claim at the port of entry. In the first quarter of 2003, two-thirds of all asylum support applications from in-country applicants were refused (Home Office, 2003c). Those forced into homelessness in those freezing winter days included a Rwandan woman who had been regularly raped and beaten by Tutsis in a refugee camp, a young Angolan suffering from trauma after his father was shot dead, his mother and sister raped by soldiers and he was interrogated and beaten, and a Somali who lost 14kg in weight and became psychologically disturbed through having to sleep rough and defecate in parks (Webber, 2003). As well as subjecting asylum claimants to destitution and degradation, the provisions further stigmatise and marginalise them, giving a further fillip to tabloid campaigns and racist attacks.

THROWING THEM OUT

In August 2002 police and immigration officers broke down the doors of a mosque and seized the Ahmadi family, Afghans with two young children who had taken sanctuary there, for removal to Germany (CARF, 2002b). The action was highly publicised, and clearly intended to send a message to others to go quietly. Another high profile deportation occurred the following year, when the Ay family, a Kurdish mother and her four children, were forcibly removed to Germany in August 2003.[28] Since 1999, the British government has been trying to increase removals of rejected asylum seekers and others with no permission to stay in the country from 12,500 to 30,000 annually. 'Snatch squads' of immigration officers, with new powers to use force, were introduced, as were special charter flights, to prevent disruption of commercial flights by deportees and their supporters, who have mounted noisy and sometimes successful protests in airports and occasionally on aircraft (CARF, 2000e). The physical measures have been accompanied by new laws preventing those whose claims are deemed 'clearly unfounded' from appealing refusal of asylum before they leave the country, and subjecting other claimants to 'fast-track' and 'expedited track' procedures. There are proposals further to curtail legal protection against removal by cutting down appeals, by amalgamating the two tiers of appeal against immigration and asylum decisions, and by reducing public funding for appeals (Department of Constitutional Affairs, 2003).

The British emphasis on removal is replicated across Europe. The EU has for many years had working groups on expulsion which have attempted to coordinate a Europe-wide removals programme. Under its aegis, member states have initiated mass deportations on charter flights (Statewatch, 2003), and the latest scheme, proposed by the Italian presidency in July 2003 (Italian Republic, 2003), is that officers in plainclothes drive unmarked police cars across the EU to dump rejected asylum seekers in 'safe' countries outside Europe, using 'legitimate force' to prevent escape.

Removal of rejected immigrants and asylum seekers has on occasion been accompanied by force, sometimes fatal. In the most notorious British case, Joy Gardner was handcuffed, manacled and then asphyxiated by 3 metres of sticky tape when police came to deport her on a Sunday morning in August 1993 (CARF, 1993; Amnesty International, 1994). (In the UK, unlike the US, police have historically played a major role in immigration enforcement – a role they are very keen to lose in the interests of police/community relations.) At least six others have met a similar fate during attempted deportations elsewhere in Europe (Fekete, 2003), while in the UK another four people have died fleeing immigration officers who came knocking at the door (CARF, 2000d). Many asylum seekers have attempted suicide – some successfully – when issued with removal notices (MFCVT, n.d.) And since no one systematically monitors what happens to rejected asylum seekers returned to countries ruled by brutal regimes, or to countries in the grip of civil war, the true toll of death and suffering caused by the wrongful refusal of asylum remains unknown.

Removal – and exclusion – can also permanently separate families. Many asylum seekers, and others seeking to remain in the country, marry or enter relationships and have children here, from whom they are forced to part, as the imperatives of immigration control trump family values.[29] In 1983, three British women complained to the European Court of Human Rights (ECHR) that the British government was violating their right to family life – the right to have their husbands live with them in Britain – by imposing this rule.[30] The government's argument that such restriction was necessary in the interests of 'the economic well-being of the country' was accepted, and the control of immigration to protect the domestic labour market was held by the court to be a reasonable justification for the separation of families.[31] Now that labour shortages have scuppered that argument, the justification is the need to prevent 'queue-jumping' – the need for 'managed migration'.

THE RATIONALE FOR CONTROL

All immigration control is predicated on the idea that unrestricted immigration is socially harmful. But the movement of people from one country to another is clearly not an evil *per se*, as the movement of drugs or guns might be. Indeed, when research is done into the economic impact of immigration, it is found to benefit both the host economy – migrants tend to be young and dynamic, contribute more than they take out, and frequently create employment – and the country of origin, to which immigrants send remittances (Glover et al., 2001). In the US, this was recognised in Carnegie's 'golden stream' in the 1880s (see Cornelius et al., 1995); the US, historically a country of immigration, has always practised 'managed migration' (as opposed to 'zero immigration') policies. British studies have also found that refugees tend to be highly educated and qualified, with skills and experience that are grossly undervalued and underused (Refugee Council, 1997).

Of course, not all immigration is controlled. Since 1973, when Britain joined the European Economic Community, the country and its labour market has been wide open to any EU (and since 1993, EEA)[32] citizen who wants to work here. The two most common reasons given for regulation – to protect the indigenous labour market, and to prevent 'disorder' by regulating immigration are dis-applied to European migrants.[33]

It is only in the last five years or so that European politicians have acknowledged Europe's need for migrant labour, as the demographic realities of ageing populations have sunk in. In July 2002 European Commission President Romano Prodi said:

> In the European countries, immigration is indispensable ... for a simple reason. No German, no Italian, no French of the younger generation wants to do night shifts in a hospital. No one wants to work in agriculture or public works. And so immigration is obviously needed. (*Migration News*, August 2002)

Australian immigration minister Philip Ruddock told a British audience in December 2001 that: 'Those who close their doors to outsiders ... face a bleak future of declining and ageing populations, introspection and cultural attenuation' (ibid.) The language of control has shifted from 'zero immigration' to 'managed migration' – which essentially means cherry picking the most highly educated and qualified migrants with skills useful to post-industrial economies, and rejecting the rest. The Home Office's new 'Highly Skilled Migrants Programme' is presented as a genuine opportunity for economic migrants to migrate lawfully to the UK, but, like other points-based systems in Canada, Australia and the US, demands a high level of skill, qualification or salary. In a globalised world, the unrestricted, autonomous immigration of the poor to rich countries must be controlled to sustain the global system which keeps rich countries rich by exploiting the poor. As Sivanandan has said, 'poverty is the new Black' (Sivanandan, 2001).

Poverty is, however, too crude a rationale for exclusion. It shames. Politicians, on the whole, have not castigated immigrants and asylum seekers simply for being poor.[34] So poverty is coded; the 'numbers game' – first played in the UK in the 1960s against black immigrants – uses the language of flooding. Both Enoch Powell's notorious 'river of blood' speech of 1968 and Margaret Thatcher's 1979 election campaign speech that Britons feared being 'swamped' by people from a different culture – memorably articulated and mobilised popular racism about immigrants from the 'new Commonwealth' countries of Asia and the Caribbean. In an apparently deliberate echo of Thatcher's notorious 1979 speech, Home Secretary David Blunkett told the BBC in April 2002 that the segregation of asylum seekers in camps ('accommodation centres') was necessitated by the 'swamping' of local schools and medical facilities by asylum seekers, and in July 2003 the language was echoed by former minister Stephen Byers, according to whom Labour's traditional supporters feared that 'in some way their national identity is under threat' (*Guardian*, 31 July 2003).

The institutionalised racism of controls which excluded black people from the UK in the 1960s and 1970s was reinforced by the racist myths deployed to justify them, by politicians who whipped up fears about illegality, criminality and disease (IRR, 1979). The myths deployed against asylum seekers from the 1990s to date have used all these stereotypes, as well as 'scrounging', 'economic migration' (a term of abuse in this context), subversion and terrorism. In responding to the refugee crises of the 1980s onwards, governments have avoided using the word 'refugee', instead defining asylum seekers in terms of their (necessary) illegality, and using that illegality to denounce them as 'illegals' and 'bogus'. Even Jack Straw, the Home Secretary who instigated the inquiry into the racist killing of Stephen Lawrence and who prides himself on his anti-racism, notoriously reviled Roma from the Czech Republic, historical holocaust victims fleeing vicious skinhead violence, claiming in 1998 that there were no genuine asylum seekers among them (CARF, 1998; CARF, 1999b). This was at a time when the press in Dover, where Czech Roma asylum seekers were arriving, was running stories week after week with headlines such as: 'Wash this human sewage down the drain' (*Dover Express*, 1 October 1998). A barrage of tabloid headlines during March 2000, such as 'Britain's had enough', 'Time to kick the scroungers out' and 'We need deportations on a large scale' led to a Home Office announcement that new powers would be sought to 'clamp down on gypsy beggars', although police confessed they had all the powers they needed (CARF, 2000c). During the 2001 general election campaign, when Conservative MPs indulged in a barrage of anti-asylum and racist invective, David Blunkett, then Education Secretary, responded by promising that if he became Home Secretary he would 'blitz asylum cheats' but as Home Secretary, he was as good as his word – but his measures 'blitz' all asylum seekers without discrimination (ibid.). As the Campaign Against Racism and Fascism said:

> the principle that politicians have a social responsibility not to inflame public opinion against minorities was happily discarded as journalists and politicians ... justified verbal attacks on asylum seekers on grounds of defending British values of freedom of speech. The established link between racially charged campaigning and racial attacks was not even discussed. (CARF, 2001b)

The Commission for Racial Equality has on occasion begged politicians to tone down their 'furious exchanges' on race and asylum issues (*Observer*, 3 December 2000). In Kent, the Association of Chief Police Officers (ACPO) has called for fair treatment of asylum seekers, demanding an end to 'racist expressions' which would not be tolerated towards any other minority. Police said that ill-informed adverse media coverage contributed to a rise in racial tension and increased the risk of public disorder (*Guardian*, 23 January 2001; *Guardian*, 1 March 2001).

The constant denigration of asylum seekers, together with Home Office policies such as dispersal which treat them as problematic and unwanted, gives the green light to tabloid racism and creates the climate for physical attacks.[35] In Hull, dispersed asylum seekers from Bosnia, Iraq and Afghanistan barricaded themselves in a supermarket in August 2000 following a spate of over 180 racial attacks including stabbings and arson attacks, in which a 19-year-old was stabbed in the chest and a 26-year-old lost the sight of one eye. A year later another asylum seeker had his throat slashed (*Guardian*, 3 June 2002). In August 2001, Kurdish asylum seeker Firsat Dag, from Turkey, was stabbed to death in a racist attack in Glasgow, where he had been 'dispersed'. Another Kurdish refugee, Davoud Naseri, from Iran, was stabbed in the back two days later (*Guardian*, 11 August 2001). In Sunderland, Iranian asylum seeker Peiman Rahmani was killed in a racist attack in August 2002. The British National Party has been campaigning there and has put up a number of candidates for the local council since dispersal of asylum seekers started there two years ago. The Medical Foundation for the Care of Victims of Torture disclosed an alarming dossier of attacks against its patients in August 2001, including refugees being slashed across the face with knives in Sunderland, a man almost garotted to death in Hull, two men in Coventry being attacked and beaten by a 40-strong gang in the town centre, a man's jaw broken in Stockton, and a TV set hurled from a tower block at an asylum seeker's family in Glasgow (*Guardian*, 9 August 2001). In 2003, racist attacks became 'routine' in Plymouth, with an average of 22 to 30 racist incidents each month against Iraqi, Zimbabwean, Afghan, Somali and Chinese asylum seekers. In April 2003, attacks on Zimbabwean asylum seekers in Portsmouth were reported; in June, severe racial violence erupted in Wrexham.

The surge in racist violence has not restricted itself to asylum seekers but, in the highly charged racial climate created by the politicians and the media, has spilled over into the whole black community. (In fact, racial violence against the settled black community has never gone away, as the deaths of Stephen Lawrence, Michael Menson, Rumi Surage, Farhan Mire, Joseph Alcendor and many others testify: CARF, 2000a.) A 'chronology of racism' compiled by CARF showed that in the month from 9 December 2000 to 7 January 2001, Conservative leader William Hague claimed that 'soft' policing of black communities was causing an increase in crime; shadow Home Secretary Anne Widdecombe said she would 'lock up all asylum seekers', shadow minister Michael Heseltine said 'bogus asylum seekers were cheating British people', and there were derogatory reports on asylum and illegal immigration in the *Mail*, the *Sunday Telegraph*, the *Independent on Sunday*, the *Sunday Mirror*, *The Times* and the *Mail on Sunday* (CARF, 2001a). In that month, there were six fatal or near-fatal attacks – on asylum seekers and settled black people, including a 13-year-old schoolboy left lying unconscious, covered with blood and wounds in Sussex, an Algerian businessman who had his throat slit in London's Soho, and a Rotherham taxi-driver.

Then, in a final twist, racial violence itself is used by politicians as a further reason for ever more restrictive policies. Just as in Germany the spate of neo-nazi attacks on asylum hostels in the early 1990s led to a change in the constitution removing the automatic right to claim asylum (CARF, 1992), so in the UK attacks on asylum seekers were used to justify the policy of dispersal and the attempts to bring down the numbers of asylum seekers (IRR, 2000). The *Independent* characterised Blunkett's 'swamping' remarks as appeasement of racism in April 2002 (*Independent*, editorial, 25 April 2002). Appeasement of popular racism and, more importantly, the tabloid press which disseminates it lay behind Prime Minister Blair's pledge in February 2003 to halve asylum numbers 'by September' (*Guardian*, 8 February 2003). But popular racism has been an excuse for anti-immigrant policies since well before Enoch Powell (see Foot, 1964; Nicol and Dummett, 1990).

TOWARDS NATIONAL SECURITY STATES

European immigration policy has, since the 1970s, been indissolubly linked with 'law and order' policies to counter drugs, organised crime and terrorism (Bunyan, 1991; Fekete and Webber, 1994) and immigrants and asylum seekers have long been targeted for surveillance and harassment by security services working with the security services of the countries they have fled from. There is ample evidence of collaboration between the security services of the UK, France, Switzerland and Germany on the one hand, and Turkey and Algeria on the other, to the extreme prejudice of refugees from the latter countries (Fekete and Webber, 1996). The UK's anti-terrorist legislation in 1998 and 2000 fuzzed the boundaries between terrorism and overthrow of tyranny on the one hand,[36] and terrorism and legitimate political activity on the other,[37] and made support for liberation movements abroad a perilous endeavour.

But the measures affected or proposed in the wake of 11 September 2001 are truly totalitarian. In the US, the USA PATRIOT Act was passed to justify the selective enforcement of deportation orders based on national origin and ethnicity, the round-ups of Arab and Muslim non-citizens for 'voluntary' interrogation by the Department of Homeland Security (DHS) and Federal Bureau of Investigation (FBI), and proposals to relax the limitations on FBI surveillance and infiltration of religious and political groups (ACLU, 2002). Regulations were passed allowing individuals to be detained for an unspecified 'reasonable time', interpreted as weeks or even months, without recourse to any court. Up to 2,000 foreigners, mostly Arabs or Muslims, are believed to have been held in secret detention pending deportation since

11 September 2001. Federal courts ordered the Justice Department to name all suspects held without charge (*Independent*, 28 August 2002). But the Supreme Court overruled them and upheld secret deportation hearings for post-11 September detainees in May 2003.[38] In March 2003, the DHS blocked the release of Haitian refugees whose release on bail was ordered by the Board of Immigration Appeals – the first time national security reasons had been used against Haitians (Lawyers Committee for Human Rights, 2003). Meanwhile, FBI officials publicly reflected on the utility of torture for reticent suspects – one of the few actions absolutely prohibited in international humanitarian law, no matter what the circumstances (*The Times*, 22 January 2001).

In the UK, the government formally derogated from the provisions of the European Human Rights Convention, which guarantee the right to liberty, so as to intern indefinitely foreign 'suspected international terrorists' who could not be deported. The Court of Appeal upheld the derogation as lawful in October 2002.[39] Meanwhile, the EU has given security services unlimited access to all personal information on asylum seekers, and is creating a Europe-wide database on all non-Europeans within the EU, involving a massive extension of the EU's security system, and the removal of all protections in extradition, allowing potential return to states where torture or the death penalty is practised (Fekete, 2002).[40]

These policy responses have been justified by an anti-Muslim and (in Europe) anti-immigrant racism, which suggests all Muslims are extremists and immigrant communities are backward. Immigration policies are 'increasingly shaped by a discourse that posits European values as under threat from non-European cultural practices within, and anti-western civilisations without' (Fekete, 2002). Racial and religious attacks against Muslims on both continents have increased. And as national security imperatives take over more and more aspects of civil society, the foundations of refugee and human rights protection, painfully built out of the horrors of nazism and Stalinism after the Second World War, and with them the values of universalism themselves, are being fundamentally undermined.

10
Workplace Injury and Death: Social Harm and the Illusions of Law

Steve Tombs

ROUTINE WORK-RELATED HARM AND CRIMINAL LAW

Work kills. It kills workers and members of the public through acute injury and chronic illness. The scale of this routine killing – deaths occur across all industries, all types of companies – is almost incomprehensible. In May 2002, the ILO estimated that 2 million workers die each year through work-related accidents and diseases – a figure which it said is 'just the tip of the iceberg' (Takala, 2002: 6). Thus, latest ILO estimates for the year 2000 show that annually there are 2 million work-related deaths – more than 5,000 every day – and for every fatal accident there are another 500–2,000 injuries, depending on the type of job. In addition, the ILO said for every fatal work-related disease there are about 100 other illnesses causing absence from work (ibid.).

According to these ILO figures, the biggest killer in the workplace is cancer, causing roughly 640,000 or 32 per cent of deaths, followed by circulatory diseases at 23 per cent, then accidents at 19 per cent and communicable diseases at 17 per cent. Asbestos alone takes some 100,000 lives annually (ibid.: 4). Twelve thousand children die each year working in hazardous conditions (ibid.: 6). Moreover, these deaths, injuries and illnesses are unequally distributed, with a particularly heavy toll of dead and injured occurring in developing countries where large numbers of workers are concentrated in primary and extraction activities such as agriculture, logging, fishing and mining (ibid.: 2–3). And *within* the most developed economies, there are also good theoretical reasons and some empirical evidence (see Slapper and Tombs, 1999: 83, and more recently, for example, Steenland et al., 2003) to indicate that these deaths, injuries and illnesses disproportionately fall upon members of the lowest socio-economic groups.

The ILO has also made several calculations as to the economic costs of these phenomena, concluding that compensation figures indicate that approximately 4 per cent of the world's GDP disappears with the cost of diseases through absences from work, sickness treatment, disability and survivor benefits. The loss in GDP resulting from this reality is 20 times greater than all official development assistance to developing countries (Takala, 2002: 7).

Moreover, the *impacts* of these economic costs are differentially distributed. Thus, for example, occupational health and safety compensation schemes differ enormously – while workers in Nordic countries enjoy nearly universal coverage, 'only 10 per cent or less of the workforce in many developing countries is likely to benefit from any sort of coverage. Even in many developed countries, coverage against occupational injury and illness may extend to only half the workforce' (ibid.).

Notwithstanding the kind of data presented above, it is important to be clear that, in fact and of importance in itself, relatively little is known about the numbers of people killed by work activities – a lack of knowledge that says a great deal about the priorities of the societies in which we live. To take deaths from work-related disease, the official statistics do not begin to capture the scale of physical harm wreaked by employing organisations. However, it is possible to highlight the *sheer scale* of deaths involved. To take but one small category of deaths in one country – deaths from asbestos exposures in the UK. The HSE noted that in 2000, there were 1,628 deaths from mesothelioma, an asbestos-related cancer, and 186 death certificates mentioning asbestosis (Health and Safety Executive, 2002: 17). In fact, as the HSE itself recognises (ibid.), actual deaths related to asbestos exposure are far, far higher. Asbestos-related deaths continue to rise in this country (not to peak until around 2025, according to the British government), years after the demise of the industry (the worst affected group are men born in the 1940s), and 70 years after the first official recognition of the cancer-causing properties of this magic mineral. Thus:

> excess deaths in Britain from asbestos-related diseases could eventually reach 100,000 ... One study projected that in western Europe 250,000 men would die of mesothelioma [just *one* asbestos-caused cancer] between 1995 and 2029; with half a million as the corresponding figure for the total number of West European deaths from asbestos. (Tweedale, 2000: 276)

A later study extrapolates from current asbestos-related deaths and concludes that more than 3 per cent of men in Europe will die of asbestos-related diseases in the next ten to 20 years (Randerson, 2001).

Thus, asbestos-related deaths are not simply a matter of historical record – the industry remains vibrant globally. Even more chillingly, 'asbestos is only one of a number of hazardous substances in our lives' (Tweedale, 2000: 277). In many respects, it is one of the safest – since there is now generally accepted knowledge regarding its deleterious health effects and it is highly regulated, at least in most advanced capitalist economies.

If there are *some* technical – though these are much more significantly overlain by political and social – reasons for this lack of knowledge with respect to deaths from work-related *ill health*, then one might expect that deaths from work-related *injuries* would be much more accurately recorded. This is not the case. For example, despite HSE claims that fatality data are virtually complete, recent work indicates that there are closer to 1,500 occupational fatalities per year, using official data and the HSE's own categories (Tombs, 1999). By way of comparison, it is worth noting that the annual number of homicides in England, Wales and Scotland stands in recent years between 700 and 850 – an apt comparison, since the HSE's own evidence indicates that 'management failure' is the cause of about 70 per cent of occupational fatalities (Bergman, 2000: 31–2), indicating that there is at least a criminal case to answer.

Reference to this point has been to deaths. And while most recent (albeit provisional) HSE figures record 633 fatal occupational injuries for 2001/2, these fatalities are only the most visible forms of physical harm caused by work-related activities. Much more common are major and minor ('over-three-day') injuries.[1] According to most recent HSE data, there were 28,383 major injuries and 127,979 over-three-day injuries to workers in Britain in 2001/2 (Health and Safety Executive, nd: 24); members of the public suffered 14,362 non-fatal occupational injuries (ibid.).

Yet even these official data fail to capture the extent of physical harm caused by working in the fourth most developed economy in the world. While the HSE has long been aware of the significant scale of underreporting of injuries (major and over-three-day), recent use of the Labour Force Survey (LFS) has produced evidence of levels of injury that far outweigh 'official' injury data. Based upon the discrepancies between 'official' and LFS data, the HSC has concluded recently that, 'overall, employers report about 44 per cent of the non-fatal injuries that they should report' (Health and Safety Commission, 2002: 1).

Indeed, following the addition of questions on occupational injury as a supplement to the LFS, it has now been estimated that official data records 'less than 5 per cent' of injuries to the self-employed (ibid.: 7). Moreover, even this recognised level of underreporting still in principle excludes three potentially significant, if somewhat overlapping, areas of occupational injuries, namely those incurred by workers in the illegal economy, as well as by home- and child-workers (see, for example, O'Donnell and White, 1998, 1999).

However, these deaths and injuries do not involve 'merely' *physical* harms. They have widespread, if largely unrecognised, financial, psychological, as well as social effects. Yet, it is the financial costs of injuries and ill health which have been the focus of recent attention by official organisations and interest groups. Thus the HSE and governments have, for almost a decade, sought (erroneously – see Cutler and James, 1996), to argue the 'business case' for improved health and safety (Health and Safety Executive, 1993, 1994; Davies and Teasdale, 1994; Health and Safety Commission, 2000), seeing the costs to companies of injuring and causing illness as a lever to raise standards of compliance! In this context, it has been estimated that the cost of injury and ill health is £18 billion a year (see, for example, Health and Safety Commission, 2000, passim). Yet one of the contradictions within such an argument is that employers do not *actually* meet the costs of workplace injuries and illness. Most of the £18 billion cost of workplace injury and illness is paid for by the government and the victims. Even the HSE itself estimates that employers, who cause the health and safety risks, pay between £3.3 billion and £6.5 billion (TUC, 2003). In other words, costs associated with injuries and ill health represent a massive socialisation of the costs of private production, in effect a massive redistribution of wealth from the poor to the rich. That is, through supporting the cost of industrial injury benefit, health and other social services, paying higher insurance premiums, paying higher prices for goods and services so that employers can recoup the costs of downtime, retraining, the replacement of plant and so on, private industry is subsidised on a massive scale by employees, taxpayers and the general public. This in turn has knock-on effects on government's ability to use revenue from general taxation for more socially productive purposes.

Of course, such bald statistics of deaths or losses to corporate profits or GDP mask a wide array of searing, but less quantifiable, social and psychological harms. Families and communities are subjected to trauma in the event of death and injury. Children lose fathers, spouses lose partners, sports teams lose coaches and players, church and social clubs lose their members, and workers lose their colleagues – to the extent that such psychological and social costs are immeasurable. Moreover, such losses and harms have effects across generations, so that, for example, children who experience poverty following the death of the main wage earner are themselves more likely to grow up in conditions of relative insecurity, a condition then more likely to be experienced by their own offspring.

Further, the psychological trauma heaped upon the bereaved is often magnified greatly by the consistent inability of the state, through the criminal justice system, to provide 'answers' as to why someone who leaves for work either does not return, or returns in a considerably less fit condition.[2] And if the state cannot provide such answers to the bereaved – and given the levels of investigation, for example, which are documented later in this chapter, this inability is an institutionalised one – then the accountability that men and women are led to expect that they will secure from the criminal justice system is almost entirely lacking.[3] The bulk of this chapter is devoted to an analysis of some of the key dimensions of the systematic discrepancies between the promise of the law and criminal justice system, and the realities of the protection and accountability that these actually offer in relation to workplace safety and health.

To be clear at the outset, while occupational safety and health protection falls squarely within the criminal law, criminalisation in practice has never formed a central part of states' agendas. In general, across developed economies, the records of protection in relation to workers' health and safety have been, and continue to be, poor. Indeed, notwithstanding the general (and, some would say, increasing) reluctance on the part of states to intervene in the activities of corporations, even within the general rubric of regulation, the regulation of occupational safety and health is likely to be even more *relatively* ineffective, since it tends to impinge upon 'the most minute details of production', rendering such regulation fundamentally 'antagonistic to the logic of firms within a capitalist economy' (Szasz, 1984: 114).[4] Thus it is possible to agree with Snider when she notes it is *generally* the case that:

> states will do as little as possible to enforce health and safety laws. They will pass them only when forced to do so by public crises or union agitation, strengthen them reluctantly, weaken them whenever possible, and enforce them in a manner calculated not to seriously impede profitability. (Snider, 1991: 220)

That is, all things being equal, the preference of capital is for less rather than more regulation, and this preference is more or less reflected through states' practices and rhetoric. Thus it is important to recognise that, historically, health and safety legislation, and any improvements in enforcement, have been *forced upon* states by pro-regulatory forces and, notably, by trades unions, the representative organisations with the key interest in this area.

In the UK, the most recent, and still the key, overarching piece of relevant legislation is the Health and Safety at Work Act 1974, an Act informed by the philosophy of self-regulation. According to this principle, criminal law and its enforcement has a key, but minor, role to play in ensuring occupational health and safety protection – the principal responsibility for achieving protection is to be left to those who create and work with the risks, namely employers and employees (see Tombs, 1995).

Two points need to be emphasised here. First, this philosophy therefore places an enormous onus upon the balances of power – within and beyond workplaces – between capital and labour. At the policy level, self-regulation is linked to a system of tripartism, so that employees and employers determine policy within the Health and Safety Commission – though this is clearly an organisation in which employers' interests predominate, which is highly conservative, and tends towards less rather than more protection (Dalton, 2000). At the level of workplaces, the balance of power is intimately related to the level and strength of workers' organisation, not least because subsidiary legislation – notably the 1977 Safety Representatives and Safety Committees Regulations – grants formal roles to trade union representatives in the organisation of health and safety.

Second, in terms of the instrumental functions of law, one must be clear that any system of self-regulation is predicated upon a range of credible enforcement techniques to which regulators have access and which thus allow an escalation in severity of sanctions in response to uncooperativeness on the part of the regulated. In essence, this is an enforcement philosophy based ultimately on the principle of deterrence. Such an enforcement process, however, can only function effectively where escalation towards greater punitiveness and the sanctions that are formally at the disposal of regulators are both credible. Central here is that the state maintains a minimal level and threat of presence within workplaces – thus, that it actually inspects and, following a complaint or incident, is able credibly to respond to these in the form of an investigation. Yet both historically and – as the following analysis indicates – contemporaneously, it is difficult to see this whip of punitive enforcement as credible in the context of an HSE which is increasingly advocating a movement away from external control.

ENFORCING THE LAW?

The main body of this chapter presents some of the results of a detailed statistical audit undertaken into the work of the Health and Safety Executive – the government body with primary responsibility for enforcing health and safety law in Britain.[5] More specifically, it examines the work undertaken by the HSE's 'operational inspectors' – that is to say those inspectors who actually inspect workplaces, investigate reported injuries, and decide whether or not to impose enforcement notices or to prosecute.

This chapter does not scrutinise the work of *all* of the HSE's inspectors – it only looks at those that work in the HSE's Field Operations Directorate (FOD). FOD is the largest directorate within the HSE and its 419 Field Inspectors (which represent two-thirds of all the HSE's Field Inspectors) are responsible for enforcing the law in 736,000 premises concerned with construction, agriculture, general manufacturing, quarries, entertainment, education, health services, local government, crown bodies and the police. The tables in this chapter have been compiled after analysing raw HSE data. It is the first time that such an audit has been undertaken.

It considers the activities of these inspectors over a five-year period, between 1 April 1996 and 31 March 2001, examining specifically:

1. the number of premises that they inspect;
2. the number of reported incidents that they investigate;
3. the number of enforcement notices that they impose;
4. the number of organisations and individuals that they prosecute; and
5. the level of sentencing following successful prosecutions.

It further documents how the levels of inspection, investigation, notices and prosecution differ between five industry groupings – agriculture, construction, manufacturing, energy and extractive industries, and the service sectors; between different parts of the country; and in each of the last five years. It also notes the level of fines imposed by the courts after conviction.

Contacts and inspections

A contact refers to an occasion an inspector makes some form of contact with premises. There are 14 types – the main ones being contacts involving 'inspection', investigations, 'advice' and 'enforcement'. This analysis shows that between 1996/97 and 2000/1, there was a 13 per cent decrease in the total number of contacts with premises by inspectors (Table 10.1).

Table 10.1 Total number of HSE contacts, 1996/97–2000/1

Year	Total contacts
1996/97	194,650
1997/98	178,267
1998/99	176,229
1999/2000	169,959
2000/1	169,876

There was, however, no consistent pattern in this decline. There were, for example, three HSE areas – the South, South West and Scotland East – where there was an increase. In the other 15 HSE areas, the decreases ranged from less than 1 per cent in Greater London (with 91 fewer contacts) to a decrease of 36 per cent in South Yorkshire (with 3,377 fewer contacts). A decrease in inspector contacts existed in all industrial sectors – though the Energy/Extractive sector suffered the greatest percentage decline of 34 per cent.

Of the 14 different types of contact that can be made by inspectors, the analysis undertaken showed that it was 'inspections' that suffered the greatest decline – a reduction of 41 per cent (Table 10.2). Under the rubric of 'inspection' are all planned and unplanned *preventative* inspections of existing, new and transient premises. This 41 per cent reduction represented a decrease of 48,300 inspections throughout Britain.

Table 10.2 Number of 'inspection' contacts by industry, 1996/97–2000/1

Industry	1996/97	2000/1	Percentage difference
Construction	37,774	17,908	– 52
Manufacturing	34,660	26,460	– 24
Agriculture	13,484	6,542	– 52
Energy/Extractive	2,596	1,397	– 46
Service	28,642	16,550	– 42
TOTAL	**117,156**	**68,857**	**– 41**

The decline in inspections ranged from 52 per cent in the Marches to 18 per cent in the South and from 52 per cent in Construction to 24 per cent in Manufacturing. The analysis also sought to determine how many *workplaces* FOD inspectors actually contacted, and in particular inspected, last year, and found that in 2000/1, one in nine registered workplaces had a contact, of some kind, with a FOD inspector. Again there were wide variations between industrial sectors and Health and Safety Executive areas. While one in five construction sites had a contact, it was one in twelve premises in the Agriculture sector, and while one in six registered premises had a contact in Merseyside, it was one in ten in East Anglia. Moreover the analysis showed that only one in 20 premises throughout Britain actually had an *inspection* in 2000/1. This ranged from one in ten in Construction to one in 36 in the Service sector, and from one in 13 in the North West to one in 33 in the Northern Home Counties.

Investigations

This analysis indicated that the reason for the sharp decline in the number of inspections was that there had been an increase in the number of investigations into reported incidents. However, as set out below, these levels still remain extremely low. This is significant in itself, since investigations are important, first, to ensure that any unsafe practices that resulted in the incident may be stopped, and, second, that evidence can be collected to determine if a criminal offence on the part of the company, organisation or individual has been committed. Thus, failures to investigate impact upon both prevention and criminal accountability.

The analysis shows that until recently a large number of reported deaths were not investigated. In the five-year period a total of 75 worker deaths were not investigated – 15 in Construction; 15 in Manufacturing; one in Agriculture; one in the Energy/Extractive sector; and the remaining 43 in the Service sector. This lack of investigation has reduced from 12 per cent (40 deaths) in 1996/97 to 3 per cent (seven deaths) in 2000/1. In the same period a total of 212 deaths of members of the public were not investigated – with all but two of these being in the Service sector. This lack of investigation has reduced from 48 per cent (115 deaths) in 1996/97 to 10 per cent (18 deaths in 2001).

Certain kinds of the most serious injuries are defined as 'major injuries'. This analysis shows that between 1996/97 and 2000/1, the percentage of reported major injuries to workers that were investigated almost doubled from 11 per cent to 19 per cent. This percentage also represents an increase in the actual number of major injuries investigated from 2,532 to 4,335; however, this increase still means that last year *81 per cent of major injuries were not investigated*. Indeed, looking at the whole five-year period, some of the injuries to the most vulnerable workers remained uninvestigated. There was no investigation into 905 of the 1,144 reported major injuries to trainees or 126 of the 164 injuries to those involved in work-experience.

In April 2000, following criticism by a Parliamentary Select Committee Report (Select Committee on Environment, Transport and Regional Affairs, 2000), FOD piloted a new investigation criteria policy – which has now been formally approved throughout the HSE – which sets out what types of incidents inspectors should investigate. The analysis shows that although the new policy requires them to have investigated the following worker injuries in 2000/1, a substantial number of cases remained uninvestigated. For example:

- 16 out of 62 amputations of hand, arm, foot or leg;
- 337 out of 633 injuries resulting from contact with moving vehicles;
- 69 out of 178 injuries involving electricity;
- 569 out of 1,384 falls from a height of over two metres; and
- 1,327 out of 2,396 industrial diseases.

Industry and HSE Area comparisons

How consistent is the level of investigations across industries and HSE Areas? In 2000/1, levels of investigation ranged from 41 per cent in Agriculture to 10 per cent in the Service sector (Table 10.3). This means that a major injury to an Agricultural worker was four times more likely to be investigated than an injury to a Service sector worker.

Table 10.3   Number of reported and investigated major injuries to workers, by industry, 2000/1

Industry	Number reported	Number investigated	Percentage investigated
Agriculture	647	262	41
Manufacturing	7,240	1,974	27
Construction	4,636	1,073	23
Extractive/Energy	297	65	22
Service	9,618	958	10
TOTAL	**22,438**	**4,332**	**19**

In 2000/1, only 13 per cent of major injuries (267 of 2,005) involving Transport – part of the Service sector – were investigated.

The differences between the Service and Agricultural sectors are partly explained by the high level of reporting in the Service sector and the low level of reporting in Agriculture.

It is less easy to explain the inconsistent levels of investigation in different parts of the country. These ranged from 26 per cent in the

Marches to 11 per cent in Greater London. Even though East Anglia and Scotland East had lower numbers of reported injuries than Greater London, the HSE investigated far more in the former areas – 112 in the case of Scotland East and 73 in the case of East Anglia.

What injuries are uninvestigated?

How serious are the injuries that are not investigated? This analysis shows that some of the most serious injuries remain uninvestigated, including in 2000/1, for example, 72 asphyxiations (44 per cent of the total), 31 electrical shocks (35 per cent of the total), 333 burns (57 per cent of the total) and 418 amputations (41 per cent of the total).

Looking at just one injury – that of amputations – there are great differences in investigation rates from one part of the country to another. While, a similar number of amputations were reported in both North East and Greater London in 2000/1 (63 and 62 respectively), only 29 out of 62 amputations were investigated in Greater London (42 per cent) compared to 40 out of 63 amputations in North East (64 per cent).

Most injuries result from trips and, perhaps unsurprisingly, few of these are investigated. However, looking at all other types of injuries (that is, those not resulting from trips) 74 per cent of major injuries still remain uninvestigated. In 2000/1, around 40 per cent of injuries resulting from contact with electricity, contact with moving machinery, high falls over 2 metres and drowning, suffocation or asphyxiation – a total of 1,303 out of 3,214 injuries – were not investigated.

There are even serious divergences in the investigation levels of particular incidents. In 2000/1, while 44 per cent of explosions in the Manufacturing industry were investigated, this compared with only 22 per cent in the Construction sector and while 80 per cent of high falls in the North East were investigated, only 36 per cent were investigated in Greater London.

'Over-three-day' injuries

An over-three-day injury is an injury (other than one defined as a major injury) that results in a worker being off work for more than three consecutive working days. The rate of investigation into over-three-day injuries is far lower than the level of investigation into major injuries – 5 per cent compared to 19 per cent in 2000/1. The number and percentage of over-three-day injuries investigated did, however, increase significantly over the five-year period – from 2,803 to 4,378. Again there is wide disparity in the investigation levels in different sectors (Table 10.4). The difference between the 2000/1 levels of investigation in the Manufacturing sector (7 per cent) and Service sector (2 per cent) is particularly noteworthy, since there were a similar number of reported injuries. Although there were 18,000 fewer injuries in Manufacturing, inspectors investigated over twice the number of injuries.

Table 10. 4 Number of reported and investigated over-three-day injuries by industry, 2000/1

Industry	Number reported	Number investigated	Percentage investigated
Agriculture	1,416	166	12
Manufacturing	37,127	2,624	7
Construction	9,753	478	5
Extractive/Energy	1,304	49	4
Service	55,023	1,061	2
TOTAL	**104,623**	**4,378**	**4**

Dangerous occurrences

Certain sorts of incidents – whether they cause an injury or not – are defined as 'dangerous occurrences'. Investigation into such occurrences is crucial in the state's own terms, which place an emphasis upon prevention – for dangerous occurrences allow unsafe conditions to be rectified often without the cost of injury to a worker or member of the public being incurred, and without thus raising more vocal calls for resort to formal sanctions or prosecution. Dangerous occurrences fall into two different categories – those that result in death and injury and those that do not. In order to avoid counting incidents that have been previously included in the injury sections above, and in order to take on the regulators in terms of their own rhetorical commitments, the following analysis considers only those dangerous incidents that did not result in death or injury.

The analysis shows that the level of investigation into dangerous occurrences increased from 26 per cent in 1996/97 to 31 per cent in 2000/1 (Table 10.5). Two notable changes took place in the five-year period. The rate of investigation of dangerous occurrences in the Service sector rose dramatically from 20 per cent in 1996/97 to 35 per cent in 2000/1, even though there were 99 more reported incidents in 2000/1 than five years earlier. At the same time, however, the number of dangerous occurrences investigated in the Energy/Extractive sector declined in this period by 7 per cent even though the same number of dangerous occurrences was reported in both years. In 2000/1, 70 per cent of dangerous occurrences remained uninvestigated. In that year, investigation levels ranged from 47 per cent in Agriculture to 17 per cent in the Energy/Extractive sector and from 54 per cent in the Marches to 18 per cent in Scotland East.

Table 10.5   Number of reported and investigated dangerous occurrences by industry, 2000/1

Industry	Number reported	Number investigated	Percentage investigated
Agriculture	60	28	47
Manufacturing	1,072	381	36
Construction	1,208	342	28
Service	1,035	366	35
Extractive/Energy	394	67	17
TOTAL	**3,769**	**1,184**	**31**

It is notable that the South East and Marches had almost the same number of reports (154 and 157 respectively) but the Marches investigated over 50 more dangerous occurrences than the South East.

The analysis also found that, in 2000/1, among the following dangerous occurrences not investigated were the following:

- 73 out of 128 building collapses;
- 146 out of 224 plant fire and explosions;
- 179 out of 230 flammable liquid releases;
- 88 out of 126 incidents involving a release of biological agent; and
- 592 out of 944 incidents involving failure of lifting machinery.

Industrial diseases

Certain forms of occupational diseases must be reported to the HSE. In 2000/1 there were 2,396 reported cases of industrial disease, of which 1,069 (45 per cent) were investigated. This was a rise of over 20 per cent from the investigation levels in 1996/97. This percentage increase took place even though the total number of disease reports had increased dramatically. However, it still means that over 55 per cent of reported industrial diseases were not investigated.

As with all the other reported incidents, the level of investigation depended on the industry and the HSE area in which the incident took place. So, while in 2000/1 almost 69 per cent (133 out of 194) of industrial diseases were investigated in the West Midlands, only 14 per cent (34 out of 236) were investigated in the North East.

Table 10.6 Number of reported and investigated industrial diseases by industry, 2000/1

Industry	Number reported	Number investigated	Percentage investigated
Agriculture	16	10	63
Service	642	366	58
Construction	194	96	50
Manufacturing	1,289	555	43
Extractive/Energy	255	42	17

Which industrial diseases were not investigated? In 2000/1 significant numbers of the most common industrial diseases were not investigated including 590 of 889 hand-arm vibrations, 221 of the 477 cases of occupational dermatitis, and 89 of the 161 cases of carpal tunnel syndrome.

Enforcement notices

In the course of the five years under analysis, the level of improvement notices has increased by 73 per cent (from 3,721 to 6,462) and prohibition notices by 20 per cent (from 3,605 to 4,315). In 1996/97, the number of improvement and prohibition notices was almost identical, but by 2000/1 over 2,000 more improvement notices had been imposed than prohibition notices. The number of Crown notices imposed was very small – a total of 65 throughout the five-year period – only twelve improvement notices and two prohibition notices in 2000/1.

The biggest percentage increases in the use of improvement notices was in Construction (with an increase of 192 per cent) and the Energy/ Extractive sector (an increase of 487 per cent), though both sectors started from particularly low levels of notices in 1996/97.

There was an increase in the use of improvement notices in all HSE areas – though this ranged from 162 per cent in the North West (an increase of 159) to 4 per cent in the West Midlands (an increase of just ten). And while the South had an 82 per cent increase in the use of prohibition notices, there were four HSE areas – Northern Home Counties (minus 1 per cent), Greater London (minus 9 per cent), North Midlands (minus 12 per cent) and West Midlands (minus 26 per cent) – where the level of prohibition notices decreased.

Are these notices the results of inspections into workplaces or investigations into reported incidents? In the five years only 343 investigated incidents resulted in improvement notices (75 in 2000/1) and only 473 resulted in prohibition notices (76 in 2000/1). While one incident may result in more than one notice, it is clear that most notices are the result of inspections

In 2000/1, only 27 deaths resulted in an improvement notices and 35 in a prohibition notice.

Prosecution

An inspection or an investigation into a reported incident (death, injury, dangerous occurrence, and so on) can result in more than one company, organisation or individual being prosecuted. In addition each of those prosecutions (or 'cases') may allege that more than one offence (or 'breach') has been committed.

A single death or injury can therefore result in one or more prosecutions. This analysis is not concerned with the total number of cases or breaches alleged after investigations, but with the total number of *incidents* that have resulted in *at least one* organisation or individual being prosecuted. Here, a prosecution that has resulted in at least one conviction counts as though the incident itself has resulted in a conviction.

Data in this section cover reported incidents that took place between 1996/97 and 1998/99. It does not cover deaths beyond this period due to the time lag between date of death and completion of prosecution that would mean that some incidents subsequent to April 1999 may not have yet come to court.

Prosecutions following deaths

The percentage of investigated worker deaths in 1998/99 that resulted in a prosecution was 33 per cent (83 out of 250), a rise of 8 per cent from 1996/97. This percentage increase also reflects an actual increase in the total number of deaths that resulted in a prosecution – from 70 to 83 (Table 10.7).

The rates of prosecution differ considerably between different industries and HSE areas. Whilst the percentage of manufacturing deaths in 1998/99 that resulted in prosecution was 53 per cent, prosecutions followed only 41 per cent of Construction deaths, 22 per cent of Service sector deaths and 10 per cent of Agricultural deaths. While 60 per cent of 1998/99 deaths in the West Midlands (nine out of 15) resulted in a prosecution this compared with only 10 per cent (two out of 20) of deaths in the South West.

The percentage of investigated deaths of members of the public that resulted in prosecution was a third of the number of prosecuted worker deaths – an average of 7 per cent throughout the three-year period. So in 1998/99, only 14 out of 134 investigated deaths resulted in a

prosecution. In some HSE areas prosecution was almost non-existent
– for example, in North and West Yorkshire none of the 23 investigated
deaths resulted in criminal charges. Very few of the investigated deaths
over the three-year period – nine out of 854 deaths – resulted in the
prosecution of a company director or senior manger.

Table 10.7 Number of prosecutions and convictions following deaths of workers,
1996/97–1998/99

Year	Number investigated	Number prosecuted	Percentage prosecuted	Number convicted
1996/97	285	70	25	68
1997/98	254	78	31	75
1998/99	250	83	33	82

Prosecutions following major injuries

Analysis of the data shows that, compared to deaths of workers, a much
smaller percentage of investigated major injuries to workers resulted in
prosecution – in 1998/99 it was only 11 per cent (297 out of 2,740) – and
that the percentage hardly changed in the three-year period.

There remained, however, considerable divergence in the prosecution
rates in different HSE areas and industries. In 1998/99, 20 per cent of
major injuries in Wales (34 out of 169) resulted in a prosecution while
in the North Midlands the rate was only 6 per cent (nine out of 155).
And while in Manufacturing 167 out of 1,372 (12 per cent) investigated
major injuries resulted in prosecution, in the Energy/Extractive sector,
rather startlingly, only one out of 32 resulted in criminal charges
(Table 10.8).

Table 10.8 Number of prosecutions following major injuries to workers in 1998/99,
by industry

Year	Number investigated	Number prosecuted	Percentage prosecuted	Number convicted
Manufacturing	1,372	167	12	165
Construction	658	80	12	79
Service	479	36	9	36
Agriculture	199	13	7	13
Extractive/Energy	32	1	3	1

Only four out of 7,982 major injuries that took place between 1996/97
to 1998/99 resulted in the prosecution of a company director or senior
manger. However, 13 employees were prosecuted.

As with deaths, the level of prosecution after major injuries to the public is far less than those suffered by workers – though there has been about a three-fold increase in the percentage of prosecutions in the three-year period from 2 per cent in 1996/97 (14 out of 576 investigations) to 6 per cent in 1998/99 (34 out of 549).

Other prosecutions

The number of dangerous occurrences that resulted in prosecution is very small – 39 out of 927 (4 per cent) in 1998/99. Prosecution levels are low in every industry and HSE area, albeit with wide variations in rates between HSE areas and sectors. As for investigated reports of industrial diseases, less than 1 per cent of these resulted in prosecutions. Over the three-year period only eleven of the 1,404 investigated ill health incidents investigated resulted in prosecution.

Sentencing

Sentencing following deaths

In the three years between 1996/97 and 1998/99, the average fine following a death has more than doubled from £28,908 to almost £67,000. The data indicate that this is the result of two factors. First, there has been an increase in the number of cases that have resulted in sentencing in the Crown Court – an increase from 40 per cent to 60 per cent; and second, the average fine imposed by the Crown Court for each death has nearly doubled from about £55,000 to £100,000 (Table 10.9).

Table 10.9   Sentences following deaths of workers, 1996/97–1998/99

Year	Number of convictions	Total average fine (£)[6]	Number in Magistrates' Courts	% in Magistrates' Courts	Average fine in Magistrates' Courts (£)	Average fine in Crown Courts(£)
1996/97	70	29,000	43	61	12,000	55,000
1997/98	75	43,000	42	56	11,000	82,000
1998/99	82	67,000	33	40	15,000	100,000

The level of fines imposed by the courts varies depending on the HSE area and industry. In the case of deaths that took place in 1998/99, in Manufacturing the average fine was £108,000 per death while in the Service sector it was only £16,000. And while convictions following two deaths in the North West in 1998/99 resulted in an average fine of £343,500, convictions following three deaths in Scotland West resulted in an average fine of £7,083.

The average fine following convictions of deaths of members of the public are about half the level following worker deaths – £33,200 following a prosecution for a death in 1998/99.

Sentencing following major injuries

The average fines relating to major injuries to workers are much lower than those relating to worker deaths – in 1998/99, six times less – and the average level of fines did not increase over the three-year period. The relatively low level of fines is linked to the high percentage of prosecutions – over 80 per cent in all three years – that resulted in sentencing in the Magistrates' Court (Table 10.10).

Table 10.10 Sentences following major injuries to workers, 1996/97–1998/99

Year	Number of convictions	Total average fine (£)[7]	Number in Magistrates' Courts	% in Magistrates' Courts	Average fine in Magistrates' Courts (£)	Average fine in Crown Courts(£)
1996/97	201	10,000	176	86	6,300	26,900
1997/98	291	8,000	253	87	6,900	12,000
1998/99	294	11,000	239	81	9,000	14,800

Other sentencing

The average fine following a dangerous occurrence has more than doubled over the three years from £12,900 to £28,300. One of the reasons for this is that more cases are sentenced in the Crown Court. There are again big variations in HSE area and industry. While six convictions in the North West resulted in an average fine of £71,000, in six HSE areas the average fines were less than £10,000.

The level of fines following industrial diseases has decreased by over 75 per cent over the three-year period – from £24,100 in 1996/97 to £5,600 in 1998/99.

CONCLUSION

Two sets of conclusions suggest themselves based upon the above analysis. One set of conclusions is internal, that is, regarding the enforcement of law within the state's own terms – recalling that the promises of law in the area of occupational health and safety protection are already highly limited. A second set of conclusions stand external to this analysis, and raise more general issues about the relationship between the state, law and social harm. Each of these is now considered in turn.

Several conclusions internal to the data presented here clearly emerge, that call into question the ability of the state to do that which it claims for itself. In brief, the data analysis presented in this chapter highlights the following concerns.

First, the inability of the HSE to deliver any form of consistency across both enforcement areas and industry sectors in levels of inspection, investigation and prosecution. One of the 'promises' of law is that it will be enforced consistently and, while it is clearly documented in other substantive areas that in spite of the consistent reassertion of this promise it remains unfulfilled, the analysis here confirms that this illusion extends to the area of health and safety law enforcement. Of course, consistency does not mean uniformity. So, for example, differences in levels of investigation or prosecution across different HSE industries or regions no doubt partly reflect the different types of health and safety problems that beset different sectors or reflect differences in the types of economic activity which predominate within different regions respectively. Somewhat differently, differing levels of sentencing across regions may reflect different cultures among regional judges or magistrates, or different class biases reflected in court practices. But none of these possible variables removes the need for the HSE, in particular, or government, in general, to be open about and thus potentially be accountable for, or indeed to seek to explain, such wide variations.

Second, it is clear from the data presented above that, notwithstanding the woefully inadequate level of reporting of injuries referred to in the introduction to this chapter, even on the basis of the limited subset of injuries actually reported to the HSE, that only a tiny percentage of these are ever investigated. Thus, for example, in 2000/1, 41 per cent of amputations, 44 per cent of asphyxiations, 67 per cent of burns and 40 per cent of the injuries resulting from contact with electricity, contact with moving machinery and high falls were simply not investigated. It is difficult to imagine a Chief Constable being able plausibly to defend such levels of failure to investigate, even cursorily, assaults on the part of their police forces.

Third, taking at face value the stated mission of the HSE – to *prevent* injury and disease rather than prosecute after the event, a mission statement perfectly consistent with the Robens philosophy regarding health and safety regulation (James and Walters, 1999, passim) – then one would expect an emphasis to be placed upon the investigation of dangerous occurrences – 'near misses' – yet 70 per cent of these are not investigated.

Fourth, as the above analysis demonstrates, there are insurmountable problems in the HSE's strategy of reorganising priorities within the framework of relatively fixed resources. As the above data have indicated, increasing levels of investigation have only been achieved alongside decreases in inspection. It is worth noting, in fact, that while the years from which the data presented here was drawn were ones in which there was, overall, a small increase in government resourcing of the HSE, this agency currently faces cutbacks, which are certain to affect its enforcement capability (Prospect, 2003). Of course, almost any organisation is likely to face resource constraints, but there are specific reasons for accepting, as Braithwaite and Fisse have argued with respect to agencies designed to regulate the activities of business more generally, that state regulators will never have the resources to enforce regulatory law effectively (Braithwaite and Fisse, 1987). But to accept this – and there are good empirical and theoretical reasons for doing so – is not to accept, as the Health and Safety Commission and Executive appear to have done, that there is no need even to attempt to argue for more adequate resources.

This latter point leads us into a second set of conclusions, external to the data presented in this chapter but following from it, conclusions which raise more general issues about the relationship between the state, law and social harm. This chapter adds to the body of evidence that clearly indicates that the criminal law *does not* offer effective occupational health and safety protection. Indeed, this is unsurprising since it has taken as a starting point, a premise, the vast body of evidence that attests to the fact that the criminal law *cannot* offer effective occupational health and safety protection. Yet this is not an argument for eschewing struggles around the law and its enforcement. Elsewhere in this volume (Hillyard and Tombs, Chapter 2), it was argued that while a social harm approach is clearly distinct in analytical and practical terms from a focus upon the nature and use of criminal law, such an approach does not 'deny the politically progressive tactic of approaching crime, law and criminal justice as sites or objects of struggle, which facilitate the development of focused political action'. Thus, 'raising issues of social harm does not entail making a simple, once-and-for-all choice between representing these as *either* crimes *or* harms'. While much of this chapter has proceeded on the basis that there is institutionalised condoning of widespread violence in terms of offences against health and safety law, and ultimately has pointed to an acceptance that, in any practical sense, much of this offending is and will remain beyond the scope of the law and its enforcers to deal with, this should not lead us to abandoning arguments for more adequate law and its more effective enforcement. Without entering into details here,[8] I would like to reiterate that the criminal law when aimed at offending organisations has important actual or potential qualities:

- in the area of corporate offending, the law retains some deterrent potential, since it is aimed at organisations that claim rationality for themselves and operate on the basis of calculability, as well as being managed by individuals with careers, prestige and status to protect;
- criminal law retains a symbolism as a means of marking out socially unacceptable forms of behaviour and outcomes, an important quality given the fact that many companies, regulators, academics and, to some extent, members of the public, cling to the ideological assumption that corporate crimes are not 'real' crimes; and
- for all its failings, it is clear that the use of the criminal law is that which the victims of corporate violence turn to as a means of achieving accountability and justice – not least because of the law's own claims.

However, as was emphasised in the introduction to this chapter, and as should now also be clear in terms of the scale of officially recorded harms upon which this chapter has focused, criminalisation has never formed a key part of the state's agenda. From the very rationale and enforcement philosophy of the HSE, through to the levels of inspection and investigation that it has achieved or is likely to achieve even with greater resources, to the outcomes of cases successfully pursued through the courts, the law's *promise* with respect to protecting workers and members of the public from work-related death, injury and disease is a very limited one, more or less an illusion. It is for these reasons that a social harm approach is useful in the context of seeking to mitigate the violent effects of capitalist production. Beyond a potential ability to document more adequately the scale of carnage wreaked through such activity, a social harm approach points to a range of other, potentially productive, strategies for mitigating such violence that are beyond – but not in contradiction to – the use of criminal law. In particular, such approaches are likely to point to mechanisms (including the use of law) to empower those who are most likely to be the victims of particular harms.

Thus, in the context of occupational safety and health, the weight of available evidence now indicates that the one most effective means of making workplaces safer is for these to be unionised and to have union-appointed safety representatives (James and Walters, 1999: 83). This one piece of evidence itself emphasises the fact that securing safer and healthier working environments is based upon redressing balances of power within and around workplaces. Within workplaces, this means wresting power away from employers and their claims regarding their rights to manage in an unhindered fashion. Beyond workplaces, this means challenging those ideologues who portray the protection of workers and the public as matters of nanny-state 'red tape'. And while the law – from criminal law but through public and social policy – has some role to play in these developments, these are issues of a more general struggle towards a more democratic and socially just society. To the extent that a social harm perspective might help us critically dissect and ultimately shed the illusions of law, then it may help us to further the struggle to mitigate the violence of working.

11

Prime Suspect: Murder in Britain

Danny Dorling

Murder is part of our everyday lives. Depending on the television schedules, we are exposed to far more fictional murders per day in Britain than actually occur across the whole country in a week, a month or even a year. The few actual murders that take place (between one and two a day on average) are brought vividly to our attention through newspapers, radio and television news. Some murders are deemed more newsworthy than others; thus murders of young men may appear to be occurring nearer to you, because they appear on your local news only. Some children and some women appear to be murdered further away, but no less frequently, because their deaths receive more coverage. Cinema films are full of murder, as are many of our favourite novels. The release of crime statistics related to violence bumps lesser stories down the schedules and sees successive Home Secretaries promising to get tougher. A couple of murders per year are even deemed worthy for comment by our Prime Minister. Murder sells the media. It buys votes through fear. Its presence almost certainly leads to many of us curtailing our daily activities, treating strangers in strange ways, avoiding travelling through parts of towns and cities, worrying who our children will meet. Our daily exposure to the fact and fiction of murder seeps into our subconscious and alters our attitudes and behaviour. A majority of people in Britain have traditionally favoured a return of the death sentence for the perpetrators of this rarest of crimes. They would sanction this murder, because they see murder as the isolated acts of individuals and so they think that if you kill the killer the killing goes away. What though, really lies behind murder?

A classic, and ever more popular, way in which murder is portrayed is through the eyes of its victims. The pathologist has taken a lead role in the story of murder, which they tell through the bodies and reconstructed lives of their silent witnesses, second only to the murder detective. What would we see if we were to take that approach, but

178

not with one murder, a dozen, or even the hundred or so that the most experienced of murder professionals can have dealt with over their working lives, but with the thousands of murders that have taken place across the whole country over many years? Such an approach has the disadvantage of reducing each event to just a short series of facts, and turning detailed individual stories into numbers and rates. However, it has the advantage of preventing extrapolation from just a few events to produce unjustified generalisations and encourages us to look deeper for the root causes of murder. It also makes us treat each murdered victim as equal, rather than concentrating on the most complex, unusual or topical of murders, and it can be turned back into individual stories of particular people in places and times. This chapter attempts to illustrate the advantages of such an approach to the study of murder. To follow this story you need to follow the twists and turns of homicide statistics, social indexes and population estimates, rather than modus operandi, suspects, bodies and weapons; but this is just as much a murder story as the conventional one. This, however, is a factual story of 13,000 murders rather than one, and of a search for underlying rather than superficial causes.

This chapter is structured through asking five simple questions:

1. who is murdered?
2. when were they murdered?
3. where were they murdered?
4. with what were they murdered and, finally,
5. why were they murdered?

The killer, as is traditional, is not revealed until the end and, as is tradition, there is a twist to the plot. But, although this story is told in a dispassionate way, it is a story of real people and actual events. The story behind the thousands of murder stories is more a testament to our shared inhumanity than a thriller. Murder, behind the headlines, is the story of the connected consequences to our collective actions. Murder, despite being the rarest of crimes, tells us in the round a great deal about millions of us who will never be even remotely connected to such a death directly.

WHO IS MURDERED?

Between January 1981 and December 2000, approximately 13,140 people were murdered in Britain, on average 1.8 per day. The number is approximate because about 13 per cent of deaths which were initially

recorded as murder are later determined not to have been murders
and thus the numbers are revised periodically (these deaths have been
excluded here). Similarly, deaths not thought to have been murders can
subsequently be reclassified as murder. Figure 11.1 shows the rates of
murder in Britain by single year of age and sex.

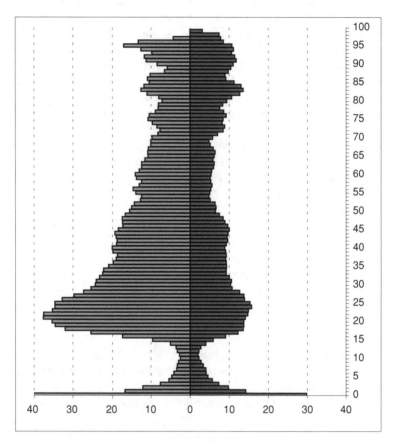

Figure 11.1   Rate of murder per million per year, Britain, 1981–2000, by sex and age

Notes: graph shows rate of murder per million per year, for the years 1981–2000, males on left,
females on the right, by age.

Figure 11.1 was constructed through examining all the records
of deaths in England and Wales and Scotland and identifying those
where the cause of death was either recorded as homicide (according
to the International Classification of Diseases (ICD) ninth revision,

E960–E969) or death due to injury by other and unspecified means (E988.8) which mainly turn out later to be homicides (Noble and Charlton, 1994). Each of these deaths was then given a probability of being a murder according to the year in which death occurred such that the total number of deaths classified here as murder sums exactly in England and Wales to the number of offences currently recorded as homicides per year (Table 1.01 in Flood-Page and Taylor, 2003; see also Home Office, 2001). It was assumed that the annual probabilities that a death initially recorded as homicide continues to be viewed as homicide would be applicable also to deaths in Scotland, although the system of initially coding cause of death differs in that country. The population denominators used to calculate the rates shown in Figure 11.1 are derived from mid-year estimates of the population and the data have been smoothed for death occurring over age two.

Figure 11.1 tells us many things. The overall 20 year average British murder rate that can be calculated from it of 12.6 murders per year per million people is of little meaning for anything other than international comparisons (British rates are low), for reassuring the population (99.88 per cent of people are not murdered), or for scaring them (you are 176 times more likely to be murdered than to win the lottery with one ticket). More usefully, the rate for men, at 17 per million per year is roughly twice that for women (at nine per million per year). The single age group with the highest murder rate is boys under the age of one (40 per million) and then men aged 21 (38 per million are murdered per year). A quarter of all murders are of men aged between 17 and 32. A man's chance of being murdered doubles between ages ten and 14, doubles again between 14 and 15, 15 and 16, 16 and 19 and then does not halve until age 46 and again by age 71 to be roughly the same then as it stood at age 15. Rates rise slightly at some very old ages for both men and women although at these ages the numbers of deaths attributed to murder are very small (as the population falls).

We often tend to concentrate far more upon the characteristics of the direct perpetrators and the immediate circumstances leading up to murder than on the characteristics of the victims or the longer-term context in which murder occurs. For instance, 50 per cent of female homicide victims killed by men are killed by their current or former male partner; it is almost always parents but occasionally other family or acquaintances who kill infants; and alcohol is a factor in just over half of murders by men of men (Brookman and Maguire, 2003a). However, researchers commissioned to consider the short-term causes of homicide also know that:

there is evidence of a strong correlation between homicide rates and levels of poverty and social inequality, and it may be that, in the long-run, significant and lasting reductions in homicide can best be achieved by strategies which take this fully into account. (Brookman and Maguire, 2003b: 2)

Figure 11.1 suffers from only telling us what the chances of an average person of particular age and sex are of being murdered in Britain in a year. For any particular person those rates will vary dramatically according to knowing more about exactly who they are, where they live, and so on. Before turning to those facts the next step is to determine the importance of when they were murdered.

WHEN WERE THEY MURDERED?

Both the number of murders and the rate of murder have doubled in England and Wales in the 35 years since the official series began. Figure 11.2 shows this series (Table 1.01 in Flood-Page and Taylor, 2003). It is very likely that the numbers for the last two years will be reduced as some of these offences come to be no longer regarded as homicide in the future, but it is unlikely that they will be reduced by much. Thus, until recent years the increase in the murder rate was slowly falling. In the first half of the 1970s the smoothed murder rate rose by 22 per cent in five years, it rose by 13 per cent in the subsequent five years, by 4 per cent in the first half of the 1980s, 3 per cent in the latter half of the 1980s, 8 per cent in the first half of the 1990s and 14 per cent in the latter half of that decade. In answer to the question of when, victims are more likely to have been murdered more recently. Over half of all murders in the last 35 years took place in the last 15 of those years.

At first glance, Figure 11.2 appears to imply that murder rates have risen. However, for the majority of the population this turns out, on closer inspection, not to be the case. From here on, data for deaths occurring in the years 2001 or 2002 will not be used as we cannot yet be sure of their reliability. Instead the four five-year time periods from 1981 to 2000 will be compared (see Rooney and Devis, 1999 for more details of time trends). It is important to remember that in calculating a murder rate it is not only the number of people who are murdered that changes over time, but also the number of people living who could be murdered.

Figure 11.3 shows the percentage change in the murder rates that all contribute to the overall change shown in Figure 11.2. Most strikingly, for all ages of women other than infant girls the murder rate has either

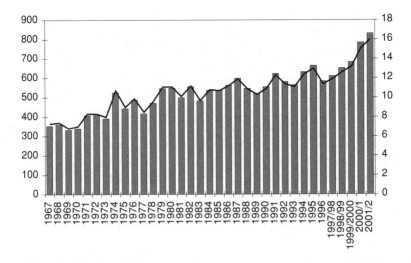

Figure 11.2 Offences currently recorded as homicide, England and Wales, 1967–2001

Notes: number of homicides per year as bars, scale on the left hand axis; rate per million people as line, scale on the right.

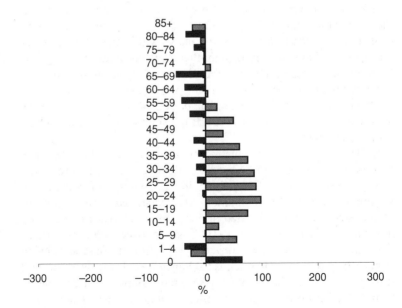

Figure 11.3 Change in the murder rate, Britain, 1981–85 to 1996–2000

Notes: light grey bars are for men, dark grey for women.

fallen or hardly changed; for women aged 65 to 69 it fell to less than half its early 1980s levels. Murder rates have also fallen for men aged 60 and above and under five. For a majority of the population, given their ages and sexes, their chances of being murdered have fallen over time, in some cases considerably. How then has the overall rate increased? For all males aged between five and 59, murder rates have increased significantly. At the extreme they have doubled for men aged 20 to 24 over the course of these two decades. The increase in the murder rate of men, and particularly young men, is enough to more than outweigh the decreases that most groups have experienced over time. Of course, this is not true of all people, and so we next turn to where these changes have occurred.

WHERE WERE THEY MURDERED?

Having considered who is most likely to be murdered given their age and sex and how these rates are changing over time, the next step in the process is to consider where these murders take place. As already touched on, it is obvious to the public at large and to criminologists who consider murder in detail that place matters. For murder, internationally it matters more where you live than who (or when) you are. Living in the US is more dangerous no matter what age you are, as compared to Britain. But then there are many places within the US with lower murder rates than places in Britain. Places are far harder to categorise than people's ages or sex, or time. However, we know that the key component to what makes one place more dangerous to live in as compared to another is *poverty*. The poorer the place you live in the more likely you are to be murdered. But just how more likely and how is that changing?

In Britain the most sensible measure of poverty is the Breadline Britain index, which can be used to calculate, for each ward in the country, the proportion of households living in poverty (Gordon, 1995). Fortunately for this study the index was calculated at the mid-point of the period we are interested in using, and includes, among other information, the results of the 1991 Census for over 10,000 local wards in Britain. For each ward we know the proportion of households living in poverty at that time. This tends to change very slowly over time and thus we can divide the country up into ten groups of wards ranging from those within which people suffer the highest rates of poverty to those in which poverty is most rare. Next, for each of the four time periods we are concerned with, we make use of the changing number of people by their age and sex living in each of these ten groups of areas.

Given that information, and applying the murder rates that people experienced in the first period throughout, we can calculate how many people we would expect to be murdered in each decile area taking into account the changing composition of the populations of those areas. Finally, if we divide the number of people actually murdered in those areas at those times by the number we would expect if place played no part, we derive a Standardised Mortality Ratio (SMR) for each area at each time.

For readers unfamiliar with this kind of approach the above paragraph was probably highly confusing. However, the results of applying this methodology are simple to interpret and also remarkable. They are shown in Table 11.1. The first line of the table should be read as saying that in the least poor areas of Britain, we find that for every 100 people we would expect to be murdered, given how many people live there, only 54 were murdered at the start of the 1980s and only 50 by the end, a fall of four per 100 expected (or 4 per cent).

Table 11.1 SMRs for murder in Britain, by ward poverty, 1981/85–1996/2000

	1981–85	1986–90	1991–95	1996–00	Change (%)
Least poor	54	59	55	50	− 4
9th decile	67	65	67	60	− 7
8th decile	62	69	68	66	4
7th decile	74	85	72	81	7
6th decile	79	77	83	88	9
5th decile	95	95	95	103	8
4th decile	112	122	125	130	18
3rd decile	119	130	148	147	28
2nd decile	151	166	191	185	34
Most poor	243	261	271	282	39
Ratio	**4.50**	**4.42**	**4.89**	**5.68**	

Note: expected values are based on 1981–85 national rates

In the five years 1981–85, people living in the poorest 10 per cent of wards in Britain were four and a half times more likely to be murdered than those living in the least poor 10 per cent. Furthermore, the SMR for murder rises monotonically (always in the same direction) with poverty: for every increase in poverty there is a rise in the murder rate, such that people living in the poorest tenth of Britain were 143 per cent more likely than average to be murdered, this rose in the successive five-year periods to 161 per cent, 171 per cent and then 182 per cent above the average SMR of 100. Most surprisingly, despite the overall national doubling of the murder rate over this time, people living in the least poor 20 per cent of Britain saw their already very low rates of murder fall further. The increase in murder was concentrated almost exclusively in the poorer parts of Britain and most strongly in its poorest tenth of wards. By the 1990s the excess deaths due to murder in the poorest half of Britain amounted to around 200 per year, that is murders that would not occur if these places experienced average rates. Just over half of that number related to excess murders among the poorest tenth of the population. The rise in murder in Britain has been concentrated almost exclusively in men of working age living in the poorest parts of the country.

WITH WHAT WERE THEY MURDERED?

What is causing these murders? How are they being committed? Is it a rise in the use of guns? This is a superficial question. It is what lies behind the murder rate that matters. A rise in drug use? Again superficial, it is what might lie behind that. Nevertheless, it is worth looking at how people by place are killed, if only to help dispel some myths. The cause of death by method is specified on the death certificates of a proportion of those who are murdered. In many cases the exact cause is unspecified. If we take those cases for which a cause is specified then five main causes account for almost all murders: a fight (ICD E960), poison (ICD E962), strangling (ICD E933), use of firearms (ICD E935) or cutting (ICD E936). Figure 11.4 shows the proportion of murders attributed to these methods and all other causes for all murders in each ward of Britain grouped by poverty rate between 1981 and 2000.

The most important myth to dispel is that of gun crimes being a key factor behind the high murder rates in poor areas. Firearms account for only 11 per cent of murders in the poorest wards of Britain compared to 29 per cent of murders in the least poor areas. The more affluent an area, the more likely it is that guns will be used when murders are committed. The simple reason for this is that there are more guns in more affluent areas. They might be legal shotguns rather than illegal handguns, but that makes them no less lethal. The use of firearms has risen in the poorest wards over the 20 years, but only by roughly an additional five murders a year (roughly one extra murder per million people living there). There has been no change in the proportion of murders committed with firearms in richer areas, despite the introduction of legislation designed to limit their use.

The most common way in which people are murdered in the poorest fifth of areas in Britain is through being cut with a knife or broken glass/bottle or (in only 4 per cent of cases, but still the largest proportion of

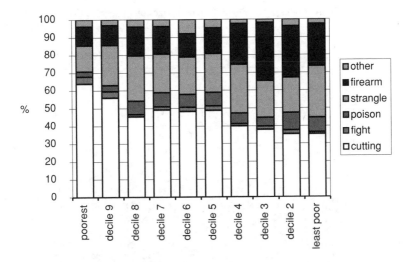

Figure 11.4   Methods of murder by ward poverty, Britain, 1981–2000

Notes: figures shows the percentage of all murders in each area by method used to kill.

any decile area) in a fight – usually through kicking. A higher proportion of people are poisoned or strangled in more affluent areas. In fact the use of poison in murder has increased its share by 15 per cent in the least poor areas over the 20 years. Perhaps those murders still occurring in more affluent areas are becoming a little more premeditated? In almost all areas the proportion of murders attributable to strangling is falling. This may well reflect the fall in the murder rate of women by men. This brief summary has concentrated on what is changing. In the round, however, much the same methods of murder are used now as were used 20 years ago, just more often in poorer areas and less often in the less poor parts of Britain.

WHY WERE THEY MURDERED?

Our final, fifth question is 'why?' Why are some people much more likely to be murdered than others and why are the rates of murder in Britain changing as they are? These are the most difficult of all the questions to address, but clearly the most important. In a way, the answer to the second part of the question – why are the rates changing as they are? – can help answer the first – why are some people much more likely to be murdered? The final table, Table 11.2, is complicated but attempts to show how the changes can be examined in much more detail to try to uncover the reasons behind the rising overall murder rate.

Table 11.2　Murder rates per million in Britain, by age/cohort, 1993–2000

				Year				
Age	1993	1994	1995	1996	1997	1998	1999	2000
11	1	1	3	3	2	1	1	3
12	1	2	4	5	3	2	3	5
13	2	3	6	6	4	3	4	6
14	5	5	6	7	6	4	5	7
15	7	8	11	12	10	9	11	11
16	13	13	17	19	17	17	19	17
17	21	21	23	24	25	26	27	26
18	24	24	27	28	28	31	35	35
19	24	25	30	31	28	30	37	42
20	26	29	32	33	30	32	41	49
21	31	33	34	34	35	36	42	51
22	32	34	34	32	33	32	34	42
23	29	31	33	31	27	27	30	34
24	26	29	33	33	29	27	30	33
25	28	30	33	34	31	27	27	30
26	27	29	31	30	28	26	29	31
27	21	23	27	27	24	25	33	36
28	20	21	26	24	21	26	35	38
29	23	23	23	20	23	30	36	37
30	24	25	24	24	26	30	30	31
31	23	24	26	27	27	26	27	30
32	24	25	25	24	25	27	29	31
33	24	28	25	21	23	27	30	32
34	22	27	26	22	21	24	31	39
35	19	25	27	21	17	22	30	36
36	20	27	29	22	18	21	25	26
37	21	26	28	23	20	19	21	24
38	20	23	26	25	21	18	21	25
39	20	23	26	26	23	22	24	25
40	22	23	24	25	25	25	25	24
41	24	22	22	23	26	25	23	24
42	22	22	21	21	24	23	22	27
43	17	20	19	17	19	22	23	25
44	15	18	19	16	18	23	22	18
45	15	19	20	19	19	21	18	13
46	16	18	19	19	18	17	15	15
47	15	17	17	16	15	16	18	18
48	13	15	16	14	16	20	21	19
49	14	16	15	14	17	21	22	20
50	17	18	15	14	16	17	17	18

Notes: the statistics in this table are the murder rates per million per year of all men in Britain by single year of age and by the year in which they were murdered (due to small number problems the statistics have been smoothed by two passes of a simple two-dimensional binomial filter). To aid reading the table cells are shaded by value. The cohort of 1965 is underlined.

Table 11.2 shows the murder rate of all men in Britain by age from eleven to 50. The table begins in 1993 because this was the first year in which deaths were recorded by year of occurrence rather than registration (year-on-year variations are unreliable before then). The rates have been smoothed slightly to make them more reliable, which has the effect of reducing the highest rates slightly. The first line of the table shows that the murder rate of eleven-year-old boys has fluctuated between one and three per million over these eight years while the murder rate of the group now most at risk of murder, 21-year-old men, has risen from 31 per million in 1993 to 51 per million by 2000. The figures in the table are shaded to allow easier reading and it is the pattern to the shading that provides our clue as to why murder rates are rising. The shading forms a triangle, and on these kinds of figures a triangle indicates what is known as a cohort effect. A cohort effect is something which affects people born in a particular year or group of years.

Take a man born in 1960. At age 33, in 1993, his cohort suffered a murder rate of 24 per million; this went up and down slightly as he aged but was still 24 per million by the time he was 40 in 2000. The murder rates that these, now older, men experience in Britain are not falling as they age, and, in general, each successive cohort is starting out with a higher murder rate at around age 20 to 21 and carrying that forward. However, for one particular group of men their murder rate is actually generally increasing as they age – men aged 35 or below in 2000, men born in 1965 and after. Why should they be different from men born in 1964 or before? Most men born in 1965 left school at the age of 16 in the summer of 1981 (some may have left at 15 slightly earlier, only a small minority carried on to take A levels). The summer of 1981 was the first summer for over 40 years that a young man living in a poor area would find work or training very scarce, and it got worse in the years that followed. When the recession of the early 1980s hit, mass unemployment was concentrated on the young, they were simply not recruited. Over time the harm caused in the summer of 1981 was spread a little more evenly, life became more difficult for slightly older men, most of the younger men were, eventually, employed. However, the seeds that were sown then, that date at which something changed to lead to the rise in murders in the rest of the 1980s and 1990s, can still be seen through the pattern of murder by age and year shown in the table. Above the cohort of 1965 line in Table 11.2 murder rates for men tend to rise as they age.

Table 11.2 concerns all men; there are too few murders and we know with too little accuracy the numbers of men by single year of age living in each ward in the country in each year to be able to produce the same exhibit for men living in poor areas. Nevertheless, we can be almost certain that this rise is concentrated in the poorest parts of Britain and is far greater there. Most worryingly, in the most recent years the rates for the youngest men have reached unprecedented levels. If these men carry these rates with them as they age, or worse, if their rates rise as have those before them, overall murder rates in Britain will continue to rise despite still falling for the majority of the population in most places.

There is no natural level of murder. Very low rates of murder can fall yet lower as we have seen for older women and in the more affluent parts of the country. For murder rates to rise in particular places, and for a particular group of people living there, life in general has to be made more difficult to live, people have to be made to feel more worthless. Then there are more fights, more brawls, more scuffles, more bottles and more knives and more young men die. These are the same groups of young men for whom suicide rates are rising, the same groups of which almost a million left the country in the 1990s unknown to the authorities, presumably to find somewhere better to live. These are the same young men who saw many of their counterparts, brought up in better circumstances and in different parts of Britain, gain good work, or university education, or both, and become richer than any similarly sized cohort of such young ages in British history. The lives of men born since 1964 have polarised, and the polarisation, inequality, curtailed opportunities and hopelessness have bred fear, violence and murder.

Why is the pattern so different for women? One explanation could be that the rise in opportunities (among them work, education and financial independence) for women outweighed the effects of growing inequalities. Extreme 'domestic' violence leading to murder, almost always of women, has fallen dramatically over this time period. Women's rates of suicide are also falling for all age groups of women and there has been no exodus of young women from Britain as the 2001 census revealed had occurred for men. Women working in the sex industry still suffer very high rates of murder, but to attempt to identify these deaths through the postcodes of the victims would be taking ecological analysis a step too far. There were also several hundred people, mostly elderly women, murdered by Harold Shipman and these deaths are not included in any of the figures here (he wrote the death certificates and only a few cases were formally investigated at his trial – and thus officially reclassified as murders). But even taking these into account, the fall in extreme violence suffered by women in Britain implies that when a group gains more self-worth, power, work, education and opportunity, murder falls.

CONCLUSION

Murder is a social marker. The murder rate tells us far more about society and how it is changing than each individual murder tells us about the individuals involved. The vast majority of the 13,000 murders that have been considered here were not carefully planned and executed crimes; they were acts of sudden violence, premeditated only for a few minutes or seconds, probably without the intent to actually kill in many cases (often those involved were drunk). There will have been hundreds of thousands of similar incidents over this time period that could just as easily have led to murder, but did not. There will have been millions of serious fights and assaults beyond this, and beyond that tens of millions, even hundreds of millions of minor acts of violence and intimidation. Murders are placed at the tip of this pyramid of social harm and their changing numbers and distributions provide one of the key clues as to where harm is most and least distributed. Behind the man with the knife is the man who sold him the knife, the man who did not give him a job, the man who decided that his school did not need funding, the man who closed down the branch plant where he could have worked, the man who decided to reduce benefit levels so that a black economy grew, all the way back to the woman who only noticed 'those inner cities' some six years after the summer of 1981, and the people who voted to keep her in office. The harm done to one generation has repercussions long after that harm is first acted out. Those who perpetrated the social violence that was done to the lives of young men starting some 20 years ago are the prime suspects for most of the murders in Britain.

12
Gendering Harm Through a Life Course Perspective

Christina Pantazis

Although women's life expectancy is increasing everywhere and women live longer than men in almost every region (UN, 1991), tens of millions of women – now referred to as the missing women – die prematurely or are never born due to manifestations of sexual discrimination: female foetuses aborted after ultrasound tests reveal their sex; newborn girls killed at birth; girl children given less food or health care than their brothers; unattended women prematurely dead of pregnancy or birth related complications; and widows slain by in-laws covetous of their property or loath to support them. (Chen, 1995: 25)

While current statistics show that women are generally living longer than ever before (see WHO, 2002b), this is only part of the picture that illustrates the passage of female lives. The experience of many female lives continues to be one lived at great risk of serious harm at all stages of life, beginning before birth and continuing into old age. Thus, the plight of the 'missing millions', first identified by Sen (1990), continues into the new millennium: each year millions of women and girls are deliberately killed or hurt and hundreds of thousands more die from deaths that could have been avoided.

This chapter examines some of the most significant harms endured by females[1] in the developing world using a life course perspective. The harms that are discussed in this chapter can result in death, disability or other serious injuries but have, so far, been ignored by the discipline of criminology. The chapter follows in four parts. The first attempts to explain why it is that criminologists have largely ignored these harms. The second develops a life course framework that is relevant to the lives of females in the developing world. The third part brings together the latest research on harms experienced by females at different stages of their lives, but due to space limitations the chapter focuses on those forms of harm which are the most significant, both in terms of extent and impact. Although space limitations do not permit an analysis of the production of harm against women and girls, my examination of the various forms of harm endured by females does allude to some common factors which contribute and continue to sustain their harmful experiences. Fourth and finally, the chapter concludes with a discussion of what the life course approach can offer to the study of social harm.

CRIMINOLOGY AND GENDERED HARM

The closest criminology comes to analysing gendered harm is in relation to interpersonal violence against women and children within families or relationships. Even so, these forms of violence have not figured highly on the priorities of the discipline of criminology, and this is especially the case with reference to developing countries.

It was not until the 1970s, with the advent of the women's liberation movement in the US and Europe, that issues relating to sexual violence, domestic violence and family violence in general started appearing on western criminology's agenda. As a result of western feminist endeavours to challenge the myth of the home and family as safe havens by excavating the private nature of violence, the state of knowledge concerning the gendered nature of violence has been greatly advanced within criminology (see, for example, Stanko, 1985; Kelly, 1988; Driver and Droisen, 1989; Russell, 1990; Dobash and Dobash, 1992; Hester et al., 1996).

Understanding male violence against women and girls in the context of unequal power relations (as opposed to individual (male) abnormality), as feminist studies have done, facilitated the opening up of possibilities for exploring the impact of male identities. Specifically, since the 1990s, there has been an emerging area of work within criminology, partly inspired by feminism, which has explored the relationships between male identities *or* masculinities and male violence, and male crime more generally (see, for example, Newburn and Stanko, 1994).

Feminist and masculinity scholars in 'engendering' criminology have made significant advances towards criminology's understanding of violence. However, the discipline's consideration of violence, if improved, continues to be narrow. The depressing picture of criminology is one that still privileges for analysis interpersonal violence between men in public places in the western world.[2] Furthermore, this is achieved in an ungendered way and, more significantly in terms of the focus of this chapter, there is an almost universal silence surrounding the harmful experiences of women and girls, particularly those living in the developing world.

It was instructive, for example, that, in undertaking the research for this chapter, recourse had to be made to other disciplines such as anthropology, medicine and development studies. Thus, in order to achieve a fuller understanding of the harmful experiences of females it is imperative that researchers cross disciplinary boundaries by stepping outside criminology. The question we should ask is why criminology neglects gendered forms of harm, as experienced by women and girls in the developing world?

This neglect can be, in part, explained in terms of the role of the discipline being largely, although not exclusively,[3] limited to analysing those forms of harms which are defined as crimes by the criminal law. Consequently, those forms of violence which are harmful but which are not criminalised are rarely the subjects of investigation by criminologists. Thus, for example, while the issue of women being killed in the course of domestic violence would fall within the confines of criminology because murder has been committed, women dying during complications in pregnancy, which may be the result of underfunded health services, would not. The effect is the same (that is, a dead woman), but the causes are such that only the former would be considered as worthy of investigation by criminologists (see Pemberton in Chapter 5 of this volume for a discussion of the limitations of the criminal law in relation to intention/omission debate). Although even then it should be emphasised that criminology has only recently begun investigating gendered issues such as domestic violence.

The role of the criminal law in constraining the remit of criminology is, however, only part of the explanation, as many of the forms of violence examined in this chapter are in fact criminalised. For example, feminists in developing countries have succeeded in making changes to the law with respect to sex selection techniques (for example, India and China), female genital cutting (for example, Kenya) and domestic violence (for example, India and Brazil). Yet, criminology continues to ignore these crimes. The other part of the explanation may relate to the fact that the enactment of laws concerning gendered harm only rarely produces convicted offenders. On the infrequent occasions where the police have undertaken an investigation of the incident and have decided to proceed with prosecution,[4] punishment is light. Courts and judges find it difficult to punish and pass severe sentences on perpetrators for activities which may be viewed as culturally legitimate and, therefore, not generally seen by society as crimes. Deep cultural attitudes can, and do, therefore remain unchallenged by the enactment of progressive legislation and criminologists are not immune to such ideas. Furthermore, the failure to produce convicted offenders means that criminologists are denied a study population on which to carry out research. As a discipline dominated by the Lombrosian project of needing to understand the causes and motivations of individual offending behaviour (see Garland, 1997), criminology has been denied access to a study population by virtue of the fact that such offenders remain absent from the criminalisation process.

Other factors, which sustain criminology's narrow focus on violence, may relate to the sexist and racist tendencies that underpin the discipline. Carol Smart, back in 1977, in her seminal book *Women, Crime and Criminology: A Feminist Critique* claimed that criminology was a discipline dominated by men who wrote on other men, for other men. Despite the achievement of significant progress since Smart's damning remarks, the discipline can still be said to be dominated by (middle-class) male researchers who study other males (usually the poor and disposed), often at the bequest of male policy-makers in government departments. Furthermore, it could also be said that the discipline is subsumed by western discourses on crime, and as a consequence marginalises issues which may be relevant to 'third world' criminology (see Banks, 2000).

The problems inherent within criminology for understanding gendered violence have given rise to the social harm perspective adopted in this chapter. Only by embracing a broader set of social harms than just those defined as violence by the criminal law can a fuller and richer understanding of the experiences of females be provided. This is particularly the case when gendered harm is understood within the context of the life course. The next part of the chapter, therefore, develops a life course approach that is relevant to understanding the experiences of females in the developing world.

DEVELOPING A LIFE COURSE FRAMEWORK

Since the 1980s, there has been a strong social science interest in the life course and life cycle. But as with most social science studies, this chapter employs a life course perspective rather than a life cycle approach, because it allows for 'more flexible biographical patterns within a continually changing social system' (Cohen, 1987: 1).

Life course writers have generally been sensitive to the notion that the life course approach cannot be applied universally: it needs to be sensitive to historical era, culture, class and ethnic group, as well as gender considerations. In particular, cultural diversity makes comparative analysis of the different stages of the life course, such as the one attempted in this chapter, fraught with difficulties. A universal agreement does not exist on what those different life stages should be[5] or how many exist over the lifetime. Nonetheless there are studies which attempt to reflect the variety of life course stages that exist to describe and understand women's experiences in different parts of the developed and developing worlds (see, for example, Katz and Monk, 1993; Sweetman, 2000). They illuminate the diverse, as well as the shared, experiences of women inhabiting different parts of the globe.

Notwithstanding some of these difficulties in undertaking a comparative exercise, this chapter utilises five broad 'stages' of the life course which are relevant to the lives of women in developing countries: prebirth, infancy, girlhood, womanhood and older womanhood.

The prebirth stage is not commonly included in studies of the life course, but it is particularly pertinent in the analyses presented in this chapter because of the large-scale harm inflicted against female foetuses. Using a medical definition, this stage of the life course represents an embryo that is more than eight weeks after conception.

Most studies of the life course begin with infancy, which represents the early stage of growth or development following birth, roughly the first year of life. During this stage, girl infants are not actively performing any social roles and they are dependent on others for survival.

It is in girlhood where roles become more properly established. Schooling typically characterises the experiences of most girls during this stage of the life course. There are, for example, over 90 per cent primary school enrolment rates and over 50 per cent secondary school enrolment rates for girls in East Asia and the Pacific, and Latin America and the Caribbean, where they are roughly equally as likely as boys to receive an education (DFID, 2001). However, mass poverty denies girls the opportunity of schooling in sub-Saharan Africa while in other regions such as the Middle East, North Africa and South Asia, poverty and discriminatory cultural attitudes towards girls combine to severely affect the extent to which they receive any schooling (Gordon et al., 2002). Middle Eastern and North African girls are 60 per cent more likely than boys to lack either primary or secondary school education, for example (ibid.). In many such societies, where sons are favoured over daughters, parents may choose not to invest in the education of girls believing that the costs outweigh the benefits (Watkins, 2001). Some girls may combine school with work (ILO, 1996) but others who are denied full access to school are put to work. Daughters may be required for unpaid agricultural and domestic labour, as well as to work outside the home in order to supplement the family's income or to pay off the family debts. Some may be contracted as bonded labourers to work on farms, in factories, sold away as domestic helpers, or trafficked abroad. Boys who are not in school may experience similar working conditions, but girls are more likely to be exposed to them.

Marriage, family formation and work are the key signifiers of womanhood. The age of first marriage for both men and women has been rising in many parts of the world, particularly in Asia and in North Africa (UNFPA, 1997) and in most countries women are delaying childbearing (Bongaarts, 1999), although as with working, getting married and starting a family may take place in late girlhood. The commencement of childbearing depends on the level of education of the mother because education generally serves to delay childbearing, as well as cultural norms related to women's social status and roles. Cultural norms in many societies often equate marriage and motherhood with female status and worth. UNFPA (1997) reports that there is enormous pressure, even among the youngest brides, to give birth soon after marriage in order to prove their fertility. Senderowitz (1995) has shown that, in other cases, cultural traditions encourage young women to demonstrate their fecundity before marriage.

Although in developing countries female involvement in the labour market is likely to occur in girlhood, it increases substantially in womanhood. According to 2001 figures, the highest rates of women in the labour force are in East Asia and the Pacific, sub-Saharan Africa, Latin America and the Caribbean. They are lowest in South Asia, the Middle East and North Africa (World Bank, 2003a). Furthermore, women will invariably combine their paid work in the formal and informal sectors with unpaid work within the home, resulting in them working much longer hours than men (UNFPA, 2002).

Differing definitions of who is considered as 'elder' in many developing countries has implications for categorising older womanhood. Western constructions of later life tend to be based on people's exit from the labour force, and their consequent retirement (see for example, Phillipson, 1987). This construction implicitly accepts the ages of 60 to 65 as a definition of an 'older' woman – the age at which women in most western countries can receive pension benefits. But this construction does not adapt well to the situation of many developing countries, because in many parts of the developing world:

chronological time has little or no importance in the meaning of old age. Other socially constructed meanings of age are more significant

such as the roles assigned to older people; in some cases it is the loss
of roles accompanying physical decline which is significant in defining
old age. (WHO, 2003: 2)

The position of many women in developing countries is that they
may continue to work well beyond the official retirement age, often until
their deaths, because they are not entitled to state support (HelpAge
International, 2002a). Even if the formal sector requires them to
retire, they may continue working in the informal economy, mostly in
agriculture.[6] However, alongside paid employment many older women
will carry out unpaid work such as child-minding and domestic work
– allowing other household members to engage in 'visible' economic
activity. Zeilinger (1999) writes, for example, that older women's care-
giving in sub-Saharan Africa renders them an important resource to
the wellbeing of their families and communities.

In summary, this section has identified five broad stages of the
life course. These stages are important because they can be utilised
in revealing the harms which females may come to experience when
passing through them. The next section examines some of the most
significant harms to which females are most at risk at different stages
of their lives.

EXPERIENCE OF HARM THROUGH
STAGES OF THE LIFE COURSE

Prebirth

In societies where sons are valued significantly more than daughters,[7]
advancements in medical technologies have made gendered harm
possible even before the birth of the child (Kusum, 1993). Prenatal
diagnostic techniques such as amniocentesis and ultrasound scans,
originally developed for detecting genetic abnormalities, have since the
1970s been regularly used as the first stage of sex-selective abortions in
East Asia, in China and South Korea in particular, but also in Singapore
and Taiwan, and in India and South Asia (Sen, 2001).

The use of such prenatal technologies in developing countries
represents a shift in technique but not necessarily in practice: in many
societies great significance has been traditionally attached to influencing
the conception of a male foetus and predicting the sex of the child
(Khanna, 1997; Junhong, 2001). However, the difference now is that
parents with a strong son preference can know, with a much greater
accuracy, the sex of their unborn child, with the result that the abortion
of the unwanted foetus is much more common.

Strong son preference occurs in patrilineal and patrilocal kinship systems mainly, although not solely, for economic reasons: sons are responsible for looking after their retired parents whereas daughters, on marriage, become responsible for the care of their husband's family. In societies where dowries are provided, girls are considered an additional economic burden. Girls can also be considered a moral burden, whose sexual chastity must be constantly protected (Khanna, 1997).

Tests for prenatal diagnosis are popular in societies preferring sons because they are relatively affordable – even to villagers (Wertz and Fletcher, 1998; Sudha and Irudaya Rajan, 1999). In their earlier study Wertz and Fletcher (1993) argued that sex selection tests were, however, especially popular with the Indian upper classes who were most eager to limit their family size to no more than two children. This group has been the hardest-pressed by demands for dowries on the marriage of their daughters. In this context, 'sex selection thus becomes a means of maintaining or raising the family's social status' argue Wertz and Fletcher (1993: 1363).

Statistics on sex selection are not easily available, but Wertz and Fletcher's (1998) survey of geneticists in 37 nations (developed and developing) found that almost half (47 per cent) of all respondents reported that they had outright requests for prenatal diagnosis to select the sex desired by parents. Majorities were reported in ten countries including Egypt (100 per cent), China (79 per cent), Sweden (75 per cent), India (70 per cent), US (62 per cent) and Turkey (55 per cent). Four of these countries (Egypt, China, India and Turkey) have a strong son preference. When geneticists were faced with a hypothetical case study of a 'couple with four healthy daughters who desired a son', one in four geneticists in both China and India said that they would perform prenatal diagnostic testing (ibid.).

In such societies with a strong son preference, sex-selective abortions (which follow prenatal diagnostic testing) are similarly popular. Kusum (1993) writes that one private clinic in a Bombay suburb is reported to have performed nearly 16,000 abortions in 1984–85 and 99 per cent of them were preceded by a sex selection test. In an earlier uncited study it was reported that between 1978 and 1982, 78,000 female foetuses were aborted after prenatal diagnostic testing (ibid.). Despite the Prenatal Diagnostic Techniques Act 1994 prohibiting prenatal diagnostics for the purpose of sex selection, inadequacies and loopholes in the law (Arora, 1996) mean sex selection testing continues in India today (Pande, 2002a). They are also popular in China, where according to Junhong (2001) 36 per cent of abortions undertaken by the women in her study were acknowledged to be female sex-selective abortions following ultrasound scans. They were most likely to occur when the previous child or children were girls or the current foetus was female.

Despite the popularity of prenatal diagnostic techniques in some countries, they present important ethical, health and social dilemmas, and harm is considered to occur not only in societies which favour boys over girls, but also in those which prefer gender-balanced families because gender selection can perpetuate gender stereotyping (Wertz and Fletcher, 1998). The issue, which is of gravest concern, is that the abortion of unwanted foetuses, following sex selection, in countries such as India and China is seriously depleting the female population. Sudha and Irudaya Rajan (1999), for example, found that for second and higher order births there are 120 or more males per 100 females in China and Korea, while for third and higher order births this increases to a staggering 185 or more for South Korea. High unbalanced sex ratios have also been found in India, and disturbingly the evidence is showing that the masculine sex ratio at birth has been spreading in recent years. Commenting on the fall in the female–male ratio of children under age six from 95 girls for 100 boys in 1991 to 93 girls per 100 boys in 2001, Sen (2001) has argued that the low female–male ratio of the Indian population is leading to a geographical split in India, with the north and east having characteristics of anti-female bias. However, this simplistic dichotomisation of India disguises within-region variations such as the 'belt of female infanticide' in the Salem/Dharmapuri/Madurai districts of Tamil Nadu argue Sudha and Irudaya Rajan (1999).

Even in the face of such population biases, others argue that sex selection follows the principle of least harm in circumstances where unwanted girls would otherwise suffer a lifetime of mistreatment (Goodkind, 1996). Prenatal sex selection, it is argued, is preferable to female infanticide or the abandonment of baby girls. Others whose speculation is based on a model of economic rationality argue that a shortage of women improves their social standing (see Arora, 1996). However, if anything, the scarcity of women relative to men should lead to more control over women's lives, not less. Khanna's historical account of the Jat community in Haryana makes this clear when she writes: 'a scarcity of women is associated with the reinforcement of purdah, increased female infanticide, the exclusion of women from education and decision-making, and the objectification of women for production and reproduction' (1997: 172).

Infancy

The greatest risk to the wellbeing of infants is disease (see Gordon in Chapter 15 of this volume). As with boy infants, girl infants face the highest risks of mortality in the population. Diseases such as pneumonia, diarrhoea, measles, malaria and malnutrition or a combination of these plague the lives of infants in developing countries to such an extent that the Infant Mortality Ratio (that is, the probability of dying before the age of one expressed per 1,000 live births) in the year 2000 was 102 for the LDCs. There are huge variations between regions with the highest ratios affecting sub-Saharan Africa (at 108 deaths per 1,000 live births) and the lowest affecting Latin America and the Caribbean (at 30 deaths per 1,000 live births). With some exceptions (e.g. India, Egypt, Jordan), which will be discussed below, boys face higher rates of infant mortality than girls and this is connected to the biological and genetic advantages girls have over boys, which allow them to be more resilient to disease (UNDESAPD, 1998). Shockingly most of infant deaths are treatable and preventable (see Gordon in Chapter 15 of this volume), but the lack of investment in healthcare resources and inadequate nutrition continue to claim millions of infant lives.

Although disease in the context of conditions of absolute poverty is the biggest killer among male and female infants (Gordon et al., 2002), girl infants face additional dangers as a direct result of their gender.

Infanticide

The practice of infanticide has been common throughout history and in many cultures of both the developed and developing worlds. While mass infanticide may belong to a specific historical era in the developed world, the killing of girls in some developing countries is still commonplace. Most victims of infanticide have been, and continue to be, female, with sex selection tending to be the main reason for infanticide (Warren, 1985). As with sex-selective abortions, India attracts the most concern with respect to infanticide, and the neglect of girls in which China is also prominent.

Female infanticide in India was historically associated with hypergamy among the uppermost castes, whereby women would marry into a sub-group above their own (Sudha and Irudaya Rajan, 1999). This made it very expensive and difficult to find a suitable husband. Since it was unthinkable for hypergamy to be transgressed or for girls to remain unmarried, girls were killed while boys were married to girls from slightly lower castes than their own in order to maximise the dowry potential. Upper caste families could, therefore, improve or extend their social-economic fortunes by having sons and acquiring dowries from daughters-in-law from suitably well-off families. Although in most cases infanticide was practised only to a small degree, in some tribes every daughter was killed so that sometimes there were no girls at all in the entire village (Premi and Raju, 1998). However, while previously only the upper castes would be involved in infanticide, the spread of the dowry to lower castes and the increasing marginalisation of women from the paid workforce have meant that other social groups are now engaging in the practice (Chunkath and Athreya, 1997).

The issue of infanticide in modern-day India came to prominence when in 1985 the leading magazine *India Today* reported instances of the practice in the Madurai district of Tamil Nadu, South India. As with the spreading of infanticide to other castes, of great concern is the finding that infanticide has spread beyond the Madurai to other districts. Chunkath and Athreya's (1997) large-scale study of infant mortality in Tamil Nadu, for example, confirmed high rates on infanticide in four districts, including Dharmapuri and Madurai where more than half of all female infant deaths and over two-thirds of neonatal deaths of female infants were the result of infanticide.

Evidence of infanticide in modern-day China has thus far been anecdotal. Das Gupta and Shuzhuo (1999) suggest that it was far more common in the past due to the country's experience of war, drought and famine. However, although Dalsimer and Nisonoff (1997) found no evidence of mothers' complicity with female infanticide, they acknowledge that it has probably occurred in China's recent history.

Discriminatory childcare practices

It is disturbing that infanticide still occurs in modern-day society, but more common is the killing of girls through discriminatory childcare practices where boys are given preference over girls in relation to food and medical care. Numerous studies now exist documenting the extent of discrimination and its deadly impacts. For example, Das Gupta's (1987) work in Punjab, India, reports a gender differential in the allocation of food, clothing and medical care to children, especially during the first two years of life, although these discrepancies were less pronounced in land-owning families. More recently, Khanna et al.'s (2003) Delhi study found that infant mortality was higher for females than for males, which they explain in terms of girls being denied medical access for treatable diseases such as diarrhoea. Chen et al.'s (1981) study in rural Matlab, Bangladesh found that girls were much more likely to be malnourished than boys as a result of female sex discrimination in the intra-family allocation of food. In China, the government's one-child policy introduced in the 1970s to limit the size of the population has been blamed for the abandonment of baby girls in government orphanages and their subsequent neglect. Even in China's best-known and most prestigious orphanage, the Shanghai Children's Welfare

Institute, 'total mortality in the late 1980s and early 1990s was probably running as high as 90 per cent' according to one non-governmental organisation (Human Rights Watch, 1996).

Although discriminatory practices such as these are normally associated with South Asia, it is probable that girls are discriminated against in other regions of the world where son preference exists. For example, one study in rural Peru reports higher female mortality patterns as a result of discrimination against females and younger children, especially infants under age one, in the allocation of medical treatments (Larme, 1997).

A recent multi-country study by the UN has confirmed that discriminatory childcare practices are responsible for imbalances in the population, but concludes that the main form of discrimination is in access to formal healthcare outside the home rather than their diet and day-to-day care (UNDESAPD, 1998). Thus in South Central Asia, there was a clear bias in favour of boys in terms of curative care: sick sons were more likely to be treated than sick daughters and to receive more effective treatment.

Girlhood

Female mortality rates decrease among older children, suggesting that beyond a certain age girls are unlikely to be killed or left to die because of son preference. Other forms of harm occur during the childhood stage of the life course. Physical and sexual abuse within the home by men – fathers, step-fathers, grandfathers, uncles – is predominantly directed against girls although many boys are also victims (UNICEF, 2000). Within the context of developing countries, two particular issues for concern have been highlighted in national and international debates. One issue is the commercial sexual exploitation of children, while the other is female genital cutting. Both of these issues are examined below.

Commercial sexual exploitation

The sexual exploitation of children covers various harmful practices including: child prostitution, trafficking and sale of children within countries and across borders for sexual purposes, and child pornography. Worldwide it is estimated that 1 million children as young as ten years of age are forced into prostitution each year and the total number of prostituted children could be as high as 10 million (Willis and Levy, 2002). Other estimates suggest that between 700,000 and 2 million women and girls are trafficked across international borders every year, although this does not include the substantial numbers who are trafficked within countries (Watts and Zimmerman, 2002). Girls are especially vulnerable to commercial exploitation because in many societies females are often treated as property.

The child sex trade is a multi-billion industry, 'built on greed and feeding on those with the least power. Children are coldly and calculatedly targeted for their marketability and cash value' (UNICEF, 2001: 1). Figures indicate that the sex industry worldwide generates an estimated $20 billion or more every year, of which $5 billion is attributed to child prostitution (cited in Willis and Levy, 2002). However, the profitability of the industry is sustained by poverty, gender discrimination, poor education, and war and conflict. Sometimes girls are enticed by promises of an education or employment, or kidnapped and then forced to work in the sex industry.

The effects of sexual exploitation of children are devastating. These are documented in Willis and Levy's (2002) study, which reports that the harmful effects of prostitution for children include not only infectious sexually transmitted diseases, pregnancy and substance abuse, but also suicide, further violence in the form of physical assault, rape and murder. They also document serious health problems, such as infants born with HIV to prostituted children.

Female genital cutting (mutilation/circumcision)

The term 'female genital mutilation' is widely used by international bodies to describe 'procedures involving partial or total removal of the external female genitalia or other injury to the female genital organs' (WHO, 1997 cited in WHO, 1998: 5). From this definition, the WHO, UNICEF and UNFPA have gone on to classify female genital mutilation according to four types. Type I involves excision of the prepuce, with or without excision of part of or the entire clitoris. Type II involves excision of the clitoris with partial or total excision of the labia minora. Type III, commonly referred to as infibulation, involves excision of part or all of the external genitalia and stitching/narrowing of the vaginal opening. Finally, Type IV is a loose category that includes pricking, piercing or incising of the clitoris and/or labia.

The term and the classification developed by the WHO, UNICEF and UNFPA include those forms of cutting that are mutilating and those that are not. While it may be an appropriate description of the extreme forms of the practice, it is not an adequate description of other forms that involve cutting but no major injury. Others use the term 'female circumcision' in preference to mutilation (see, for example, Isa et al., 1999), but this may similarly be inappropriate. Applying this term to all contexts may disguise the extent to which the practice is harmful since it implies that female and male circumcisions are analogous in the harm they can cause. I prefer, as do Cook et al. (2002), to use the term 'female genital cutting' because while being less judgemental it is still possible to discuss the serious harms which may arise from such practices.

Female genital cutting is generally undertaken in most communities between the ages of four and 14 although there is wide variation in practice (WHO, 1998). Thus, in southern Nigeria it is performed on babies in the first few months of life while in Uganda it is performed on young adult women. Typically mothers or grandmothers hold down the girl and expose her genitalia. Using a variety of instruments, such as knives, razor blades, broken glass or scissors the local village practitioner or the midwife performs the task, although among the more affluent qualified health personnel may perform the cutting in a healthcare facility.

The reasons for female genital cutting are many and varied depending on its cultural or religious context. Common reasons include customary practice or tradition, as a rite of passage from childhood to adulthood and associated with the belief that girls should be 'saved' from temptation and fidelity preserved until marriage. The practice is seen to signify cleanliness and purification. In others it is strongly related to Islam because of the significant values attached by Islam to female modesty and chastity, even though the Koran does not require females to be circumcised.

Worldwide, over 132 million women and girls have undergone genital cutting, while estimates indicate that some 2 million girls are at risk of undergoing some form of the procedure every year – approximately 6,000 per day (WHO, 1998). Female genital cutting is most common in sub-Saharan Africa (see Figure 12.1) but also occurs in the Middle East and Asia. The highest rates can be found in Somalia where prevalence rates from different surveys range from 96 per cent to 100 per cent.

The type of female genital cutting undertaken varies by country, although the most common types are Types I and II (WHO, 1998). Together they account for up to 80–85 per cent of all cases, while infibulation constitutes the remainder of all procedures. Infibulation is most widespread in Somalia, Djibouti and the Sudan, and parts of Egypt, Ethiopia, Kenya, Nigeria and Mali, where proportions of infibulated women are as high as 80 per cent (Candib, 1999). It is the most extreme form of female genital cutting involving keeping a small opening to allow the passage of urine and menstrual blood. An infibulated woman is cut open, sometimes with her husband's knife, to allow intercourse on the wedding night (Hopkins, 1999).

The physical impacts of female genital cutting have been well documented, although less well documented are the psychological

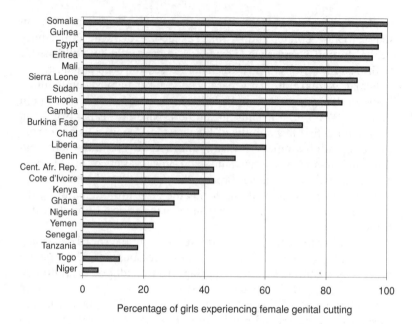

Figure 12.1   Most reliable estimates of female genital cutting

Note: based on a number of surveys carried out during the 1980s and 1990s.

Source: WHO (2001a)

and sexual impacts upon women. WHO (1998) provides a comprehensive summary of the physical consequences and complications (see
Table 12.1).

Womanhood

During womanhood females continue to experience violence, often
within their families. But the transfer of women, on marriage, from
the home of their birth families to that of their husband's means that
women now become exposed to the risk of their partner's violence
and sometimes even to the violence of their partner's families as well
(WHO, 2002c). Thus, while for many women the family can offer love,
security and support, it can also be the site of violence challenging the
idea that the family is a safe haven (Stanko, 1985).

Domestic violence

The causes of domestic violence between partners are complex. It has
been linked to individual, relationship, as well as broad community and
structural factors (WHO, 2001b), although the research base is heavily

Table 12.1   Physical consequences and complications of female genital cutting

---

Immediate complications to all Types
Death
Haemorrhage
Shock
Injury to neighbouring organs
Urine retention
Infection
Severe pain

Long-term complications of Types I and II
Failure to heal
Abscess formation
Dermoid cyst
Keloids
Urinary tract infection
Scar neuroma
Painful sexual intercourse
HIV/AIDS, hepatitis B and other bloodborne diseases
Pseudo-infibulation

Long-term complications of Type III
Reproductive tract infections
Dysmenorrhoea
Chronic urinary tract obstruction
Urinary incontinence
HIV/AIDS, hepatitis B and other bloodborne diseases
Stenosis of the artificial opening to the vagina
Complications of labour and delivery
Injury to neighbouring organs

Source: WHO (1998)

skewed towards understanding individual factors. At the individual level, witnessing marital violence as a child, heavy drinking as an adult and poor self-esteem are known risk factors in explaining why men commit violence, while at the relationship level marital conflict and male dominance have been found to be important. Furthermore, levels of unemployment and crime are risk factors at the community level, while at the structural level norms around male dominance, as well as political instability, have been found to be relevant.

While domestic violence has only recently come to be seen as a pressing social and health issue in the developing world, research has revealed that women in developing countries endure both more varied and more severe forms of abuse (Deepa et al., 2000), as well as higher rates, than men (Doyal, 1995). The violence they experience is often in the form of physical abuse, but it is also accompanied in many cases by psychological and sexual violence (Deepa et al., 2000).

The lack of an international prevalence survey of domestic violence makes comparisons between countries difficult.[8] Yet, the overwhelming finding that emerges from the WHO (2002c) comparative analysis of population-based studies carried out in different countries is that domestic violence in developing countries harms a significant proportion of women, whether in families or relationships. However, there are wide variations with women in Ethiopia and Uruguay reporting the lowest prevalence rates (10 per cent with regards to experiencing physical violence in the last twelve months) while women in the Gaza Strip report the highest (52 per cent) (ibid.).

Although potentially all women are at risk of experiencing domestic violence, some groups are more likely to experience it. One national Indian study, for example, reported that violence was significantly higher for rural women followed by women in urban slum areas than urban non-slum women, and for women in lower socio-economic classes rather than the middle or higher social classes (ICRW, 2000).

Even though in some societies women may agree with and justify the violence experienced by them, or may not consider it to be a serious form of mistreatment if it does not happen regularly, the multitude of physical, psychological and sexual health difficulties which may arise are inescapable (see Table 12.2). Health consequences can be both acute, requiring immediate treatment, but also chronic. The most serious forms of domestic violence can lead to suicide and murder.

All over the world women have been killed by their partners for the sake of their 'honour' in matters relating to marital infidelity, demanding a divorce, or even for failing to serve a meal on time. 'Honour killings' have had a particularly high profile in Bangladesh, Brazil, Ecuador, Egypt, India, Jordan, Pakistan, Morocco, Turkey, Uganda and Kenya. In Jordan, where honour killings are sanctioned by law,[9] an estimated average of 24 murders occur each year (Hawley, 2002). In Pakistan, where honour killings are most pervasive, a newspaper report cites that some 5,000 women have been burnt to death in the last five years by their husbands or in-laws in the city of Rawalpindi alone (Dawn, 2003). According to another newspaper report (BBC, 2002) the number of such killings in Pakistan appears to the increasing, while Amnesty International/USA (2003) claims that these increases are occurring because the perception of what constitutes honour has widened 'beyond defiance of sexual norms to include other forms of perceived defiance of social norms by women'. The main consideration underlying these honour killings, which cut across culture and religion, is that:

women are considered the property of the males in their family irrespective of their class, ethnic or religious group. The owner of the property has the right to decide its fate. The concept of ownership has turned women into a commodity which can be exchanged, bought and sold. (Shahid Khan, 1999, cited in Mayell, 2002: 3)

Table 12.2 Health consequences of intimate partner violence

Physical
Abdominal/thoracic injuries
Bruises and welts
Chronic pain syndrome
Disability
Fibromyalgia
Fractures
Gastrointestinal disorders
Irritable bowel syndrome
Ocular damage
Reduced physical functioning

Sexual and reproductive
Gynaecological disorders
Infertility
Pelvic inflammatory diseases
Pregnancy complications/miscarriage
Sexual dysfunction
Sexually transmitted diseases including HIV/AIDS
Unsafe abortion
Unwanted pregnancy

Psychological and behavioural
Alcohol and drug abuse
Depression and anxiety
Eating and sleep disorders
Feelings of shame and guilt
Phobias and panic disorders
Physical inactivity
Poor self-esteem
Post-traumatic stress disorder
Psychosomatic disorders
Smoking
Suicidal behaviour and self-harm
Unsafe sexual behaviour

Fatal health consequences
AIDS-related mortality
Maternal mortality
Homicide
Suicide

Source: WHO (2002c)

If women are considered the property of males, then the dowry further accentuates the commodification of women. Indeed a number of studies have linked the dowry to family violence (for example, Deepa et al., 2000). This is most dramatically evidenced in the criminal statistics which show that despite the 1961 Dowry Prohibition Act there were 6,700 dowry-related deaths in India in 1999 (Pande, 2002b), and that between 1987 and 1991 there was a 170 per cent increase in these types of murders (cited in ICRW, 2000). This could simply reflect an increase in the reporting of such deaths, but more than likely it represents a real increase in response to the rise in dowry inflation which has occurred in recent years (*The Economist*, 2003).

Maternal deaths

While women are at risk of deliberately inflicted harm from their husbands or intimate partners, these relationships are also those which give rise to the most significant cause of death and disability among women of reproductive age in developing countries. Complications during pregnancy and childbirth are the main reasons why women of reproductive age die at higher rates than men. The WHO (1992) has defined maternal death as the death of a woman while pregnant or within 42 days of termination of pregnancy, irrespective of the duration and site of pregnancy, from any cause related to or aggravated by the pregnancy or its management but not from accidental or incidental causes.

The most common cause of maternal mortality is haemorrhage, but infection, long or obstructed labour, toxaemia, pregnancy hypertension and abortion claim further lives (Sloan et al., 2001). It is certain that some of these factors are strongly linked to the lack of skilled attendants at delivery (see, for example, AbouZar and Wardlaw, 2001). Even more certain are the structural causes such as chronic disease and malnutrition, poverty, isolation and unwanted pregnancies cited by McCauley et al. (1994).

Estimating the extent of maternal mortality is fraught with difficulties,[10] but on the basis of an improved measure of maternal mortality by the WHO, UNICEF and UNFPA (WHO, 2001c), it has been estimated that throughout the world more than half a million women will die each year because of complications in pregnancy and childbirth. Further, for every woman who dies in pregnancy or childbirth, 30 women suffer injury, infection or disease, leading to at least 15 million women a year suffering this type of damage (UNICEF, 2003). Of the 515,250 annual deaths, 53 per cent take place in Africa, 42 per cent in Asia, 4 per cent in Latin America and the Caribbean and less than 1 per cent in the more developed world (Table 12.3).

Table 12.3 WHO/UNICEF/UNFPA estimates of maternal mortality by region, 1995

Region	Maternal Mortality Ratio (MMR) (maternal deaths per 100,000 live births)	Number of maternal deaths	Lifetime risk of maternal death
Africa	1,000	273,000	1 in 16
Asia*	280	217,000	1 in 110
Latin America and Caribbean	190	22,000	1 in 160
Europe	28	2,200	1 in 2,000
Oceania	260	560	1 in 260
Northern America	11	490	1 in 3,500
World Total	400	515,250	1 in 75

Note: * excludes Japan and New Zealand/Australia

Source: adapted from WHO (2001c)

However, estimates of Maternal Mortality Ratio (MMR), which take into account the number of live births allowing more reliable comparisons between countries, reveal the extent of the harm faced by African women. Figure 12.2 shows how these rates differ among countries. The highest five MMRs are all in Africa, with Ethiopia at 1,800 maternal deaths per 100,000 live births compared to the UK ratio of only ten per 100,000 live births. The fact that MMRs are consistently high across so many developing countries makes maternal mortality the health statistic with the largest disparity between developed and developing countries.

The effects of a mother's death or disability can have significant implications for the family and the wider community. A million or more children are left motherless each year due to women dying from pregnancy-related causes. As a result, older women are often left with the burden of taking care of orphaned grandchildren. Motherless children are likely to get less healthcare and education as they grow up, and children who survive their mother's death are significantly more likely to die within two years than children with two living parents (Safe Motherhood, 1998).

Older womanhood

Women who have survived the previous stages of life may have little to look forward to in later life. The abuse of older people, unlike violence against women and children, has only very recently been recognised as a global problem, although it is likely to intensify in the context of

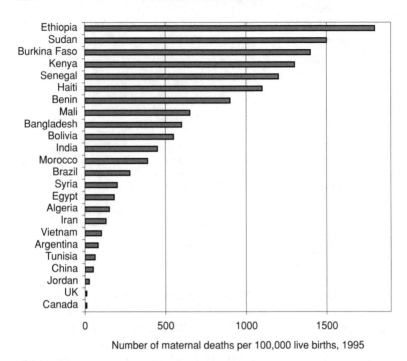

Figure 12.2   Maternal Mortality Ratio (maternal deaths per 100,000 live births) for a
selected number of countries, 1995

Source: WHO (2001c)

a growing older population. International agencies commonly define
elder abuse as: 'a single or repeated act, or lack of appropriate action,
occurring within any relationship where there is an expectation of
trust which causes harm or distress to an older person' (WHO, 2002d).
This definition allows for different dimensions of elder abuse to be
considered. However, the first attempt to define and classify elder abuse
in a developing country was provided by workshops and focus groups
in South Africa in the 1990s (WHO, 2002c). Elder abuse was defined
as encompassing various forms of violence including physical abuse,
emotional and verbal abuse, financial abuse, sexual abuse, neglect,
accusations of witchcraft and abuse by systems (WHO, 2002c). This
spectrum of elder abuse includes those forms which are normally
considered in western typologies (for example, physical, emotional,
sexual and neglect), as well as cultural customs, institutional and
societal abuse.

In a study by WHO (2002e) with INPEA,[11] *Missing Voices*, older people primarily blamed governments and structural factors for the mistreatment they experienced in their homes, in public and in healthcare institutions:

> Participants frequently mentioned issues such as budget cuts, wrong priorities in public spending, cutbacks in health care, and insufficient supervision of health care institutions as concrete instances of governments' failure in fulfilling their responsibilities towards older people. (WHO, 2002e: 10)

Country reports differed in the label they attached to describe such abuse, but many of the participants saw societal abuse as the most serious and saw it as the root cause of the violence they experienced at the personal level (ibid.). In Kenya, for example, respondents blamed their offspring's mistreatment on the deteriorating economic conditions (Nhongo, 2001). Participants in the Argentinian study defined social abuse as age discrimination, manifested particularly in inadequate pensions. Pensions, which were already considered meagre, have recently been lowered in Argentina with the result that many of the elderly now find it difficult to afford even the basic necessities of life (WHO, 2002e). On the other hand, in the Indian study, participants linked abuse to very severe acts of violence, which they said was abnormal and did not occur in their communities. Not a single person was willing to label 'lack of emotional support', 'neglect by family members', 'feeling of insecurity', 'loss of dignity', 'maltreatment' and 'disrespect' by the family as abuse (Soneja, 2001). The author of the Indian study reported that 'defining abuse was a problem'.

These discussions offer interesting insights into the differing notions of abuse from elderly people's perspectives in different country settings. However, to date there are no cross-national studies on the prevalence of such violence and very few countries systematically collect statistics relating to the abuse of older people. Consequently our knowledge of the extent of elder abuse is extremely scant and patchy. However, the recent report from UN Secretary General, Kofi Annan (UNESC, 2002), cites figures from Argentina, where 45 per cent of urban dwellers claimed mistreatment, for whom psychological abuse was the most frequently reported form. In Brazil, 35 per cent of respondents reported psychological, physical or financial abuse and a much higher 65 per cent reported 'social violence', which included negative treatment on the grounds of age, specifically in relation to government regulations.

Although these figures are not disaggregated by gender, the risks of elder abuse are inherently gendered. For example, Aitken and Griffin (1996), writing from a UK perspective, set out a very clear case for viewing elder abuse as a gendered phenomenon, not least because most elderly victims are women. This is supported by Da Silver's (2001) research into elder abuse in Mozambique which shows that women are more frequently abused than men when it comes to accusations of witchcraft (61 per cent versus 28 per cent); psychological and emotional abuse (68 per cent versus 43 per cent); and violations of basic rights (52 per cent versus 37 per cent).

Sexual abuse

Other studies similarly support the gendered nature of elder abuse. HelpAge International (2002b) reports that in the Latin American region, it is the older women who are the most frequent victims of sexual abuse by family members under the influence of drugs and alcohol. It cites another study of the townships of the Cape Flats, South Africa, where the prevalence of sexual abuse outnumbers all other types of abuse:

> When you are a mother ... left behind with children who are boys, there is one amongst your children ... he wants to sleep with you and wants that you must not talk about it ... you are afraid because you do not have the strength. He does that thing he pleases. (Older women, in Keikelame and Ferreira, 2000, cited in HelpAge International, 2002b: 11)

Witchcraft

Furthermore, in Africa accusations of witchcraft have been mainly directed at older women who embody physical characteristics considered to be associated with witches, for example, grey hair, wrinkles, bags under their eyes (HelpAge International, 2002b). Following accusations of witchcraft, women are often physically attacked, forced out of their homes and attempts are made to take from them whatever resources they might have (ibid.). Sometimes it results in murder. For example, in Tanzania an estimated 500 women are murdered every year.

CONCLUSION

This chapter has shown that, as a discipline, criminology has ignored the plight of women and girls in developing countries. This dearth within criminology has been somewhat compensated by recognition in the health, development and anthropological literatures. However, even in these literatures there has been a tendency to neglect the harm experienced by older women, as well as the life course impact of gendered harm. It is crucial that the emerging perspective of social harm takes on board both the neglect of gendered harm in the context of development, as well as how these harms are affected by different stages of the life course.

A life course approach offers many important insights into a social harm perspective. First, it can be utilised to show that women and girls face a lifetime experience of harm. Kusum (1993), for example, has noted prenatal diagnostic techniques have facilitated the bias against females from the 'womb to the grave' rather than just the 'cradle to grave'. A life course approach can therefore sensitise the researcher to the pervasiveness of harm against females and the stages which expose females to particular harms.

Second, a life course perspective can focus attention on the experiences of *all* females because it does not prioritise one phase of the life course over another. In particular, it can result in focusing attention on previously ignored harms such as abuse of older women. In the contexts of a growing elderly population and the feminisation of old age it is important that such imbalances are readdressed. Thus, one potential that a life course lens can offer a social harm perspective is that it allows for equity in the analysis and treatment of violence as experienced by women in different phases of the life course.

Third, a life course approach can reveal the extent to which women's harm is a cumulative experience. The cumulative experience of harm has important implications for women's long term wellbeing. Crucially it points to the knock-on effect which one type of harm, experienced at an earlier phase of the life course, can have on later phases. The experience of infibulation in girlhood, for example, may place women in later life at a higher risk of experiencing other harms. It is associated with complications in pregnancy – which we have seen may result in disability and even death. When for so many women the risks of mortality are acquired during girlhood, it is important that the social harm perspective takes into account just how one stage of the life course can impact on another.

While the causes of gendered harm were not the focus of this chapter, the final point I wish to end on is that the emerging paradigm of social harm will need to grapple with understanding the complexities of the aetiology of harm against women and girls. The roots of female harm are complex, multi-faced, and interrelated. Crucially they relate to the interactions between patriarchy and economic interests and are manifested in law, customs, religion, tradition and societal norms more generally.

The solutions to gendered harm are as complex as the problems. A social harm perspective will need to look beyond the narrow confines of criminal justice solutions which have had little impact up until now in ameliorating harmful practices and consequences, and look towards those proffered by other disciplines which have focused on these issues. As the development theorist Amartya Sen has argued:

> respect and regard for women's well-being is strongly influenced by such variables as women's ability to earn an independent income, to find employment outside the home, to have ownership rights and to have literacy and be educated participants in decisions within and outside the family. (1999: 191)

ACKNOWLEDGEMENTS

I would like to thank Tom Hore for his helpful comments on drafts of this chapter.

13
Heterosexuality as Harm: Fitting In[1]

Lois Bibbings

INTRODUCTION (FOREPLAY?)

Sexuality, along with other aspects of identity and behaviour such as gender, race and ethnicity, are fundamental to and underpin both our understandings of life and our experiences. Indeed, sexuality, sexual activities and identities are often the source of controversy and the subject of much (often heated and polarised) debate. Much of this discussion centres upon different conceptions of morality, normality and naturalness. Thus, while certain sexualities, behaviours and the people associated with them are more likely to be considered 'right', others are marginalised and/or castigated. Although there are cultural variations in dominant notions of sexuality, it is most often heterosexuality which is privileged or, more particularly, certain conceptions of heterosexuality. The result is that, in various ways, harm[2] can be said to be caused to those who fail to fit in through various forms of normalisation, discrimination, marginalisation, exclusion and punishment. This chapter examines this notion. It begins with a discussion of some of the dominant aspects of western heterosexuality and then focuses upon a few specific examples of harm in the context of the family and medicine.

The idea that constructions of heterosexuality can inflict harm is by no means new. Feminists, gender and sexuality scholars have alerted us to a range of such hurts (see, for example, Rich, 1980; Jeffreys, 1990 and 1996; Wittig, 1992). Such accounts describe the pervasiveness of the heterosexual imperative as well as the damage it causes. This chapter revisits this territory and, in doing so, seeks to provide a starting point for a harm-based analysis. The aim, however, is not to argue that heterosexuality causes only hurt; to suggest that it is innately, uniformly or solely harmful would be fallacious. Thus, the focus upon harm by no means constitutes a denial that heterosexuality can be a source of pleasure. Also, despite its frequent portrayal as a global norm, heterosexuality is not a fixed, monolithic or universal concept. Rather it is a historically, culturally and geographically contingent construction. Thus, while heterosexuality might (in general terms) be described as a hegemonic ideology, analysis of the cluster of ideas associated with this label and examination of its effects must recognise that we should more accurately be speaking about heterosexualit*ies* (see, for example, Smart, 1996: 170). Such heterosexualities could, for example, include models which foreground women's position, readmit female pleasure and are woman-centred (see, for example, Segal, 1994; Hollway, 1996). However, while recognising this, my purpose in this chapter is not to construct different models of heterosexuality but rather to highlight some of the ways in which notions of heterosexuality can impact upon people in harmful ways. Therefore, I will use the singular form of the word to denote the negative aspects of hegemonic heterosexuality highlighted below.

This form of harm-focused analysis is potentially helpful in terms of understanding and explaining a broader conception of hurt beyond that caused by events which are defined as crimes. Indeed, criminalisation can (in many ways) be a significant cause of harm. In the present context, for example, the crimes associated with gay male activities have proved damaging both to the individuals prosecuted and punished and to those forced to hide from the public gaze in an attempt to avoid such maltreatment.

Undertaking a harm-based approach may also prove to be politically important as a means of advocating change and planning strategy. Yet any such attempt to categorise the harms caused by a particular cluster of ideas is also problematic. Identifying and separating out a single cause of harm risks excluding the bigger picture – what, for example, of race, class, culture, ethnicity, and so on. This is not to say that heterosexuality is not implicated in harm, but merely that any attempt to explain people's lived experiences has at least to recognise the countless other variables and influences which impact upon individuals and groups. Further, identifying something as harmful where many of those 'harmed' do not identify their position as being one of victimhood (and may even embrace their 'harm') can be deeply problematic and should not be a course that is adopted lightly. Indeed, the silencing of voices of dissent or celebration can cause hurt not least by denying the agency of individuals; it should be remembered that heterosexuality is not merely ideological but also shapes and refers to a collection of bodily practices, values, beliefs, behaviours and experiences.[3]

Consequently, it may be important to consider the possible effects of naming something as harmful, not least if the purpose in so naming is to draw attention to hurt and to attempt to improve the lives of those it affects. If this only serves to perpetuate the harm and alienate the 'harmed', then any benefit of the approach is potentially lost. Strategic and political considerations should, thus, form the background to using the nomenclature of harm and in some instances it may be important to consider varying the language and tone used as well as showing respect for those involved and their perspectives.

WESTERN HETEROSEXUALITY (THE REAL THING?)

We have been cock-sure of many things that were not so.

Rose, 1999/2000: 4

To attempt to divide us into rigid categories ... is like trying to apply the laws of solids to the state of fluids.

Bornstein, 1994: 69

Despite its instability as a concept, a number of general, sometimes contradictory, observations can be said to characterise contemporary understanding of heterosexuality in western states (although there are of course local differences). Primarily, it is infrequently named and is often rendered invisible by its supposed normality and naturalness. Beyond this, heterosexuality clearly concerns sexuality – but it does not merely relate to sexual activity. Conceptions of sex, gender and the prioritising of heterosexuality are intimately interlocking, mutually dependant and mutually defining concepts. Thus, while the focus of this chapter is upon heterosexuality, it is also very much concerned with sex and gender, so there are close links between some of the harms highlighted here and those raised by Pantazis in Chapter 12 of this volume. In fact, many, if not all, of the latter could be conceptualised as heterosexual harms.

Most obviously, in sexual terms heterosexuality is supposedly the only appropriate form of sexual expression; it *is* sex. Hence, real sexuality is being 'other-sexual' or desiring the other sex (Wilton, 1996); fundamentally it requires a man and a woman – it is sexed and gendered. 'Real sex' is more specific, however. It requires sexual intercourse, the *penetration* of a vagina *by a penis*. The language itself is significant here, it is the male member which *penetrates*, while the female role is merely to be a cavity; for example, there is no talk of a vagina actively enveloping (or consuming) a penis. Thus, the very description of real sex conceptualises it as something someone with a penis *does* to someone with a vagina. Indeed, the pervasiveness of this definition makes it

difficult to find a way to speak of intercourse without mentioning the
'p' word. In the present context, I have chosen to use this terminology
in order to emphasise its significance as well as the need to find a range
of definitions of intercourse which would include penetration alongside
a number of alternatives.

This type of penetration alone (in some versions of heterosexuality)
is often viewed as being 'natural' and real. In part, because sex is
sometimes deemed to be 'for' reproduction, real sex is legitimated by
this link. For others heterosex is God given:

> Obviously the penis belongs in [or in some accounts 'to' or 'with'] the
> vagina; that this is something fundamental to the way God has made
> us. (The Right Rev. Graham Dow, the Bishop of Carlisle, *Newsnight*,
> BBC2, 16 June 2003)[4]

Other activities, even when they involve a woman and a man, may
be sexual but they are often not considered to be actual sex. Thus,
we have the word 'foreplay' to describe everything else and 'virgin' to
apply to those who have not taken part in heterosex. Here the idea of
female pleasure and, in particular, the role of the clitoris go largely
ignored. In addition, penile penetration of other orifices located within
a female body are often not what we understand as heterosex, as the
most traditional legal definitions of rape illustrate.[5] There is little
agreement as to how these sexual activities, which are less than real or
'full' sex but take place between women and men, should be conceived.
To some they are not even truly heterosexual or are not things one could
contemplate a heterosexual couple doing:

> there is a profound difference between heterosexual sex and anal sex
> which I must underline. One is an extremely dangerous activity; the
> other involves dangers, but not in the serious medical sense to which
> reference has been made. (Baroness Young, 619 House of Lords 165,
> col. 62, 13 November 2000)

Here anal sex is completely other from heterosex. Yet this view is not
universally held. Anal sex is considered to be a desirable heterosexual
activity by some women and men, particularly, according to popular
culture, by men[6] – although not necessarily solely by men:

> Heterosexual behaviour does not always equal 'straight'. When I strap
> on a dildo and fuck my male partner, we are engaged in 'heterosexual'
> behaviour, but I can tell you that it feels altogether queer, and I'm

sure my grandmother ... would say the same. (Carol Queen, quoted in Hemmings, 1993: 132)

This is perhaps not a commonly held perspective but it is clear that some view heterosexual behaviour far more broadly than the Bishop of Carlisle and Baroness Young. Indeed, magazines and popular sex guides advocate play, experimentation and improved technique to enhance heterosexual activities (for example, see Comfort, 2002). However, even here real sex tends still to mean one thing and be privileged – albeit in a wide range of potential positions – despite the fact that, as Stevi Jackson points out:

There is nothing intrinsic to male and female anatomy which ... privileges certain sexual practices above others. There is no absolute reason why the conjunction of a penis and a vagina has to be thought of as penetration, or as a process in which only one of those organs is active. (Jackson, 1996: 33)

Nevertheless, heterosexual anal sex is likely to be conceived of as less unacceptable than male-on-male penetrative engagement. Indeed, the latter has been more likely to attract criminal liability and punishment than the former (see for example *ADT* v. *United Kingdom*).[7] Thus, the ownership of the orifice is often conceived of as being more important than the actual orifice involved; an anus or mouth has a sex which must be other. In this model gay male sex is supposedly unacceptable, unnatural and evil. Indeed, this perspective has been intensified by misinformation and propaganda describing AIDS as the 'gay plague' (for example, see American Family Association c. 1983, quoted in Patton, 1985: 850). Moreover, it seems to be a perversion of the norm in that it apes heterosexuality by focusing upon penetration but not of the straightway (the vagina). Confusingly though, the fact that it involves something akin to real sex can make it more offensive, to some men more threatening and yet also more understandable in terms of a desire to penetrate.

What then of lesbians? If sex is penetration and, more specifically, the penetration of a vagina by a penis then what is 'lesbian sex'? Or to pose this question in its most common form: 'What do lesbians do?' Is it ever sex or can it only amount to foreplay? Can heterosexuality take lesbians seriously? Lesbians, then, fail to fit in; in fact they fail to fit together. As Wilton (1996) has pointed out, this heterocentric perspective leads people to ask, 'Who is the man?' in an attempt to impose difference or to straighten homosexuality. However, lesbianism has tended to be viewed as less troubling than male-on-male sex perhaps, in part, precisely because heterosexuality dictates that there is nothing akin to real sex involved (Herek and Capitanio, 1996; Kite and Whitley, 1998). As a result, lesbian sex has tended to be more likely to escape criminalisation than gay male sex. Instead, lesbianism is sometimes considered chic or viewed as being titillating for the heterosexual male – although in some contexts concerns are raised about its unnaturalness and its troubling or threatening nature (for example, where lesbian parenthood is concerned, see S.B. Boyd, 1992; Beresford, 1998).

Sexuality, though, is not a question of falling into one category or another – of always being either homosexual or heterosexual – of being *monosexual*. Sexual identities, thoughts and/or experiences are not this clear cut as both desires and actions can cut across these supposedly bordered orientations. Yet the tendency or need is to talk not of people as *sexual* but as having or embodying a *particular sexuality*. A person is straight or gay and we need to know who they are. They might have had little lapses, indulged in adolescent, drunken or curious experimentation, opted for 'situational homosexuality' (behavioural bisexuality) or have mistaken, denied or hidden their true selves, but these are all temporary situations – their sexuality is concrete and knowable. This is not to say that the label 'bisexual' does not exist, but rather that it seems often to be viewed as a way of saying that an individual is undecided, confused or even unstable. Seemingly, bisexuality (like, as we shall see, intersex) is sometimes taken to signify an identity-in-the-making rather than something which is complete. It can be hard to categorise as an identity and stereotype because it refuses to fit the hetero/homo binary which requires a desire for *either* men or woman. Or as Moshe Shokeid (2001) puts it: 'You Don't Eat Indian and Chinese Food at the Same Meal'.

Thus, as Rust suggests, sexuality needs to be reconceptualised in order to create space for bisexuality – otherwise (conceptually at least) it remains a non-identity or an invisible identity (2000: 207–9; see also Yoshino, 2000).[8] Consequently, those who *identify as* bisexual occupy an uneasy position in relation to both heterosexuals and homosexuals and may suffer the effects of 'biphobia' as a result. However, comparatively little scientific attention has been paid to bisexuality or to societal attitudes to bisexual people and often biphobia has been assumed to be identical to homophobia. Studies suggest that the latter is not the case. For example, within the lesbian community there is a tendency to be suspicious or dismissive of bisexual women (see, for example, Rust, 1993; Garber, 1995: 20–1; Esterberg, 1997). Also, although gay and lesbian activists and support organisations often now tend to include bisexual people,[9] some gay activists see any talk of bisexuality as diluting the coherence of the community. This they feel can be particularly damaging – especially in a time of attack (Tisdale, 1998). In terms of heterosexuals one US study found that, although there was a high degree of correlation between biphobia and homophobia, negative attitudes about bisexuals, particularly in men, were more prevalent than negative attitudes about lesbians or gay men. This suggests that, as the study concluded, biphobia and homophobia should be considered related, but distinct, phenomena (Eliason, 1997).

However, as the above discussion suggests, heterosexuality is not just about sexual activity and sexual orientation; it is also more generally about ways of being. Its ontology is dimorphic (occurring in two distinct forms) and hierarchical; one can only be male and masculine or female and feminine (in that order). Each of these categories is often rigidly delineated in terms of the behaviour and the bodily geography which is required – and everyone *must* be one or the other. The male always comes first, is dominant and the norm against which the Other is measured. He is active, thrusting, firm bodied, aggressive, impregnable and has a penis. The female comes second (if she comes at all), is problematic in her difference, is passive, soft and leaky bodied, retiring, impregnatable, has a vagina and lacks a penis. We know from the classics of sexology that he is the hunter, she the hunted, naturally resisting and fearing capture but in reality enjoying it (see, for example, the analysis in Jeffreys, 1990: 119). Thus, however often repeated, 'no' really means 'yes'. More generally, heterosexuality tends to prioritise certain femininities and masculinities and foregrounds male dominance – in this conception it is a male-centred ideology (although not one that advantages all men).

Just as notions of heterosexuality, sex and gender are overlapping, so too are our understandings of sex and gender. Indeed, even the conventional wisdom that sex is the biological while gender is the socially constructed is problematic. As Jackson and Scott among others argue, sexual differences should be seen as social cultural practices (Jackson and Scott, 2001). Nature does not determine what a female or male body is. Thus (supposedly biological) sex is as much a social construct as is gender and in semiotic terms 'sex', 'gender', 'woman', 'man', 'male' and 'female' have no inherent significance until different cultural meanings are ascribed to them (see, for example, Delphy, 1984: 144; Butler, 1990). Indeed, we know that some cultures do not restrict their understandings of sex identity to male and female and that some are far more accepting than others of the mutability of both sex and gender (see, for example, Edgerton, 1964; Williams, 1986; Herd, 1996). This, however, makes it all the more difficult (linguistically and conceptually) to analyse the concepts 'sex' and 'gender'. If they are so interwoven, would it not be more accurate to talk of 'sex and gender' as one thing? Does this reconceptualisation require a commentator to conflate the two, despite the fact that they are still widely understood to be distinct? For present purposes the latter observation provides the answer. Thus, while I agree that sex and gender are not discrete, in this chapter I have sought to use 'sex' when I am talking about that which is so often considered to be biological, and 'gender' when I refer to what is usually described as being socially constructed. However, given the nature of the subject matter, this separation tendency is undermined or disrupted.

Transgender[10] and, in particular, transsexual and intersex people disrupt our understandings of sex and gender. Whatever their sexuality, intersex and transsexual people sometimes pose very significant dilemmas for heterocentric societies. Such individuals challenge the notion that we can categorically know, once and for all, the sex, gender and sexuality of a person and, consequently, they present dangers for the supposedly natural binaries that are assumed to underpin heterosexuality. Thus, often there are attempts in law and medicine to 'fix' the sex and gender of a person in an appropriate and clearly bounded identity.

Many transsexual people tend to adopt very conventional, congruent sex and gender identities (albeit sometimes because they are forced to do so in order to gain access to 'reassignment' and social acceptance), although some opt for a 'third sex' identity or resist categorisation. Transsexual people may be bisexual, gay, lesbian, straight, they may be non-operative, pre-operative, or have undergone partial or complete reassignment. Nevertheless, all transsexual people still pose problems for the heterosexual order in that they are viewed as electing to pervert nature, to alter the (supposedly biological) sex (and gender) they were born with. Consequently, they are often seen as dysfunctional, as a category of homosexual, and as their birth certificate sex; their identity is denied. They can face a range of obstacles from accessing (free) medical procedures (however, see Dyer, 1999; *R.* v. *North West Lancashire HA Ex p. A*)[11] and changing their sex for legal purposes, to facing discrimination in society (for example, see *Guardian*, 15 August 2003) and the workplace (for example, see *Croft* v. *Consignia Plc*[12] and the mixed messages in *Chief Constable of West Yorkshire* v. *A*).[13] Thus, there is resistance to transgendered people in society as a whole. Beyond this, there is also (at the very least) distrust from some sectors of the lesbian and gay community. For example, Ann Ogborn, a transgender activist who identifies as bisexual, goes so far as to refer to the attitude of some in the gay community as 'genocidal' (quoted in Greenberg, 1993: 51–2; see further Rose, 1999/2000: 50–2).

Intersex, too, challenges definitions of sex and gender and, thus, also of heterosexuality. P.-L. Chau and Jonathan Herring discuss some of the difficulties intersex can pose for social, medical and legal orthodoxy, and emphasise three crucial points. First, that it is not possible to classify everyone in scientific terms as either clearly male or female. However, this does not mean that it is hard to find out whether an intersex person is male or female. Instead, even knowing everything there is to know about a person does not help because not all people do not fall into the accepted bodily description of male or female. Second, alternative classifications do not work. It is not accurate to talk of three sexes, as there is a vast and diverse range of intersex conditions. Moreover, a scale of maleness and femaleness would be unsatisfactory as in some respects a person may be classified as male and in other aspects female. Third, they point out that intersex, far from being an illness, is in fact natural in human and non-human animals (just as same-sex sex is), thus it should not be assumed that 'treatment' is the appropriate response (Chau and Herring, 2002: 332).

In intersex, then, hormones, social identity, observed characteristics (the phenotype) of the individual, and the various biological criteria are not always congruent. However, a wider point can be emphasised: bodies vary, and even within the assumed boundaries of the usual there are massive differences. One need only cite differences in breast size and the size of the visible part of the clitoris among those categorised as female and differences in penis size in those categorised as male. Indeed, hormonal levels also vary considerably and fluctuate throughout a lifetime. This variety might mean that, for example, a particular man might have lower levels of testosterone than a particular woman does. Yet both society and medicine tend to assume that women and men can be unproblematically defined, identified and clearly distinguished without any need for testing and measuring. It is only when unignorable variations are identified that questions are asked and even here, once asked, they are often swiftly swept away.

This need for certainty represents a fear of the liminality which intersex people embody – their existence denies the truth of simple, natural binaries and, thereby, threatens the basis of the heterosexual order. Thus, as we shall see, where ambiguity exists, action is often taken to ensure that a person is, in so far as this is possible, fitted into one sex and its matching gender.

HETEROSEXUALITY AS HARM (MISSFITS?)

Hatred, prejudice, lack of understanding, marginalisation, homophobia and, more generally, the pressure or compulsion to conform cause harm in different spheres of activity and in many varied ways. Indeed, attitudes in themselves can be hurtful and there is evidence that negative attitudes to 'non-heterosexuals' are pervasive in some societies. For example, recent studies in the US have consistently revealed that, despite some shifts over the last 30 years, most adults still hold negative attitudes towards homosexual behaviour, viewing it as wrong and unnatural (Herek and Capitanio, 1996; Yang, 1997). In addition, in a 1992 national survey over half the heterosexual respondents expressed disgust for gay men and lesbians (Herek, 1994). Further, the US study of attitudes to bisexuals suggested that those who were homophobic were highly likely to be biphobic as well (Eliason, 1997). Despite this, there are studies that suggest that most Americans believe that gay people should not be denied employment or basic liberties. There is, however, a reluctance to treat homosexual people in the same ways as heterosexual people. Thus, for many of those who favour some level of recognition, same-sex domestic partnerships are considered acceptable, while same-sex marriages are opposed (Yang, 1997).

The range of hurts caused by heterosexuality is broad. Here I have chosen to be selective and to focus upon a very few examples relating to the family and medicine. This leaves out many of the most obvious aspects of heterosexuality as harm, although some of these are mentioned elsewhere in this chapter. Most notably, the significant harm caused by the criminalisation of 'unheterosexual' activities is omitted, as is the failure of criminal law to protect from or react to hate crime directed at homosexuals.

The harms discussed below vary in severity and, while some affect large numbers, others only directly impact upon relatively few individuals. The latter are included because of their extreme nature and because they are particularly revealing in terms of both heterosexuality and heterosexuality as harm. I have focused upon examples from the west and, in particular, the United States and England and Wales because of cultural variations in the construction of appropriate sexuality.

A recent trend, however, has been the move towards attempting to legislate to lessen, remove or punish some of the harm caused to some 'non-heterosexuals'. Some of these developments are mentioned below. While such moves are in general terms a positive step they will not guarantee an end to prejudice, discrimination and hatred. In addition, these developments are often the result of compromise and thus, while they purportedly seek to mitigate harm, they often still perpetuate heterocentricity. However, they do constitute a significant reversal in states which previously used law (or the absence of law) to discriminate against, oppress and exclude those who did not fit.[14]

Thus, in some jurisdictions the law (criminal and civil) which once caused harm to 'non-heterosexuals' is at least purporting to remove hurt by decriminalising 'homosexual practices', criminalising anti-gay hate crime, making discrimination illegal and recognising some rights for those who fail to fit in.

The family

Although the idea of the family is culturally contingent, conceptions of the familial often tend to be heterocentric. Notions of the family in the west tend to focus upon a cosy heterosexual unit, which may take different forms but is assumed to have at its core a woman and man, married or unmarried, who cohabit in a sexual relationship and reproduce. In this model it is often assumed that the man provides and the woman supports him, is primary carer for the children and does most of the domestic labour. Despite the fact that an increasing number of living arrangements and relationships do not conform to this model, those who appear to fail to reflect this heterocentric ideal still risk less favourable treatment and criticism or condemnation. For example, in *B* v. *B*[15] the English judiciary found it difficult to understand why a father would give up paid employment to stay at home and look after his child (see further Collier, 1995: 196–7). But it is those 'families' that are judged completely to fail to be heterosexual which tend to come in for the most attention. For example, in England and Wales the infamous Section 28 of the Local Government Act 1988 continued to prohibit local authorities from 'promoting' either homosexuality or the acceptability of 'pretended family relationships' (lesbian and gay relationships) until its repeal (Section 122 Local Government Act 2003). The message here was that some families were not real and, therefore, could only falsely purport to be in any way familial.

The construction and regulation of marriage provides a wealth of illustrations of the harm which heterosexuality causes. For example, same-sex marriage remains largely unrecognised. Although not all couples want a right to marry, this excludes many not only from selecting this public and legal recognition of their relationships but also from a range of benefits that result from marriage (for example, inheritance provisions, pension entitlement, tax allowances, immigration, asylum). In England and Wales, gay marriages remain unrecognised, although in June 2003 the government published a consultation document proposing a new legal status of 'registered partner' (Women and Equality Unit, 2003). Although the document does suggest that registered civil partners would acquire a package of rights and responsibilities, it is not clear whether registered gay couples are to be offered exactly the same legal rights as married couples. Moreover, it is not presently envisaged that this would apply to heterosexual couples who reject marriage. Thus, the current proposals, while an improvement, maintain marriage as the privileged preserve of the other-sexual by excluding the same-sexual and effectively penalising other-sex couples who do not espouse the truly heterosexual union.

The partnership (compromise) model seems to be an emerging trend in a number of western jurisdictions. Some EU member states and US states, Canada and Australia have introduced some form of civil partnership registration scheme. Denmark introduced the first civil partnership registration scheme in 1989. The degree of rights attached to the different schemes varies, and some allow heterosexual couples to opt in.

In the US, gay marriage is unrecognised (however, see the discussion of transsexual marriage below) and 37 states have enacted anti-same-sex marriage laws (which affect lesbian, gay, bisexual, transsexual and potentially some intersex people). However, ten states and the District of Columbia provide health insurance benefits to the domestic partners of government employees.[16] Only in Vermont can couples enter into civil unions and receive the same state benefits as married couples (15 VSA 1201–1207). Despite this, all same-sex couples are denied the more than 1,000 federal benefits and protections of marriage.

Nevertheless, there are some signs of a liberalisation of attitudes in the US, although it seems that this shift is unlikely to be reflected in federal policy. There is some evidence of support for a limited form of civil union, although many remain wary and hostile towards the idea of gay marriage (see, for example, Kaylan, 2003). As to the future, state courts in Massachusetts and New Jersey are poised to decide lawsuits challenging the non-recognition of same-sex marriage, and a similar case in Indiana which was initially dismissed is expected to be appealed.[17] However, members of the House of Representatives have proposed a ban on gay marriages to counter the trend for some states to grant legal recognition to gay unions.[18] In addition, President George Bush has stated that he wants to 'codify' marriage to ensure it stays 'between man and woman' (*Guardian*, 1 August 2003).

However, some countries are moving in the opposite direction. Until very recently only the Netherlands allowed gay couples to marry (introduced in 2000). On 30 January 2003 the Belgian parliament passed a law allowing same-sex marriages which came into force in May 2003.[19] More recently, the Canadian position has shifted. The provinces of Ontario and British Columbia now allow same-sex couples to marry and many such unions have already taken place.[20] More significantly, the Canadian government has since announced that the Canadian legislature will consider legislation to permit marriage by same-sex couples nationwide.[21]

Transsexuals (and occasionally intersex people) also sometimes fail to fit into marriage law provisions, whether they are bisexual, straight, lesbian or gay. The infamous English case of *Corbett* v. *Corbett*[22] illustrates some of the heterocentric attitudes and opinions which harm transsexuals and others. The decision is dated and its legal status is currently, to say the least, highly questionable following two decisions by the European Court of Human Rights and a recent House of Lords' Statement of Incompatibility under the Human Rights Act 1998.[23] However, *Corbett* technically still represents the current state of English law, although it seems that this is set to change, and the attitudes which the case embodies are unfortunately by no means eradicated.

In *Corbett* Ormrod J., a judge with a medical background, prioritised biological sex; a man was always a man and could never marry another man even were 'he' to identify as female and/or undergo a full 'sex-change'. In so deciding he discussed the role of a woman in marriage. In his view this is to be in possession of a *natural cavity* which is capable of receiving a male member – to have the 'capacity for natural sexual intercourse is an essential element' (105). Yet it seems that, as the Court of Appeal had already found, a woman whose body cannot permit intercourse without medical intervention can be deemed capable of intercourse and marriage because of both her (natural) sex and the possibility of treatment.[24] From this approach sex is fixed at birth by doctors; a man is always a man and a woman is always a woman. The only exception to this statement relates to intersex people who, perhaps because their liminality is perceived to be *natural* rather than a *matter of choice*, are more likely to be legally recognised in their 'chosen' sex.[25]

In *Corbett* there was no contemplation of the possibility of not identifying an individual as being either a male or a female. There was a need to divide and distinguish, fixing sex and gender identity from birth (perhaps) so that one (or more precisely a man) can know the sex/gender of the person he is penetrating. Thus, it is not the artificially constructed vagina that is at issue but rather the perception that the person involved *is still* male and for the purposes of sex will always be male regardless of the fact that he might lack a penis and have a vagina. This decision excludes the possibility of any sex other than the penetration of a 'natural' vagina being real or natural sex, prevents same-sex marriage, stops (some) transsexuals marrying and thereby causes harm. However, the strange, narrow and ill thought out logic of *Corbett* does not mean that a transsexual person cannot be married or

marry. If the individual was already validly married to someone of the
opposite sex in their pre-change days the marriage is still valid and will
only be terminated in divorce or other proceedings unrelated to their
transsexual identity – despite the fact that the marriage *may* appear to
be a same-sex union. Also, a transsexual person can technically marry
anyone as long as that person is of the opposite sex to their birth sex
– to all outward appearances and to the couple themselves, the marriage
in this case *may* again be a same-sex union. In addition such a union
may be between two transsexuals.

In England and Wales proposed legislation offers the possibility of
both alleviating and perpetuating harm.[26] The Draft Gender Recognition
Bill 2003 allows for a person to apply for a gender recognition certificate.
In order to be successful certain conditions need to be met and, in
particular, the person must be able to prove both their gender dysphoria
and their 'new' identity using expert medical evidence (clause 2). So the
process is likely to be extremely onerous, as there is a need repeatedly
to prove identity – initially to the psychologists and medics who decide
upon their 'condition' and 'treatment', then to the medics who give
evidence about their identity, and finally to the panel of psychologists,
medics and lawyers who assess their application (Schedule 1). Where a
full certificate is issued the person becomes for all intents and purposes,
including marriage, the 'acquired gender' (clause 5). However, while
this would grant some recognition for some transsexuals, it perpetuates
marriage as being the preserve of heterosexuality and reaffirms the
binary nature of sex and gender as a person always has to be legally
categorised as female or male. Thus, where at the time of application
a person is validly married to a person of their 'acquired gender', an
interim certificate will be granted until the marriage is annulled or
dissolved or the spouse dies (clause 3). Once a full certificate is granted a
person can marry in their 'acquired gender' – that is they can only marry
a person of the opposite sex to their newly recognised identity. In terms
of keeping up appearances at least, wherever possible, marriage is only
for other-sex couples and all people have to be categorised as female
or male. However, the Bill does not provide a foolproof formula for
achieving this. In fact, it could be used in such a way as to make it at least
theoretically possible for all transsexual people to marry (should they
choose to do so), whatever their sex, gender or sexuality. Thus, without
a full certificate a validly married couple could remain married and,
presumably, a transsexual person without recognition could marry in
their birth sex. Also, an application for a certificate (if successful) would
allow a transsexual person to marry in their 'acquired gender'. However,
some transsexual people may either fail to fit into the proposed model

or be forced to choose between marriage and recognition. For example, a male-to-female transsexual may wish to be recognised as a woman but might also desire to be married to another woman.

In the US, the legal position varies considerably from state to state and is often incoherent. In the main, confusion arises because of failure to consider transsexuals in legislation – old marriage laws talk of a union between a man and a woman (without definition) while defence of marriage statutes focuses upon prohibiting lesbian and gay unions. As a result, the courts are left to grope a pathway through the issues with little or no guidance apart from their own often limited and confused understandings of sex, gender and sexuality. The result is a fairly haphazard and confusing tapestry of responses. For example, on 21 February 2003 in Clearwater, Florida, a judge ruled that Michael Kantaras, a female-to-male transsexual, was legally male at the time of his marriage to a woman and so a divorce could be granted.[27] Here not only was there a change of legal identity and, thereby, a valid marriage but also Kantaras was awarded primary custody of the couple's two children.

In contrast, Texas law prohibits same-sex and, thus, transsexual marriage (Tex. Fam. Code Ann. 2.001(b)). The legal position is, therefore, effectively the same as it has been in England and Wales under *Corbett*. For example, in 1999, an appellate court in San Antonio, Texas, invalidated a seven-year marriage between Christine Littleton, a transsexual woman, and her deceased husband.[28] Ironically, given that a dominant theme of the *Littleton* decision was to ensure the prevention of (supposedly) same-sex marriage,[29] as an unintended result of *Littleton* some same-sex marriages within Texas became legal. Thus, on 16 September 2000, Ms Jessica Wicks and Ms Robin Manhart Wicks were legally married in San Antonio because their original birth certificates categorised them as 'girl' and 'boy' respectively (*San Antonio Express-News*, 7 September 2000). Another unanticipated result of *Littleton* is that married couples who were forced by doctors to divorce as a condition of surgery are now able to remarry (see further Frye and Meiselman, 2001: 1034).

Medicine

There are many possible historical and contemporary examples of attempts to tame, punish and/or remould the body, to inscribe straightness upon the flesh as well as the mind. Such instances could be said to include many strategies aimed at making women and men fit in – not least to each other. Thus, various social, cultural, legal and medical pressures or interventions have sought and still seek to heterosexualise the bodies and minds of women and men. There are many such examples in the field of medicine. For example, doctors have often sought to 'cure' people by punishing their bodies for their failure to conform or by reconfiguring them in the hope of producing more (appropriately) heterosexual behaviour and desire – or at least eradicating homosexual desire with scant or a warped regard for autonomy. Indeed, it was not so long ago that homosexuality was defined as a psychiatric illness requiring treatment.[30]

Attempts to ensure and enforce heterosexual conformity among men and women, girls and boys have also sometimes resulted in the removal or reshaping of healthy body parts. Clitoridectomy (a form of female circumcision) has been used by doctors in the US and Europe (contradictorily) to 'cure' hysteria as well as perceived frigidity and nymphomania (Showalter, 1991: 130). In addition, at least one doctor undertook female genital alterations to correct what he felt was a failure to evolve sufficiently on the part of the female of the species with devastating results (*New York Times*, 11 December 1988 and 26 January 1989).

Men too have had healthy body parts removed. The perceived need to curb male 'self abuse' in part led the US medical establishment in the twentieth century (and still to a significant extent today) to see the practice of infant male circumcision as routine. According to this approach, masturbation was immoral and unhealthy, it distracted men from their natural duty (to achieve satisfaction through the normal heterosexual channel, thereby not wasting their seed), and could lead to homosexuality and impotence. The removal of the foreskin, it was assumed, would reduce the urge to masturbate as the effort required to reach orgasm would be all the greater given the lack of a retractable and highly sensitive foreskin (see further Gollaher, 1994). Today, amid conflicting evidence of the potential medical benefits of routine circumcision (see, for example, Council on Scientific Affairs and American Medical Association, 1999; Szabo and Short, 2000; Warner, 2000; Lamptey, 2002), the procedure is still fiercely defended by the US medical establishment and is still practised routinely in hospitals, although the incidence has decreased (see Dritsas, 2001). Indeed, many circumcised men see nothing wrong with early circumcision as a routine practice.[31] Nevertheless, this position is under attack from anti-circumcision organisations. Such groups see the unnecessary circumcision of babies and young boys, who are unable to consent to the procedure, as an abuse of human rights, an attack on their masculine identity and as the limiting of their sexual potential; and as male genital mutilation.[32]

Intersex people have also found that their bodies have been redesigned without their consent. Although there have been some recent shifts in notions of good practice (see, for example, British Association of Paediatric Surgeons, 2001), in medicine the identification of any variation from the usual in terms of biological sex tends often to result in decisions to 'correct' the body as soon as possible. The idea in this model of treatment is that the sex should be 'fixed' as soon as possible to ensure sexual congruence in the physical characteristics of the baby or child. This is based upon a Freudian assumption that sex-identity is learnt as a result of growing up with a particular body. The individual concerned is, thus, often not given any choice in the decision, which can be considered to be largely or entirely a medical matter. As soon as ambiguity is detected (often at birth) investigations into the different indications of sex are carried out, the condition is diagnosed and, as each condition is constructed in such a way that it indicates the sex, the sex is 'chosen'. The sex is then described as a certainty, despite the fact that the different indicators of sex are not congruent, and non-essential genital surgery is often advocated and performed at this point. In addition, intersex individuals and their parents have often been lied to or misled by doctors in order avoid suffering. As a result, some intersex people make startling and traumatic discoveries in later life.[33]

Early non-essential surgical intervention, an approach still followed by some specialists, also prioritises the need for a body to have the potential to participate in heterosex from the earliest age. The assumption then is that the individual will (or must) be straight. Thus, while tests and exploratory surgeries may be performed to establish the different indicators of sex, sometimes the outward appearance is the basis of the final decision. For example, a baby diagnosed as a boy with a micro penis may well be *made into* a girl, the penis being removed as soon as possible and a vagina constructed either at a very young age or during puberty when hormone treatment would also begin. Parents, assuming they accepted the medical view, would be told they had a girl and to bring her up accordingly, hence hopefully completing the transformation from intersex to female/feminine (and heterosexual). Part of the justification for this, put most crudely, is given below. The description recounts the experiences of a mother whose daughter was diagnosed with Partial Androgen Insensitivity Syndrome (which can produce an enlarged clitoris or micro penis) and had surgery at three months:

The paediatrician tried to explain about ambiguous genitalia. He also said that she would probably be brought up female since it is harder, 'to make a pole than a hole.' I find it incredible that I didn't

say anything to him about his insensitive comment. I can only think
that we were both still in shock.[34]

So it seems that the final test of maleness is sometimes based upon
a medical prediction of a penis's ability to penetrate a vagina. Here
heterosexual assumptions cause very definite harm, as Iain Morland
explains:

> The child is sexed retrospectively on the basis of their presumed
> future heterosexual relationships – relationships which are in turn
> considered to be organised around and authenticated by penis-vagina
> penetration ... this is not always the case – not only may people
> be homosexual, but they may also be heterosexual and nonchalant
> towards penis-vagina penetration. (Morland, 2002)

In addition, the potential for orgasm is often very low down the list of
doctors' priorities, if indeed it is considered at all when tissue is removed
and reshaped. For example, when of a group of intersex specialists were
asked how they defined successful intercourse for an intersex woman
and how many of the girls treated had actually had an orgasm, one
responded as follows: 'Adequate intercourse was defined as successful
vaginal penetration' (see the comments of John P. Gearhart in Bailez
et al., 1992: 684). Here again all that is required is a receptive hole and
there is no consideration of the role of the clitoris/penis and no regard
for the effects of clitoral/penile reduction upon pleasure. Unsurprisingly,
research shows that such procedures can have significant negative effects
upon women and their sex lives (Minto et al., 2003).

This rush to inflict heterosexuality, sex and gender upon the body
seems to highlight a fear of liminality embodied in a single human
form. Why do we not allow the individual to choose at some later date
what should or should not be done, if anything? This view has led
campaigners to take their lead from the anti-circumcision movements
and rename early (medically unnecessary) alterations as harm – as
'intersex genital mutilation'.[35]

CONCLUSION (CLIMAX?)

Just as the 'new theorisation of heterosexuality ... invites a radical
rethinking of many concepts we use to theorise social relations', so
too does a focus upon the social harm which heterosexuality causes
(Richardson, 1996: 2). In this chapter I have sought to develop ways
of applying a social harm analysis to constructions of heterosexuality

using a few examples. However, there are of course many other spheres to which this approach could usefully be applied. For example, one could focus upon work, health, education, politics, the media, social life and the construction of gay and straight spaces. In relation to health one could argue that heterosexual prejudices might contribute to high suicide rates among young bisexual and gay men (Remafedi et al., 1998). In the field of reproductive technology Steinberg (1996) has argued that the regulation of treatments such as IVF seeks to reproduce heterosexuality and exclude both 'non-heterosexuals' and those who are deemed to be inappropriately heterosexual. Similarly, in relation to the provision of school sex education, harm could be identified in the tendency to focus upon heterosexuality and, in particular, real sex (see generally Bibbings, 1996b – the law is now contained in the Education Act 1996). This can mean that the only point at which gay male sex is mentioned is in the context of AIDS, while lesbianism might not be mentioned at all. As a result, lesbian and gay pupils can feel excluded and, in some cases, despised (see, for example, Mac An Ghaill, 1991: 295; Stafford, 1995). This was a particular concern in England and Wales when Section 28 (Local Government Act 1988) made educators fearful of mentioning homosexuality – despite the fact that this law did not apply to schools. It remains to be seen what if any effect its repeal will have. In addition, the focus on real sex means that the role of the clitoris and the subject of female pleasure are often not considered in lessons. Consequently, female sexuality is portrayed as being a matter of plumbing, prevention and pregnancy (Bibbings, 1996b).

However, as I have suggested, the process of identifying the harms caused by heterosexuality should not be undertaken lightly. Not only is there a danger of being overly reductive by describing a concept as solely harmful but there is also the possibility of causing harm by denying the experiences and beliefs of some women and men. Thus, the application of a social harm analysis to heterosexuality requires a sense of outrage (sometimes) tempered by a sensitivity of approach and an awareness of difference as well as a recognition that heterosexuality as ideology has both positive and negative aspects and as lived experience can be a source of pleasure.

This chapter comments upon the law and policy development up until 31 August 2003.

14
Children and the Concept of Harm

Roy Parker

There are two ways in which the concept of harm has been and is applied to the condition of children. One concerns the harm that children suffer and the other the harm that they are considered to do. The balance between the two in public policy and popular debate has altered over the years; but both have continued to contribute to one of the most significant ambiguities in attitudes towards children, ambiguities that reflect the unsettled demarcation of childhood.

CHILDREN AS VICTIMS OF HARM

Current disquiet about child abuse, paedophilia, drugs and genetic damage emphasises the need to protect children from harm. Yet the categories of such harms are both various and changing. In terms of interventions by the state there has been one important distinction: that between the harm that may befall a child within its family and that which is inflicted in other settings. Although steps had been taken to protect children from excessive and crippling labour by the middle of the nineteenth century it was not until 1889[1] that there was any legislation which aimed at safeguarding them within their family, and even then such protection was largely restricted to physical cruelty.[2] Indeed, the identification of neglect, as it is now understood, waited upon the reduction of widespread destitution and a significant decline in infant and child mortality. Until then, broadly speaking from the 1920s onwards, neglect was often indistinguishable from the conditions enforced upon a large number of families by their unrelenting poverty. Much the same applies in the poverty-stricken countries of the world today, where signs of 'neglect' – that is, parental neglect – are impossible to separate from the effects of destitution, famine, disease, exploitation and international indifference (Townsend, 1993).

The shifting tide of social concern

There have been times, in the early years after the Second World War, for example, when it was widely assumed that the issue of harm to children was largely a problem of the past, and that with economic recovery, better health and social provision, as well as the fruits of education, it would continue to decline in importance. Here, for instance, is a statement to parliament in the first part of the 1950s in response to a working party's report on children neglected or ill-treated in their own homes: 'There is comparatively little ill-treatment, [and] ... deliberate neglect is found in a small minority of cases only ...'[3]

This, of course, may have reflected official complacency. On the other hand there were organisations, such as the Women's Group on Public Welfare,[4] that pressed, albeit unsuccessfully, for a major inquiry to be set up to examine the extent and nature of child neglect. It is impossible to know with hindsight whether these anxieties, or the government's apparent complacency, were justified.[5] Matters may well have been improving with close to full employment and, earlier, because a large number of men were away from home serving in the armed forces during and after the war. This suggestion is supported by the fact that whereas the majority of convictions for cruelty to children in the 1930s were of men, during the war years this was substantially reversed. In 1938 three-fifths of the 301 people convicted were men. By 1943 the total had risen to 669, of which 76 per cent were women. The pattern of the 1930s (and before) was not restored until after 1948.[6]

Indeed, the whole question of the gendered nature of harm to children deserves the fuller attention that it is now receiving.[7] For example, when, as in the inter-war years, concern was principally expressed about neglected children, rather than about those who were abused in other ways, its explanation frequently took the form of an indictment of mothers, and especially mothers of low intelligence.[8] The responsibility of fathers was not (and is not) called into question when the problems of child neglect are uppermost. By contrast, when the emphasis is upon physical or sexual abuse, as it now tends to be, fathers, step-fathers, male partners and men generally become the centre of concern, even though little action, short of prosecution and imprisonment, is taken to deal with the problem.

The shift to a preoccupation with physical and sexual abuse rather than with neglect dates in Britain from the mid-1970s; that is, with the 'discovery' (partly facilitated by advances in medical technology, especially radiology) of the 'baby-battering' syndrome; by the spate of public inquiries into children's deaths at the hands of their parents or while in public care, and by the gradual availability of statistical information about child abuse that had not existed hitherto. Voluntary organisations, like the National Society for the Prevention of Cruelty to Children (NSPCC), began to publish data[9] and local authorities were required to set up registers which provided some basis for gauging the scale and nature of child abuse.

Today, relatively little attention is paid to neglect at the policy level.[10] There are at least five reasons for this. First, it has arisen because so many resources have been ploughed into dealing with what seems to be a veritable plague of physical and especially sexual abuse. Secondly, neglect is less to the fore because governments are loth to confront the political implications of dealing with it, touching as they do upon poverty, family disintegration, maternal health, food policies and other far-reaching matters.[11] By contrast, the political responses to other forms of abuse can be contained within a much narrower compass. Child physical and sexual abuse does not call for the same kind of across-the-board shifts in policy.

There is a third and related reason why concern about parental neglect is less prominent than might be expected. It is that much of it is comparatively low level, albeit potentially terribly cumulative. As Stevenson has concluded, although such parenting is often 'on the edge of "not good enough"' the neglect which follows is rarely wilful, reflecting instead a range of problems that are associated with a generally chaotic lifestyle in which children are denied adequate daily care (Stevenson, 1998: 3). Despite the longstanding character of this kind of neglect, social workers and others are often reluctant to view the parents (typically mothers) as culpable, holding out hopes that, with help, matters will improve.

Fourthly, abuse rather than neglect is likely to be emphasised when the spotlight of public inquiry falls upon the mis-use of children in residential care, as it has done more recently.

Finally of course, abuse, especially sexual abuse, rather than neglect, has captured so much attention because the media more readily seize upon it, thereby increasing the pressure on governments to respond.

However, there are signs of a change in practice, if not in policy. For example, in England the annual proportion of cases involving neglect that were placed upon child protection registers rose from 29 per cent in 1994 to 46 per cent in 2001 (Department of Health, 2001). Of course, definitions may have altered, but even that suggests that more attention is beginning to be paid to neglect.

One important development in the classification of harms to children has been the inclusion of emotional abuse, although it still only accounted for 18 per cent of child protection registrations in 2001 (Department of Health, 2001). Admittedly, from the legislation of 1933, the offence of causing a child 'unnecessary suffering' included their 'mental derangement'; but this implied a specific psychiatric illness.[12] The idea of emotional harm is more nebulous and although a child's deprivation of love and consistent care has been well recognised as a harm (certainly since Bowlby's work in the 1940s[13]), it has not been regarded as a sufficient ground for public intervention unless extreme. This is partly because of the difficulty of establishing the severity (and hence the harmfulness) of such experiences, but also because of its usually private nature within the family. Nevertheless, it is now generally agreed that the long-term harm that children are likely to suffer from physical or sexual abuse or from neglect frequently stems from the psychological damage that accompanies these mis-uses or from witnessing discord and violence. Post-traumatic stress disorder certainly affects children as much as it does adults.[14] The considerable overlap between emotional damage and other forms of abuse makes it unlikely that it will stand alone, although when it is recorded in child protection registers it is not often enumerated in combination with other risks.

It is highly likely that the extent and repercussions of emotional abuse far exceed what is popularly understood as harm. This becomes vividly apparent when the connection is made between the concept of harm and that of impaired development. Of course, impairments may arise for reasons other than the emotional turmoil in a child's life. Nevertheless, it is crucially important to emphasise what damage 'significant harms' can do to normal development, whether they be psychological, physical, educational or social. Although the Children Act 1989 defines harm rather imprecisely as 'ill-treatment or the impairment of health or development' (sect. 31.9) it is plain that the *consequential* effect of harm should be taken into account when, for example, assessing a child's needs.

There is also the matter of where the principal responsibility for such damage lies. Is it assumed to implicate both mothers and fathers (some of whom may be absent) or perhaps certain siblings? And what about the emotional damage wrought by unsympathetic styles of teaching, by bullying at school, by insensitive substitute care or by the penal system? In terms of the last of these harms the recent (2002) success of the Howard League for Penal Reform in challenging the Home Office ruling that the Children Act 1989 does not apply to young people in prison establishments is of considerable significance, raising as it does questions about their protection from harm and the way in which their needs should be met.

Structural harms

Thus far the discussion of harm to children has concentrated upon those aspects that reflect a concern with *specific* children at risk of maltreatment or neglect by identifiable individuals or sometimes (as in the rare cases of ritual abuse)[15] by small groups. This is a quite proper approach, but it is nonetheless narrow and does not cover what might be regarded as the *general* or structural harm inflicted upon children by a variety of environmental factors. There are, for example, the ill-effects of air pollution (some of which especially affect children);[16] the dangers created by traffic and the design of roads; the lack of safe play spaces or housing that pays scant regard to children's needs.[17]

However, beyond such harms as these stands a market, and an increasingly international market (Townsend, 1993), that disregards the harm that both its methods of production and its selling strategies can do to children. Of course, in one important respect the market pays increasingly close attention to boosting and manipulating child and adolescent consumption. One of the harms that may well be done by the drive to create *specific* markets for the young, with goods and fashions that are deliberately contrived to mark them off from older people, is the rupture of generational solidarity, the possible repercussions of which are only gradually being acknowledged and which touch not only children and young people but others as well.

The emphasis upon the harms inflicted upon individual children by *individuals* has the effect of relieving governments (and others) of the need to address the more politically contentious issue of the harms that arise from the structural arrangements of society. Furthermore, it is also possible to identify what might be termed *policy* harms. These are the harms that may be done to certain children as a result of initiatives that are either argued to be in their interest, but are not, or which simply fail to take them into account. The emigration of unaccompanied children to Canada and Australia by philanthropic agencies from the 1870s to the 1960s, often with governmental support, illustrates the first of such harms.[18] There are also many instances of the second variety; that is, harms which arise because the negative impact of policies upon children is glossed over. The poll tax was one such instance in as much as it was levied at a flat rate irrespective of family income or family size. Later, there was the example of the cut in lone parent benefits in 1997, driven largely by the desire to provide an incentive for single mothers to re-enter the labour force and hence reduce social security expenditure.[19]

There is another important sense in which issues concerning harm to children are having, and may increasingly have, wider repercussions on social organisation. It is now patently obvious, for example, that the *fear* of harm befalling children – at the hands of paedophiles, through traffic accidents, as a consequence of the drug culture or as a result of the unruly and bullying behaviour of other children – is influencing life-styles, not only for children but also for parents and others charged with their care. Indeed, it may be that anxieties about the pervasive presence of harm will have more far-reaching consequences than the incidence of actual harm. Furthermore, these misgivings may well already be spilling over into an undue and stifling (for both the child and the parents) pre-occupation with the avoidance of *all* potential risks to children, however remote the possibility of their occurrence. Such over-protection is likely to constrain children's opportunity for unsupervised play which, in its turn, can have adverse effects upon their social and cognitive development.[20]

Although many of the most high-profile risks are statistically rare, particular risks of harm are unevenly distributed: by class, by area, by ethnicity, by age and by gender. In order to understand the specific likelihood of harm befalling a child we need an epidemiology of harm, not least in order to counterbalance the impression conveyed by the media that it is essentially random and hence pervasive. In fact, one of the faces of the unacceptable inequalities that distort the lives of children is the *unequal* risk of their being harmed.

Children, harm and law

One of the problems that confronts courts, and those who have to decide about the severity of harm, and thus about what steps, if any, need to be taken to protect a child, is the meaning of the evidence. Adcock (1998) points out the important distinction between evidence of abuse and evidence of the *effects* of that abuse, especially when these effects, such as impaired development, are not immediately apparent. The problem is increased in those cases where young people do not feel able to report the harms done to them until adulthood, while there are doubtless others who never reveal what they have suffered. Furthermore, the consequences of different forms of harm are liable to vary from child to child. There is also the fact that single incidents of abuse may not be regarded as of sufficient gravity to justify the removal of a child or the provision of family support; but when they persist they can lead to severe harm.[21] The problems of both assembling and weighing 'the evidence' are brought into sharp relief in, for example, the Children Act 1989 which contains provision for a court to make a care order not only when harm has occurred but also when there is the *likelihood* of a child suffering significant harm because the care being given is not what it would be reasonable to expect a parent to provide, or because the child is 'beyond parental control'.

Thus various professionals are called upon to make judgments not only about whether the harm that a child suffers, or may suffer, is 'significant' enough in terms of the 1989 Act to bring the case to court, but also about what to do to deal with a lower level of harm. Furthermore, it is clear that the evidence that is required in order to justify interventions to protect a child from harm is of a different order from that which is required to bring a successful action against the agents of that harm, added to which there is the question of their assumed culpability, particularly that of neglectful mothers who may be oppressed by poverty, depression, marital violence, ill-health and a general sense of hopelessness.[22]

Take, for example, Foetal Alcohol Syndrome – the malign effects upon children's physical, behavioural and intellectual development caused by their exposure to alcohol before birth. These are clearly harms inflicted upon a child by the behaviour of the mother during her pregnancy. However, the consumption of alcohol is not illegal, so there is no crime involved. Yet the long-term damage to the child may be as grave as the abuses that do qualify for the criminal register (see for example, Mok, 1987; McNamara et al., 1995). The same kind of situation may be seen in the case of expectant mothers who smoke. However, when it comes to pre-natal exposure to proscribed drugs such as marijuana, heroine or cocaine the matter is complicated by the over-lying criminal implications. Certainly, babies are likely to be harmed by the drug abuse of their mothers, although different drugs, and different ways of taking them, pose somewhat different risks. For example, direct injection into a vein courts the danger of HIV infection. Likewise, the combination of drugs (including alcohol and tobacco) patently increases the risk of damage being done to the unborn child, damage that continues to manifest itself after birth.[23]

The concept of harm to a child therefore goes well beyond the limited range of circumstances that calls for criminal, or indeed civil, proceedings. Some might argue that that range should be enlarged, particularly with regard to the corporate harms inflicted upon children; others tend towards the view that the perpetrators are themselves the victims of the childhood harms that they have suffered and that, for this reason, resort to the criminal law is inappropriate and unjust. Whatever balance is struck it is evident that, at least in the case of children, a distinction has to be made between harm and crime; but, in addition, the nature of the relationship between the two has to be more carefully considered than hitherto. The political ramifications of concentrating upon the one rather than the other have to be recognised, as do those that follow from the different ways in which each is regarded. For example, as has been suggested, governments will tend to shrink from a more comprehensive definition of harm, foreseeing that its adoption would require far-reaching alterations to prevailing social and economic practices as well as to the law. The case of children and divorce (or separation) illustrates the point.

In the 1980s Wallerstein and her colleagues produced two of the most influential books on children and divorce. *Surviving the Breakup* traced, over five years, how children coped with the trauma, recording their hurt, distress and anger (Wallerstein and Kelly, 1980). The follow-up study *Second Chances* pursued the enquiry up to 15 years after the split and found that many of these effects had persisted (Wallerstein and Blakeslee, 1990). Nevertheless, many of the children seem to have established stable and fulfilling lives for themselves; but the long-term consequences proved hard to predict. If time *had* healed how then should the harm have been conceived in the first place? Does relatively short-lived *distress* (in divorce or in other situations) amount to a harm? And what about the distress experienced by children prior to the actual divorce or separation when there is obvious parental conflict?

What, in any case, is the justification for the state to intervene in such situations? At the moment in England and Wales it does so only to the extent that when parents divorce the 'arrangements' for the children have to be specified and, where custody is disputed, that a welfare report has to be provided for the court. Yet the views of the children are rarely canvassed and the divorce is almost never impeded by any misgivings about the present or future wellbeing of the children. And, of course, many unmarried parents separate without having to explain to any court the arrangements that they intend to make for their children.

This, as do many other examples, poses the question of the nature of harms and which of them, actual or potential, are considered significant enough for the state to step in, either to prevent or to minimise them.

CHILDREN AS HARMERS

The protection of children from harm is only one side of the coin. The other is the longstanding disquiet about the harms that children cause, or are believed to cause. Indeed, this concern has been an abiding influence on public policy, even though it has been more prominent at some times than others. However, responses to that concern have been hedged around by assumptions about the essential innocence of children and hence about the *extent* to which they should be held accountable for what they do. This has been evident in the debates concerning the appropriate age at which criminal responsibility should be set.

Children and criminal responsibility

In 1933 the age of criminal responsibility was raised from seven to eight, where it remained until 1964 when it went up to ten (except in Scotland). That is where it has stayed despite sporadic attempts to have it lifted, most notably in the late 1960s. Nevertheless, certain dispensations are available.[24] Between ten and 14 children are not considered to have reached an age of discretion (*doli incapax*) and are thus assumed to have a reduced criminal responsibility, although they may be prosecuted if there is sufficient evidence of criminal intent. Likewise, different disposals may be made at different ages. Under 16 years the offender might be sent to a local authority secure unit or to a secure training centre under the auspices of the Youth Justice Board depending upon the length of the detention and training order (DTO) and their age. Once they have reached 16 there is more agreement about a young person's culpability, reflected in the fact that, if convicted, they may be sent to a young offenders' institution within the penal system. Not until 18 can a young person be tried in an adult court.

These examples illustrate how variable the legislative arrangements are in response to similar childhood behaviour. Notwithstanding this variety the criminal law remains a blunt instrument for dealing with children who engage in harmful behaviour. In the first place there are those under the age of criminal responsibility to be considered. How are they to be dealt with? One course is provided in the Crime and Disorder Act 1998 which allows magistrates to impose child safety orders under family proceedings. These are specifically intended for those below the age of ten and place them under the supervision of 'a responsible officer'. There are several grounds upon which such orders may be made: for example, that the child has committed an act which, had he been ten or over, would have constituted an offence, or that he has caused (or is likely to cause) 'harassment, alarm or distress' to people outside his household. Together with child safety orders the 1998 Act permits local authorities to impose curfews upon unaccompanied children under ten being in certain areas between 9.00pm and 6.00am. However, so far, only one council has used this provision.

It is the case, of course, that an order committing such disruptive young children to the care of a local authority could be made if there were compelling evidence that they had *also* been significantly harmed (or exposed to that risk). However, since the Children Act 1989 it is not possible for a court to make a care order solely on the grounds that a child is 'beyond control'.

Even in the case of offending children over the age of criminal responsibility there is a reluctance to invoke the criminal law and its potential sanctions. For example, because of their children's immaturity and reduced degree of responsibility parents may be held responsible instead, and thus become the focus of official intervention. It is they, it is argued, who are to blame for the deficient upbringing of their children. This view is reflected in the parenting orders that were introduced in the Crime and Disorder Act. These can be made in any court proceedings where, for example, an anti-social behaviour order is imposed on a child or young person, where a child under 16 has committed an offence, or where a parent is convicted for failing to ensure that their child goes to school. The order requires the parent(s) to attend for such counselling and guidance as may be specified by 'the responsible officer', and further obligations may be added. The move to hold parents responsible for the disorderly behaviour of their children can also be seen in proposals that, under certain circumstances, they be denied social security benefits, or lose the tenancy of their council house.

Children 'out of control'

Yet another approach to children who are out of control and offending revolves around the school. It is based upon the conviction that school provides a profoundly important means of inculcating desirable values, of imposing a discipline or simply of keeping children 'off the streets'.[25] Certainly, it is now apparent that much of the vandalism, street crime and substance abuse for which children are responsible involves those who are not at school when they should be, or who have been excluded. Hence the emphasis upon combating truancy and upon the provision of special units for those who cannot be accommodated in the ordinary classroom because of their disruptive behaviour.

Not surprisingly none of this is new. For instance, at much the same time that the campaign to protect children from parental cruelty was gaining momentum in the second half of the nineteenth century other movements to secure greater control over disorderly and delinquent children were gathering pace. The rapid expansion of reformatories and industrial schools (later to become approved schools) provides a good example, especially the latter. From 1857 onwards courts could send children below the age of 15 to an industrial school until they were 16. The grounds upon which such orders could be made were extensive and did not require that the child had committed an offence. Indeed, the main aim at the time appears to have been to deal with vagrancy and

begging as well as with predatory groups of youngsters in the major
cities. The purpose was to 'sweep up' wandering street urchins or those
who 'were known to frequent the company of thieves'.[26]

The scale of the development of reformatories and industrial schools
gives an indication of the extent of the contemporary anxiety about
juvenile disorder and its longer-term consequences. By 1883, for
example, there were 61 reformatories containing some 5,500 boys and
girls and 141 industrial schools housing almost 19,000.[27] Numbers
then remained steady and only eventually fell under the impact of
compulsory education and the reluctance of central government to
meet the rising costs.

Thus, concern about children being out of control in their communities
is a familiar story. Yet there remains a tension in policy about what to
do in response to the theft, vandalism and aggressive behaviour engaged
in by the young. While there are regular calls for less 'lenient' treatment
for those who wreak havoc in their neighbourhood there continues to
be a reluctance to respond in too punitive a manner. Perhaps the most
sympathetic treatment of the issue is to be found in the white paper
published by the in-coming Labour government in 1964.[28] In *The Child,
the Family and the Young Offender* three proposals were prominent.
First, it was argued that the age of criminal responsibility should be
raised to 16. Secondly, local family councils (along the lines of the
children's panels that were established in Scotland) were to be set up
by local authorities to deal with those under 16 'as far as possible in
consultation and agreement with the parents'. Only if that proved to
be unproductive would the case be referred to a family court. Thirdly,
a new family support service was proposed in order to help forestall
delinquency. As far as possible, therefore, children under 16 were to be
placed 'outside the ambit of the criminal law and the courts' (Home
Office, 1965).

These reforms met with strong opposition from influential groups
such as the magistracy. This led the government to issue a revised white
paper in 1968 – *Children in Trouble* (Home Office, 1968) – which put less
emphasis upon the involvement of families and lowered the proposed
age of criminal responsibility to 14. Most of the recommendations of
this second white paper were carried forward into the 1969 Children and
Young Persons Act, although raising the age of criminal responsibility
to 14 was not made mandatory but vested in the discretion of the
Home Secretary and, even then, the approval of parliament was to
be obtained for any movement above twelve. No Home Secretary has
invoked these powers. However, even though many parts of the Act
remained unimplemented by the newly elected Conservative government

it did put others into force which shifted the response to juvenile delinquency towards non-custodial treatments in the community. For example, police cautioning almost doubled between 1969 and 1973 in England and Wales – from 45,000 to 87,000.

The 1969 Children and Young Persons Act (and the preceding white papers) captured much of the ambiguity in public attitudes towards children who offend or who are disorderly. The report of the Expenditure Committee which reported on the Act in 1975 did so even more clearly (Expenditure Committee, 1975). The intention of the Act, it pointed out, was to abolish the distinction between the deprived and the deliberately offending child; but that rested upon the assumption that juvenile crime (and, by implication, disorder) arose from mental or emotional disturbance generated within the family. Many of those who gave evidence challenged this interpretation, or considered that it applied to only a small minority of those involved. A widely expressed view held that juvenile crime was more closely related to social and material factors; that is, to poverty and other forms of social deprivation. Yet others, such as the magistrates and their clerks, argued that most children (whether deprived or not) committed wrongful acts that harmed others in the 'full knowledge of their nature'. They needed to have the consequences 'sharply brought home to them'. It was feared that more tolerance and understanding could well lead to an increase in juvenile crime. Furthermore, as the committee concluded, there was 'a limit to the amount of delinquent behaviour which society is prepared to tolerate' and to say that children 'grow out of crime' was small comfort to their victims.

That was, and is, the political nub of the problem of juvenile disorder, a fact recognised in the (Labour) government's observations on the Expenditure Committee's report. It was admitted that there was a basic dilemma:

On the one hand there is a strongly felt and understandable demand for the public to be protected from serious and persistent, albeit youthful, offenders. On the other hand there is a widespread revulsion against holding young people in secure custody, especially custody of the kind that resembles prison. (House of Commons, 1976: 2)

Despite the clamour for more punitive responses to the anti-social behaviour of certain children there is still a strong (and often paradoxical) belief that they are more sinned against than sinning, especially the younger ones. Yet, that being accepted, there remains the problem of what this interpretation implies for modes of intervention.

Clearly, there are different types of anti-social behaviour; it happens at different ages and it may or may not become persistent or more grave.[29] For example, it may be that there are some harms that children do (singly or in groups) that should be regarded as significant but which tend to be dismissed as the result of high spirits, natural naughtiness or as pranks that get out of hand. Parents tend to claim that their offspring have been led astray by others. Some behaviour may be none of these things but rather a warning sign of a more deep-seated malaise that calls for resolute steps to be taken; for example, in the enhancement of parenting skills or in the provision of child and family therapy.

Of course, the malaise in question can be seen as more far-reaching; that is, as a symptom of much wider ills in the prevailing social and economic order. But that diagnosis, although highly credible, demands the kind of comprehensive political response that governments are unwilling or unable to make and which, if they did, would only gradually bear fruit. Instead, various aid for the improvement of certain communities is offered: support such as special funding for 'action' areas or zones, the rehabilitation of run-down housing or the establishment of training schemes for young unemployed school-leavers. Some of these initiatives do make a difference, although not necessarily to the harmful behaviour of the young.

Thus, the question of what to do about this harmful behaviour is enmeshed in a tangled politics that is obliged to juggle with the often-contradictory attitudes towards such wrongdoing, attitudes that reflect deep-rooted (but historically recent) notions about childhood innocence, about parental responsibility, about freely chosen intent and about the fragile nature of social order. Of course, the extent to which such influences affect policies towards disorderly children varies, shaped as they are by the media's love of sensation, by the power of pressure groups, by the fashionable interpretations of the time and, not least, by the harm in question.

Whatever the current responses may be one thing remains clear; namely, that in the process of harming, and in its consequences, children are likely also to be harmed or to harm themselves, the effects of the harms that they may already have suffered thereby being aggravated. Indeed, those who approach these issues from a child development perspective stress the harms that are done to their own development by a child's harmful behaviour towards others.

CONCLUSION

Thus far we have referred to 'the two sides of the coin' – the harm done to children and the harm that they cause. Of course, the matter is not as straightforward as this implies. There is a connection, but a connection that is complicated and variable. Ample evidence exists that those children whose behaviour harms others (often termed conduct disorder) have frequently been harmed themselves, although the harms are not necessarily physical or sexual. Typically, these children come from families where affection is lacking, where discipline hardly exists or is inconsistent, where violence is endemic, and where life in general is chaotic. In some cases children will have been socialised (by parents or peers, or by both) into a pattern of deviant and anti-social behaviour, an apprenticeship that it is not unreasonable to include in the catalogue of harms.

However, it is of the utmost importance to recognise that although children who harm have often been harmed (albeit in a variety of ways) it is far less common for those who suffer harm then to engage in harmful behaviour, at least not in a direct fashion. The difference between these two statements tends to pass unnoticed. Whether or not the harmed child harms depends upon many factors: upon the circumstances and the nature of the harm inflicted upon them, upon temperament and, not least, upon gender. A substantial majority of those who subsequently behave in anti-social ways are boys, doubtless for a combination of biological and social reasons.

Whatever the nature and extent of the connection between harm and harming its existence has profoundly affected the debate about the place of children in the criminal justice system and about the relevance of that system at all. How should children whose delinquent behaviour is attributable to the past ills that have befallen them be dealt with? Is the notion of criminal intent a sustainable concept? And what about the most heinous crimes? Should the issue turn upon questions of justice, the efficacy of sanctions, or a child's needs?

Sometimes extreme examples make matters clearer. For instance, how should child soldiers who have committed terrible crimes be treated? Many will have been forceably inducted by warring militias and sometimes by states, in blatant contravention of the UN Convention on the Rights of the Child.[30] Such children are widely regarded as victims (certainly by international aid agencies) and, once free from their lives of violence, are assumed to need special help and support, not punishment. Yet some children will have volunteered to fight for what they have come to believe is a legitimate cause. Surely they are victims too in the light of the *chain* of events that shaped their decision?[31] Might not similar conclusions be drawn with respect to the children whose harmful behaviours do not occur in such extreme situations?[32]

What needs to be acknowledged is that there is an intricate network of overlapping harms that children may suffer, only some of which fall into the criminal justice system. Furthermore, society's responsibility to treat as well as to punish cuts across a variety of legislation, much of which does not deal with crime. Yet the cross-cutting of criminal and non-criminal legislation is not unique to children, as has been made plain in other chapters. Nevertheless, children do provide a sensitive barometer of attitudes towards both harms suffered and harms done.

In the light of this discussion what can be concluded about the notions of crime and harm as they relate to children, and how might these be applied in a more global context than has been possible here?

First, there are many cases where the criminal justice system is an inappropriate and, it can be argued, morally unjustified way of responding to the harms that children do. It may also be an inappropriate response to those who inflict harm upon them, either because the fact of being harmed in childhood is regarded as a ground for mitigation or for other reasons. There will remain, however, 'inexcusable' crimes and certainly the level of public tolerance places a limit on what it is politically possible to excuse.

Secondly, much of this discussion has focused upon the harms perpetrated by identifiable individuals. Yet considerable harm is done to children by apparently impersonal processes. These harms are less likely to be classified as crimes: typically they are the harms done to children by corporate bodies, including states, whether by commission or omission.[33]

Finally, were the *full* range of harms inflicted upon children better documented and understood, and their relative severities gauged, more appropriate policies might be adopted, both nationally and internationally. How, for example, do we fit into our analysis the fact that half of the world's children under five live in *absolute* poverty? Should this not be regarded as much a crime against humanity as the horrors of war, horrors that children suffer together with the poverty that is so often its accompaniment? Understandably, in this country we approach the question of harm to children through the narrow perspective of the 1989 Children Act; but many harms remain invisible or ignored, sometimes for fear of the implications of revealing them and sometimes through the want of information. Some should certainly rank as crimes, even though those responsible may be difficult to bring to book. In general, however, the exploration of the nature of harm must be central to the formulation of policies for the protection of children and for the enhancement of their physical and psychological development, whether they be classified as the harmed or the harmers.

15
Poverty, Death and Disease

Dave Gordon

This chapter examines some of the harm caused by mass poverty in both developing and industrialised countries. Poverty is currently the world's largest source of social harm; it causes more death, disease, suffering and misery than any other social phenomenon. Poverty is now a bigger scourge on humanity than plague, pestilence or famine. Yet there is no need for any person in the twenty-first century, anywhere, to starve, go without clean drinking water, toilets or access to basic healthcare and education. Providing poor people with all these things would not have any significant (or even noticeable) impact on the lifestyles of the 'rich'. Poverty is not an 'act of god' nor 'inevitable', it is a political choice. What is lacking is not sufficient money but the political will to end poverty. This chapter will examine why poverty continues to persist and grow when governments have repeatedly committed themselves to alleviating and then eradicating poverty for the past 40 years. These arguments have considerable implications for a theory of social harm and the critical need to challenge the concept of intentionality/guilty mind.

POVERTY AND HEALTH

Poverty is the main cause of ill health on the planet. The *1995 World Health Report* (WHO, 1995) states that the world's most ruthless killer and the greatest cause of suffering on earth is listed in the latest edition of WHO's International Classification of Diseases (ICD), an A to Z of all ailments known to medical science, under the code Z59.5. It stands for extreme poverty:

> Poverty is the main reason why babies are not vaccinated, clean water and sanitation are not provided, and curative drugs and other treatments are unavailable and why mothers die in childbirth. Poverty is the main cause of reduced life expectancy, of handicap and

disability, and of starvation. Poverty is a major contributor to mental illness, stress, suicide, family disintegration and substance abuse.

Poverty wields its destructive influence at every stage of human life from the moment of conception to the grave. It conspires with the most deadly and painful diseases to bring a wretched existence to all who suffer from it. During the second half of the 1980s, the number of people in the world living in extreme poverty increased, and was estimated at over 1.1 billion in 1990 more than one-fifth of humanity. For most of its victims the only escape from poverty is an early grave. Poverty provides that too: while life expectancy is increasing in most developed countries, it is actually shrinking in some of the poorest of all

For most of the people in the world today every step in life, from infancy to old age, is taken under the twin shadows of poverty and inequity, and under the double burden of suffering and disease. For many millions of people for whom survival is a daily battle, the prospect of a longer life may seem more like a punishment than a prize. (WHO, 1995: 1)

Jacobson has stated that:

Two out of three women around the world presently suffer from the most debilitating disease known to humanity. Common symptoms of this fast-spreading ailment include chronic anaemia, malnutrition and severe fatigue. Sufferers exhibit an increased susceptibility to infections of the respiratory tract. And premature death is a frequent outcome. In the absence of direct intervention, the disease is often communicated from mother to child with markedly higher transmission rates among females than males. Yet, while studies confirm the efficacy of numerous prevention and treatment strategies, to date few have been vigorously pursued. (1993: 3)

The disease she is referring to is poverty.

It has long been known that poverty and deprivation can kill and maim. The evidence that poverty and inequality in material wellbeing underlie inequalities in health is now overwhelming (Gordon et al., 1999; Shaw et al., 1999). Evidence, which has accrued since the mid-1980s lends further support to the conclusion of the UK *Black Committee on Inequalities in Health*[1] in 1980 that:

While the health care service can play a significant part in reducing inequalities in health, measures to reduce differences in material standards of living at work, in the home and in everyday social and community life are of even greater importance. (Townsend and Davidson, 1982: 165)

The 1998 *World Health Report* argued succinctly:

on the unfinished agenda for health, poverty remains the main item. The priority must be to reduce it in the poorest countries of the world, and to eliminate the pockets of poverty that exist within countries. Policies directed at improving health and ensuring equity are the keys to economic growth and poverty reduction. (WHO, 1998b: 8)

The reason for the WHO's prioritisation of poverty reduction as a primary mechanism for improving the health of the world's population can be clearly understood by examining the age at death profiles of the populations in developed and developing countries. Figure 15.1 shows that the majority of men and women in developed countries (where poverty is relatively low) are more than 75 years old when they die. Whereas, in developing countries – where poverty is much greater – the highest number of deaths each year is in the under five age group. People in industrialised countries normally die in old age whereas in developing countries more than 55 million babies and young children died between 1990 and 1995 (over 10 million a year), mainly as a result of poverty. These are mainly avoidable deaths.

It should also be noted from Figure 15.1 that since the majority of the world's population lives in developing countries there are more deaths in all age groups in the developing world than in industrialised countries.

ONLY THE GOOD DIE YOUNG? – WHAT KILLS CHILDREN

Despite the fact that United Nations organisations produce a lot of statistics on how many children die each year and from what causes, these statistics are often little more than educated guesses. The sad reality is that many governments treat their poor populations with indifference (see Pemberton in Chapter 5 of this volume). Many poor children are born, become sick and die without ever being recorded by 'official' agencies. The very existence of these children remains known only to their families and local communities. Not a single country in the developing world has a comprehensive register of the cause of child deaths (Lopez et al., 2001). Since 99 per cent of child deaths occur in the developing countries, what is known about why these children died

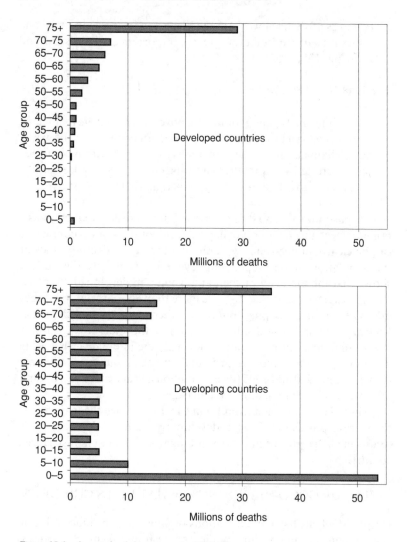

Figure 15.1   Age at death by age group, 1990–95

Source: UNFPA (1998)

are estimates usually based upon relatively small sample surveys of the dead children's parents (Black et al., 2003).

Figure 15.2 shows the estimated underlying causes of 10.7 million deaths for children younger than five in 2000, using the epidemiological model of Black et al., (2003), for 42 developing countries.

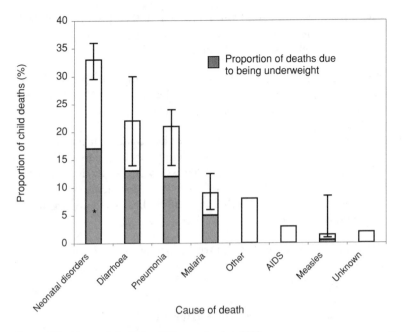

Figure 15.2   Cause of death for children under five, 2000

Note: bars show estimated confidence interval *. Additional work is in progress by Black et al. (2003) to establish the specific contribution of being underweight to neonatal deaths.

Most of the estimated 10 to 11 million deaths of young children in the world each year are the result of just a few causes. Neonatal disorders (birth asphyxia, infections, prematurity and tetanus), diarrhoea, respiratory disease (particularly pneumonia) and malaria account for 85 per cent of deaths (Black et al., 2003). It is estimated that two-thirds of these deaths could be prevented by medical interventions that are both readily available and feasible (that is, inexpensive) in developing countries, for example, low technology interventions such as breastfeeding, oral rehydration therapy, antibiotics and insecticide treated mosquito nets (Jones et al., 2003).

Figure 15.2 also illustrates that malnutrition was a contributing factor in approximately half of the deaths of young children in 2000. Despite the fact that in 1974, under the auspices of the Food and Agriculture Organisation (FAO) of the United Nations, ministers representing 133 countries met in Rome for the World Food Conference and unanimously voted for an integral fight against hunger. They endorsed Henry Kissinger's[2] objective that:

within a decade no child will go to bed hungry, [...] no family will fear for its next day's bread and [...] no human being's future and well being will be stunted by malnutrition.

This integral fight against hunger was designed to help fulfil the binding commitment that all nations had made in the 1948 Universal Declaration of Human Rights Article 25(1)

Everyone has the right to a standard of living adequate for the health and well-being of himself and of his family, including food, clothing, housing and medical care and necessary social services, and the right to security in the event of unemployment, sickness, disability, widowhood, old age or other lack of livelihood in circumstances beyond his control.

So why is there so much malnutrition in a twenty-first-century world that is wealthy and where there is plenty of food? The following two sections examine this issue.

THE PRICE OF LIFE

Most people assume that the cost of saving the lives of the millions of children who die each year from preventable causes would be so large that it would require a significant change in the living standards of people in developed countries to pay for it. The exact cost (like the numbers of children who die) is of course unknown; however, in 1997 the United Nations Development Programme (UNDP, 1997) estimated the annual cost over ten years of providing every person in the world with basic social services (Table 15.1).

Table 15.1   The cost of achieving universal access to basic social services

Need	Annual cost (US$ billions)
Basic education for all	6
Basic health and nutrition	13
Reproductive health and family planning	12
Low-cost water supply and sanitation	9
Total for basic social services	40

The UNDP estimated the additional cost of achieving basic social services for all in developing countries at about $40 billion per year over ten years (1995 to 2005). This is less than 0.2 per cent of world income and represents about 1 per cent of developing country income. The cost of providing basic health and nutrition for every person in the world was estimated at just $13 billion per year for ten years. This seems a very large amount of money but, to put it in perspective, in 2000 the US population spent $11.6 billion on dog and cat food (Euromonitor International, 2001). Europe and the US combined spend a lot more on pet food than is needed to provide basic health and nutrition for the world's people (Gordon, 2002).

The distribution of income in the world is highly polarised and has been growing more unequal, particularly during the 1980s and 1990s. Figure 15.3 shows the estimated world income distribution by quintile groups, the shape of the income distribution has been ironically compared with a champagne glass.

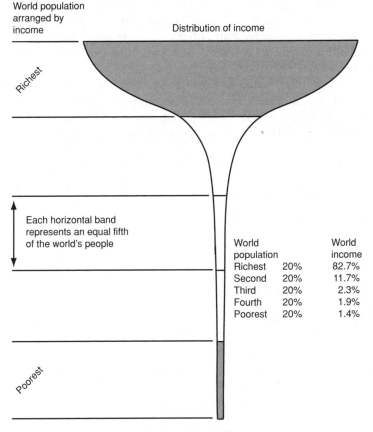

Figure 15.3 Champagne glass of income distribution

Source: World Bank (1998/99)

The stem of the glass is getting thinner. In 1960 the income of the wealthiest fifth was 30 times greater than that of the poorest fifth; now it's more than 80 times greater. A relatively minor redistribution of income from the richest 20 per cent to the poorest 20 per cent of the world's population would make a dramatic change in the extent and severity of poverty and the resulting social harm.

The income distributions shown in Figure 15.3 are based upon aggregated economic statistics. However, significant improvements in the volume, coverage and quality of household survey data that occurred during the 1990s have recently allowed the analysis of income data on a global scale based upon the directly measured income of households, rather than on their inferred incomes from national accounts (Milanovic, 2002). Analyses are so far available for both 1988 and 1993 and data for later years are currently being assembled. Figure 15.4 shows the global distribution of per capita household incomes in 1993 and graphically illustrates both the global distribution of income inequality, as well as some of the disparities that also occur within countries (for example, between urban and rural China).

The most striking feature of Figure 15.4 is the two poles of the income distribution. The 'poorest' income peak represents 2.4 billion people (about 45 per cent of the world's population) whose mean income is less than US$1,000 (adjusted for spending power, by Purchasing Power

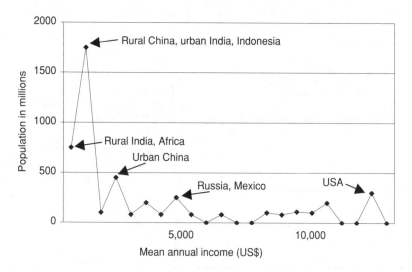

Figure 15.4   World per capita income distribution

Source: redrawn from Milanovic (2002).

Parity (PPP)) and includes the populations of both urban and rural India and Indonesia and rural China. The 'rich' peak, with incomes above US$PPP11,500, represents 0.5 billion people (about 13 per cent of the world's population) and includes the US, Japan, Germany, France and the UK. Three-quarters of the world's income inequality is explained by income differences between countries and the remainder by disparities within countries (Milanovic, 2002).

Between 1988 and 1993, global income inequality increased with the poorer 75 per cent of the world's population becoming poorer in real terms (wherever they lived) and the 'poorest' 5 per cent suffering from an income reduction of almost a quarter. By contrast, the richest 5 per cent of the world's population's incomes increased by 12 per cent over the same period. The latest, incomplete world income data show that the increase in income inequality continued during the 1990s (Pearce, 2002). There is, however, no inevitability that income inequality will continue to increase across the world. The increasing polarisation of income is not an inevitable consequence of economic growth (Atkinson, 2002). The rising income inequality is a result of political choices, of deliberate economic and social policies, and not an 'act of god' or the 'market' (Townsend, 1993; Townsend and Gordon, 2002). Ending poverty is largely a matter of political will (Gordon, 2000). It is not a problem of lack of money or scientific knowledge on how to eradicate poverty.

HOW DOES POVERTY KILL?

Although Figure 15.2 shows the 'medical' cause of death of young children in the world the underlying cause of their deaths is a result of the squalid living conditions experienced by the majority of children in the developing world. Recent research for UNICEF (Gordon et al., 2003) has shown that over 1 billion children – more than half the children in developing countries – suffer from severe deprivation of basic human need and over a third (674 million) suffer from absolute poverty (two or more severe deprivations).[3]

This research has produced the first ever scientific measurement of child poverty in the developing world based on the internationally agreed definition of absolute poverty adopted by the governments of 117 countries at the 1995 World Summit for Social Development (Langmore, 2000). Absolute poverty was defined as:

a condition characterised by severe deprivation of basic human needs, including food, safe drinking water, sanitation facilities, health, shelter, education and information. It depends not only on income but also on access to services. (United Nations, 1995, Chapter 2, Para. 19)

The research findings showed that:

- Over a third of children have to live in dwellings with more than five people per room or which have mud flooring.
- Over half a billion children (31 per cent) have no toilet facilities whatsoever.
- Almost half a billion children (25 per cent) lack access to radio, television, telephone or newspapers at home.
- Over 20 per cent of children (nearly 376 million) are using unsafe (open) water sources or have more than a 15-minute walk to water.
- Over 15 per cent of children under five years in the developing world are severely malnourished, over half of whom (91 million children) are in South Asia.
- 265 million children (15 per cent) have not been immunised against any diseases or have had a recent illness causing diarrhoea and have not received any medical advice or treatment.
- 134 million children aged between 7 and 18 (13 per cent) are severely educationally deprived – they have never been to school.

Table 15.2 shows the distribution of absolute poverty and severe deprivation of basic human needs for children in the five developing regions of the world (as defined by UNICEF).

Severe deprivations of basic human need are highly likely to have serious adverse consequences for the health, wellbeing and development of children. Severe deprivations harm children in both the short term and the long term. Many of the absolutely poor children surveyed will have died or had their health profoundly damaged as a direct consequence of their appalling living conditions. Many others will have had their development so severely impaired that they may be unable to escape from a lifetime of grinding poverty. The high death rates of young children in developing countries (see Figure 15.1) are a direct result of these impoverished living conditions.

POVERTY AND SOCIAL JUSTICE

The leaders of the world have repeatedly committed themselves to eradicating poverty over the past 40 years. Unfortunately, they have singularly failed to act despite the necessary technological and economic

Table 15.2 Percentage of children living in absolute poverty and severe deprivation, by region

Region	Absolute Poverty (2+ severe deprivations)	Severely Deprived (1+ severe deprivations)	Severely Shelter Deprived	Severely Sanitation Deprived	Severely Information Deprived	Severely Water Deprived	Severely Food Deprived	Severely Health Deprived	Severely Education Deprived
Sub-Saharan Africa	65	83	62	38	39	53	19	27	30
South Asia	59	82	45	61	40	18	27	23	19
Middle East & North Africa	40	65	45	26	23	24	12	14	23
Latin America & Caribbean	17	35	23	17	10	7	5	7	3
East Asia & Pacific	7	23	8	5	7	10	5	3	1
Developing World	37	56	34	31	24	21	15	14	13

Note: percentages for health and food deprivation are for the population aged under five and for education deprivation it is for the population aged 7 to 18.

Source: Gordon et el. (2003)

resources being available to fulfil these commitments. This section discusses the ideology of political leaders which facilitates the making of grand commitments to combat world poverty followed by inactivity. An understanding of this ideological position is important for a theory of social harm.

At the beginning of the twenty-first century the United Nations General Assembly voted to adopt the *Millennium Declaration*,[4] paragraphs 11 and 12 of which stated:

> 11. We will spare no effort to free our fellow men, women and children from the abject and dehumanising conditions of extreme poverty, to which more than a billion of them are currently subjected. We are committed to making the right to development a reality for everyone and to freeing the entire human race from want.
> 12. We resolve therefore to create an environment – at the national and global levels alike – which is conducive to development and to the elimination of poverty.

In the *Millennium Declaration* (paragraph 19) the world's governments set themselves the following specific target (among several other specific targets):

> To halve, by the year 2015, the proportion of the world's people whose income is less than one dollar a day and the proportion of people who suffer from hunger and, by the same date, to halve the proportion of people who are unable to reach or to afford safe drinking water ...
> By the same date, to have reduced maternal mortality by three-quarters, and under-five child mortality by two-thirds, of their current rates.

Yet, so little action has been taken by 2003, only three years after the *Millennium Declaration*, that the World Bank Chief Economist (Nicholas Stern) warned that most of the *Millennium Development Goals* would not be met.[5] This is just the latest example of the failure of governments to honour both their moral and legal commitments to eliminate poverty. For example, since 1976, Article 11 of the *International Covenant on Economic, Social and Cultural Rights* places a 'legal' duty on signatories to provide international aid to end hunger and poverty.[6] It requires that:

> 1. The States Parties to the present Covenant recognize the right of everyone to an adequate standard of living for himself and his

family, including adequate food, clothing and housing, and to the continuous improvement of living conditions. The States Parties will take appropriate steps to ensure the realization of this right, recognizing to this effect the essential importance of international co-operation based on free consent.

2. The States Parties to the present Covenant, recognizing the fundamental right of everyone to be free from hunger, shall take, individually and through international co-operation, the measures, including specific programmes, which are needed.

The 148 countries, which are signatories to the covenant, have simply failed in their legal duties to fulfil these basic social and economic rights. So how is this inactivity, which results in a clear gross violation of human rights, justified? It is probably not just a result of simple indifference[7] to the plight of the 'poor', let alone a deliberate plan to cause starvation and child death. The violation of economic and social rights and the consequent poverty is partly a result of a neo-liberal philosophical position which equates justice and liberty with freedom from intentional coercion (Plant, 2000). Intentionality is seen as the key concept for defining 'liberty' just as it is also the central concept used for defining 'crime' in the criminological literature – for example, crime usually requires both a harmful act and intentionality/guilty mind.[8]

To take this argument about intentional coercion to its extreme would mean that a family starving in rural sub-Saharan Africa has more 'freedom' than say Bill Gates' family, as the African family are not being intentionally coerced into paying 'taxes'. Its neo-liberal exponents argue that although the operation of the market may result in mass poverty (or lack of social and economic rights), since it is not the 'intention' of anyone that this should happen – no injustice occurs. Redistributive policies, which may help fulfil economic and social rights obligations in international law, would reduce freedom and liberty as they require what is seen as an 'arbitrary' bureaucratic decisions on resource allocation by the state (Hayek, 1979).

Further civil and political rights are viewed by neo-liberal commentators as essentially about protecting negative liberties, for example, the right to life, the right not to be imprisoned without due process, freedom of speech, and so on. In order for these civil and political rights to be met, the state has a duty of abstinence, for example, not to kill, imprison and prevent free speech, and so on. By contrast, social and economic rights are argued to be positive rights – freedom to rather than freedom from – which require a right to resources. Neoliberals argue that this presents unrealistic duties on the state, as there is no clear limit to the need for health, education and welfare, for example (Plant, 2000).

Hayek developed this argument to its logical conclusion, that societies had no obligation to meet the social and economic needs of people, as societies did not exist. In his 1979 Heidelberg lecture, he argued that the word 'social' had no objective meaning as an adjective or a noun; he stated that nobody knows what the 'social' in fact is. Hayek concluded that a social market economy is no market economy, a social constitutional state is no constitutional state, a social conscience is not conscience and that social justice is not justice (Piper, 1997).

Margaret Thatcher, then UK Prime Minister, spelt out the logic of this argument in simple terms:

> I think we've been through a period where too many people have been given to understand that if they have a problem, it's the government's job to cope with it. 'I have a problem, I'll get a grant.' 'I'm homeless, the government must house me.' They're casting their problem on society. And, you know, there is no such thing as society. There are individual men and women, and there are families. And no government can do anything except through people, and people must look to themselves first. It's our duty to look after ourselves and then, also to look after our neighbour. People have got the entitlements too much in mind, without the obligations. There's no such thing as entitlement, unless someone has first met an obligation. (1987)

These neo-liberal arguments reject the very notion of economic and social rights and therefore any responsibility to eliminate poverty via the redistribution of resources. There are no obligations that any of the millions of young children who die each year as a result of poverty could meet to gain an entitlement to life. Doyal and Gough succinctly summarise this point when they say: 'to put this another way, in order to act successfully people again need physically to survive' (1984: 15).

Plant (2000) defends the concept of social and economic rights by arguing that unintended but 'foreseeable' consequences are also important to 'liberty' and social justice. For example, it is foreseeable that privatisation of health systems will cause damage to the healthcare of the less well off as the market will not adequately provide all the healthcare they need. The 'poor' have a human right to health, so privatisation of healthcare would reduce freedom and liberty.[9]

Furthermore, civil and political rights require extensive resources for their fulfilment, for example, a police force, criminal justice system, electoral system, and so on. So, civil and political rights also require resource allocation decisions to be made by the state and not just abstinence from interfering with these rights.

International human rights agreements and conventions argue that all human rights are indivisible, for example, civil, political, economic and social rights are not separable. It is all too clear that the millions of young children who die unnecessarily each year will never get to exercise their civil and political rights – they will never vote – as the violation of their social and economic rights results in their untimely deaths. They have no civil and political rights because they do not have their social and economic rights fulfilled.

However, indifference and neo-liberal biases of political elites cannot fully explain why so little has been done to alleviate the harm of world poverty. There are also psychological factors which can result in harmful decisions by policy-makers. In particular omission bias and a preference for indirect harm over direct harm have been shown to cause errors in decision-making (Royzman and Baron, 2002). In omission bias, people are unwilling to reach a desired outcome through a harmful act – even when the harmful act is fairly trivial and the desired outcome is very important (Spranca et al., 1991; Baron, 1998). For example, parents who will not vaccinate their babies because of the risk of the vaccination being harmful, even though the 'objective' risk of harm to the baby from the disease is much greater (Ritov and Baron, 1990; Meszaros et al., 1996). Similarly, policy-makers are unwilling to risk the likely small political harm of redistributing 0.2 per cent of the world's income to the 'poorest' (the amount needed to provide basic social services for all) even though they may desire an end to world poverty.

CONCLUSION

This chapter has shown that millions of people die from preventable causes each year due to their impoverished living conditions. Over 1 billion children suffer from severe deprivation of basic human need. Despite the necessary economic and technical resources being available and repeated international commitments by policy-makers to eliminate poverty little has changed over the past decades. The world has grown more unequal and there are more 'poor' people. Poverty is thus the greatest cause of social harm, suffering and death in the twentieth century.

Political elites lack the political will to end the social harm of poverty. One of the key reasons for this is the concept that poverty is an unintentional consequence of the actions of global economic systems

– particularly market systems. The harm of poverty is therefore often viewed as unfortunate but not as unjust – as no one intended this harm to happen. Unless the ideology of intentionality is challenged then the harm of poverty is likely to continue. A social harm perspective represents a major advance on other judicial/criminological theories as it allows all harmful outcomes to be treated as of equal consequence – whether intended or unintended. However, unlike utilitarianism, it examines harm from a socially realistic perspective. Thus social harm provides a sociological rather than an abstract philosophical theory. It would be immoral and unjust to treat a few tens of thousand child murders as of greater consequence than the millions of preventable child deaths that result from poverty.

ACKNOWLEDGEMENTS

I would like to thank my colleagues in the Centre for the Study of Poverty and Social Justice at Bristol University and particularly Simon Pemberton for his helpful comments and advice.

16
Conclusion:
'Social Harm' and its Limits?

FROM CRIMINOLOGY TO SOCIAL HARM?

On the basis of the preceding chapters, we are now able to state somewhat more clearly than we were in the first chapter of this volume just what may be entailed in the enterprise of a discipline based around a concept of social harm. Indeed, we can do so briefly at this point, since the chapters, taken together, provide a clear, albeit not exhaustive, statement of the range of areas and types of substantive concerns, variety of methodological approaches and political trajectory entailed in a social harm perspective.

First, and perhaps most clearly, the chapters have demonstrated a concern with a wide range of social harms: the harm caused by mass poverty in both developed and developing industrialised countries; the gross violations of human rights of millions of people every year at the hands of their own states leading to permanent injuries or death; the harm inflicted on women and girls who are deliberately killed or hurt because of their gender; the harmful working practices which cause death on a large scale; the harm caused by the dominant notions of sexuality and the privileging of heterosexuality in particular; the harm arising directly from the 'war on migration' leading to the deaths of thousands on the land, sea and in the air as they travel across borders to reach more prosperous parts of the world; the harm caused to children; and the harm caused by pollution, food poisoning and miscarriages of justice.

Second, the book has highlighted various ways in which harms can be analysed. For example, Parker has looked at a particular category – children – and explored the harm done to them and the harm they do to others. Similarly, Pantazis focused on women and girls and systematically explored the harm done to these two groups using a life course perspective. Webber has concentrated upon policy and has shown how policy, far from being benign, is directly responsible for harm. Tombs focused on a specific context – work – and explored the role of the Heath and Safety Executive in preventing harm.

Third, the book has explored a number of conceptual and theoretical issues concerning harm. Salmi developed a detailed typology for the classification of harm. Hillyard and Tombs explained much of the harm in the world by locating the cause firmly at the feet of the pursuit of a neo-liberal economic paradigm. Bibbings and Pantazis, however, have shown that not all harm stems directly from the political economy of the globalised world but is directly related to customs, traditions and dominant ideologies. Ward argued for a conceptualisation of state harm which can be embraced within criminology rather than beyond it. Pemberton and Sim looked at two particular phenomena associated with harm: the extent of moral indifference most people show towards the sufferings of others; and state defined images of victimisation. Dorling in his analysis of murder showed clearly that murder rates are related to broader economic and political decisions, raising fundamental philosophical and jurisprudential questions about where responsibility lies for murder. These and other chapters have therefore begun the task of developing conceptual and theoretical issues around the notion of harm.

Fourth, the book has raised a number of methodological issues for those concerned with social harm. Methods of this enterprise would include the attempt to chart and compare social harms through qualitative research techniques such as locally based interviewing, and the production of life histories and biographies, as well as utilising existing data. There are now numerous databases which provide information on some aspect of harm. These include the census, morbidity and mortality data, poverty indices, measures of pollution and air quality, workplace and labour market data. There is also a large amount of crime data, from police recorded crimes to victim surveys, which can be compared with these data to provide an objective assessment of the amount of harm caused by crime and other causes. New research needs to be carried out to produce objective measures of what people consider are the most harmful events so that an index of harm can be produced.

Fifth, in political terms, each of the chapters has pointed to the limiting, stultifying and mystificatory effect of both political and academic discourse around a particular form of social harm. Webber's chapter, for example, showed how migration policies are causing death on a massive scale. However, in the official discourse no connection is made between the bodies which are washed up on the shores or drop from the skies and the policies adopted in national parliaments to stop the movement of people, nor is there any discussion of the way neo-liberal economic policies are producing ever-increasing inequalities so that it is inevitable that people will try to escape poverty and destitution and attempt to find a new life for themselves and their families. Parker too showed how certain policies, which were suggested to be in the best interest of the child, caused massive harms, such as the British government's support for the emigration of unaccompanied children to Canada and Australia by philanthropic agencies or the poll tax which was levied irrespective of family size. Similarly, Sim highlighted the mystification which occurs in relation to the death of state servants, such as the police and prison officers.

The chapters have also drawn attention to the importance of language. Collisions on the road resulting in the death of drivers or passengers are described as 'accidents', notwithstanding that one of the drivers may have been drunk or using their mobile phone. Deaths arising from pollution are quaintly referred to as 'deaths brought forward'. Imagine the uproar if the police in their annual reports talked about the number of 'deaths brought forward' as a result of homicides. Where larger numbers of people are killed in a single incident it is referred to as a disaster, suggesting some sudden misfortune for which no one is responsible. Yet, the disaster may have been far from sudden. It may have been totally predictable because some piece of machinery had not been maintained or the demand to increase profits meant that basic safety procedures were ignored. In a very different context, Bibbings showed how the language of sexuality is underlain with numerous assumptions prioritising certain femininities and masculinities and foregrounds male dominance.

The problem, however, goes much further than the limiting, stultifying and mystificatory effects of the discourse. Many instances of substantial harm involve silences, denials, lies and cover-ups by governments. The olive oil scandal in Spain, described in Chapter 3, for example, shows how far a state may be prepared to go to cover up the truth in order to protect certain interests and as a consequence allows many more deaths of its own citizens to occur. There are other examples throughout the book where harms are denied.

While the critique offered by a social harm perspective in terms of the limits of current academic disciplines is not *confined* to criminology, the ubiquitous demands across these chapters for a shift from a focus upon crime and law to social harm, and from analyses and explanations located in pathological individuals or malfunctioning institutions to more structurally based modes of inquiry, analysis and prescription, do impinge *particularly significantly* upon criminology. Indeed, as we believe many of the chapters presented here have demonstrated, one key advantage that a social harm approach might have over criminology, however, is that, to usurp a (rather horrendous) Blairite phrase, it might have greater potential for 'joined up' analysis and prescription. That is, understanding and treating harm requires reference to a range of disciplines and spheres of social, public and economic policy. This approach has much more potential for a multi-disciplinary perspective than criminology, and therefore also the potential to escape from the constraints of narrow subject-based confines which criminology finds difficult to achieve. Further, a social harm approach would draw upon the experiences and voices of a range of professionals and social groups, including, for example, doctors, accountants, police, lawyers, economists, trade unions, non-governmental organisations, and so on.

One of the key legacies of critical criminology has been to demonstrate the problems of attempting to treat behaviours defined as crime through the criminal justice system – that is, critical criminologists have long recognised, as did much of the social positivism from the 1930s onwards, that 'crime' has social and economic 'causes' which must be addressed at that level. The problem for criminologists, however, is that while pointing to the need for understanding of, and reforms in, areas beyond 'criminal justice', they are inevitably drawn back to proposing reforms of the criminal justice system and to understanding crime through an (albeit ameliorated) criminological discourse. Criminology necessarily entails some privileging of law and criminal justice – even if only, to borrow a famous phrase, 'in the last instance'! And of course it was precisely this ultimate privileging that led many critical criminologists – for example, some Marxists and feminists – to abandon the criminological enterprise altogether. By contrast, social harm has fewer theoretical constraints than the notion of crime; for example, a harm perspective could be developed to have something meaningful to say about human rights and distributional justice theory, a potential unlikely to be realised within the discipline of criminology.

What is more, given that the birth of criminology was located in the emergence of a concern to seek the causes of crime – and thus the 'remedies' for crime – within individuals (Pasquino, 1991), it is unsurprising that criminology and criminal justice remain infected with individually based analysis, explanation and 'remedy'. We would argue that this remains the case despite decades of resistance to these notions from within the discipline of criminology itself. In other words, for us, criminology cannot entirely escape such discursive practices because this is what it is, where it was born, how it has been constructed.

A social harm approach, by contrast, starts from a different place. It begins with a focus upon the *social* origins of harms, upon the structures that produce and reproduce such harms, albeit that these harms are refracted through, suffered by, individuals. Of course, to utilise the social as a departure for explanation and theorising need not, and for us does not, entail a rejection of the need to account for human agency. But it is to accept a view of the world that sees human agency as highly delimited by structures, structures which must be known and of which we must provide accurate accounts. If this is a defining characteristic of a social harm approach, then there is immediately potential for charting a theoretical and prescriptive trajectory which is quite different from that which criminology has (necessarily) followed.

THE LIMITS OF A SOCIAL HARM APPROACH?

From our critique of criminology in Chapter 2, through to the systematic setting out of the limitations of this discipline in the chapters that constitute this volume, the clear trajectory of this text points towards the abandoning of criminology in favour of a social harm approach. It seems appropriate in the conclusion, however, to consider the theoretical and political *attractions* of retaining a focus upon crime, law and criminal justice, and to pay attention to some of the *problems* consequent upon a focus on the concept of social harm. It is to a brief sketch of these tasks that we turn.

In short, it might be argued that a key advantage of retaining a commitment to criminology and crime is that, for all its attendant problems, reference to law points to some readily defined standard against which some social actions and omissions are judged as always of some seriousness; to speak of crime is to invoke certain (though clearly not homogeneous or fixed) social and political meanings. While criminalisation is rightly treated as a problematic process by many criminologists, the politics of criminalising certain activities – for example, certain activities of states and corporations, or behaviours against women or ethnic minorities – has been progressive, acting as a focus of, and thus further contributing to the development of, 'organised public resentment' and thus social change. Further, it might be argued: that law and established forms and processes of legal reasoning direct attention to the identification of offenders through locating responsibility; that law and established forms and processes of legal reasoning can, and at times do, direct attention to establishing means of redress for victims of wrongs and offences; and that law invokes a range of sanctions (and/or forms of state monitoring) where its violation has been 'proven'; moreover, these do not tend to *preclude* other forms of responses or resistances to social harms, nor indeed to crimes themselves. All of these may be used as arguments for retaining a commitment to criminology.

These objections lead to the claim that 'social harm' – certainly in contrast to crime – appears to be a generalised, amorphous term, covering an enormous range of quite heterogeneous phenomena. However, one of the major advantages of a social harm perspective is precisely that it has the potential to have a much greater degree of ontological reality than is possible with the notion of crime. For example, there are international agreements on the meaning of death, serious and minor injuries, disease and financial loss – and there are compilations of comparable statistics on these subjects, produced by a range of organisations, representing different disciplines – for example, the International Labour Organisation, World Health Organisation, the European Union, and so on. By contrast, given that one of the most prevalent 'crimes' in the UK is 'failure to pay the TV licence', while the most common crime in Turkey is 'being rude to a public official', there is not even a theoretical prospect of being able to make meaningful international comparisons of the extent of crime, except in relation to a relatively small sub-set of 'crimes'.

Nevertheless, it may still be argued that if the criminalising processes that cohere around the label crime are at least related in some way to 'organised public resentment', then this cannot necessarily be said for many 'harms'. However, this argument is rather less convincing when one recalls how processes of criminalisation are overwhelmingly directed at so-called lower class offenders, while white-collar, corporate and state offenders have consistently managed to evade these. Indeed, Christie's argument regarding what constitutes a 'suitable enemy' indicates that these effects are necessary rather than contingent aspects of criminal justice systems. In analysing 'the suitable enemy', Christie questions the possibility of law and order campaigns against white-collar criminals. 'Who has heard of a society using police force against its rulers?' According to Christie, it is hard to imagine the same extraordinary rules of the zero-tolerance game – provocation, infiltration, the police pretending to be businessmen, bugging of telephones, payment to informers, the complete stripping by customs officers of business executives, and intimate body searches – being applied to economic as opposed to, for example, drugs crimes (Christie, 1986: 56; Alvesalo, 1998).

A further objection to a social harm approach might be that, if the concept of harm is a relatively open one, and if this may indeed be productive, as we have claimed (above), then this also makes it potentially fraught with danger. There are at least three forms, or sources, of this danger, one more significant than the others.

One is the problem of majoritarianism, the problem that harms become defined socially by their being recognised as problems by a majority of the population – so that certain groups such as 'asylum seekers' or 'aggressive beggars' or practices such as congestion charging or environmental taxes might become defined as 'social harms'. Now, certainly, where one seeks to access people's experiences of harms, then there is a danger – though one that may be avoided – of simply accessing and reproducing manifestations of racism, sexism, and so on. Yet the real danger here is in an approach to such data which takes such views unproblematically, letting popular views 'speak for themselves'; thus, people's experiences must inform, but cannot constitute, a social harm approach, nor indeed any social science.

Second, and related, is that techniques which seek to access experience are still more likely to produce data about relatively manifest harms, or the superficial manifestations of harms, rather than more latent harms. Again, this is a problematic, though not necessary, tendency – thus, for example, a social harm approach might develop a critical epidemiology which is able to access deleterious health effects which are the result of environmental harms irrespective of whether a given population explicitly recognises either such health effects or any relationship between these and forms of environmental harm.

A third problem is that, if what constitutes social harm is relatively open, then this makes it particularly open to contestation – and thus a social harm approach might be a disciplinary area particularly prone to being fashioned by relatively powerful social and political interests. Again, this is a powerful potential objection to an embracing of the term harm as the central object of academic focus. Yet if we accept that all forms of academic work are produced within a power/knowledge network, then it is also long established within critical social science that academic work which begins with an explicit recognition of this nexus, and indeed starts from a political position of resistance, emancipation and social justice, is best placed to mitigate its infection by the demands and concerns of 'the powerful' (more generally, see Tombs and Whyte, 2002).

In the context of the above concerns, the distinction drawn by Hulsman between different kinds of 'problematic situations' seems a particularly useful analytical device. Thus, following Hulsman, we would want to distinguish between: those situations 'which are considered problematic by all those directly concerned'; those 'which are considered problematic by some of those directly involved, and not by others'; and those 'not considered problematic by those directly involved, but only by persons or organisations not directly involved' (Hulsman, 1986: 35).

The objection regarding the lack of clarity in the object of a social harm approach may take some more explicitly epistemological form. One version of this objection may be that to speak of social harm is simply to reflect a moral or political viewpoint, so that one descends into mere moralising or political posturing. There is some superficial force to these claims. Certainly, for example, the charge of moral entrepreneurialism is one that has frequently been directed at those who have sought to focus upon corporate crimes (Shapiro, 1983; Nelken, 1997), to the extent that academics pursuing this area of study have been labelled 'corporate crime crusaders' (Shapiro, 1983). In response to this objection, however, it seems to us that if to adopt a definition of harm is partly a moral choice, then we must accept that *to adopt a definition of crime as the guiding criterion of a field of study is equally a moral choice* – and this is no less the case simply because such a choice rarely receives (or seems to require) any justification since it is produced by, coheres with, and is reinforced by, the power of criminological discourses. Thus one response to the charge of political or moral entrepreneurialism which proponents of a social harm approach may attract is simply to accept it, but to counter that at least such choices can be made openly and explicitly, in a way that renders them liable to justification, contest and debate – which is in stark contrast to the choices entailed in retaining a commitment to criminology, choices masked by reference to an apparently objective focus around criminal law (itself sometimes rationalised by reference to it being some – albeit imperfect – form of collective consciousness, or national morality, or socially agreed sense of justice, and so on).

Further, in the context of objections regarding a potential moral relativism, we would argue that a notion of harm which is rigorously operationalised and reflects the concerns of the population would carry considerable political force because of its democratic articulation. The Paddington rail disaster illustrates only too well the way in which the public's perception and definitions of harm can counter the official discourses emanating from government or the private corporations. People who use the railways in Britain experience on a daily basis the reality of a declining service, crumbling physical condition and the increasing reality of a major incident. And they associate this with privatisation, which is why in the aftermath of the disaster, there emerged calls for renationalisation. And this is not to say that rail users look back to the days of British Rail with rose-tinted spectacles, since those who remember British Rail recall years of underinvestment by the state, aspects of overbureaucratisation, and hence a service which was never as good as it should have been. But it is also their experience to be even more concerned regarding railways that are run for a profit, so that rail users reject the bland statements made by operating companies and Railtrack that safety comes before profits. They know that privatised railways produce the potential for mass harm; and it is precisely such knowledges that a social harm approach would attempt to access, and to take seriously.

The other objections raised above, regarding the practices and procedures entailed in law for the identification of offenders, location of responsibility, establishment of means of redress for victims, the invoking of a range of sanctions, and so on, seem to us to have somewhat less force. Of course these *are* characteristics of criminal justice and legal systems. The point is, of course, that none of these have been used with any degree of vigour or consistency – despite the exigencies of many criminologists – beyond dealing with 'conventional' offences and offenders, while even where they have been used their effects have hardly, as we have noted above, been successful (at least, that is, according to their stated rationales). Holding out hope that this situation might change through ever greater pressure from within criminology is at best highly optimistic, at worst illusory.

As an instance, here, we can take the vast amount of criminological and criminal justice efforts expended in recent years with various forms of informal, restitutive and community-based legal responses to wrongs and offences (Abel, 1982a, 1982b; Matthews, 1988; Johnstone, 2001). It is noteworthy that, while these vary, they tend to seek to establish themselves within the terrain of, but significantly altering, criminal justice systems. It is at least worth considering the extent to which such theorising and practice might be more successful were it to abandon reference to crime, law and criminal justice – the terrain of criminology – altogether, and instead begin from the viewpoint of the redress of harm. Indeed, freed from the narrowing shackles of criminal justice, such a starting-point would allow the determination or development of more novel, imaginative and effective forms of prevention rather than being fixated with redress. Whereas criminology necessarily takes adequate 'redress' as it starting-point, a major advantage of the social harm perspective is precisely that it facilitates a shift in emphasis from 'redress' to 'prevention'. It is surely better to prevent harm than to provide fair redress once it has occurred: criminal justice is largely reactive; a social harm approach has real potential to be both proactive and emancipatory.

Notes

CHAPTER 1

1. The new discipline was termed Zemiology, from the Greek Zemia, meaning harm. It has since been described as 'horribly named' (Hil and Robertson, 2003). Others prefer the word 'Zemiotics'. For the purposes of this book we used the more easily understood term social harm.
2. We are indebted for one anonymous reviewer of the book proposal for this expression.

CHAPTER 3

1. 29 per cent of black American men, 17 per cent of Mexican-Americans and 4 per cent of white American males will go to prison at least once (Williams, 2003: 17).
2. What follows in this section is heavily indebted to Pearce and Tombs (2003).
3. And parallel to the WTO and regional agreements such as NAFTA run industry-based agreements – see, for example, the Energy Charter Treaty, which seeks to expand the power of oil and other energy multinationals through the extension of WTO rules to non-WTO countries (Project Underground, 2001).
4. This legal privilege has already been used successfully by corporations, notably against legislation designed to protect the environment (see Pearce and Tombs, 2003, for examples).
5. It has been calculated that 'the top 500 transnational corporations are responsible for 30 per cent of the world's gross product, 70 per cent of world trade, and 80 per cent of world investment' (Smith et al., 1999: 212).
6. On this point, it is worth noting that recent years have seen the appearance of useful empirical studies in the context of considerations of the regulation of occupational health and safety – which have sought to document through particular case-studies the ways in which, and the effects to which, such discourses of globalisation may be used by already powerful companies, not least at moments when they seem most vulnerable to greater state and pro-regulatory scrutiny (Woolfson et al., 1996; Whyte and Tombs, 1998; Whyte, 1999).
7. The G-7 was made up of the world's seven richest industrial countries – the United States, Japan, Germany, France, Britain, Italy and Canada – whose leaders have been meeting regularly since 1975 in an annual summit to discuss problems in the world economy. Since the entry of Russia to such discussions in 1991, this summit has been recast as the G-8.
8. See the contributions by Salmi in Chapter 4 and Pemberton in Chapter 5 of this volume.
9. Edited by Vicente Navarro, published quarterly by Baywood Publishing Company, New York.

10. Other forms of harms generated in the production and distribution of goods are discussed at various points throughout this text. See, for example, Parker's discussion in Chapter 14 of the range of harms located in the market, where children are specially targeted to boost child and adolescent consumption, or Tombs's consideration in Chapter 10 of occupationally produced death, injury and illness.

11. These were sites of extreme environmental hazard, originally designated in a 1986 US Federal Act, which required companies to internalise clean-up costs (see Barnett, 1994).

12. It should be noted that Finland experienced a recession in the early part of the 1990s which was more severe than that experienced by any other OECD country since the war, and greater than Finland's own depression of the 1930s; the effects of this recession, and indeed of the 'recovery' from it during the 1990s, have been marked (see Andersson et al., 1993; Kiander and Vartia, 1996).

CHAPTER 4

1. This chapter is adapted from Jamil Salmi (1993).

2. See for example: Conquest (1971), Medvedev (1976), Carrère d'Encausse (1978) Conquest (1979) and Heller and Nekrich (1986).

CHAPTER 5

1. This point will be developed later in the chapter.

2. The Schwendingers' (1975) approach utilised an innovative social harm approach to define state crime as the infringement of human rights, which encompassed categories such as racism, sexism and economic exploitation.

3. An example of indifference as an implicit cause of harm is the recent actions of the US government at the WTO. The member countries of the WTO are currently involved in negotiations to allow developing countries to import 'generic' drugs for any condition which undermines public health. However, agreement over Trade and Related Property Rights (TRIPS) has been jeopardised by the American veto. Among the sufferers of the many diseases which the population of the African continent endures, this agreement would potentially offer relief to the 29.4 million people currently living with HIV/AIDS in sub-Saharan Africa (UNAIDS-WHO, 2002). Clearly, unlike the genocide perpetrated by the Nazis in 1940s Germany, the US government is not responsible for the AIDS epidemic in Africa. However, the US government should be morally accountable for possessing the capability to intervene and alleviate human suffering, yet remaining indifferent to this harm in the interests of capital. The indifference of the US government has been secured through their relationship with the pharmaceutical industry, evidenced in the industry's £39 million donation to the Republican's mid-term election campaign (*Guardian*, 20 February 2003).

4. See the accounts of Imam (1994), Chossudovsky (1997) and Lynas (2000) for descriptions of the devastating effects of these policies.

5. Furthermore, the report noted that during the period 1995 to 1999, 81 per cent of the population of LDCs in the sample lived on less than the equivalent of $2 a day (UNCTAD, 2002a).

6. In the context of late modernity Bauman seeks to develop this notion of unconditional responsibility (Bauman, 1995). Bauman contends that late modernity structures

different forms of human togetherness, and these have dominated the moral form of 'being for the other'. 'Being for' is the antithesis of reason, because it is dominated by concerns of sentiment, emotion and feeling (1995: 52). Bauman argues that the polemic notions of reason and sentiment define one another, 'for reason to be rule governed – its opposite the unruly must be unreason – sentiment' (1995: 53). Sentiment represents the randomness, the spontaneity which is deemed destructive to order, which rationality wishes to counteract.

7. In Titmuss's (1970: 239) classic comparative study of blood donation, he noted one of the effects of market-oriented systems is to 'free' actors from any sense of obligation for the other regardless of the other's ability to reciprocate. This removes any sense of collectivity.

8. Bauman has made cogent arguments for the use of universal rights to check the immorality of growing inequality: 'In a world of global dependencies with no corresponding global polity and few tools of global justice, the rich of the world are free to pursue their own interests while paying no attention to the rest ... the issue of a universal right to a secure and dignified life, and so to universal (truly cosmopolitan) standards of justice, must be confronted point blank before the subtleties of cultural choices may come back into their own' (Bauman, 2001).

9. Nils Christie's (1993) seminal thesis notes that integral to this shift in penal policy is the growing privatisation of the criminal justice system. Consequently these interests have underpinned the increasing criminalisation of the redundant 'reserve army of labour' in western society. The social construction of the criminal code and criminalisation provides this system of wealth accumulation with an endless supply of 'raw material' and profit.

10. The link of poverty and criminality is not new. Historically policies such as the 'poor law' have been based upon this nexus. However, in the context of recent history with the demise of the 'post-war consensus', welfare based solutions have become colonised by those of the criminal justice process.

CHAPTER 6

1. Animals, too, have welfare interests (Feinberg, 1984) and obviously suffer enormous harm at the hands of the state (for example, the mass slaughter of UK cattle during the recent foot-and-mouth disease outbreak (Campbell and Lee, 2003)). I am not certain whether harm to animals falls within the concept of *social* harm.

2. It seems doubtful whether the concept of state crime, as Green and I have formulated it, can usefully be applied to many events before the Second World War. For example, it would be highly anachronistic to describe the Atlantic slave trade (at least for the first three centuries of its existence) as either 'deviant' or – in any socially significant sense – a 'violation of human rights' (see Drescher, 1996). It might be an interesting project to consider whether a modified version of the concept is of any value in discussing some of the more brutal excesses of nineteenth-century colonialism.

3. BBC News, 15 March 2001; Holsti (1996: 114); *Financial Times*, 19 October 2000.

4. I am indebted to Louk Hulsman for discussions on this point.

5. Between 1960 and 1990, the ratio of the income of the richest fifth of the world's population to that of the poorest fifth increased from 30 to 1 to 60 to 1; and to 74 to 1 by 1997 (Cilliers, 1999).

6. Bauman's one-sided emphasis on the bureaucratic, rational character of the Holocaust is problematic (Burleigh, 1997), but does offer insight into the morally deforming effects of modern structures of state power.

CHAPTER 8

1. These are concepts that are built around 'fictions or empty pretences' (Beck, cited in Bauman, 2002: 82).

2. There are too many to list here but there are a number of texts that should be mentioned which have focused on: the normality of male violence towards women and children (Stanko, 1990); the extent of racial violence (Bowling, 1998) and violence towards gay men and lesbian women (Corteen et al., 2001); the identification of masculinity in the reproduction of violent structures of domination and subordination (Sim, 1994; Collier, 1998); the brutal role of the state in repressing populations in different countries identified by critical anthropologists (Scheper-Hughes, 1992); the question of how violence is defined including structural and institutional violence carried out by states, governments and corporations (Pearce and Tombs, 1998; Cohen, 2001; Barak, 2003; Green and Ward, 2004); and the use of state repression in maintaining an inequitable social order in Northern Ireland (Hillyard, 1995). In addition, between 1997 and 2002, the Economic and Social Research Council (ESRC) opened up the debate (only to some extent, however, as the violence generated through corporate crime and state crime was still noticeable for its absence) by funding a number of research projects arising out of the Violence Research programme headed by Betsy Stanko, a trenchant critic of the individualised, positivist paradigm (ESRC, 1998). Finally, a number of readers have been published which again have utilised both an interdisciplinary approach to the issue while focusing on the need for a wide-ranging definition of what constitutes violence (Kleinman et al., 1997; Steger and Lind, 1999; Stanko, 2002).

3. This marginalisation has been recently challenged by the emergence of 'convict criminology' in the US (Ross and Richards, 2003).

4. The text by Liebling and Price (2001), described on its back cover as 'the most important book for the prison service of the past thirty years', even managed to avoid dealing with the negative aspects of the work of prison officers altogether. They noted that the book 'concentrated on the best aspects of prison officer work and very little on the "dark" side. This is consistent with our aims. There is a case for more contemporary empirical work on poor performance, abuses of power and "where things go wrong", but this is not our present task' (ibid.: 108). One wonders what the reaction would have been if a critical criminologist had written a book concentrating on the repressive and coercive side of the work of prison officers.

5. This chapter concentrates on the question of deaths and injuries to prison and police officers. There is a broader issue to be discussed which is outside the scope of this chapter, relating to the comparison between deaths and injuries in these occupations with other occupations. The Home Office has published some work in this area (Budd, 1999) which argued that police officers face the highest risk of assault, but there are a range of methodological issues relating to this study including the lack of definition and consideration of violence committed by employers and the different pressures involved in the reporting and non-reporting of violence and threats of violence when the police are compared with other occupations (personal communication, Dave Whyte).

6. It is important to comment on the question of official statistics and in particular the data concerning deaths and injuries to state servants. Given the immense political, cultural and symbolic significance surrounding such deaths, it might be assumed that detailed official data regarding these deaths would be available in order to identify not only trends and processes, but also what lessons could be learned so

that strategies could be developed to reduce the future risks that might confront them. However, the data concerning such deaths are incomplete and fragmented. For example, in a personal communication from the prison service, a spokesperson pointed out that their electronic records with respect to deaths and assaults on prison officers 'only go back as far as 1990. While they do contain earlier incidents, I could not guarantee their accuracy' (personal communication, HM Prison Service, 13 June 2000). In a further personal communication, the data on prison officer deaths were traced back to 1988 but the researcher doubted that this was 'a true record of all events since 1988, but are all that we know of' (personal communication, HM Prison Service, 22 December 2000). The incomplete nature of the data makes it difficult, but not impossible, to compare different occupational groups across different time spans as different years have been used as the base years for the collection of these data.

7. There are similar methodological issues here with respect to comparing different time-spans but the general point remains valid. It is also worth noting that between 1998 and 2001, out of the 104 individuals who died in police custody the majority – 81 – had been arrested for non-violent offences (personal communication, Simon Pemberton).

8. At the time of writing, July 2003, the latest figures available for offences against prison discipline indicated that in 2001 there were 6,800 'proven assaults' in prisons, an increase of 450 compared with 2000. The figures are not broken down between assaults on staff and assaults on prisoners. However, the Home Office does indicate that the increase between the two years was 'in line with the increase in the prison population in 2001 so the overall rate of violent offending remained the same. *The overall rate of violent offences has remained fairly constant over the last ten years*' (Home Office, 2003b: 133, emphasis added).

9. See note 6 above.

10. See note 6 above.

11. There are other interesting comparisons that can be made. For example, in three forces – the Met, West Midlands and Greater Manchester – the number of officers dismissed between 1998–99 and 2000–1 was 197. This far outstripped police officer deaths which numbered 75 (figures adapted from *Hansard*, 22 January 2002: col. 843).

12. It is also worth noting that the police are not beyond injuring themselves in order to achieve convictions. See Norris (1993: 135) for a description of how officers, in the force he researched, engaged in the 'gross misuse of force' against a suspect and then used violence against each other to exaggerate the case against him (thanks to Dave Whyte for pointing this reference out to me). The study by Smith and Gray for the Policy Studies Institute in the early 1980s also found that 'fighting and violence are not a regular occurrence in the working lives of most police officers'. At the same time, 'many police officers see violence as a source of excitement and glamour' (Smith and Gray, 1983: 87).

13. At the time of writing in July 2003, the Manchester branch of the Police Federation proposed that members of the public who are stopped and searched should be handcuffed 'in a bid to reduce the number of serious assaults on officers ... Suspects can lash out and if the officer had the power to handcuff them automatically it makes it safer not just for the officer but also that person' (*Manchester Metro News*, 25 July 2003). No figures were produced to support the claimed relationship between the use of stop and search powers and serious injuries sustained by the police. Thanks to Dave Whyte for the cutting.

14. Zygmunt Bauman has made the point that the modern television industry, in particular, with its emphasis on the idolisation of personalities, is central to the propagation of a culture which is orientated towards finding "'biographical solutions to systemic problems'" (Bauman, 2002: 179). This provides an interesting elaboration upon Mathiesen's original insight into the synoptic nature of modern social control practices.

15. After trenchant criticism, the proposal was dropped from the government's legislative programme in November 2002 but with a promise that ministers still intended to introduce the legislation in the future (*Independent*, 15 November 2002). It is also worth noting that the legislative programme, announced in the Queen's speech in the autumn of 2002, reinforced the discourse of respectability by placing the 'victim at the centre of criminal justice policy'. However, this initiative had been preceded by a letter from the Home Secretary, David Blunkett, stating that those who had experienced work injuries or had been involved in disasters would not be included in the category of victims. Thanks to Steve Tombs for this observation.

16. In May 2003, the Home Secretary announced that victims of crime were to be given a voice in the sentencing process (*Guardian*, 10 May 2003).

17. In the case of the police, 17 had been murdered since 1945; five between 1958 and 1964 when the Homicide Act was still in place, and two in 1963 before the Act was abolished. Since its abolition, four had been killed; three of whom were murdered in a single incident at Shepherds Bush in 1966. In terms of prison officers, one had been murdered in 1965 while 'incidents of violence against prison officers had not increased' (Callaghan, cited in Block and Hostettler, 1997: 265).

CHAPTER 9

1. Commonwealth citizens had never before been subject to visa controls – in fact they had only been subject to immigration controls at all since 1962, and until 1988 were given preferential treatment in some areas such as family reunion (see Nicol and Dummett, 1990; Macdonald and Webber, 2001).

2. In 1995, the EU adopted a regulation requiring member states to impose visa requirements on nationals of countries on a common list. This regulation was replaced by Council Regulation (EC) 574/99 of 12 March 1999 determining the third countries whose nationals must be in possession of visas when crossing the external borders of the member states.

3. The 1951 UN Convention on Refugees requires refugees to be outside their own country in order to be recognised as such, so many countries, including the UK, refuse to grant visas to would-be refugees, although the UK now appears to be moving towards a US-style refugee quota system, in which the government sets an annual quota and UNHCR assesses eligibility in camps in or near the refugee-producing countries. The concept of 'diplomatic asylum' is very unevenly recognised, and has hardly been accepted at all by western countries since the 1950s (see Goodwin-Gill, 1996: 173).

4. Although the Act provides for the possibility of an asylum claim, there are few safeguards in place to ensure that claims can be made and entertained before removal (see CMRA, 2002).

5. Carrier sanctions were contained in the 1990 Agreement implementing the Schengen Accord of 1985, and were made compulsory throughout the EU in June 2001. All aspiring member states are obliged to adopt legislation imposing penalties: EU

Council (2001b), adopted under Title IV of the Treaty of European Union (as amended by the Amsterdam Treaty). The UK opted in to the directive.

6. In 2002, the Immigration and Naturalisation Service (INS) imposed its largest ever fine of $56,100 on Qantas for bringing in 17 undocumented Chinese immigrants from Melbourne to Los Angeles (Davis University, 2002).

7. Section 3A of the Immigration and Asylum Act 1999 allowed immigration officers to grant or refuse leave to enter the UK before passengers' arrival there. In May 2003 the Court of Appeal ruled that the practice of preventing would-be asylum seekers from leaving their country of origin by pre-screening controls was not racially discriminatory and did not offend against the 1951 Refugee Convention, which only protected refugees once they had left their own country; *European Roma Rights Centre* v. *Immigration Officer, Prague and Secretary of State for the Home Department* [2003] EWCA Civ 666.

8. The authority-to-carry scheme is contained in the 2002 Nationality, Immigration and Asylum Act, and is modelled on a US scheme.

9. The EU's Eurodac Convention allows for rapid exchange of fingerprint information by member states to allow them to check identity details of asylum seekers and illegal migrants. In the UK, the 2002 Act extends the types of physical data immigrants in specified categories can be asked to provide.

10. An estimated 3,000 villages in the southeast were destroyed by security forces in operations against Kurdish insurgents in the 1990s; verbal support for a separate Kurdish state is a terrorist offence, and torture remains endemic (see for example, the Home Office country assessment April 2003, on <www.ind.homeoffice.gov. uk/default.asp?PageId=88>).

11. Apart from the ACP countries, these include Egypt, Lebanon, Algeria, Armenia, Georgia, Azerbaijan, Uzbekistan, Croatia, FYROM, Hong Kong, Macao, Sri Lanka (see Peers, 2003a, 2003b).

12. *Sale* v. *Haitian Centers Council*, 113 S Ct 2549, 509 US 155 (1993).

13. Umberto Bossi told *Corriere della Sera* on 16 June 2003 that force should be used: 'After the second or third warning, boom ... the cannon roars, the cannon that blows everyone out of the water' (cited in ERB, 2003b).

14. See <www.raf.mod.uk/news/news_jun03>, <www.andalucia.com/news>. Ulysses is one of 17 joint border-policing operations; others include Triton, Orca, Deniz and Rio IV (see EU Council, 2003).

15. See *Guardian*, 16 April 2002; ERB, 1999; <www.gras.at/schengen/s0.html>.

16. In the UK, the maximum sentence for assisting illegal entry (smuggling) was increased to 14 years in 1999. 'Humanitarian' smugglers are sentenced to between six and 18 months' imprisonment, while commercial smugglers get three to five years, depending on the numbers, the degree of organisation and other factors (see Macdonald and Webber, 2001: 14.31). It is also a criminal offence simply to bring an asylum seeker to the UK to enable him or her to claim asylum, without any element of smuggling; conviction of smuggling requires proof of gain.

17. EU JHA (1997); see also Tampere Conclusions of October 1999 No 23, in Statewatch (1999), and the proposed Directive and Framework Decision on preventing the facilitation of unauthorised entry and stay, agreed May and September 2001 and awaiting adoption, EU Council (2001a).

18. *R* v. *Uxbridge Magistrates ex parte Adimi* [1999] INLR 490. As a result of the High Court's declaration that the practice was illegal, hundreds of asylum seekers had their convictions quashed and received compensation.

19. Karamjit Singh Chahal was alleged to be involved in Sikh terrorism, although no details of the allegation were ever given. He won his case in the European Court of Human Rights, which said he had a right to be given reasons for the detention and a right to challenge it through the courts. *Chahal* v. *UK* (1996) 23 European Human Rights Reports 413.

20. See <www.ncadc.org>; <www.sundayherald.com/35920>; <news.bbc.co.uk/1/hi/scotland/3131637>.

21. Activists who have sought to expose conditions in detention have been punished by transfer to prison. Cameroonian asylum seeker Gabriel Nkwelle (now a recognised refugee) was moved from Rochester, to Haslar, to maximum security prison Belmarsh, after a series of articles on detention conditions (see CARF, 2002a).

22. For case papers from the Campsfield Nine case, *R* v. *Ozidede and Others*, in which nine detainees were charged following disturbances at the detention centre, see <www.closecampsfield.org.uk>.

23. Sir John Donaldson, Master of the Rolls, in *Gurinder Singh Dhillon* v. *Home Secretary* (1987) cited in Ashford, 1993.

24. *Kandasamy Balakrishnan* (1987) in Ashford, 1993.

25. *Secretary of State for the Home Department* v. *Saadi and Others* [2002] UKHL 15; <www.parliament.the-stationery-office.co.uk/pa/ld199697/ldjudgmt/ldjudgmt>.

26. *R (on the application of Gezer)* v. *NASS* [2003] EWHC Admin; see 'UK should hang its head in shame over treatment of asylum seekers', <ncadc.org.uk> 17 April 2003.

27. In *R (Q and Others)* v. *Secretary of State for the Home Department* [2003] EWCA Civ 364, 18 March 2003 the Court of Appeal said that refusal of support did not *necessarily* breach asylum seekers' human rights, but in *R* (on the application of S, D, T) v. *Secretary of State of the Home Department* [2003] EWHC 1941 (Admin), 31 July 2003, the High Court held that in denying support, the Home Office violated the applicants' human dignity and subjected them to inhuman and degrading treatment.

28. For the Ay family campaign see the National Coalition of Anti-Deportation Campaigns website, <ncadc.org>.

29. The UK government has issued reservations to the UN Convention on the Rights of the Child, which expressly state that the welfare of children is secondary to immigration control.

30. *Abdulaziz, Cabales and Balkandali* (1985) 7 European Human Rights Reports.

31. The government was, however, found guilty of sex discrimination for not erecting similar obstacles to the entry of foreign wives, which it promptly did. The right to family life, like rights to liberty, fair trial, free expression, assembly and association, are defined in international conventions like the International Covenant on Civil and Political Rights (ICCPR) and the European and American regional human rights conventions as qualified rights. This qualification allows governments to interfere with them if such interference pursues a legitimate aim, is prescribed by law and is 'necessary in a democratic society in the interests of national security, public safety or the economic well-being of the country, for the prevention of disorder or crime, for the protection of health or morals, or for the protection of the rights and freedoms of others'. The European and Inter-American human rights courts balance these qualified rights against states' rights to control the entry of non-nationals but the ECHR frequently finds expulsion of immigrants, particularly 'integrated aliens', to be in breach of family and private life rights; see e.g. *Moustaquim* v. *Belgium* (1991)

13 EHRR 43, *Beldjoudi* v. *France* (1992) 14 EHRR 801, *Boultif* v. *Switzerland* [2001] 33 EHRR 10.

32. The EEA (European Economic Area) comprises the 25 EU countries and Norway, Lichtenstein and Iceland. Swiss nationals also enjoy the same free movement rights across the EU. In addition, Association Agreements with a number of central and eastern European states (many of which joined the EU on May 2004) give reciprocal rights to their nationals and EU nationals to set up businesses in each other's territory.

33. The European Court of Justice held, in the case of *Pieck* [1981] QB 571 that EC nationals irregularly in another member state could not be deported for the infraction.

34. Although the German slogan 'The boat is full' was borrowed from the far-right Republikaner in the early 1990s to justify stopping the 'flood' of asylum seekers, and *Der Spiegel* had a headline which ran: 'The onslaught of the poor'.

35. CARF, bimonthly from 1991 to 2001 and then quarterly, and the Institute of Race Relations' quarterly *European Race Bulletin*, detail political and press racism and racist violence to asylum seekers in each issue (see in particular CARF, 1991, 1993, 1999a, 2000b, 2001b).

36. Article 1 of the International Covenant on Civil and Political Rights 1966 upholds the right to self-determination, and armed liberation movements such as the African National Congress (ANC) and the Palestine Liberation Organisation (PLO) have in the past achieved recognition by the UN. The very broad definition of terrorism in the 2000 Terrorism Act, the list of organisations proscribed by that Act (and now, the longer list proscribed by the EU and the even longer one proscribed by the US) make all armed struggle 'terrorism'.

37. Again, by the extremely broad definition of 'terrorism' in the UK and the EU, which covers any urban protest which involves violence to people or property.

38. See <www.lchr.org/media/2003_alerts>.

39. See <www.statewatch.org/news>. The Appeal Court overruled the Special Immigration Appeals Commission (SIAC), which had found the derogation unlawful, because it discriminated against foreign nationals. For SIAC decision see Norton-Taylor, 'Right ruling, wrong reason' in the *Guardian*, 1 August 2002.

40. An extradition agreement was signed between the US and the EU in June 2003. The House of Lords Select Committee on the European Communities expressed concern at the lack of human rights protection in the agreement. A separate treaty with the UK goes much further, allowing the US to demand extradition from the UK without providing prima facie evidence. See 'UK parliament Select Committee issues critical report on EU-US agreements', 'New UK-US extradition treaty' on <www.statewatch.org/news/2003/july>.

CHAPTER 10

1. What constitutes a 'major injury' is defined in legislation and includes certain forms of fracture, amputation, dislocation, loss of sight, strain, burn, electrical shock, asphyxiation, poisonings and concussion. Minor injuries are work-related injuries which fall outside of these categories, but which cause the injured to be absent from work for three or more days.

2. Of course, the inability and/or institutional reluctance of state bodies to provide 'answers' in relation to the production and reproduction of private troubles and public issues has been well documented, not least by critical criminologists. Notable

here has been a critical focus upon the role of coroners' courts and the inquest system; see, for example, Scraton and Chadwick, 1987; Scraton 1999.

3. The misery heaped upon the bereaved, and their desperate struggle for 'answers', is clear from the work of the Centre for Corporate Accountability (CCA). The CCA was established as a not-for-profit organisation in 1999, and seeks to promote worker and public safety through addressing law enforcement and corporate accountability. While the CCA's activities fall into three main categories – advice, research and advocacy – its key activities are its Work-Related Death Advisory Service, and a similar service relating to workplace injuries, each of which provides free, independent and confidential advice to families on how to ensure that deaths (and injuries) are properly investigated and that evidence is subjected to proper prosecution scrutiny. For further details on these services, see <www.corporateaccountability.org/death_advice.htm> and <www.corporateaccountability.org/injury_advice.htm>

4. This is not to deny that there are good empirical and theoretical reasons why more effective safety regulation *can* be functional for capital, albeit under certain conditions, for certain companies, over limited periods of time (Pearce and Tombs, 1998: 283–5).

5. The analysis was undertaken by the CCA on behalf of the public services trade union UNISON. I am grateful to each organisation for their kind permission to use this data so extensively. Of course, the views expressed here are my own, and do not in any way represent views of either the CCA or UNISON. The data which form the bulk of this chapter are taken from a much more detailed report (see Unison/CCA, 2002) which is available at <www.corporateaccountability.org/HSEReport/index.htm>.

6. Average fines have been rounded up to the next thousand.

7. Average fines have been rounded up to the next thousand.

8. But see Pearce and Tombs, 1998: chapters 7 and 9.

CHAPTER 12

1. My focus in this chapter is on gender with explicit reference to females, though this approach is not a negation of the harmful experiences that males experience because of their gender.

2. For example, the British Crime Survey is heavily influenced by explanations of victimisation which focus on the life style approach. This tends to exaggerate the importance of public violence at the expense of violence which occurs in private, behind hidden doors.

3. For example, the critical criminology tradition has been a strong advocate for extending the definition of crime to incorporate human rights violations. For example, Schwendinger and Schwendinger (1975) proposed that crime could be defined as violations of fundamental human rights – which are based on a set of moral values.

4. For example, in Tamil Nadu, North India, George (2000) writes that where a case of female infanticide has been reported to the police, it has not usually resulted in a successful prosecution. Very often, reports are filled in days after the discovery and are incomplete. With many other crimes being committed, female infanticide cases are not rigorously pursued.

5. For example, Monk and Katz (1993) write that the Comanches have been reported as identifying five stages, the Kikuyu six for males and eight for females, the Andaman Islanders 23 for men and the Incas ten.

6. The ILO has estimated that about 40 per cent of people over 64 years of age in Africa and about 25 per cent in Asia remain in the paid labour force.

7. According to Warren (1985), son preference involves some or all of the following desires: (1) that if there were to be only one child in the family, that one be male; (2) that if there were to be several children, that there be more boys than girls; and (3) that the first-born child be male. There are cultural variations in son preference, with developing countries, particularly in Asia and Africa, exhibiting the strongest preference. But son preference is also prevalent, although not dominant, in the US and western Europe, as well as those countries which are experiencing rapid economic development such as Korea and Taiwan (ibid.; see also Das Gupta and Shuzhuo, 1999) and China (Dalsimer and Nisonoff, 1997).

8. WHO is currently carrying out a multi-study on women's health and domestic violence against women (Garcia-Moreno, 2003). Preliminary results are not currently available.

9. According to Article 340 of the criminal code, 'a husband or a close blood relative who kills a woman caught in a situation highly suspicious of adultery will be totally exempt from sentence'. Article 98 guarantees a lighter sentence for male killers of female relatives who have committed an 'act which is illicit in the eyes of the perpetrator'.

10. Maternal deaths may be misclassified, cause of death may not be reported, and countries may not have a reliable system of civil registration for recording vital events including deaths.

11. Countries included Argentina, Brazil, India, Kenya, Lebanon, as well as Canada, Austria and Sweden.

CHAPTER 13

1. Thanks go to the editors for their patience, support and helpful comments. In addition, I am grateful to Richard Huxtable for (what he would doubtless describe as) his penetrating insights, to Sharon Cowan for an alcohol-fuelled conversation about intersex and to F. Howerd for the first *double entendre* loaded draft.

2. I have chosen not to define 'harm' explicitly as I am wary of delimiting the concept at the outset. Instead, the chapter seeks to identify and describe particular hurts, while leaving space for the further development of notions of harm.

3. For example, identifying female circumcision/genital mutilation and cosmetic surgery as harm can in itself sometimes be both overly reductive and harmful (Bibbings, 1995, 1996a, 1999 and 2001).

4. Commenting upon Canon Dr Jeffrey John's (brief) appointment as the first openly but non-practising gay Anglican Bishop (he was persuaded to withdraw his acceptance of the Reading bishopric).

5. For example, see the English and Welsh definition of rape as sexual intercourse, s.1 Sexual Offences Act 1956 (as subsequently amended). The law on sexual offences is soon to be changed (Sexual Offences Bill 2003).

6. A fascination with heterosexual anal sex is evident from the pages of men's magazines such as *Loaded* or *FHM*.

7. [2000] 2 F.L.R. 697.

8. Asexuality poses further questions about non-identity and invisibility but is not considered in this chapter.

9. For example, the International Lesbian and Gay Association describes itself as being 'dedicated to achieving equal rights for lesbians, gay men, bisexuals and transgendered people everywhere', <www.ilga.org>.

10. 'Transgender' is an umbrella term which is generally taken to include transsexual, transvestite and intersex people.
11. [2000] 1 W.L.R. 977.
12. [2002] I.R.L.R. 851 (EAT).
13. [2003] 1 All E.R. 255 (CA).
14. Perhaps the most significant recent development is the US Supreme Court finding that sodomy laws are unconstitutional. *Lawrence* v. *Texas* 123 S. Ct. 2472 (2003). See also the South African Constitutional Court's decision in *National Coalition for Gay and Lesbian Equality* v. *Minister of Justice* 1999 (1) SA 6 (CC).
15. [1985] FLR 166, [1985] Fam Law 29.
16. See generally <www.hrc.org/familynet> and <www.hrc.org/issues/family>.
17. <www.hrc.org/stateaction/index.asp>.
18. <www.hrc.org>.
19. See <www.womenandequalityunit.gov.uk/discrimination/partnership.htm>.
20. *Halpern* v. *Canada (Attorney General)* (2003) 225 D.L.R. (4th) 529; *Barbeau* v. *Canada (Attorney General)* (2003) 228 D.L.R. (4th) 416.
21. <www.hrc.org/familynet/chapter.asp?article=759>.
22. [1971] P 83, [1970] 2 All ER 33.
23. *I* v. *UK* (25680/94) [2002] 2 F.L.R. 518 [2002], (2003) 36 E.H.R.R. 53; *Goodwin* v. *UK* (28957/95) [2002] I.R.L.R. 664, (2002) 35 E.H.R.R. 18; *Bellinger* v. *Bellinger* [2003] UKHL 21, 2 All ER 593, [2003].
24. *SY* v. *SY* [1963] P 37.
25. See, for example, *W* v. *W* (Nullity: Gender) [2001] Fam 111, [2001] 1 FLR 324.
26. The shift was sparked in part by *I* v. *UK*, *Goodwin* v. *UK* and *Bellinger* v. *Bellinger* (mentioned above).
27. Circuit Court of the Sixth Judicial Circuit, Pasco County, Florida, Case No.: 98–5375CA. Available at <www.genderlaw.org>.
28. *Littleton* v. *Prange* 9 SW3d 225. All attempts to overturn this decision have thus far been unsuccessful. See Frye and Meiselman (2001), ftns.3, 231 for a summary of the various actions.
29. See *Littleton* at 225, 226–27.
30. For example, the American Psychiatric Association only dropped this diagnosis in 1973 (see Herek, 2000: 19).
31. See, for example, the few defences of circumcision at <www.cirp.org/pages/feedback. html>.
32. See, for example, <www.cirp.org> and <www.Nocirc.org>.
33. See further, for example, Dreger (1998) on medical approaches to intersex. For an account of later-life trauma see 'Fora's Story' <www.medhelp.org/www/ais>.
34. Gayle's Story, <www.medhelp.org/www/ais/>.
35. See, for example, <www.isna.org> and <www.ukia.co.uk>.

CHAPTER 14

1. The Prevention of Cruelty to Children Act, 1889.
2. For a fuller account see Parker (1995).
3. Public Record Office (PRO), MH 102/1966.
4. See Women's Group on Public Welfare (1948) and ibid.
5. This was the conclusion reached by a joint committee of the BMA and the Magistrates' Association, saying: 'It is impossible to make any definite assessment of parental cruelty and neglect. As social standards are raised any instance of

individual cruelty tends to become more obvious and to attract more publicity. It seems probable that cases of extreme cruelty are less, but who can know how much mental cruelty exists?' (BMA, 1956: 1–2).

6. Ibid., appendix 1, table B(i); p. 58.

7. For an excellent discussion see L. Gordon (1989) and Swift (1995), especially chapter 6, 'Neglect as Failed Motherhood'.

8. This was linked with the eugenics movement, many of the assumptions of which found expression in reports such as that of the Brock Committee (1933).

9. NSPCC, *Research Briefing: Child Abuse*, London, various dates.

10. An excellent discussion of this issue is to be found in Stevenson (1996, 1998). 'Neglect', as she says, 'has been neglected' (1998: 13).

11. For evidence of this reluctance see, PRO, MH 102/1966. In the case of food policy the changes introduced by the 1980 Education Act provide a relevant example. Prior to this legislation school meals had to conform to prescribed nutritional standards. Thereafter, local authorities were left 'free to decide the form, content and price' of these meals. That de-control is likely to have contributed to the worsening diets of school children, partly through the effects of higher prices and partly through the widening of the choices that they can make as a result of 'self-service' as well as a result of their greater use of commercial outlets. See, Department of Health (1989).

12. Children and Young Persons Act, 1933; sect. 1.

13. See Bowlby (1951, 1971) and also Rutter's (1970) critical review.

14. See for a brief review of this and other issues connected with harm, Bentovim (1998). Also consult Black et al. (1997) especially chapters 10c and 11b.

15. See, La Fontaine (1994).

16. This is dealt with in WHO (2002a: 67–72).

17. For an early example see Jephcott (1971).

18. For accounts of these trans-shipments see Parr (1980), Wagner (1982), and, more recently, Health Committee (1997).

19. Some offsetting steps were taken later in raising children's allowances in the income support and tax systems.

20. See for a discussion of this and related issues Guldberg (2000).

21. See, Bentovim (1998) for a brief classification of harms and their respective likely consequences.

22. For a wider and influential analysis of the issue see Ryan (1971).

23. For a more general review of the effect of foetal and infant experience on later disease see Barker (1992).

24. Internationally the age of criminal responsibility varies between seven and 18. It is also interesting to note how different religions deal with the issue of moral responsibility. Jesuit doctrine puts it at seven, while in Judaism a boy's barmitzvah at 13 is accompanied by his father's statement that he is then no longer responsible for his son's behaviour: literally, 'Blessed be he who has freed me from the punishment that this one must have'. In Shari'ah law a child is not held to be responsible until reaching puberty.

25. These two latter functions of schools have been stressed by such radical commentators as Illich (1973) and Meyer (1983).

26. See Parker (1990).

27. See 27th Report of the Inspector of Reformatory and Industrial Schools of Great Britain, c.4147, 1884; pp 22 and 32.

28. The white paper was based upon Lord Longford's report for the Labour Party (Labour Party, 1964).

29. For a review of the research evidence on these matters see Rutter et al. (1998).

30. The Convention was approved in 1989 and has been ratified by nearly 200 countries. One of its clauses prohibits children under 15 from being recruited into armed forces.

31. For a brief review of the evidence on war and children see Nikapota (1997: 161–4). For a study of the effects of incarceration in Nazi concentration camps see Hicklin (1946).

32. In this respect it might be noted that the Law Lords in Britain have recently ruled that sentences on children who have murdered should take account of their welfare and not just the punishment. For a report see the *Independent*, 23 November 2002.

33. For an up-to-date example see, ITS (2003) accessible at <www.warchild.ca>. For example: 'The Gulf War and twelve years of economic sanctions have had a devastating effect on Iraq's health infrastructure, resulting in a significant decline in the health and well being of Iraqi children' (ibid.: 11).

CHAPTER 15

1. Republished by Townsend and Davidson (1982).

2. Henry Kissinger was the 56th Secretary of State of the United States from 1973 to 1977 and was awarded the Nobel Peace Prize in 1973. In the same year that he gave the commitment at the World Food Conference that no child will go to bed hungry he also wrote National Security Study Memorandum 200 (Kissinger, 1974) which argued that population growth in the LDCs was a grave threat to US national security and outlined a covert plan to reduce population growth in those countries through birth control, and also, implicitly, war and famine, for example by using food as a weapon (see also Brewda, 1995).

3. Gordon et al. (2003) analysed survey data on nearly 1.2 million children in 46 countries collected mainly during the late 1990s, this is the largest, most accurate survey sample of children ever assembled.

4. <www.un.org/millennium/declaration/ares552e.htm>.

5. <www.theglobeandmail.com/servlet/story/RTGAM.20030924.wbank0924/ BNStory/International> See also World Bank (2003b).

6. The *International Covenant on Economic, Social and Cultural Rights* came into force in 1976 and has since been signed and/or ratified by virtually every country in the world (148 countries as of 2 November 2003). See <www.unhchr.ch/pdf/report.pdf> for details.

7. Research has shown that people who have never lived in poverty are more likely to blame poverty on the inadequate actions and moral failings of the 'poor' (for example, see Gordon and Pantazis, 1997; Kreidl, 2000). However, it seems likely that many modern political elites have at least some concern for people living in poverty.

8. The relationship between intentionality, moral acts and crime has a long history and is sometimes traced to Thomas Aquinas's doctrine of double effect: Nothing hinders one act from having two effects, only one of which is intended, while the other is beside the intention. Now moral acts take their species according to what is intended, and not according to what is beside the intention, since this is accidental. Accordingly the act of self-defence may have two effects, one is the saving of one's life, and the other is the slaying of the aggressor. Therefore this act, since one's

intention is to save one's own life, is not unlawful, seeing that it is natural to everything to keep itself in 'being', as far as possible. And yet, though proceeding from a good intention, an act may be rendered unlawful, if it be out of proportion to the end (cited in Woodward, 2001).

9. Plant (2000) rejects the principles of the doctrine of double effect, that foreseeable harmful acts are permissible if they are unintended consequences of some other action. The intention of privatisation of healthcare is not to harm the poor.

BIBLIOGRAPHY

Abel, R. L. (1982a) *The Politics of Informal Justice: Volume One. The American Experience* (New York: Academic Press).

Abel, R. L. (1982b) *The Politics of Informal Justice: Volume Two. Comparative Perspectives* (New York: Academic Press).

AbouZar, C. and Wardlaw, T. (2001) 'Maternal Mortality at the End of the Decade: Signs of Progress', *Bulletin of the World Health Organisation*, vol. 79, no. 6.

ACLU (2002) 'Press Release', 24 January. <www.aclu.org>

Action Against False Allegations of Abuse (2000) *You Could Be Next to be Falsely Accused of Sexual Abuse*, AAFAA, 25 February. <www.aafaa.org.uk>

Action Against False Allegations of Abuse (2002a) *Home*, AAFAA, 25 February. <www.aafaa.org.uk>

Action Against False Allegations of Abuse (2002b) *History*, AAFAA, 4 July. <www.aafaa.org.uk>

Adcock, M. (1998) 'Significant Harm: Implications for Local Authorities', in M. Adcock and R. White (eds) *Significant Harm: Its Management and Outcomes*, 2nd edition (Croyden: Significant Publications).

Ahlstrom, D. (2002) '6,600 Britons May Have form of BSE', *Irish Times*, 20 September.

Aitken, L. and Griffin, G. (1996) *Gender Issues in Elder Abuse* (London: Sage).

Alvesalo, A. (1998) 'They Are Not Honest Criminals', *Organised Crime and Crime Prevention: What Works?*, Rapport fra NSFKs 40 forskeseminar (Copenhagen: Scandinavian Research Council for Criminology).

Alvesalo, A. (1999) 'Meeting the Expectations of the Local Community on Safety – What About White-Collar Crime?', Paper Presented at the 27th Annual Conference of the European Group for the Study of Deviance and Social Control, Palanga, Lithuania, 2–5 September.

Alvesalo, A. and Tombs, S. (2002) 'Working for Criminalisation of Economic Offending: Contradictions for Critical Criminology?', *Critical Criminology: An International Journal*, vol. 11, no. 1.

Amnesty International (1993) 'Unlawful Killing of Detained Asylum Seeker Omasese Lumumba', EUR 45/13/93, November.

Amnesty International (1994) 'Cruel, Inhuman or Degrading Treatment During Forcible Deportation', EUR 45/05/94, July.

Amnesty International (1997) 'No Flights to Safety: Carrier Sanctions; Airline Employees and the Rights of Refugees', ACT 34/021/1997, 1 November.

Amnesty International (2003) 'Australia Factsheet 15'. <www.amnesty.org.au/refugees/ref-fact15>

Amnesty International/USA (2003) *Pakistan: Violence Against Women in the Name of Honour*. <www.amnestyusa.org/countries/pakistan/reports/honour/overview2.html>

Anderson, P. (2000) 'Editorial. Renewals', *New Left Review*, no. 1, January/February.

Andersson, J. O. (1996) 'Fundamental Values for a Third Left', *New Left Review*, no. 216, March/April.

Andersson, J. O., Kosonen, P. and Vartiainen, J. (1993) *The Finnish Model of Economic and Social Policy: From Emulation to Crash* (Abö: Akademi).

ARC (1999) *Out of Sight, Out of Mind: A Report on the Dispersal of Asylum Seekers in the UK* (London: Asylum Rights Campaign).

Aretxaga, B. (2000) 'A Fictional Reality: Paramilitary Death Squads and the Construction of State Terror in Spain', in J. A. Sluka (ed.) *Death Squad* (Philadelphia: University of Pennsylvania Press).

Arora, D. (1996) 'The Victimizing Discourse: Sex Determination and Policy', *Economic and Political Weekly*, vol. 31, no. 7, 17 February.

Ashford, M. (1993) *Detained Without a Trial: A Survey of Immigration Act Detention* (London: Joint Council for the Welfare of Immigrants).

Atkinson, A. B. (2002) 'Is Rising Income Inequality Inevitable? A Critique of the "Transatlantic Consensus"', in P. Townsend and D. Gordon (eds) *World Poverty: New Policies to Defeat an Old Enemy* (Bristol: Policy Press).

Backers, S. (2001) 'Risking it All: The Implications of Refugee Smuggling', *Race & Class*, vol. 43, no. 1.

Baggot, R. (2000) *Public Health. Policy and Politics* (London: Macmillan).

Bailez, M. M., Gearhart, J. P., Migeon, C. and Rock, J. (1992) 'Vaginal Reconstruction After Initial Construction of the External Genitalia in Girls with Salt-Wasting Adrenal Hyperplasia', *Journal of Urology*, vol. 148, no. 3.

Ballinger, A. (2000) *Dead Woman Walking* (Aldershot: Ashgate).

Banks, C. (ed.) (2000) *Developing Cultural Criminology: Theory and Practice in Papua New Guinea* (Sydney: Institute of Criminology).

Barak, G. (2003) *Violence and Nonviolence: Pathways to Understanding* (Thousand Oaks, CA: Sage).

Barker, D. J. (ed.) (1992) *Foetal and Infant Origins of Adult Disease* (London: British Medical Journal).

Barlow, M. and Clarke, T. (2001) *Global Showdown* (Toronto: Stoddart).

Barnett, H. (1994) *Toxic Debts and the Superfund Dilemma* (Chapel Hill: The University of North Carolina Press).

Baron, J. (1998) *Judgment Misguided: Intuition and Error in Public Decision Making* (New York: Oxford University Press).

Bauman, Z. (1989) *Modernity and the Holocaust* (Cambridge: Polity).

Bauman, Z. (1995) *Life in Fragments: Essays in Postmodern Morality* (Oxford: Blackwell).

Bauman, Z. (1998) *Work Consumption and the New Poor* (Buckingham: Open University Press).

Bauman, Z. (2000) 'Social Issues of Law and Order', *British Journal of Criminology*, vol. 40, no. 2.

Bauman, Z. (2001) 'Quality and Inequality', *Guardian*, 29 December.

Bauman, Z. (2002) *Society Under Siege* (Cambridge: Polity).

BBC (2002) 'Rise in Pakistan "Honour" Killings', *BBC News*, 1 February.

Beck, U. (1992) *Risk Society: Towards a New Modernity* (London: Sage).

Becker, H. (1963) *Outsiders* (Glencoe: Free Press).

Becker, J. (1996) *Hungry Ghosts: China's Secret Famine* (London: J. Murray).

Beckmann, A. (1999) '"Life-Worlds" of Consensual "SM" Versus the Social Construction of "Sadomasochism" and its "Socio-Legal Control"', Paper Presented at Annual

Conference of the European Group for the Study of Deviance and Social Control, Palanga, Lithuania, 2–5 September.

Beckmann, A. and Cooper, C. (2003) 'Conditions of Domination: Reflections on the Harms Generated by the British Educational System', Paper Presented at the 'Tough on Crime – Tough on Freedoms?' Conference, Chester College, 22–24 April.

Beetham, D. (1991) *The Legitimation of Power* (Basingstoke: Macmillan).

Beijing Review (2002) 'Beijing Review', 3 January.

Bentham, J. (1970) *Of Laws in General* (London: Athlone Press).

Bentovim, A. (1998) 'Significant Harm in Context', in M. Adcock and R. White (eds) *Significant Harm: Its Management and Outcomes*, 2nd edition (Croyden: Significant Publications).

Beresford, S. (1998) 'The Lesbian Mother: Questions of Gender and Sexual Identity', in L. J. Moran, D. Monk and S. Beresford (eds) *Legal Queeries: Lesbian, Gay and Transgender Legal Studies* (London: Cassell).

Bergman, D. (2000) *The Case for Corporate Responsibility. Corporate Violence and the Criminal Justice System* (London: Disaster Action).

Bhaskar, R. (1998) *The Possibility of Naturalism*, 3rd edition (London: Routledge).

Bibbings, L. (1995) 'Female Genital Mutilation and the Law', in J. Bridgeman and S. Millns (eds) *Law and Body Politics: Regulating the Female Body* (Aldershot: Dartmouth).

Bibbings, L. (1996a) 'Touch: Socio-Cultural Attitudes and Legal Responses to Body Alteration', in L. Bently and L. Flynn (eds) *Law and the Senses: Sensational Jurisprudence* (London: Pluto).

Bibbings, L. (1996b) 'Gender, Sexuality and Sex Education', in N. Harris (ed.) *Children, Sex Education and the Law* (London: National Children's Bureau).

Bibbings, L. (1999) 'Feminist Dilemmas: Female Genital Mutilation', in A. Buckwald and M. Raab-Pir (ed.) *24 Feministischer Juristinnentag* (Munich: Druck).

Bibbings, L. (2001) 'Criminalising Tradition: The Practices Formerly Known as Female Circumcision', in P. Alldridge and C. Brants (eds) *Personal Autonomy, the Private Sphere and the Criminal Law – A Comparative Study* (Oxford: Hart).

Birnberg, B. (1998) 'Why the Law Failed Derek Bentley', *The Times*, 4 August.

Black, D., Newmann, M., Harris-Hendricks, J. and Mezey, G. (1997) *Psychological Trauma: A Developmental Approach* (London: Gaskell).

Black, R. E., Morris, S. S. and Bryce, J. (2003) 'Where and Why Are 10 Million Children Dying Every Year?', *Lancet*, vol. 361.

Blad, J. R., van Mastrigt, H. and Uildriks, N. A. (1987) *The Criminal Justice System as a Social Problem: An Abolitionist Perspective* (Rotterdam: Erasmus University).

Block, B. and Hostettler, J. (1997) *Hanging in the Balance* (Winchester: Waterside Press).

Blum, W. (2000) *Rogue State: A Guide to the World's Only Superpower* (London: Zed Books).

BMA (1956) *Cruelty to and Neglect of Children* (London: British Medical Association).

Bongaarts, J. (1999) 'The Fertility Impact of Changes in the Timing of Childbearing in the Developing World', *Population Studies*, vol. 53, no. 3.

Bornstein, K. (1994) *Gender Outlaw – On Men, Women and the Rest of Us* (New York, London: Routledge).

Boukovsky, V. (1972) *Une nouvelle maladie mentale en URSS: l'opposition* (Paris: Editions du Seuil).

Bowlby, J. (1951) *Maternal Care and Mental Health* (Geneva: WHO).

Bowlby, J. (1971) *Attachment and Loss*, vols 1 and 2 (Harmondsworth: Penguin).

Bowling, B. (1998) *Violent Racism* (Oxford: Oxford University Press).

Box, S. (1983) *Power, Crime and Mystification* (London: Tavistock).

Boyd, C. (1992) 'Case Study: The Zeebrugge Car Ferry Disaster', in W. Frederick, J. Post and K. Davis (eds) *Business and Society: Corporate Strategy, Public Policy and Ethics* (New York: McGraw Hill).

Boyd, S. B. (1992) 'What Is a Normal Family?', *Modern Law Review*, vol. 55, no. 2.

Braithwaite, J. (1995) 'White-Collar Crime', in G. Geis (ed.) *White-Collar Crime. Classic and Contemporary Views*, 3rd edition (New York: The Free Press).

Braithwaite, J. (2000) 'The New Regulatory State and the Transformation of Criminology', *British Journal of Criminology*, vol. 40, no. 2.

Braithwaite, J. and Fisse, B. (1987) 'Self-Regulation and the Control of Corporate Crime', in C. D. Shearing and P. C. Stenning (eds) *Private Policing* (Beverly Hills: Sage).

Breitman, R. (1999) *Official Secrets: What the Nazis Planned, What the British and Americans Knew* (London: Penguin).

Brewda, J. (1995) 'Kissinger's 1974 Plan for Food Control Genocide', *Executive Intelligence Review*, vol. 22, no. 49. <www.larouchepub.com/other/1995/2249_kissinger_food. html>

British Association of Paediatric Surgeons (2001) *Statement of the Working Party on the Surgical Management of Children Born with Ambiguous Genitalia.* <www.baps. org.uk>

Brock Committee (1933) *Report of the Departmental Committee on Sterilisation*, cmd. 4485 (London: HMSO).

Brookman, F. and Maguire, M. (2003a) *Reducing Homicide: A Review of the Possibilities* (London: Home Office). <www.homeoffice.gov.uk/rds/pdfs2/rdsolr0103.pdf>

Brookman, F. and Maguire, M. (2003b) *Reducing Homicide: Summary of a Review of the Possibilities*, Home Office Research Development and Statistics Directorate, Occasional Paper No. 84 (London: Home Office). <www.homeoffice.gov.uk/rds/ pdfs2/occ84homicide.pdf>

Budd, T. (1999) *Violence at Work: Findings from the British Crime Survey* (London: Home Office).

Buncombe, A. (1999) 'Court Frees Three Over Killing of Newsagent', *Independent*, 8 December.

Bunyan, T. (1991) 'Towards an Authoritarian European State', *Race & Class*, vol. 32, no. 3.

Burleigh, M. (1997) *Ethics and Extermination: Reflections on Nazi Genocide* (Cambridge: Cambridge University Press).

Butler, J. (1990) *Gender Trouble: Feminism and the Subversion of Identity* (New York: Routledge).

Callaghan, J. and Tunney, S. (2000) 'Prospects for Social Democracy: A Critical Review of the Arguments and Evidence', *Contemporary Politics*, vol. 6, no. 1.

Campbell, D. and Lee, R. (2003) '"Carnage by Computer": The Blackboard Economics of the 2001 Foot and Mouth Epidemic', *Social & Legal Studies*, vol. 12, no. 4.

Candib, L. (1999) 'Incest and Other Harms to Daughters Across Cultures: Maternal Complicity and Patriarchal Power', *Women's Studies International Forum*, vol. 22, no. 2.

CARF (1991) 'Playing the Race Card', *CARF*, vol. 5, Nov.–Dec.

CARF (1992) 'After Hoyerswerda: The New Political Consensus in Germany', *CARF*, vol. 8, May–Jun.

CARF (1993) 'Defying the Reparation Plan', *CARF*, vol. 16, Sep.–Oct.

CARF (1998) 'No Safety for Roma', *CARF*, vol. 41, Dec. 1997–Jan. 1998.

CARF (1999a) 'Breaking Down Borders', *CARF*, vol. 51, Aug.–Sep.

CARF (1999b) 'Learning the Lessons of Dover', *CARF*, vol. 52, Oct.–Nov.

CARF (2000a) 'Racially Motivated Murders – Known or Suspected – Since 1997', *CARF*, vol. 54, Feb.–Mar.

CARF (2000b) 'Beware: Media Lies Fuel Racism', *CARF*, vol. 55, Apr.–May.

CARF (2000c) 'Stop the Bogus Nationalism', *CARF*, vol. 55, Apr.–May.

CARF (2000d) 'Deportations: More Violence, More Deaths', *CARF*, vol. 57, Aug.–Sep.

CARF (2000e) 'How to Stop a Deportation', *CARF*, vol. 57, Aug.–Sep.

CARF (2001a) 'Killer Politics', *CARF*, vol. 60, Feb.–Mar.

CARF (2001b) 'Licence to Hate', *CARF*, vol. 62, Jun.–Jul.

CARF (2002a) 'The Knock on the Door', *CARF*, vol. 66, Feb.–Mar.

CARF (2002b) 'No Borders', *CARF*, vol. 68, Autumn.

CARF (2003) 'Yarl's Wood: Profit Before Lives?' *CARF*, vol. 72, Autumn.

Carlen, P. (1992) 'Criminal Women and Criminal Justice: The Limits to, and Potential of, Feminist and Left Realist Perspectives', in R. Matthews and J. Young (eds) *Issues in Realist Criminology* (London: Sage).

Carlen, P., Gleeson, D. and Wardhaugh, J. (1992) *Truancy: The Politics of Compulsory Schooling* (Buckingham: Open University Press).

Carrère d'Encausse, H. (1978) *L'Empire eclaté* (Paris: Flammarion).

Cassen, B. (1981) 'Révolte et désarroi en Grande Bretagne', *Le Monde Diplomatique*, August.

Chau, P.-L. and Herring, J. (2002) 'Defining, Assigning and Designing Sex', *International Journal of Law Policy and the Family*, vol. 16, no. 3.

Chen, L., Huq, E. and D'Souza, S. (1981) 'Sex Bias in Family Allocation of Food and Health Care in Rural Bangladesh', *Population and Development Review*, vol. 7, no. 1.

Chen, M. (1995) 'The Feminisation of Poverty', in N. Heyzer, with S. Kapoor and J. Sandler (eds) *A Commitment to the World's Women: Perspectives on Development for Beijing and Beyond* (New York: UNIFEM).

Chibnall, S. (1977) *Law and Order News* (London: Tavistock).

Chomsky, N. (1989) *The Culture of Terrorism* (London: Pluto).

Chomsky, N. (1999) *Profit Over People. Neo-Liberalism and Global Order* (New York: Seven Stories Press).

Chossudovsky, M. (1997) *The Globalisation of Poverty: Impacts of IMF and World Bank Reforms* (Goa: Other India Press).

Christie, N. (1977) 'Conflicts as Property', *British Journal of Criminology*, vol. 17, no. 1.

Christie, N. (1982) *Limits to Pain*, 3rd edition (Oxford: Martin Robertson).

Christie, N. (1986) 'Suitable Enemies', in H. Bianchi and R. van Swaaningen (eds) *Abolitionism. Towards a Non-Repressive Approach to Crime* (Amsterdam: Free University Press).

Christie, N. (1993) *Crime Control as Industry: Towards Gulags, Western Style* (London: Routledge & Kegan Paul).

Christie, N. (2000) *Crime Control as Industry: Towards Gulags, Western Style*, 3rd edition (London: Routledge).

Chunkath, S. and Athreya, V. (1997) 'Female Infanticide in Tamil Nadu: Some Evidence', *Economic and Political Weekly*, vol. 32, no. 17, April.

Cilliers, J. (1999) 'In Structural and Terminal Imbalance?', *UN Chronicle Online*, vol. 36, no. 4.

Clarke, M. (1998) *Citizens' Financial Futures: The Regulation of Retail Financial Investment in Britain* (Aldershot: Ashgate).

CMRA (2002) 'Committee for Migration and Refugees Brief: Issues Affecting Asylum' (Washington: Committee for Migration and Refugee Affairs, InterAction). <www.interaction.org>

COEA (Council for Economic Advisors for the President's Initiative on Race) (1998) *Changing America: Indicators of Social and Economic Well Being by Race and Hispanic Origin* (Washington: GPO).

Cohen, A. K. (1956) *Delinquent Boys* (London: Routledge & Kegan Paul).

Cohen, G. (ed.) (1987) *Social Change and the Life Course* (London: Tavistock).

Cohen, R. (2002) 'An Epidemic of Neglect: Neglected Diseases and the Health Burden in Poor Countries', *Multinational Monitor*, vol. 23, no. 6. <www.multinationalmonitor.org/mm2002/02june/june02corp1.html>

Cohen, S. (1981) 'Footprints on the Sand: A Further Report on Criminology and the Sociology of Deviance in Britain', in M. Fitzgerald, G. McLennan and J. Pawson (eds) *Crime and Society. Readings in History and Theory* (London: Routledge/Open University).

Cohen, S. (1988) 'The Failures of Criminology', in S. Cohen (ed.) *Against Criminology* (New Brunswick: Transaction Books).

Cohen, S. (1993) 'Human Rights and Crimes of the State: The Culture of Denial', *Australian and New Zealand Journal of Criminology*, vol. 26, no. 2.

Cohen, S. (2001) *States of Denial: Knowing About Atrocities and Suffering* (Cambridge: Polity).

Collier, R. (1995) *Masculinity, Law and the Family* (London: Routledge).

Collier, R. (1998) *Masculinities, Crime and Criminology* (London: Sage).

Comfort, A. (2002) *The New Joy of Sex*, updated edition (London: Mitchell Beazley).

Committee of Public Accounts (1999) *Managing Sickness Absence in the Prison Service* (London: HMSO).

Committee on the Medical Effects of Air Pollutants (1998) *Report: The Quantification of the Effects of Air Pollution on Health in the United Kingdom* (London: Department of Health).

Conquest, R. (1971) *The Great Terror: Stalin's Purge of the Thirties* (London: Penguin).

Conquest, R. (1979) *Kolmya: The Arctic Death Camps* (Oxford: Oxford University Press).

Cook, R., Dickens, B. and Fathalla, M. (2002) 'Female Genital Cutting (Mutilation/Circumcision): Ethical and Legal Dimensions', *International Journal of Gynaecology*, vol. 79.

Cooper, C. (2002) *Understanding School Exclusion: Challenging Processes of Docility* (Nottingham: Education Now).

Cornelius, W., Martin, P. and Hollifield, J. (eds) (1995) *Controlling Immigration: A Global Perspective* (California: Stanfield University Press).

Cornell, D. (1995) *The Imaginary Domain: Abortion, Pornography and Sexual Harassment* (London: Routledge).

Corrigan, P. and Sayer, D. (1985) *The Great Arch* (Oxford: Blackwell).

Corteen, K., Moran, L., Skeggs, B. and Tyrer, P. (2001) 'Property, Boundary, Exclusion: Making Sense of Heterocentric Violence and Safer Spaces', *Social and Cultural Geography*, vol. 2, no. 4.

Council of Europe (1991) 'Recommendation 1163 (1991): Arrival of Asylum Seekers at European Ports', Parliamentary Assembly of the Council of Europe. <www.assembly. coe.int>

Council of Europe (2000a) *Recommendation 1449 (2000): Clandestine Migration from South of the Mediterranean into Europe*, Parliamentary Assembly of the Council of Europe. <www.assembly.coe.int>

Council of Europe (2000b) *Recommendation 1467 (2000): Clandestine Immigration and the Fight Against Traffickers*, Parliamentary Assembly of the Council of Europe. <www.assembly.coe.int>

Council on Scientific Affairs and American Medical Association (1999) *Report 10: Neonatal Circumcision* (Chicago: American Medical Association).

Cox, R. W. (1993a) 'Gramsci, Hegemony and International Relations', in S. Gill (ed.) *Gramsci, Historical Materialism and International Relations* (Cambridge: Cambridge University Press).

Cox, R. W. (1993b) 'Structural Issues of Global Governance: Implications for Europe', in S. Gill (ed.) *Gramsci, Historical Materialism and International Relations* (Cambridge: Cambridge University Press).

Crainer, S. (1993) *Zeebrugge: Learning from Disaster* (London: Herald Families Association).

Criminal Justice System Online (2003) *CJS Aims & Objectives*. <www.cjsonline.gov. uk/access/working/aims.html> (accessed 12 August 2003)

Cronin, H. (1967) *The Screw Turns* (London: John Long).

Cutler, T. and James, P. (1996) 'Does Safety Pay? A Critical Account of the Health and Safety Executive Document: "The Costs of Accidents"', *Work, Employment & Society*, vol. 10, no. 4.

Da Silver, T. (2001) *The Elderly and Human Rights: Abuse of the Elderly in Mozambique* (Cambridge MA: Carr Centre for Human Rights Policy, John. F. Kennedy School of Government, Harvard University).

Dalsimer, M. and Nisonoff, L. (1997) 'Abuses against Women and Girls Under the One-Child Family Plan of the People's Republic of China', in N. Visvanathan, L. Duggan, N. Laurie and N. Wiegersma (eds) *The Women, Gender and Development Reader* (London: Zed Books).

Dalton, A. (2000) *Consensus Kills* (London: AJP Dalton).

Das Gupta, M. (1987) 'Selective Discrimination Against Female Children in Rural Punjab', *Population and Development Review*, vol. 13, no. 1.

Das Gupta, M. and Shuzhuo, L. (1999) 'Gender Bias in China, South Korea and India 1920–1990: The Effects of War, Famine and Fertility Decline', *Development and Change*, vol. 30.

Davies, N. (2002a) 'Cosy Relationship Keeps Corporates Happy But Could Cost £20 Billion in Taxes', *Guardian*, 23 July.

Davies, N. (2002b) 'Poor Leadership, Missed Chances and Billions Down the Drain', *Guardian*, 24 July.

Davies, N. (2002c) 'The Scandal of Our Craven Tax Collectors', *Guardian*, 17 October.

Davies, N. V. and Teasdale, P. (1994) *The Costs to the British Economy of Work Accidents and Work-Related Ill-Health* (London: HSE Books).

Davis University (2002) *Migration News*, vol. 9, no. 5.

Dawn (2003) 'Rawalpindi: "5000 Women Burnt to Death in Five Years"', *Dawn*. <www. dawn.com/2003/06/28/local44.htm>

De Haan, W. (1996) 'Abolitionism and Crime Control', in J. Muncie, E. McLaughlin and M. Langan (eds) *Criminological Perspectives: A Reader* (London: Sage).

298 BEYOND CRIMINOLOGY

de Waal, A. (1997) *Famine Crimes: Politics and the Disaster Relief Industry in Africa* (Oxford: James Currey).

Deepa, N., Chambers, C., Shah Kaul, M. and Petesch, P. (2000) *Voices of the Poor: Crying Out for Change* (New York: Published for the World Bank, Oxford University Press).

Delphy, C. (1984) *Close to Home: A Materialist Analysis of Women's Oppression* (London: Hutchinson).

Department of Constitutional Affairs (2003) *Public Consultation on Proposed Changes to Publicly Funded Immigration and Asylum Work, June 2003*, (London: DCA).

Department of Health (1989) *The Diets of British School Children*, Report of the sub-committee of the Committee on Medical Aspects of Food Policy (London: HMSO).

Department of Health (2001) *Children and Young People on Child Protection Registers, Year Ending 31 March 1994, England*, and *31 March, 2001* (London: Department of Health).

Department for International Development (2001) *The Challenge of Universal Primary Education* (London: DFID).

Department of Transport, Local Government and the Regions (2002) *Road Accident Casualties* (London: DTLR). <www.dft.gov.uk/stellent/groups/dft_transstats/documents/page/dft_transstats_024293.hcsp>

Dobash, R. and Dobash, R. (1992) *Women, Violence and Social Change* (London: Routledge & Kegan Paul).

Donohoe, M. (2003) 'Causes and Health Consequences of Environmental Degradation and Social Injustice', *Social Science & Medicine*, vol. 56, no. 3, February.

Downes, D. (1997) 'What the Next Government Should Do About Crime', *Howard Journal*, vol. 36, no. 1.

Doyal, L. (1995) *What Makes Women Sick: Gender and the Political Economy of Health* (Basingstoke: Macmillan).

Doyal, L. and Gough, I. (1984) 'A Theory of Human Need', *Critical Social Policy*, vol. 4, no. 10.

Doyal, L. and Gough, I. (1991) *A Theory of Human Needs* (Basingstoke: Macmillan).

Dreger, A. D. (1998) '"Ambiguous Sex" – or Ambivalent Medicine?', *The Hastings Centre Report*, vol. 9, no. 3.

Drescher, S. (1996) 'The Atlantic Slave Trade and the Holocaust: A Comparative Analysis', in A. S. Rosenbaum (ed.) *Is the Holocaust Unique? Perspectives on Comparative Genocide* (Boulder: Westview).

Dritsas, L. S. (2001) 'Below the Belt: Doctors, Debate, and the Ongoing American Discussion of Routine Neonatal Male Circumcision', *Bulletin of Science, Technology and Society*, vol. 21, no. 4.

Driver, E. and Droisen, A. (1989) *Child Sexual Abuse: Feminist Perspectives* (London: Macmillan).

Dyer, C. (1997) 'Birmingham Six to Sue Tory MP', *Guardian*, 19 March.

Dyer, C. (1999) 'Blanket Ban on Treating Transsexuals is Ruled "Unlawful"', *British Medical Journal*, vol. 319, 7 August.

The Economist (2003) 'A Suitable Price: The Rising Cost of Marrying Up', 14 June.

Edgar, K., O'Donnell, I. and Martin, C. (2003) *Prison Violence* (Cullompton: Willan).

Edgerton, R. (1964) 'Poket Intersexuality: An East African Example of the Resolution of Sexual Incongruity', *American Anthropologist*, vol. 66, no. 6, part 1.

Edmond, G. and Mercer, D. (1997) 'Scientific Literacy and the Jury: Reconsidering Jury "Competence"', *Public Understanding of Science*, vol. 6, no. 329.

Edney, R. (1997) 'Prison Officers and Violence', *Alternative Law Journal*, vol. 22, no. 6.

Eliason, M. J. (1997) 'The Prevalence and Nature of Biphobia in Heterosexual Undergraduate Students', *Archives of Sexual Behaviour*, vol. 26, no. 3.

Ellis, S. (1999) *The Mask of Anarchy: The Destruction of Liberia and the Religious Dimension of an African Civil War* (New York: New York University Press).

Epstein, R. (1989) *Takings: Private Property and the Power of Eminent Domain* (Cambridge, MA: Harvard University Press).

ERB (1999) *European Race Bulletin*, no. 31, November.

ERB (2001) *European Race Bulletin*, no. 38, October.

ERB (2003a) 'Death at the Border: Who Is to Blame?' *European Race Bulletin*, no. 44, July.

ERB (2003b) 'Return at the Border, Interception at Sea', *European Race Bulletin*, no. 44, July.

Esping-Anderson, G. (1999) *Social Foundations of Post-Industrial Economies* (Oxford: Oxford University Press).

ESRC (1998) *Taking Stock, Violence Research Programme* (Swindon: ESRC).

Esterberg, K. G. (1997) *Lesbian and Bisexual Identities: Constructing Communities, Constructing Selves* (Philadelphia: Temple University Press).

EU Council (2001a) *Proposal for Directive and Framework Decision on Preventing the Facilitation of Unauthorised Entry and Stay.* <www.statewatch.org/semdoc>

EU Council (2001b) *Directive 2001/51 on Carrier Sanctions*, OJ 2001 L 187/45.

EU Council (2002) *Proposal for a Comprehensive Plan to Combat Illegal Immigration and Trafficking of Human Beings in the EU*, 6621/1/02, 27 February.

EU Council (2003) *Road Map for Follow-Up to Conclusion of the European Council Seville*, 6023/4/03, May. <www.statewatch.org/semdoc>

EU JHA (1997) *Joint Action to Combat Trafficking in Human Beings and Sexual Exploitation of Children*, 97/154/JHA, 27 February (Brussels: Justice and Home Affairs Committee). <www.statewatch.org/semdoc>

Euromonitor International (2001) *Pet Foods and Accessories in the USA 2001* (London: EO). <www.majormarketprofiles.com>

Expenditure Committee (1975) *Eleventh Report from the Expenditure Committee, Session 1974–75, The Children and Young Persons Act, 1969*, vol. I 'Report' and vol. II 'Evidence', HC 534 – I and II (London: HMSO).

False Allegations Support Organisation (2002) *Yes it Might*, False Allegations Support Organisation, 30 July. <www.false-allegations.org.uk/page2.html>

Feeley, M. M. and Simon, J. (1992) 'The New Penology: Notes on the Emerging Strategy of Corrections and its Implications', *Criminology*, vol. 30.

Fein, H. (1990) 'Genocide: A Sociological Perspective', *Current Sociology*, vol. 38, no. 1.

Feinberg, J. (1984) *Harm to Others* (Oxford: Oxford University Press).

Feitlowitz, M. (1998) *A Lexicon of Terror: Argentina and the Legacies of Terror* (Oxford: Oxford University Press).

Fekete, L. (2000) 'The Dispersal of Xenophobia', *European Race Bulletin*, vol. 33/34, August.

Fekete, L. (2001) 'The Emergence of Xeno-Racism: The Three Faces of British Racism', *Race & Class*, vol. 43, no. 2.

Fekete, L. (2002) 'Racism: The Hidden Cost of September 11', *European Race Bulletin* (Special Issue).

Fekete, L. (2003) 'Deaths During Forced Deportations', January. <www.irr.org.uk>

Fekete, L. and Webber, F. (1994) *Inside Racist Europe* (London: Institute of Race Relations).

Fekete, L. and Webber, F. (1996) 'From Refugee to Terrorist', *Race & Class*, vol. 38, no. 2.

Feller, E. (1989) 'Carrier Sanctions and International Law', *International Journal of Refugee Law*, vol. 1.

Fevre, R. (2000) *The Demoralisation of Western Culture: Social Theory and the Dilemmas of Modern Living* (London: Continuum).

Fitzgerald, M. and Sim, J. (1982) *British Prisons* (Oxford: Blackwell).

Flood-Page, F. and Taylor, J. (2003) *Crime in England and Wales 2001/2002: Supplementary Volume* (London: Home Office).

Foot, P. (1964) *Immigration and Race in British Politics* (Harmondsworth: Penguin).

Foot, P. (2002) 'Hanratty's Appeal Is Over, But Justice Is Yet to be Done', *Guardian*, 3 May.

Ford, R. (1998a) 'Motorists Awarded Conviction Payouts', *The Times*, 25 June.

Ford, R. (1998b) '£200,000 for Man Beaten by Police into Confession', *The Times*, 20 January.

Foucault, M. (1977) *Discipline and Punish. The Birth of the Prison* (London: Allen Lane).

Foucault, M. (1979) *History of Sexuality*, vol. 1 (London: Allen Lane).

Foucault, M. (1980a) 'Prison Talk', in C. Gordon (ed.) *Power/Knowledge. Selected Interviews and Other Writings 1972–1977* (London: Harvester Wheatsheaf).

Foucault, M. (1980b) 'Two Lectures', in C. Gordon (ed.) *Power/Knowledge: Selected Interviews and Other Writings 1972–1977* (London: Harvester Wheatsheaf).

Friedrichs, D. (1992) 'White-Collar Crime and the Definitional Quagmire: A Provisional Solution', *Journal of Human Justice*, vol. 3, no. 2.

Friedrichs, D. (ed.) (1998a) *State Crime: Defining, Delineating and Explaining State Crime*, vol. 1 (Aldershot: Ashgate).

Friedrichs, D. (ed.) (1998b) *State Crime: Exposing, Sanctioning and Preventing State Crime*, vol. 2 (Aldershot: Ashgate).

Fritzell, J. (1993) 'Income Inequality Trends in the 1980s: A Five Country Comparison', *Acta Sociologica*, vol. 36, no. 1.

Froud, J., Haslam, C., Johal, S., Leaver, A. Williams, J. and Williams, K. (1999) 'The Third Way and the Jammed Economy', *Capital & Class*, vol. 67, Spring.

Frye, P. R. and Meiselman, A. D. (2001) 'Same-Sex Marriages Have Existed Legally in the United States for a Long Time Now', *Albany Law Review*, vol. 64, no. 3.

Fukuyama, F. (1989) 'The End of History', *National Interest*, no. 16.

Fukuyama, F. (1992) *The End of History and the Last Man* (New York: Avon Books).

Galeano, E. (1981) *Les Veines ouvertes de l'Amérique latine* (Paris: Editions Plon).

Garber, M. (1995) *Vice Versa: Bisexuality and the Eroticism of Everyday Life* (New York: Simon & Schuster).

Garcia-Moreno, C. (2003) 'From Research to Action: WHO Multi-Country Study on Women's Health and Domestic Violence Against Women', Paper Presented at Gender and Women's Health, Economic and Social Science Research Council (ESRC) seminar series, 24–25 April.

Garfinkel, I. and McLanahan, S. (1988) 'Feminisation of Poverty: Nature, Causes and a Partial Cure', in D. Tomaskonic-Devey (ed.) *Poverty and Social Welfare* (Armonk, NY: M.E. Sharpe).

Garland, D. (1992) 'Knowledge in Criminal Justice and its Relation to Power', *British Journal of Criminology*, vol. 32, no. 4.

Garland, D. (1996) 'The Limits of the Sovereign State', *British Journal of Criminology*, vol. 36, no. 4.

Garland, D. (1997) 'Of Crimes and Criminals: The Development of Criminology in Britain', in M. Maguire, R. Morgan and R. Reiner (eds) *The Oxford Handbook of Criminology*, 2nd edition (Oxford: Clarendon).

Garland, D. (2001) *The Culture of Control: Crime and Social Order in Contemporary Society* (Oxford: Oxford University Press).

Gatswatch (2001) *GATS – What Is Fact and What Is Fiction? A Civil Society Response to the WTO's Publication 'GATS – Fact and Fiction'*. <www.gatswatch.org/docs/rebuttal/html>

Geffen, I. (1999) 'Costing Injustice', *Guardian*, 29 June.

George, S. (2000) *Female Infanticide in Tamil Nadu, India: From Recognition Back to Denial?* <www.hsph.harvard.edu/Organizations/healthnet/SAsia/suchana/0225/george.html>

Getty, J. A. and Naumov, O. V. (2000) *The Road to Terror: Stalin and the Self-Destruction of the Bolsheviks, 1932–1939* (New Haven: Yale University Press).

Gewirth, A. (1978) *Reason and Morality* (Chicago: University of Chicago Press).

Gewirth, A. (1982) *Human Rights: Essays on Justification and Applications* (Chicago: University of Chicago Press).

Gibbons, E. D. (1999) *Sanctions in Haiti: Human Rights and Democracy under Assault* (Washington, DC: The CSIS Press).

Giddens, A. (1991) *The Consequences of Modernity* (Stanford, CA: Stanford University Press).

Gill, S. (1990) *American Hegemony and the Trilateral Commission* (Cambridge: Cambridge University Press).

Gill, S. and Law, D. (1993) 'Global Hegemony and the Structural Power of Capital', in S. Gill (ed.) *Gramsci, Historical Materialism and International Relations* (Cambridge: Cambridge University Press).

Gillan, A. (2001) 'Innocent "Dumped Like Sacks of Garbage"', *Guardian*, 14 March.

Gilroy, P. (2002) *There Ain't No Black in the Union Jack*, 2nd edition (London: Routledge).

Gilroy, P. and Sim, J. (1987) 'Law, Order and the State of the Left', in P. Scraton (ed.) *Law, Order and the Authoritarian State* (Milton Keynes: Open University Press).

Gioia, D. (1996) 'Why I Didn't Recognise Pinto Fire Hazards: How Organisational Scripts Channel Managers' Thoughts and Actions', in M. Ermann and R. Lundman (eds) *Corporate and Governmental Deviance: Problems of Organisational Behaviour in Contemporary Society* (Oxford: Oxford University Press).

Glover, S. Gott, C., Loizillon, A., Portes, J., Price, R., Spencer, S., Srinivasan, V. and Willis, C. (2001) *Migration: An Economic and Social Analysis*, Home Office Development and Statistics Directorate (London: HMSO).

Goldblatt, D. (1997) 'At the Limits of Political Possibilities: The Cosmopolitan Democratic Project', *New Left Review*, vol. 225, September/October.

Gollaher, D. (1994) 'From Ritual to Science: The Medical Transformation of Circumcision in America', *Journal of Social History*, vol. 28, no. 1.

Goodkind, D. (1996) 'On Substituting Sex Preference Strategies in East Asia: Does Prenatal Sex Selection Reduce Postnatal Discrimination?', *Population and Development Review*, vol. 22, no. 1.

Goodman, J. (1999) 'Is Michael Stone Innocent of the Two Russell Murders?', *Daily Mail*, 13 March.

Goodwin-Gill, G. (1996) *The Refugee in International Law*, 2nd edition (Oxford: Clarendon).

Gordon, A. and Suzuki, D. (1990) *It's a Matter of Survival* (Toronto: Stoddart).

Gordon, D. (1995) 'Census Based Deprivation Indices: Their Weighting and Validation', *Epidemiology and Community Health*, vol. 49, supplement 2.

Gordon, D. (2000) 'Inequalities in Income, Wealth and Standard of Living', in C. Pantazis and D. Gordon (eds) *Tackling Inequalities: Where Are We Now and What Can Be Done?* (Bristol: Policy Press).

Gordon, D. (2002) 'The International Measurement of Poverty and Anti-Poverty Policy', in P. Townsend and D. Gordon (eds) *World Poverty: New Policies to Defeat an Old Enemy* (Bristol: Policy Press).

Gordon, D., Davey Smith, G., Dorling, D. and Shaw, M. (1999) *Inequalities in Health: The Evidence Presented to the Independent Inquiry into Inequalities in Health* (Bristol: Policy Press).

Gordon, D., Nandy, S., Pantazis, C., Pemberton, S. and Townsend, P. (2002) *The Nature and Distribution of Child Poverty in Developing Countries*, Unpublished report to UNICEF.

Gordon, D., Nandy, S., Pantazis, C., Pemberton, S. and Townsend, P. (2003) *Child Poverty in the Developing World* (Bristol: Policy Press).

Gordon, D. and Pantazis, C. (eds) (1997) *Breadline Britain in the 1990s* (Aldershot: Ashgate).

Gordon, L. (1989) *Heroes of Their Own Lives* (London: Virago).

Gottschalk, P., Gustafsson, B. and Palmer, E. (1997) 'What's Behind the Increase in Inequality? An Introduction', in P. Gottschalk, B. Gustafsson and E. Palmer (eds) *Changing Patterns in the Distribution of Economic Welfare: An International Perspective* (Cambridge: Cambridge University Press).

Gramsci, A. (1971) *Selections from the Prison Notebooks* (London: Lawrence and Wishart).

Gramsci, A. (1999) *A Gramsci Reader: Selected Writings, 1916–1935*, D. Forgacs (ed.) (London: Lawrence and Wishart).

Graves, D. (1997) 'Crucial Evidence of Fabrication Was Overlooked', *Electronic Telegraph*, 2 February. <www.telegraph.co.uk>

Gray, J. (1998) *False Dawn: The Delusions of Global Capitalism* (London: Granta).

Gray, N., Laing, J. and Noaks, L. (2002a) *Criminal Justice, Mental Health and the Politics of Risk* (London: Cavendish).

Gray, N., Laing, J. and Noaks, L. (2002b) 'Risk, the Professional, the Individual, Society and the Law', in N. Gray, J. Laing and L. Noaks (eds) *Criminal Justice, Mental Health and the Politics of Risk* (London: Cavendish).

Greater London Council (1982) 'Greater London Council Rejects Commissioner's Report', *Policing London*, vol. 3, October.

Green, A. (1995) *Fitting Up: An Analysis of the Manufacture of Wrongful Convictions*, Unpublished PhD thesis, Keele University.

Green, P. (1990) *The Enemy Without: Policing and Class Consciousness in the Miners' Strike* (Milton Keynes: Open University Press).

Green, P. (2002) 'A Question of State Crime?', in P. Scraton (ed.) *Beyond September 11: An Anthology of Dissent* (London: Pluto).

Green, P. and Ward, T. (2000) 'State Crime, Human Rights and the Limits of Criminology', *Social Justice*, vol. 27, no. 1.

Green, P. and Ward, T. (2004) *State Crime: Governments, Violence and Corruption* (London: Pluto).

Greenberg, S. (1993) 'The Next Wave', *The Advocate*, 13 July.

Greider, W. (2001) 'The Right and US Trade Law: Invalidating the 20th Century', *The Nation*, 15 October.

Guldberg, H. (2000) 'Child Protection and the Precautionary Principle', in J. Morris (ed.) *Rethinking Risk and the Precautionary Principle* (Oxford: Butterworth-Heinemann).

Gurr, T. R. (1986) 'The Political Origins of State Violence and Terror: A Theoretical Analysis', in M. Stohl and G. A. Lopez (eds) *Government Violence and Repression: An Agenda for Research* (Westport, CT: Greenwood Press).

Gustafsson, B. and Palmer, E. (1997) 'Changes in Swedish Inequality: A Study of Equivalent Income, 1975–1991', in P. Gottschalk, B. Gustafsson and E. Palmer (eds) *Changing Patterns in the Distribution of Economic Welfare: an International Perspective* (Cambridge: Cambridge University Press).

Gustafsson, B. and Uusitalo, H. (1990) 'The Welfare State and Poverty in Finland and Sweden from the Mid-1960s to the Mid-1980s', *Review of Income and Wealth*, vol. 36, no. 3.

Hacking, I. (1995) *Rewriting the Soul* (Princeton: Princeton University Press).

Hacking, I. (1999) *The Social Construction of What?* (Cambridge, MA: Harvard University Press).

Hale, D. (2002) *A Town Without Pity* (London: Century).

Hall, S. (1988) *The Hard Road to Renewal* (London: Verso).

Hall, S., Critcher, C., Jefferson, T., Clarke, J. and Roberts, B. (1978) *Policing the Crisis: Mugging, the State and Law and Order* (London: Macmillan).

Hallsworth, S. (1999) 'All that Glitters Is Not Gold: On the Uses and Abuses of Crime and Disorder Audits', *Radical Statistics*, no. 72, Autumn.

Harman, C. (1996) 'Globalisation: A Critique of a New Orthodoxy', *International Socialism*, vol. 73.

Hattenstone, S. (2002) 'I'm Dead Inside', *Guardian*, 17 June.

Hawley, C. (2002) 'Jordanian Women Fight "Honour Killings"', *BBC News*. <news.bbc. co.uk/1/hi/world/middle_east/1778891.stm>

Hayek, F. A. (1979) *Law, Legislation and Liberty. A New Statement of the Liberal Principles of Justice and Political Economy, vol. 3. The Political Order of a Free People* (London: Routledge and Kegan Paul).

Hayner, P. (2001) *Unspeakable Truths – Confronting State Terror and Atrocity* (London: Routledge).

Hazell, R. (1974) *Conspiracy and Civil Liberties: A Cobden Trust Memorandum*, Occasional Papers on Social Administration, No. 55 (London: The Social Administration Research Trust).

Health Committee (1997) *Third Report of the Health Committee, Session 1997–8, The Welfare of Former British Child Migrants*, vols I and II (Evidence), HC 755 – I and II (London: HMSO).

Health and Safety Commission (2000) *Revitalising Health and Safety. Strategy Statement* (London: DETR).

Health and Safety Commission (2002) *Levels and Trends in Workplace Injury: Reported Injuries and the Labour Force Survey* (London: HSC). <www.hse.gov.uk/statistics/2002/lfsfct01.pdf>

Health and Safety Executive (1993) *The Costs of Accidents at Work* (London: HSE Books).

Health and Safety Executive (1994) *The Costs to the British Economy of Work Accidents and Work-Related Ill-Health* (Sudbury: HSE Books).

Health and Safety Executive (2001) *Health and Safety Statistics 2001/01* (London: HSE Books).

Health and Safety Executive (2002) *Health and Safety Statistics Highlights 2001/02* (London: HSE). <www.hse.gov.uk/statistics/overall/hssh0102.pdf>

Health and Safety Executive (nd) *Health and Safety Statistics Highlights 2001/02*. <www.hse.gov.uk/statistics/overall/hssh0102.pdf>

Heller, M. and Nekrich, A. M. (1986) *Utopia in Power: The History of the Soviet Union from 1917 to the Present* (New York: Summit Books).

HelpAge International (2002a) *State of the World's Poor 2002* (London: Help Age International).

HelpAge International (2002b) *Gender and Ageing Briefs* (London: Help Age International).

Hemmings, C. (1993) 'Resituating the Bisexual Body', in J. Bistow and A. R. Wilson (eds) *Activating Theory: Lesbian, Gay, Bisexual Politics* (London: Lawrence and Wishart).

Henry, S. (1991) 'The Informal Economy: A Crime of Omission by the State', in G. Barak (ed.) *Crimes of the Capitalist State* (New York: Suny Press).

Henry, S. and Milovanovic, D. (1996) *Constitutive Criminology. Beyond Postmodernism* (London: Sage).

Her Majesty's Chief Inspector of Prisons (1998) *Campsfield House Detention Centre: Report of an Unannounced Short Inspection 13–15 October 1997* (London: Home Office).

Her Majesty's Chief Inspector of Prisons for England and Wales (2002) *HM Prison Dartmoor. Report of an Unannounced Follow-Up Inspection 17–21 September 2001* (London: Home Office).

Her Majesty's Inspectorate of Constabulary (1997/98) *Officer Safety: Minimising the Risk of Violence* (London: Home Office).

Her Majesty's Prison Service (2001) *Annual Report and Accounts April 2000 to March 2001* (London: The Stationery Office).

Herd, G. (ed.) (1996) *Third Sex, Third Gender: Beyond Sexual Dimorphism in Culture and History* (New York: Zone Books).

Herek, G. M. (1994) 'Assessing Attitudes Toward Lesbians and Gay Men: A Review of Empirical Research with the ATLG Scale', in B. Greene and G. Herek (eds) *Lesbian and Gay Psychology* (Thousand Oaks, CA: Sage).

Herek, G. M. (2000) 'The Psychology of Sexual Prejudice', *Current Directions in Psychological Science*, vol. 9, no. 1.

Herek, G. M. and Capitanio, J. (1996) '"Some of My Best Friends": Intergroup Contact, Concealable Stigma, and Heterosexual's Attitudes Towards Gay Men and Lesbians', *Personal and Social Psychology Bulletin*, vol. 22, no. 4.

Hester, M., Kelly, L. and Radford, J. (eds) (1996) *Women, Violence and Male Power: Feminist Activism, Research and Practice* (Buckingham: Open University Press).

Hicklin, M. (1946) *War-Damaged Children: Some Aspects of Recovery* (London: Association of Psychiatric Social Workers).

Hil, R. and Robertson, R. (2003) 'What Sort of Future for Critical Criminology', *Crime, Law and Social Change*, vol. 39, no. 1.

Hill, A. (2001) 'I Won My Freedom, But Those Years in Jail Smashed My Life to Bits', *Observer*, 18 March.

Hillyard, P. (1995) 'The Political Economy of Socio-Legal Research', Paper Presented at the Annual Conference of the Socio-Legal Association, University of Leeds, 27–29 March.

Hillyard, P. (2002) 'In Defence of Civil Liberties', in P. Scraton (ed.) *Beyond September 11: An Anthology of Dissent* (London: Pluto).

Hillyard, P., Gordon, D. and Pantazis, C. (forthcoming) *An Atlas of Crime and Justice* (Cullompton: Willan).

Hillyard, P. and Sim, J. (1997) 'The Political Economy of Socio-Legal Research', in P. Thomas (ed.) *Socio-Legal Studies* (Aldershot: Dartmouth).

Hillyard, P., Sim, J., Tombs, S. and Whyte, D. (2004) 'Leaving a "Stain Upon the Silence": Critical Criminology and the Politics of Dissent', *British Journal of Criminology*, vol. 44, no. 3.

Hillyard, P. and Tombs, S. (1999) 'From Crime to Social Harm? Criminology, Zemiology and Justice', Paper presented at the 27th Annual Meeting of the European Group for the Study of Deviance and Social Control, Palanga, Lithuania, 2–5 September.

Hillyard, P. and Tombs, S. (2001) 'From Crime to Social Harm? Criminology, Zemiology and Justice', Paper presented at the Socio-Legal Studies Association Annual Conference, University of Bristol, 3–5 April.

Hirst, P. Q. and Thompson, G. (1996) *Globalisation in Question* (Cambridge: Polity).

Holdaway, S. and Rock, P. (1998) 'Thinking About Criminology: Facts are Bits of Biography', in S. Holdaway and P. Rock (eds) *Thinking About Criminology* (London: UCL Press).

Hollway, W. (1996) 'Recognition and Heterosexual Desire', in D. Richardson (ed.) *Theorising Heterosexuality* (Buckingham: Open University Press).

Holsti, K. (1996) *The State, War and the State of War* (Oxford: Oxford University Press).

Home Office (1965) *The Child, the Family and the Young Offender*, cmnd. 2742 (London: HMSO).

Home Office (1968) *Children in Trouble*, cmnd. 3601 (London: Home Office).

Home Office (1997) *Statistics of Offences Against Prison Discipline and Punishments England and Wales 1996*, cm. 3715 (London: HMSO).

Home Office (2001) *Review of Information on Homicide: A Discussion Document* (London: Home Office). <www.homeoffice.gov.uk/rds/pdfs/provhomicideinfo.pdf>

Home Office (2003a) *Crime in England and Wales, 2002–2003* (London: Home Office). <www.homeoffice.gov.uk/rds/pdfs2/hosb703.pdf>

Home Office (2003b) Prison Statistics England and Wales 2001, CM 5743 (London: Home Office).

Home Office (2003c) *Asylum Statistics, First Quarter 2003* (London: TSO).

Home Secretary (2003) 'Statement on Zones of Protection', 27 March. <www.ind.homeoffice.gov.uk>

Hopkins, S. (1999) 'A Discussion of the Legal Aspects of Female Mutilation', *Journal of Advanced Nursing*, vol. 30, no. 4.

House of Commons (1976) *Eleventh Report from the Expenditure Committee, Session 1974–75, The Children and Young Persons Act, 1969*, vol. I 'Report' and vol. II 'Evidence', HC 534 – I and II, 1975 (London: HMSO).

Hulsman, L. (1986) 'Critical Criminology and the Concept of Crime', in H. Bianchi and R. van Swaaningen (eds) *Abolitionism. Towards a Non-Repressive Approach to Crime* (Amsterdam: Free University Press).

Human Rights Watch (1996) *Death by Default: A Policy of Fatal Neglect in China's State Orphanages*. <www.hrw.org/summaries/s.china961.html>

Hutton, W. (1995) *The State We're In* (London: Jonathan Cape).

ICRW (2000) *Domestic Violence in India: A Summary of a Multi-Site Household Survey* (Washington: International Centre for Research on Women).

Illich, I. (1973) *Deschooling Society* (Harmondsworth: Penguin).

ILO (1996) *Child Labour, Targeting the Intolerable* (Geneva: International Labour Organisation).

Imam, A. (1994) 'SAP Is Really Sapping Us', *The New Internationalist*, no. 257. <www.newint.org/issue310/flesh.htm>

INNOCENT (2002) *Fighting Miscarriages of Justice since 1993*, INNOCENT, 21 February. <www.innocent.org>

IRNA (2001) 21 May. <www.hambastegi.org>

IRR (1979) *Police Against Black People* (London: Institute of Race Relations).

IRR (1999) *European Race Bulletin*, no. 31, November.

IRR (2000) *European Race Bulletin*, no. 33/34, August.

Isa, R., Shuib, R. and Othman, S. (1999) 'The Practice of Female Circumcision Among Muslims in Kelantan, Malaysia', *Reproductive Health Matters*, vol. 7.

Italian Republic (2003) 'Draft Initiative of the Italian Republic for a Council Directive on Assistance in Cases of Transit by Land in the Context of Removal Measures by Member States Against Third-Country Nationals', 3 July. <www.statewatch.org/news>

ITS (2003) *Our Common Responsibility: The Impact of a New War on Iraq Children* (Toronto: International Study Team War Child Canada). <www.warchild.ca>

Jackson, R. H. (1990) *Quasi-States: Sovereignty, International Relations and the Third World* (Cambridge: Cambridge University Press).

Jackson, S. (1996) 'Heterosexuality and Feminist Theory', in D. Richardson (ed.) *Theorising Heterosexuality* (Buckingham: Open University Press).

Jackson, S. and Scott, S. (2001) 'Putting the Body's Feet on the Ground: Towards a Sociological Reconceptualisation of Gendered and Sexual Embodiment', in K. Backett-Milburn and L. McKie (eds) *Constructing Gendered Bodies* (Harlow: Palgrave).

Jacobson, J. L. (1993) 'Women's Health: The Price of Poverty', in M. Koblinsky, J. Timyan and J. Gay (eds) *The Health of Women. A Global Perspective* (Boulder: Westview Press and The National Council for International Health).

James, P. and Walters, D. (eds) (1999) *Regulating Health and Safety at Work: The Way Forward* (London: IER).

Jantti, M. and Ritakallio, V.-M. (1997) 'Income Inequality and Poverty in Finland in the 1980s', in P. Gottschalk, B. Gustafsson and E. Palmer (eds) *Changing Patterns in the Distribution of Economic Welfare: An International Perspective* (Cambridge: Cambridge University Press).

Jasanoff, S. (1995) *Science at the Bar* (Cambridge, MA: Harvard University Press).

Jefferson, T. (1990) *The Case Against Paramilitary Policing* (Milton Keynes: Open University Press).

Jeffreys, S. (1990) *Anticlimax: A Feminist Perspective on the Sexual Revolution* (London: The Women's Press).

Jeffreys, S. (1996) 'Heterosexuality and the Desire for Gender', in D. Richardson (ed.) *Theorising Heterosexuality* (Buckingham: Open University Press).

Jephcott, J. (1971) *Living in High Flats* (Edinburgh: Oliver and Boyd).

Jessop, B. (1982) *The Capitalist State* (Oxford: Martin Robertson).

Jessop, B. (1990) *State Theory: Putting the Capitalist States in their Place* (Cambridge: Polity).

Johnstone, G. (2001) *Restorative Justice: Ideas, Values, Debates* (Cullompton: Willan).

Jones, G., Steketee, R., W. Black, R. E., Bhutta, Z. A. and Morris, S. S. (2003) 'How Many Child Deaths Can We Prevent This Year?' *Lancet*, vol. 362.

Jones, K. (1982) *Law and Economy: The Legal Regulation of Corporate Capital* (London: Academic Press).

Jones, R. (2002) 'Pensions Green Paper. Forget Retiring to the Seaside and Thoughts of a World Cruise – it's B&Q for the Lot of You', *Guardian*, 18 December.

Junge, M. (2001) 'Zygmunt Bauman's Poisoned Gift of Morality', *British Journal of Sociology*, vol. 52, no. 1.

Junhong, C. (2001) 'Prenatal Sex Determination and Sex-Selective Abortion in Central China', *Population and Development Review*, vol. 27, no. 2.

JUSTICE (1989) *Miscarriages of Justice* (London: Justice).

Kaldor, M. (1999) *New and Old Wars: Organised Violence in a Global Era* (Stanford, CA: Stanford University Press).

Katz, C. and Monk, J. (eds) (1993) *Full Circles: Geographies of Women over the Life Course* (London: Routledge & Kegan Paul).

Katz, J. (1988) *Seductions of Crime: Moral and Sensual Attractions in Doing Evil* (New York: Basic Books).

Kauzlarich, D. and Kramer, R. C. (1998) *Crimes of the American Nuclear State: At Home and Abroad* (Boston, MA: Northeastern University Press).

Kauzlarich, D., Matthews, R. A. and Miller, W. J. (2001) 'Toward a Victimology of State Crime', *Critical Criminology*, vol. 10, no. 3.

Kaylan, M. (2003) 'The Way We Live Now', *Wall Street Journal*, 8 August.

Kelly, L. (1988) *Surviving Sexual Violence* (Cambridge: Polity).

Khanna, R., Kumar, A., Vaghela, J., Sreenivas, V. and Puliyel, J. (2003) 'Community Based Retrospective Study of Sex in Infant Mortality in India', *British Medical Journal*, vol. 327, 19 July.

Khanna, S. (1997) 'Traditions and Reproductive Technology in an Urbanizing North Indian Village', *Social Science Medicine*, vol. 44, no. 2.

Kiander, J. and Vartia, P. (1996) 'The Great Depression of the 1990s in Finland', *Finnish Economic Papers*, vol. 9, no. 1.

Kim, J. Y., Millen, J. V., Irwin, A. and Gershman, J. (eds) (2000) *Dying for Growth: Global Inequality and the Health of the Poor* (Monroe, MN: Common Courage Press).

Kissinger, H. A. (1974) *National Security Study Memorandum 200, Implications Of Worldwide Population Growth for U.S. Security and Overseas Interests* (Washington: National Security Council). <www.kzpg.com/Lib/Pages/Books/NSSM-200/28-APP2.html>

Kite, M. E. and Whitley, B. E. J. (1998) 'Do Heterosexual Women and Men Differ in Their Attitudes Towards Homosexuality? A Conceptual and Methodological Analysis', in G. M. Herek (ed.) *Stigma and Sexual Orientation: Understanding Prejudice Against Lesbians, Gay Men, and Bisexuals* (Newbury Park, CA: Sage).

Kleinman, A., Das, V. and Lock, M. (eds) (1997) *Social Suffering* (Berkeley: University of California Press).

Kreidl, M. (2000) 'Perceptions of Poverty and Wealth in Western and Post-Communist Countries', *Social Justice Research*, vol. 13, no. 2.

Kusum, K. (1993) 'The Use of Pre-Natal Diagnostic Techniques for Sex Selection: The Indian Scene', *Bioethics*, vol. 7, no. 2/3.

La Fontaine, J. (1994) *The Extent and Nature of Organised and Ritual Abuse* (London: HMSO).

Labour Party (1964) *Crime – A Challenge to Us All* (London: Labour Party).

Lacey, N. (2002) 'Legal Construction of Crime', in M. Maguire, R. Morgan and R. Reiner (eds) *The Oxford Handbook of Criminology*, 3rd edition (Oxford: Oxford University Press).

Lacey, N. and Wells, C. (1998) *Reconstructing Criminal Law: Texts and Materials* (London: Butterworths).

Lamptey, P. R. (2002) 'Reducing Heterosexual Transmission of HIV in Poor Countries', *British Medical Journal*, vol. 324, 26 January.

Langmore, J. (2000) 'Reducing Poverty: The Implications of the 1995 Copenhagen Agreement for Research on Poverty', in D. Gordon and P. Townsend (eds) *Breadline Europe: The Measurement of Poverty* (Bristol: Policy Press).

Larme, A. (1997) 'Health Care Allocation and Selective Neglect in Rural Peru', *Social Science Medicine*, vol. 44.

Law Commission (1996) *Legislating the Criminal Code: Involuntary Manslaughter*, Report No. 237 (London: HMSO).

Lawyers' Committee for Human Rights (2003) 21 March, 27 May. <www.lchr.org/media/2003_alerts>

Lee, M. (1998) *Youth, Crime and Police Work* (Basingstoke: Macmillan).

Leonard, T. (1997) 'Euphoria Gives Way to Anger Over Lost Years', *Electronic Telegraph*, 2 February. <www.telegraph.co.uk>

Levi, M. (1988) *Of Rule and Revenue* (Berkeley: University of California Press).

Liebling, A. and Price, D. (2001) *The Prison Officer* (Winchester: Waterside Press).

Lilly, J., Cullen, F. and Ball, R. (1989) *Criminological Theory* (Newbury Park, CA: Sage).

Lopez, A. D., Ahmad, O. B., Guillot, M. Inoue, M. Ferguson, B. D. and Salomon, J. (2001) *Life Tables for 191 Countries for 2000: Data, Methods, Results*, GPE Discussion Paper Number 40 (Geneva: WHO).

Lord Chancellor's Department (1998) *Judicial Statistics Annual Report* (London: HMSO).

Lord Chancellor's Department (1999) *Judicial Statistics Annual Report* (London: HMSO).

Lord Chancellor's Department (2000) *Judicial Statistics Annual Report* (London: HMSO).

Lynas, M. (2000) 'Letter from Zambia', *The Nation*, 14 February. <www.past.thenation.com/cgibin/framizer.cgi?url=http://past.thenation.com/issue/000214/0214lynas.shtml>

Lyon, J. (2003) 'Managing to Work in Prisons', *Prison Report*, vol. 61, June.

Mac An Ghaill, M. (1991) 'Schooling, Sexuality and Male Power: Towards an Emancipatory Curriculum', *Gender and Education*, vol. 3, no. 3.

MacArthur, J. (2001) *The Selling of 'Free Trade'* (Berkeley: University of California Press).

Macdonald, I. and Webber, F. (2001) *Immigration Law and Practice*, 5th edition (London: Butterworths).

MacEwan, A. (1999) *Neo-Liberalism or Democracy? Economic Strategy, Markets and Alternatives for the 21st Century* (London: Zed Books).

MacGregor, S. (1999) 'Welfare, Neo-Liberalism and New Paternalism: Three Ways for Social Policy in Late Capitalist Societies', *Capital and Class*, vol. 67, no. 47.

Madden, A. (2002) 'Risk Management in the Real World', in N. Gray, J. Laing and L. Noaks (eds) *Criminal Justice, Mental Health and the Politics of Risk* (London: Cavendish).

Maguire, M., Morgan, R. and Reiner, R. (1994) *The Oxford Handbook of Criminology* (Oxford: Oxford University Press).

Maguire, M., Morgan, R. and Reiner, R. (eds) (1997) *The Oxford Handbook of Criminology*, 2nd edition (Oxford: Clarendon).

Mahmood, C. K. (2000) 'Trials by Fire: Dynamics of Terror in Punjab and Kashmir', in J. A. Sluka (ed.) *Death Squad* (Philadelphia: University of Pennsylvania Press).

Mandel, M. (2002) 'This War Was Illegal and Immoral, and it Won't Prevent Terrorism', in P. Scraton (ed.) *Beyond September 11: An Anthology of Dissent* (London: Pluto).

Marchak, P. (1999) *God's Assassins: State Terrorism in Argentina in the 1970s* (Montreal: McGill-Queen's University Press).

Mathiesen, T. (1990) *Prison on Trial* (London: Sage).

Mathiesen, T. (1997) 'The Viewer Society: Michel Foucault's "Panopticon" revisited', *Theoretical Criminology*, vol. 1, no. 2.

Matthews, R. (1988) *Informal Justice* (London: Sage).

Mayell, H. (2002) 'Thousands of Women Killed for Family "Honour"', *National Geographic News*, 12 February.

McCauley, A. P., Robey, B., Blanc, A. K. and Geller, J. S. (1994) *Opportunities for Women Through Reproductive Choice*, Population Reports, Series M, No. 12, Population Information Program (Baltimore: Johns Hopkins School of Public Health). <www.jhuccp.org/pr/m12edsum.shtml#top>

McClintock, M. (1985) *The American Connection* (London: Zed Books).

McNamara, J., Grimes, E. and Bullock, A. (1995) *Bruised Before Birth: Parenting Children Exposed to Parental Substance Abuse* (London: BAAF).

Medvedev, R. (1976) *Let History Judge* (Nottingham: Spokesman Books).

Merseyside Against Injustice (2002) *About Us*, 14 July. <website.lineone.net/~mai5/>

Meszaros, J. R., Asch, D. A., Baron, J., Hershey, J. C., Kunreuther, H. and Schwartz-Buzaglo, J. (1996) 'Cognitive Processes and the Decisions of Some Parents to Forego Pertussis Vaccination for their Children', *Journal of Clinical Epidemiology*, vol. 49, no. 6.

Meyer, P. (1983) *The Child and the State: The Intervention of the State in Family Life* (Cambridge: CUP and Maison des Sciences de l'Homme).

MFCVT (n.d) 'Suicide in Asylum Seekers and Refugees', Medical Foundation for the Care of Victims of Torture. <www.torturecare.org.uk/archivebrf/brief29>

Migration News (2002) 'Migration News', vol. 9, no. 8, August.

Milanovic, B. (2002) 'True World Income Distribution, 1988 and 1993: First Calculations Based on Household Surveys Alone', *The Economic Journal*, vol. 112.

Minto, C. L., Liao, L.-M., Woodhouse, C. R. J., Ransley, P. G. and Creighton, S. M. (2003) 'The Effects of Clitoral Surgery on Sexual Outcome in Individuals Who Have Intersex Conditions with Ambiguous Genitalia: A Cross-Sectional Study', *Lancet*, vol. 361, 12 April.

Mishra, R. (1999) *Globalisation and the Welfare State* (Cheltenham: Edward Elgar).

Mok, J. (1987) 'HIV Seropositive Babies: Implications in Planning for Their Future', in D. Batty (ed.) *The Implications of AIDS for Children in Care* (London: BAAF).

Mokhiber, R. and Weissman, R. (1999a) *Corporate Predators. The Hunt for Mega-Profits and the Attack on Democracy* (Monroe, ME: Common Courage).

Mokhiber, R. and Weissman, R. (1999b) *The Trouble With Larry*, Focus on the Corporation, 1 May. <www.lists.essential.org/focus>

Mokhiber, R. and Weissman, R. (1999c) *Make Lots of Money and Avoid Paying Taxes*, Focus on the Corporation, 8 June. <www.lists.essential.org/focus>

Monk, J. and Katz, C. (1993) 'When in the World Are Women?' in C. Katz and J. Monk (eds) *Full Circles: Geographies of Women Over the Life Course* (London: Routledge & Kegan Paul).

Moody-Stuart, G. (1997) *Grand Corruption: How Business Bribes Damage Developing Countries* (Oxford: WorldView Publishing).

Moore, M. (2002) *Stupid White Men and Other Sorry Excuses for the State of the Nation!* (London: Penguin).

Moran, J. (1998) 'The Dynamics of Class Politics and National Economies in Globalisation: The Marginalisation of the Unacceptable', *Capital & Class*, vol. 66, Autumn.

Morland, I. (2002) 'Sizing Up the Intersexed', *British Medical Journal*, Rapid Responses, 27 April. <www.bmj.com/cgi/eletters/324/7342/883#21713>

Morrison, J. (2001a) 'The Dark Side of Globalisation: The Criminalisation of Refugees', *Race & Class*, vol. 43, no. 1.

Morrison, J. (2001b) 'How Anti-Trafficking Initiatives Criminalise Refugees', *ACRF*, vol. 67, Apr.–May.

Morse, A. D. (1967) *While Six Million Died* (New York: Ace Publishing Corporation).

Muncie, J. (1999) 'Decriminalising Criminology', Paper Presented at the British Criminology Conference, Liverpool, 11–15 July.

National Audit Office (1999) *Managing Sickness Absence in the Prison Service* (London: National Audit Office).

Naughton, M. (2001) 'Wrongful Convictions: Towards a Zemiological Analysis of the Tradition of Criminal Justice System Reform', *Radical Statistics*, vol. 76.

Naughton, M. (2003a) 'How Big Is the "Iceberg"? – A Zemiological Approach to Quantifying Miscarriages of Justice', *Radical Statistics*, vol. 81.

Naughton, M. (2003b) *The Financial Costs of Miscarriages of Justice*, Report to Miscarriages of Justice Organisation Conference, House of Commons, London, 12 March.

Navarro, V. (1999) 'The Political Economy of the Welfare State in Developed Capitalist Countries', *International Journal of Health Services*, vol. 29, no. 1.

Navarro, V. (2000) *The Political Economy of Social Inequalities: Consequences for Health and Quality of Life*, vol. 1 (Amityville NY: Baywood Publishing Company, Inc).

Navarro, V. and Shi, L. (2001) 'The Political Context of Social Inequalities in Health', *Social Science and Medicine*, vol. 52, no. 3, February.

NCADC (2002) 'Newsletter 26', Apr.–Jun. (Manchester: National Coalition of Anti-Deportation Campaigns). <www.ncadc.org.uk>

NCRM (n.d.) '157 Unnecessary deaths' (Southall: National Civil Rights Movement). <www.ncrm.org.uk>

Nelken, D. (1997) 'White Collar Crime', in M. Maguire, R. Morgan and R. Reiner (eds) *The Oxford Handbook of Criminology*, 2nd edition (Oxford: Clarendon).

Newburn, T. and Stanko, E. (1994) *Just Boys Doing Business? Men, Masculinities and Crime* (London: Routledge).

Nhongo, T. (2001) *Elder Abuse in the Health Care Services in Kenya*, A Study Carried Out by HelpAge International – Africa Regional Development Centre and HelpAge Kenya, with support from WHO and INPEA. <www.who.int/hpr/ageing/Report%20Kenya.pdf>

Nicol, A. and Dummett, A. (1990) *Subjects, Citizens, Aliens and Others* (London: Weidenfeld).

Nikapota, A. (1997) 'Children in Conflict', in D. Black, M. Newman, J. Harris-Hendricks and G. Mezey (eds) *Psychological Trauma: A Developmental Approach* (London: Gaskell).

Noble, B. and Charlton, J. (1994) 'Homicides in England and Wales', *Population Trends*, vol. 75.

Nobles, R. and Schiff, D. (1995) 'Miscarriages of Justice: A Systems Approach', *The Modern Law Review*, vol. 58, no. 3.

Noland, M., Robertson, S. and Wang, T. (2001) 'Famine in North Korea: Causes and Cures', *Economic Development and Cultural Change*, vol. 49, no. 4.

Norris, C. (1993) 'Some Ethical Considerations on Field-Work with the Police', in D. Hobbs and T. May (eds) *Interpreting the Field* (Oxford: Clarendon).

NSPCC *Research Briefing: Child Abuse* (London: NSPCC – various dates).

NUT (2002) 'National Union of Teachers Briefing: Children Out of Detention'. <www.chilout.org>

O'Donnell, C. and White, L. (1998) *Invisible Hands. Child Employment in North Tyneside* (London: Low Pay Unit).

O'Donnell, C. and White, L. (1999) *Hidden Danger: Injuries to Children at Work in Britain* (London: Low Pay Unit).

Osler, D. (2002) *Labour Party Plc. New Labour as a Party of Business* (Edinburgh: Mainstream).

Outen, F. (2003) 'A Victim of its Own Success? Psychiatry and Pre-Crime Intervention', *Safer Society*, vol. 17, Summer.

Pallister, D. (1999a) 'An Injustice that Still Reverberates', *Guardian*, 19 October.

Pallister, D. (1999b) '"Confession" to Disgraced Crime Squad Led to 20-year Jail Term', *Guardian*, October 27.

Pallister, D. (2000) 'Blair's Apology to Guildford Four', *Guardian*, 6 June.

Pande, M. (2002a) 'A Price for Life', *The Hindu*, 3 February.

Pande, R. (2002b) 'The Public Face of Domestic Violence', *International Feminist Journal of Politics*, vol. 4, no. 3.

Pantazis, C. and Gordon, D. (eds) (2000) *Tackling Inequalities: Where Are We Now and What Can be Done?* (Bristol: Policy Press).

Parker, R. (1990) *Away from Home: A Short History of Child Care* (London: Barnardo's).

Parker, R. (1995) 'A Brief History of Child Protection', in E. Farmer and M. Owen (eds) *Child Protection Practice: Private Risks and Public Remedies* (London: HMSO).

Parr, J. (1980) *Labouring Children* (Montreal: Croom Helm, McGill/Queen's University Press).

Partington, M. (1997) 'Socio-Legal Research in Britain: Changing the Funding Environment', in P. Thomas (ed.) *Socio-Legal Studies* (Aldershot: Dartmouth).

Pashukhanis, E. (1978) *Law and Marxism* (London: Inklinks).

Pasquino (1991) 'Criminology: The Birth of a Special Knowledge', in G. Burchell, C. Gordon and P. Miller (eds) *The Foucault Effect: Studies in Governmentality. With Two Lectures by and an Interview with Michel Foucault* (London: Harvester Wheatsheaf).

Patton, C. (1985) *Sex and Germs: The Politics of AIDS* (Boston, MA: South End Press).

Pauly, L. W. (1994) 'Promoting a Global Economy: The Normative Role of the International Monetary Fund', in R. Stubbs and G. R. Underhill (eds) *Political Economy and the Changing Global Order* (London: Macmillan).

Pearce, F. (1976) *Crimes of the Powerful: Marxism, Crime and Deviance* (London: Pluto).

Pearce, F. (1995) 'Accountability for Corporate Crime', in P. Stenning (ed.) *Accountability for Criminal Justice* (Toronto: University of Toronto Press).

Pearce, F. (2002) 'Divided We Fall', *New Scientist*, vol. 173, no. 2328.

Pearce, F. (2003) 'Preface. Holy Wars and Spiritual Revitalisation', in S. Tombs and D. Whyte (eds) *Unmasking the Crimes of the Powerful: Scrutinising States and Corporations* (New York: Peter Lang).

Pearce, F. and Tombs, S. (1996) 'Hegemony, Risk and Governance: "Social" Regulation and the US Chemical Industry', *Economy and Society*, vol. 25, no. 3.

Pearce, F. and Tombs, S. (1998) *Toxic Capitalism: Corporate Crime and the Chemical Industry* (Aldershot: Ashgate).

Pearce, F. and Tombs, S. (2002) 'Crime, Corporations and the "New" World Order', in G. Potter (ed.) *Controversies in White-Collar Crime* (Cincinnati, OH: Anderson).

Pearce, F. and Tombs, S. (2003) 'Multinational Corporations, Power and "Crime"', in C. Sumner (ed.) *The Blackwell Companion to Criminology* (Oxford: Blackwell).

Peers, S. (2003a) 'Readmission Agreements', in N. Rogers and S. Peers (eds) *EU Immigration and Asylum Law: Text and Commentary* (Dortrecht: Kluwer).

Peers, S. (2003b) 'Readmission Agreements and EU External Migration Law', May 2003 (London: Statewatch Semdoc Observatory).

Pekkarinen, J. (1997) 'Corporatism and Economic Performance in Sweden, Norway and Finland', in J. Pekkarinen, M. Pohjola and B. Rowthorn (eds) *Social Corporatism – A Superior Economic System?* (Oxford: Clarendon).

Perrott, D. (1981) 'Changes in Attitude to Limited Liability – The European Experience', in T. Orhnial (ed.) *Limited Liability and the Corporation* (London: Croom Helm).

Phillipson, C. (1987) 'The Transition to Retirement', in G. Cohen (ed.) *Social Change and the Life Course* (London: Tavistock).

Pilger, J. (1998) *Hidden Agendas* (London: Vintage).

Pilger, J. (2002) *The New Rulers of the World* (London: Verso).

Pion-Berlin, D. (1989) *The Ideology of State Terror: Economic Doctrine and Political Repression in Argentina and Peru* (Boulder: Lynne Rienner).

Piper, N. (1997) 'F. Hayek Die unheimliche Revolution', *Die Zeit*, nr. 37, September.

Plant, R. (2000) 'Equality and Inequality in Health Care', in I. Forbes (ed.) *Health Inequalities: Poverty and Policy* (London: Academy of Learned Societies for the Social Sciences).

Police Complaints Authority (2002) *Fatal Pursuit* (London: Police Complaints Authority).

Pollin, R. (2000) 'Anatomy of Clintonomics', *New Left Review*, no. 3, May/June.

The Portia Campaign (2002) *Portia History*, February 21. <www.portia.org/History.html>

Poulantzas, N. (1978) *State Power Socialism* (London: Verso).

Power, S. (2001) *A Problem from Hell: America and the Age of Genocide* (New York: Basic Books).

Power, S. (2002) 'Bystanders to Mass Murder', *Washington Post*, 21 April.

Premi, M. and Raju, S. (1998) 'Born to Die: Female Infanticide in Madhya Pradesh', *Search Bulletin*, July–September.

Price, C. M. (1994) 'Privatization in Less Developed Countries', in P. M. Jackson and C. M. Price (eds) *Privatization and Regulation. A Review of the Issues* (London: Longman).

Project Underground (2001) *Oil, the World Trade Organisation, & Globalisation*, March 2002. <www.moles.org/ProjectUnderground/oil/wto2001_nov_b.html>

Prospect (2003) *Safety Briefing. Cut Risks, Not Safety Workers* (London: Prospect). <www.prospect.org.uk/doclib/download/245_9583656441.pdf/as/cut_risks.pdf>

Purvis, A. (2003) 'The Dangers of Cheap Meat', *Observer Food Monthly*, 10 August.

Randerson, J. (2001) 'Lingering Death', *New Scientist*, vol. 171, no. 2310.

Rawls, J. (1971) *A Theory of Justice* (Cambridge, MA: Harvard University Press).

Refugee Council (1997) *Just Existence* (London: Refugee Council).

Regan, S. (1997) 'Miscarriage: Ultimate Scenario for a Nightmare', *Scandals in Justice*, 27 May.

Reiman, J. (1979) *The Rich Get Richer, the Poor Get Prison. Ideology, Class and Criminal Justice* (Chichester: Wiley).

Reiman, J. (1998) *The Rich Get Richer and the Poor Get Prison. Ideology, Class and Criminal Justice*, 5th edition (Boston, MA: Allyn and Bacon).

Reiner, R. (1985) *The Politics of the Police* (Brighton: Wheatsheaf).

Remafedi, G., French, S., Story, M., Resnick, M. D. and Blum, R. (1998) 'The Relationship Between Suicide Risk and Sexual Orientation: Results of a Population-based Study', *American Journal of Public Health*, vol. 88, no. 1.

Reno, W. (1999) *Warlord Politics and African States* (Boulder: Lynne Rienner).

Rich, A. (1980) 'Compulsory Heterosexuality and Lesbian Existence', *Signs*, vol. 5, no. 4.

Richardson, D. (1996) 'Heterosexuality and Social Theory', in D. Richardson (ed.) *Theorising Heterosexuality* (Buckingham: Open University Press).

Rigakos, G. S. (1999) 'Risk Society and Actuarial Criminology: Prospects for a Critical Discourse', *Canadian Journal of Criminology*, vol. 41, no. 2.

Risse, T., Ropp, S. C. and Sikkink, K. (eds) (1999) *The Power of Human Rights: International Norms and Domestic Change* (Cambridge: Cambridge University Press).

Ritov, I. and Baron, J. (1990) 'Reluctance to Vaccinate: Omission Bias and Ambiguity', *Journal of Behavioural Decision Making*, vol. 3.

Roberts, Y. (1999) 'Freedom Fighter', *Guardian*, 30 September.

Robinson, S. (2000) *Marked Men: White Masculinity in Crisis* (New York: Columbia University Press).

Rock, P. (1994) 'The Social Organisation of British Criminology', in M. Maguire, R. Morgan and R. Reiner (eds) *The Oxford Handbook of Criminology* (Oxford: Oxford University Press).

Rooney, C. and Devis, T. (1999) 'Recent Trends in Deaths from Homicide in England and Wales', *Health Statistics Quarterly*, vol. 03.

Rose, K. C. (1999/2000) 'The Transsexual and the Damage Done: The Fourth Court of Appeals Opens PanDOMA's Box by Closing the Door on Transsexuals' Right to Marry', *Tulane Journal of Law & Sexuality*, vol. 9, no. 1.

Ross, J. and Richards, S. (eds) (2003) *Convict Criminology* (Belmont: Thomson/Wadsworth).

Rossigneux, B. (2001) 'Balivernes pour un massacre', *Le Canard enchaîné*, 12 December.

Royal Commission on Criminal Justice (1993) *Report*, cm. 2263 (London: HMSO).

Royzman, E. B. and Baron, J. (2002) 'The Preference for Indirect Harm', *Social Justice Research*, vol. 15, no. 2.

Ruff, A. (1989) 'The UK Immigration (Carriers' Liability) Act 1987', *International Journal of Refugee Law*, vol. 1.

Ruigrock, W. and van Tulder, R. (1995) *The Logic of International Restructuring* (London: Routledge).

Rummel, R. J. (1996) *Death by Government* (Somerset, NJ: Transaction).

Russell, D. (1990) *Rape in Marriage* (Bloomington, IN: Indiana University Press).

Rust, P. C. R. (1993) 'Neutralising the Political Threat of the Marginal Women: Lesbians' Beliefs About Bisexual Women', *Journal of Sex Research*, vol. 30, no. 3.

Rust, P. C. R. (2000) 'Bisexuality: A Contemporary Paradox for Women', *Journal of Social Issues*, vol. 56, no. 2.

Rutter, M. (1970) *Maternal Deprivation Reassessed* (Harmondsworth: Penguin).

Rutter, M., Giller, H. and Hagell, A. (1998) *Anti-Social Behaviour by Young People: The Main Messages* (Cambridge: Cambridge University Press).

Ryan, W. (1971) *Blaming the Victim* (London: Orbach and Chambers).

Ryle, S. (2002) 'Mis-Selling Bill Could Hit £15bn', *Observer Business*, 29 September.

Safe Motherhood (1998) *Maternal Mortality*. <www.safemotherhood.org/facts_and_figures/maternal_mortality.htm>

Said, E. (1993) *Culture and Imperialism* (London: Chatto and Windus).

Salmi, J. (1991) 'Education, Dissent and Freedom of Speech: How Different Governments Respond to Accusations of Human Rights Violations', *The McGill Journal of Education*, vol. 26, no. 3.

Salmi, J. (1993) *Violence and Democratic Society: New Approaches to Human Rights* (London: Zed Books).

Sanders, A. and Young, R. (2000) *Criminal Justice*, 2nd edition (London: Butterworths).

Sanders, J. (1998) *Bendectin on Trial: A Study of Mass Tort Litigation* (Ann Arbor: University of Michigan Press).

Sarat, A. (1997) 'Vengeance, Victims and the Identities of Law', *Social and Legal Studies*, vol. 6, no. 2.

Sayer, A. (1995) *Radical Political Economy. A Critique* (Oxford: Blackwell).

Schatzberg, M. G. (1988) *The Dialectics of Oppression in Zaire* (Bloomington, IN: Indiana University Press).

Scheper-Hughes, N. (1992) *Death Without Weeping* (Berkeley: University of California Press).

Schlesinger, P. and Tumber, H. (1994) *Reporting Crime* (Oxford: Oxford University Press).

Schuck, P. H. (1986) *Agent Orange on Trial: Mass Toxic Disasters in the Courts* (Cambridge, MA: Belknap Press).

Schwendinger, H. and Schwendinger, J. (1975) 'Defenders of Order or Guardians of Human Rights?', in I. Taylor, P. Walton and J. Young (eds) *Critical Criminology* (London: Routledge & Kegan Paul).

Scottish Parliament (2002) *Report of Scottish Parliamentary Visit to Dungavel Removal Centre* (London: TSO).

Scraton, P. (1999) *Hillsborough: the Truth* (Edinburgh: Mainstream).

Scraton, P. and Chadwick, K. (1987) *In the Arms of the Law: Coroner's Inquests and Deaths in Custody* (London: Pluto).

Searle, C. (2001) *An Exclusive Education: Race, Class and Exclusion in British Schools* (London: Lawrence and Wishart).

Segal, L. (1994) *Straight Sex: Rethinking the Politics of Pleasure* (London: Virago).

Select Committee on Environment, Transport and Regional Affairs (2000) *Fourth Report. Inquiry into the Work of the Health and Safety Executive*. <www.parliament.the-stationery-office.co.uk/pa/cm199900/cmselect/cmenvtra/31/3102.htm>

Sen, A. (1990) 'More Than 100 Million Women Are Missing', *New York Review*, 20 December.

Sen, A. (1999) *Development as Freedom* (Oxford: Oxford University Press).

Sen, A. (2001) 'Many Faces of Gender Inequality', *Frontline*, vol. 18, no. 22.

Senderowitz, J. (1995) *Adolescent Health: Reassessing the Passage to Adulthood*, World Bank Discussion Papers, no. 272. (Washington, DC: The World Bank).

Shapiro, S. P. (1983) 'The New Moral Entrepreneurs: Corporate Crime Crusaders', *Contemporary Sociology*, vol. 12.

Shaw, M., Dorling, D., Gordon, D. and Davey Smith, G. (1999) *The Widening Gap: Health Inequalities and Policy in Britain* (Bristol: Policy Press).

Shaw, T. (1998) 'Woman Twice Jailed for Murder is Freed', *Daily Telegraph*, 8 April.

Shiling, C. and Mellor, P. (1998) 'Durkheim, Morality and Modernity', *Theory, Culture and Society*, vol. 49, no. 2.

Shokeid, M. (2001) 'You Don't Eat Indian and Chinese Food at the Same Meal: The Bisexual Quandary', *Anthropological Quarterly*, vol. 75, no. 1.

Showalter, E. (1991) *Sexual Anarchy: Gender and Culture at the Fin de Siècle* (London: Virago).

Showalter, E. (1997) *Hystories: Hysterical Epidemics and Modern Culture* (London: Picador).

Sim, J. (1994) 'Tougher Than the Rest? Men in Prison', in T. Newburn and E. Stanko (eds) *Just Boys Doing Business? Men Masculinities and Crime* (London: Routledge).

Sim, J. (2000/2001) 'The Victimised State', *Criminal Justice Matters*, no. 42.

Sim, J. (2002) 'The Future of Prison Health Care: A Critical Analysis', *Critical Social Policy*, vol. 22, no. 2.

Sim, J. (2003) 'Whose Side Are We Not On? Researching Medical Power in Prisons', in S. Tombs and D. Whyte (eds) *Unmasking the Crimes of the Powerful: Scrutinizing States and Corporations* (New York: Peter Lang).

Sim, J., Scraton, P. and Gordon, P. (1987) 'Introduction: Crime, the State and Critical Analysis', in P. Scraton (ed.) *Law, Order and the Authoritarian State* (Milton Keynes: Open University Press).

Sivanandan, A. (2001) 'Poverty Is the New Black: The Three Faces of Racism', *Race & Class*, vol. 43, no. 2.

Slapper, G. and Tombs, S. (1999) *Corporate Crime* (London: Longman).

Sloan, N., Langer, A., Hernandez, B., Romero, M. and Winikiff, B. (2001) 'The Etiology of Maternal Mortality in Developing Countries: What Do Verbal Autopsies Tell Us?', *Bulletin of the World Health Organisation*, vol. 79, no. 9.

Smart, A. (1999) 'Predatory Rule and Illegal Economic Practices', in J. M. Heyman (ed.) *States and Illegal Practices* (Oxford: Berg).

Smart, C. (1977) *Women, Crime and Criminology: A Feminist Critique* (London: Routledse & Kegan Paul).

Smart, C. (1990) 'Feminist Approaches to Criminology, or Postmodern Woman Meets Atavistic Man', in L. Gelsthorpe and A. Morris (eds) *Feminist Perspectives in Criminology* (Milton Keynes: Open University Press).

Smart, C. (1996) 'Collusion, Collaboration and Confession', in D. Richardson (ed.) *Theorising Heterosexuality* (Buckingham: Open University Press).

Smith, D. and Gray, J. (1983) *Police and People in London, IV, the Police in Action* (London: Policy Studies Institute).

Smith, J., Bolyard, M. and Ippolito, A. (1999) 'Human Rights and the Global Economy: A Response to Meyer', *Human Rights Quarterly*, vol. 21, no. 1.

Smith, P. (1997) *Millennial Dreams: Contemporary Culture and Capital in the North* (London: Verso).

Smith, R. and Wynne, B. (eds) (1989) *Expert Evidence: Interpreting Science in the Law* (London: Routledge).

Snider, L. (1990) 'Co-operative Models and Corporate Crime: Panacea or Cop-Out?', *Crime & Delinquency*, vol. 36, no. 2.

Snider, L. (1991) 'The Regulatory Dance: Understanding Reform Processes in Corporate Crime', *International Journal of Sociology of Law*, vol. 19.

Snider, L. (2000) 'The Sociology of Corporate Crime: An Obituary (Or: Whose Knowledge Claims Have Legs?)', *Theoretical Criminology*, vol. 4, no. 2.

Snider, L. (2003) 'Captured by Neo-Liberalism: Regulation and Risk in Walkerton, Ontario', *Risk Management: An International Journal (Special Issue: Globalised Crime in a Globalised Era)*, vol. 5, no. 2.

Social Exclusion Unit (2000) *Reducing Re-Offending by Ex-Prisoners* (London: Cabinet Office).

Soneja, S. (2001) *Elder Abuse in India*, Country Report for the World Health Organisation. <www.who.int/hpr/ageing/Report%20India.pdf>

Spranca, M., Minsk, E. and Baron, J. (1991) 'Omission and Commission in Judgment and Choice', *Journal of Experimental Social Psychology*, vol. 27.

Stafford, J. M. (1995) 'In Defence of Gay Lessons', in J. M. Stafford (ed.) *Essays on Sexuality & Ethics* (Solihull: Ismeron).

Stanko, E. (1985) *Intimate Intrusions: Women's Experience of Male Violence* (London: Virago).

Stanko, E. (1990) *Everyday Violence* (London: Pandora).

Stanko, E. (ed.) (2002) *Violence* (Aldershot: Ashgate).

Statewatch (1999) 'Tampere: Globalising Immigration Controls', *Statewatch*, vol. 9, no. 5, Sep.–Oct.

Statewatch (2001) 'A Permanent State of Emergency', *Statewatch*, vol. 11, no. 5, Aug.–Oct.

Statewatch (2003) 'EU: Mass Deportations by Charter Flight', *Statewatch*, vol. 13, no. 2, April.

Steele, J. (1995) 'Ex-Soldier Jailed for Killing Is Free After 16 Years', *Daily Telegraph*, 14 July.

Steenland, K., Halperin, B., Hu, S. and Walker, J. (2003) 'Mortality from External Causes Among Employed Persons by Socioeconomic Status from 1984–1997 in 27 States', *Epidemiology*, vol. 14, no. 1.

Steger, M. and Lind, N. (eds) (1999) *Violence and Its Alternatives: An Interdisciplinary Reader* (Basingstoke: Macmillan).

Steinberg, D. L. (1996) 'Technologies of Heterosexuality: Eugenic Reproductions under Glass', in D. L. Steinberg, D. Epstein and R. Johnson (eds) *Border Patrols: Policing the Boundaries of Heterosexuality* (London: Cassell).

Steinert, S. (1986) 'Beyond Crime and Punishment', *Contemporary Crises*, no. 10.

Stenson, K. (2001) 'The New Politics of Crime Control', in K. Stenson and R. Sullivan (eds) *Crime, Risk and Justice* (Cullompton: Willan).

Stevenson, O. (1996) 'Emotional Abuse and Neglect: A Time for Reappraisal', *Child and Family Social Work*, vol. 1, no. 1.

Stevenson, O. (1998) *Neglected Children: Issues and Dilemmas* (Oxford: Blackwell).

Strange, S. (1994) 'Wake Up, Krasner! The World *has* Changed', *Review of International Political Economy*, vol. 1, no. 2.

Sudha, S. and Irudaya Rajan, S. (1999) 'Female Demographic Disadvantage in India 1981–1991: Sex Selective Abortions and Female Infanticide', *Development and Change*, vol. 30.

Sullivan, R. (2001) 'The Schizophrenic State: Neo-liberal Criminal Justice', in K. Stenson and R. Sullivan (eds) *Crime, Risk and Justice* (Cullompton: Willan).

Sumner, C. (1994) *The Sociology of Deviance. An Obituary* (Buckingham: Open University Press).

Surette, R. (1996) 'News from Nowhere: Policy to Follow: Media and the Social Construction of "Three Strikes and You're Out"', in D. Shichor and D. Sechrest (eds) *Three Strikes and You're Out: Vengeance as Public Policy* (Thousand Oaks, CA: Sage).

Sutherland, E. (1940) 'White-Collar Criminality', *American Sociological Review*, vol. 5, February.

Sutherland, E. (1945) 'Is "White-Collar Crime" Crime?', *American Sociological Review*, vol. 10.

Sutherland, E. (1949) *White-Collar Crime* (New York: Holt Reinhart and Winston).

Sweetman, C. (ed.) (2000) *Gender and Lifecycles* (Oxford: Oxfam GB).

Swift, K. J. (1995) *Manufacturing Bad Mothers: A Critical Perspective on Child Neglect* (Toronto: University of Toronto Press).

Szabo, R. and Short, R. V. (2000) 'How does Male Circumcision Protect Against HIV Infection?', *British Medical Journal*, vol. 320, 19 June.

Szasz, A. (1984) 'Industrial Resistance to Occupational Safety and Health Legislation 1971–1981', *Social Problems*, vol. 32, no. 2.

Takala, J. (2002) 'Introductory Report: Decent Work – Safe Work', Paper Presented at the XVIth World Congress on Safety and Health at Work, Vienna, 26–31 May.

Tappan, P. (1947) 'Who Is the Criminal?' *American Sociological Review*, vol. 12.

Thatcher, M. (1987) 'Interview', *Women's Own Magazine*, 3 October.

Theobald, R. (1990) *Corruption, Development and Underdevelopment* (Basingstoke: Macmillan).

Therborn, G. (1986) *Why Some Peoples Are More Unemployed Than Others* (London: Verso).

Tilly, C. (1985) 'War Making and State Making as Organised Crime', in P. B. Evans, D. Rueschmeyer and T. Skocpol (eds) *Bringing the State Back In* (Cambridge: Cambridge University Press).

Tilly, C. (1992) *Coercion, Capital and European States 990–1990* (Oxford: Blackwell).

Tisdale, S. (1998) 'Second Thoughts', *Salon Magazine*, 11 September. <www.salon.com> (excerpted at <www.bettydodson.com/bisexual.htm>)

Titmuss, R. (1970) *The Gift Relationship: From Human Blood to Social Policy* (London: George Allen and Unwin).

Tombs, S. (1995) 'Law, Resistance and Reform: "Regulating" Safety Crimes in the UK', *Social & Legal Studies*, vol. 4, no. 3.

Tombs, S. (1999) 'Death and Work in Britain', *Sociological Review*, vol. 47, no. 2.

Tombs, S. (2000) 'Official Statistics and Hidden Crime: Researching Safety Crimes', in V. Jupp, P. Davies and P. Francis (eds) *Doing Criminological Research* (London: Sage).

Tombs, S. (2002) 'Beyond the Usual Suspects? Crime, Criminology and the Powerful', *Safer Society: The Journal of Crime Reduction and Community Safety*, no. 15, Winter.

Tombs, S. and Whyte, D. (2002) 'Unmasking the Crimes of the Powerful', *Critical Criminology: An International Journal*, vol. 11, no. 3.

Tombs, S. and Whyte, D. (2003) 'Two Steps Forward, One Step Back: Towards Accountability for Workplace Deaths?', *Policy and Politics in Occupational Health and Safety*, vol. 1, no. 1.

Townsend, P. (1993) *The International Analysis of Poverty* (Hemel Hempstead: Harvester Wheatsheaf).

Townsend, P. (2002) 'Poverty, Social Exclusion and Social Polarisation: The Need to Construct an International Welfare State', in P. Townsend and D. Gordon (eds) *World Poverty: New Policies to Defeat an Old Enemy* (Bristol: Policy Press).

Townsend, P. and Davidson, N. (1982) *The Black Report* (London: Penguin).

Townsend, P. and Gordon, D. (eds) (2002) *World Poverty: New Policies to Defeat an Old Enemy* (Bristol: Policy Press).

Toynbee, P. (2002) 'The Cheek of It. Business Wants Yet More Tax Breaks', *Guardian*, 13 November.

TUC (2003) *TUC Press Release*, 18 March. <www.tuc.org.uk/pressextranet>

Tweedale, G. (2000) *Magic Mineral to Killer Dust: Turner & Newall and the Asbestos Hazard* (Oxford: Oxford University Press).

UNAIDS-WHO (2002) *AIDS Epidemic Update* (Geneva: UNAIDS).

UNCTAD (2002a) *The Least Developed Countries Report 2002* (Geneva: United Nations).

UNCTAD (2002b) *Press Release*. <www.unctad.org/en/pub/ps1ldc02.en.htm>

UNDESAPD (1998) *Too Young to Die: Genes or Gender?* (New York: United Nations Department of Economic and Social Affairs Population Division).

UNDP (1997) *Human Development Report 1997* (Oxford: Oxford University Press).

UNDP (2000) *Human Development Report 2000* (New York: Oxford University Press).

UNESC (2002) *Abuse of Older Persons: Recognising and Responding to Abuse of Older Persons in a Global Context*, Report of the General-Secretary, World Assembly on Ageing 2002, United Nations Economic and Social Council. <www.un.org/ageing/>

UNFPA (1997) *State of the World's Population 1997: The Rights to Choose* (New York: United Nations Population Fund).

UNFPA (1998) *State of the World's Population 1998* (New York: United Nations Population Fund).

UNFPA (2002) *State of the World's Population 2002: People, Poverty and Possibilities* (New York: United Nations Population Fund).

UNHCR (2000) *Reconciling Migration Control and Refugee Protection in the European Union*, October 2000 (Geneva: United Nations High Commissioner for Refugees).

UNICEF (2000) *Domestic Violence Against Women and Girls*, Innocenti Digest, No 6 United Nations Children's Fund (Florence: Innocenti Research Centre).

UNICEF (2001) *Profiting from Abuse: An Investigation into the Sexual Exploitation of Our Children* (New York: United Nations Children's Fund).

UNICEF (2003) *Maternal Mortality* (New York: United Nations Children's Fund). <www.childinfo.org/eddb/mat_mortal/>

Unison/Centre for Corporate Accountability (2002) *Safety Last? The Under-Enforcement of Health and Safety Law. Full Report* (London: Unison/Centre for Corporate Accountability).

United Nations (1995) *The Copenhagen Declaration and Programme of Action: World Summit for Social Development 6–12 March 1995* (New York: United Nations Department of Publications).

van Swaaningen, R. (1997) *Critical Criminology: Visions from Europe* (London: Sage).

van Swaaningen, R. (1999) 'Reclaiming Critical Criminology: Social Justice and the European Tradition', *Theoretical Criminology*, vol. 3, no. 1.

Vanhecke, C. (1985) 'Armero ne devait pas être détruite', *Le Monde*, 30 November.

Wagner, G. (1982) *Children for the Empire* (London: Weidenfeld and Nicolson).

Wallach, L. and Sforza, M. (1999) *The WTO: Five Years of Reasons to Resist Corporate Globalisation* (New York: Seven Stories Press).

Wallerstein, J. S. and Kelly, J. B. (1980) *Surviving the Breakup: How Children and Parents Cope with Divorce* (New York: Basic Books).

Wallerstein, J. S. and Blakeslee, S. (1990) *Second Chances* (London: Corgi).

Ward, T. (1998) 'Law's Truth, Lay Truth and Medical Science: Three Case Studies', in H. Reece (ed.) *Law and Science* (Oxford: Oxford University Press).

Ward, T. (1999) 'Psychiatric Evidence and Judicial Factfinding', *International Journal of Evidence and Proof*, vol. 3, no. 3.

Ward, T. and Green, P. (2000) 'Legitimacy, Civil Society and State Crime', *Social Justice*, vol. 27, no. 1.

Warner, J. (2000) 'Mass Circumcision: Crime Against Humanity?', *British Medical Journal*, Rapid Responses, 20 June. <www.bmj.com/cgi/eletters/320/7249/1592#8445>

Warren, M. (1985) *Gendercide: The Implications of Sex Selection* (Totowa, NJ: Rowman and Allanheld).

Watkins, K. (2001) *The Oxfam Education Report* (Oxford: Oxfam Publishing).

Watts, C. and Zimmerman, C. (2002) 'Violence Against Women: Global Scope and Magnitude', *Lancet*, vol. 359.

Weaver, M. (1997) 'Justice Provides No Comfort for Carl's Parents', *Electronic Telegraph*, 12 August. <www.telegraph.co.uk>

Webber, F. (1991) 'From Ethnocentrism to Euro-Racism', *Race & Class*, vol. 32, no. 3.

Webber, F. (2003) 'NASS: Chronicle of Failure', 24 July 2003 (London: IRR). <www.irr.org.uk/news>

Weiss, L. (1997) 'Globalisation and the Myth of the Powerless State', *New Left Review*, no. 225.

Weiss, L. (1998) *The Myth of the Powerless State* (Cambridge: Polity).

Welsh, B. (2002) 'Globalisation, Weak States and the Death Toll in East Asia', in K. Worcester, S. A. Bermanzohn and M. Ungar (eds) *Violence and Politics: Globalisation's Paradox* (London: Routledge).

Wertz, D. and Fletcher, J. (1993) 'Prenatal Diagnosis and Sex Selection in 19 Nations', *Social Science Medicine*, vol. 37, no. 11.

Wertz, D. and Fletcher, J. (1998) 'Ethical and Social Issues in Prenatal Sex Selection: A Survey of Geneticists in 37 Nations', *Social Science Medicine*, vol. 46, no. 2.

Whelan, A. (1998) 'Bridgewater Four', *The Times*, 30 July.

Whelan, A. (2002) 'Miscarriages of Justice', Paper Presented at United Against Injustice Official Launch Blackburne House, Hope Street, Liverpool, 12 October.

White, M. (1997) 'David Evans: "In the Gutter"', *Guardian*, 5 March.

WHO (1992) *International Statistical Classification of Diseases and Related Health Problems*, 10th Revision (Geneva: WHO).

WHO (1995) *The World Health Report 1995: Bridging the Gaps* (Geneva: WHO).

WHO (1997) *Female Genital Mutilation: A Joint WHO/UNICEF/UNFPA Statement* (Geneva: WHO).

WHO (1998) *Female Genital Mutilation: An Overview* (Geneva: WHO).

WHO (2001a) *Estimated Prevalence Rates for FGM, Updated May 2001* (Geneva: WHO).

WHO (2001b) *Violence Against Women*, WHO FACT Sheet No. 239 (Geneva: WHO).

WHO (2001c) *Maternal Mortality in 1995: Estimates Developed by WHO, UNICEF, UNFPA* (Geneva: WHO).

WHO (2002a) *Reducing Risks, Promoting Healthy Life* (Geneva: WHO).

WHO (2002b) *Active Ageing: A Policy Framework* (Geneva: WHO).

WHO (2002c) *World Report on Violence and Health* (Geneva: WHO).

WHO (2002d) *The Toronto Declaration on the Global Prevention of Elder Abuse* (Geneva: WHO).

WHO (2002e) *Missing Voices – Views of Older People on Elder Abuse* (Geneva: WHO).

WHO (2003) *Information Needs for Research, Policy and Action on Ageing and Older Persons: Definition of an Older or Elderly Person* (Geneva: WHO). <www.who.ch/whosis/mds/mds_definition/mds_definition_english.cfm?path=whosis,mds,mds_definition&language=english>

Whyte, D. (1999) *Power, Ideology and the Management of Safety in the UK Offshore Oil Industry*, Unpublished PhD Manuscript, Liverpool John Moores University.

Whyte, D. (2002) '"Behind the Line of Truncheons": The Production of "Valid" Knowledge in Criminology', Paper Presented at Crossing Borders, British Criminology Conference 2002, Keele University, 17–20 July.

Whyte, D. and Tombs, S. (1998) 'Capital Fights Back: Risk, Regulation and Profit in the UK Offshore Oil Industry', *Studies in Political Economy*, vol. 57.

Willheim, E. (2002) 'MV Tampa: The Australian Response', Paper Presented at the Conference Global Migrations/Domestic Reactions: A Comparative Constitutional Perspective, Oxford Brookes University, 24 May 2002.

Williams, W. L. (1986) *The Spirit and the Flesh: Sexual Diversity in Indian American Culture* (Boston, MA: Beacon Press).

Williams, Z. (2003) 'Thieves Take Stuff, That's All', *Guardian*, 21 January.

Willis, B. and Levy, B. (2002) 'Child Prostitution: Global Health Burden, Research Needs, and Interventions', *Lancet*, vol. 359, no. 9315.

Willis, P. (1977) *Learning to Labour* (Aldershot: Gower).

Wilton, T. (1996) 'Which One's the Man? The Heterosexualisation of Lesbian Sex', in D. Richardson (ed.) *Theorising Heterosexuality* (Buckingham: Open University Press).

Wittig, M. (ed.) (1992) *The Straight Mind* (Hemel Hempstead: Harvester Wheatsheaf).

Woffinden, B. (1998) 'Wrong Again: Sion Jenkins Is Innocent', *New Statesman*, 10 July.

Woffinden, B. (2001) 'Cover-Up', *Guardian Weekend*, 25 August.

Women and Equality Unit (2003) *Civil Partnership: A Framework for the Legal Recognition of Same-Sex Couples* (London: Department of Trade and Industry).

Women's Group on Public Welfare (1948) *The Neglected Child and His Family* (Oxford: Oxford University Press).

Woodward, P. A. (2001) *The Doctrine of Double Effect: Philosophers Debate a Controversial Moral Principle* (Paris: University of Notre Dame Press).

Woolfson, C., Foster, J. and Beck, M. (1996) *Paying for the Piper? Capital and Labour in the Offshore Oil Industry* (Aldershot: Mansel).

World Bank (1997) *World Development Report 1997: The State in a Changing World* (New York: Oxford University Press).

World Bank (1998/99) *World Development Report 1998/99* (Washington, DC: World Bank).

World Bank (2003a) *Data & Statistics: Gender*. <www.worldbank.org/data/databytopic/gender.html>

World Bank (2003b) *World Development Report 2004: Making Services Work for Poor People* (Washington, DC: World Bank).

WHO (1998) *The World Health Report 1998: Life in the 21st Century A Vision for All* (Geneva: WHO).

WTO (2001) *GATS – Fact and Fiction*. <www.wto.org/english/tratop_e/serv_factfiction_ehtm>

Yang, A. (1997) 'Trends: Attitudes Towards Homosexuality', *Public Opinion Quarterly*, vol. 61, no. 3.

Yoshino, K. (2000) 'The Epistemic Contract of Bisexual Erasure', *Stanford Law Review*, vol. 52, no. 2.

Young, A. (1995) *The Harmony of Illusions: Inventing Post-Traumatic Stress Disorder* (Princeton: Princeton University Press).

Young, T. (1995) '"A Project to Be Realised": Global Liberalism and Contemporary Africa', *Millennium*, vol. 24, no. 3.

Zeilinger, I. (1999) 'Family Support Systems and Older Women in Sub-Saharan Africa', in INSTRAW (ed.) *Ageing in a Gendered World: Women's Issues and Identities* (Dominican Republic: INSTRAW).

Zinn, H. (1980) *A People's History of the United States* (London: Longman).

Zvekic, U. (1998) *Criminal Victimisation in Countries in Transition* (Rome: UNICRI).

Notes on Contributors

Lois Bibbings is a senior lecturer in the School of Law at the University of Bristol

Danny Dorling is Professor of Human Geography in the Department of Geography at the University of Sheffield

Dave Gordon is Professor of Social Justice in the School for Policy Studies and Director of the Townsend Centre for International Poverty Research, both at the University of Bristol

Paddy Hillyard is Professor of Social Policy and Administration in the School for Policy Studies at the University of Ulster

Michael Naughton is a lecturer in the School of Law at the University of Bristol

Christina Pantazis is a research fellow in the School for Policy Studies at the University of Bristol

Roy Parker is Professor Emeritus of Social Policy at the University of Bristol

Simon Pemberton is an ESRC postdoctoral fellow in the School for Policy Studies at the University of Bristol

Jamil Salmi is a development economist at the World Bank

Joe Sim is Professor of Criminology in the School of Social Science at Liverpool John Moores University

Steve Tombs is Professor of Sociology in the School of Social Science at Liverpool John Moores University

Tony Ward is reader in law at the University of Hull

Frances Webber is a leading immigration barrister in London

Index

Compiled by Sue Carlton